THE SISTER ARTS

Th.

MVTA
POESIS

"Ut pictura poesis"
—Horace

"Painting is mute poetry, and poetry a
speaking picture"
—Simonides

Sister Arts

THE TRADITION OF LITERARY PICTORIALISM

AND ENGLISH POETRY FROM DRYDEN TO GRAY

By Jean H. Hagstrum

THE UNIVERSITY OF CHICAGO PRESS

CHICAGO & LONDON

THE UNIVERSITY OF CHICAGO PRESS, CHICAGO 60637
The University of Chicago Press, Ltd., London

© 1958 by The University of Chicago
All rights reserved. Published 1958
Paperback edition 1987
Printed in the United States of America
96 95 94 93 92 91 90 89 88 87   8 7 6 5 4

Library of Congress Catalog Card Number 58-11948
International Standard Book Number 0-226-31298-4

TO MY MOTHER AND THE MEMORY OF MY FATHER

Preface

I have been interested in the relations of poetry and painting as the subject of research ever since Professor Chauncey B. Tinker in 1938 published his Norton Lectures under the title *Painter and Poet*. But it was only during recent investigations of Anglo-Italian cultural relations that I became convinced that the impact of the visual arts upon the English imagination should be made the subject of a separate study that would also attempt to trace the history of *ut pictura poesis* in criticism and to define the pictorial image of neoclassical poetry. The present book is the fruit of that conviction.

I wish to express my thanks to the many who have supported my researches in Anglo-Italian relations, since they have also contributed to the present study: to the Graduate School of Northwestern University and its dean, Professor Moody Prior; to Dr. Stanley Pargellis for the grant of a Newberry Library Fellowship; to the American Philosophical Society, which made possible a summer at Yale; and to those responsible for my year in Italy as a Fulbright research scholar. I wish also to thank the staffs of several institutions for more than usual courtesy: the Deering Library at my own school, Northwestern University, the Huntington Library, the Newberry Library, and the Yale Library in this country; and in Florence the Biblioteca Nazionale, the Biblioteca Mediceo-Laurenziana, the Biblioteca Marucelliana, the Biblioteca Riccardiana, and the Archivio di Stato.

I am grateful to those of my students who have worked with me on this subject and those of my friends who have read the manuscript of this book in whole or in part. I should like to have given their stimulating suggestions the response they deserved. Richard Ellmann and Moody Prior have read the entire manuscript; Karl Olsson, Part I; and Stuart Small, the first two chapters. Carson Webster performed valuable services for me at the Frick Art Reference Library, and Bernard Weinberg permitted me to use his fine collection of Italian criticism.

JEAN H. HAGSTRUM

vii

Contents

Illustrations

The title page illustrations are from the Library of Congress copy of Bellori, *Le vite de' pittori, scultori et architetti moderni* (Rome, 1672), pp. 103, 19. One illustrates Simonides' characterization of painting as mute poetry. The other I have selected to represent poetry conceived of as a "speaking picture."

(At end of book)

Introduction

Men who cherish more than one of the arts have often made comparisons between them. Of these none has had a more important history than the comparison of painting and poetry, the two arts that have most commonly been called "sisters." In the millenniums that have intervened between Simonides of Ceos and Wallace Stevens[1] the observations on this relationship have become voluminous. Painters and critics of painting, poets and critics of poetry, philosophers of aesthetics and of history, historians of culture and of particular pictorial and poetic genres have all drawn the analogy, each to his own purpose, each on his own assumptions. The defenders of painting have sometimes assimilated it to poetry in order to make it acceptably humanistic, often for sociological as much as for philosophical reasons. At other times, like Leonardo, they have compared the two arts in order to demonstrate the superiority of graphic to verbal expression. Aestheticians, like Lessing and Croce, have been concerned with the analogy in order either to define the aesthetic value peculiar to each medium or to discover a beauty that transcends both. Some historians have sought the "time-spirit" that they believe lies behind the historical conditions of the arts, and others have attempted in a limited historical context to compare one kind of painting, the landscape, for example, with a parallel kind of poem, the descriptive.

From such works the present one differs in aim and method. It approaches the analogy from the side of literature. It strives to illuminate poetry, specifically English poetry, of whatever genre, written in the late seventeenth and early eighteenth centuries and usually called "neoclassical." It applies the methods of literary history and analysis to the pictorial imagery of that poetry and to the tra-

---

[1] "The Relations between Poetry and Painting," *The Necessary Angel* (New York, 1951), p. 160. On Simonides see below, p. 10 and n. 14.

dition out of which it grew. Its aim is thus somewhat more limited than might at first appear.

Who can deny the justice of Mario Praz's comment that about all the works of art in a given epoch there is an *air de famille?*[2] The poems of Prior, the sonatas of Corelli, and the paintings of Watteau unmistakably betray the marks of their origin in a single cultural period. And who can deny that the analysis of these family traits would be a commendable effort? But the fact is that most studies of interart parallels continue, in spite of Professor René Wellek's sensible warning,[3] to chase that will-o'-the-wisp, the *Zeitgeist,* that fades forever and forever as we move. One can scarcely avoid feeling that such studies serve the purposes of cultural mysticism, not of sober investigation. Since what is being sought—admittedly or not—is the "time-spirit" that lies behind all particular works of art and since individual artistic uniqueness tends to be neglected for the total uniqueness of the epoch, the terms of critical analysis pass undiscriminatingly from one work to another, even from one art to another.

Herbert Read finds linear style (emphasis on outline) in plastic art paralleled by alliteration ("horizontal movement across the structure of the verse") in poetry.[4] Bernard Fehr equates Pope's couplets to the stiff rectilinearity of classical plastic form and David Mallet's blank verse to the linear convolutions of the baroque.[5] Marco Mincoff sees Renaissance lyrical refrains as parallel to the repetitions in a Renaissance façade.[6] And Wylie Sypher, in a learned and at times brilliant book that is nevertheless a tissue of such correspondences as these, considers a Gothic interior a manifestation of the *sic et non* of scholastic thought, *Hamlet* a "mannerist" play, *Othello* "baroque," and so on.[7]

[2] "Modern Art and Literature: A Parallel," *English Miscellany,* V (1954), 217.

[3] "The Parallelism between Literature and the Arts," *English Institute Annual 1941* (1942), pp. 29–63.

[4] "Parallels in Painting and Poetry," *In Defence of Shelley* (London, 1936), p. 230.

[5] "The Antagonism of Forms in the Eighteenth Century," *English Studies,* XVIII (October, 1936), 193–97.

[6] "Baroque Literature in England," *Annuaire de l'Université de Sofia,* XLIII (1946–47), 27.

[7] *Four Stages of Renaissance Style* (Garden City, N.Y., 1955), pp. 25, 45, 261, and *passim.*

From the method followed in these and in other similar studies I must dissociate the present work. I am not primarily interested in the *Zeitgeist*, although I hope I have not neglected relevant cultural sociology. Nor am I willing to indulge in the kind of analogizing I have just illustrated. I have been impressed with Laurence Binyon's comment that "it is on the side of imagery that poetry comes closest into relation with painting."[8] Neglecting this patent truth, such studies as those I have passingly noted often abandon sound scholarly method. Professor Sypher, for example, finds Dryden to be an example of late baroque style. The point may be valid. (I shall in discussing this poet use the term "baroque" of certain of his verses.) But it cannot be established without reference to the poet's visual imagery. Professor Sypher is not persuasive when he finds the baroque in the highly unvisual first stanza of the first St. Cecilia's Day ode and in the abstract theological argument of the *Religio laici*.[9]

I do not wish to deny that correspondences between painting and poetry can be profound. Later on I shall try to show that the practice of pictorialism has fundamentally affected total poetic structure. But the investigator should always begin with the visual side of poetry—and thereafter keep it firmly in mind—when considering the relations between these two arts.

I wish also to distinguish my method from that of Helmut Hatzfeld's reading of French literature through its pictorial relationship in his recent *Literature through Art*.[10] Professor Hatzfeld's aim is to illuminate literature by means of art and art by means of literature, using paintings as commentaries on poems and poems as commentaries on paintings. By these comparisons the motifs and forms of each art are allegedly more fully illustrated. Professor Hatzfeld is also interested in the *Zeitgeist*. He usually confines his parallels between the two arts to works that were produced within the same predetermined epoch.

I have, however, chosen not to limit comparison in this manner. The reason is simple: the visual context of Pope's poetry, for ex-

[8] "English Poetry in Its Relation to Painting and the Other Arts," *Proceedings of the British Academy 1917–1918*, p. 383.

[9] *Op. cit.* (n. 7), pp. 256–59.

[10] (New York, 1952.) See especially the Preface and chap. vii for a discussion of method.

ample, was not composed of contemporaneous art, either English or Continental, but of masterpieces of sixteenth- and seventeenth-century Italian and Italianate painting and of antique statuary. To ignore the works he knew and liked and may have been influenced by for contemporary works produced under allegedly similar cultural conditions would seem to me to be unhistorical and illogical.

My study differs from Professor Hatzfeld's in yet another important respect: mine is devoted exclusively to literary history and analysis. I am not qualified to analyze paintings for their own or for the epoch's sake, and I gladly leave such necessary labors to the critic and historian of art. Paintings and other works of graphic art are reproduced and commented on only in connection with literary analysis.

It should always be borne in mind that literary pictorialism is more literary than pictorial. During its long history it has sometimes seemed to thrive quite independently of the visual arts. I am not trying to eliminate painting from the comparison; *ut pictura poesis* could obviously not have arisen had the art of painting not existed. In the eighteenth century knowledge of painting was widespread among poets and affected the visual imagery of their poetry. My point is simply that what we are about to examine is a literary and verbal phenomenon—a phenomenon that often *did* bear direct relation to particular paintings and particular schools of painting but that does not necessarily bear those relations. It is a way of seeing and a way of speaking that, in its long history, has created conventions and habits of its own that are sometimes quite unrelated to particular works of visual art.

Vastly different from the type of *Geistesgeschichte* and *Formgeschichte* we have been considering are two historical studies that have had considerable influence upon contemporary views of the eighteenth century: Elizabeth Wheeler Manwaring's *Italian Landscape in Eighteenth Century England* (1925) and Christopher Hussey's *The Picturesque* (1927). Of these the late Miss Manwaring's is the more scholarly and in many respects deserves the admiration it has received. But in its treatment of the earlier eighteenth century it is inadequate and perhaps even misleading. It limits the picturesque to description of landscape alone when the picturesque is a much broader concept, related to landscape in only ancillary ways. It exaggerates the influence of Claude Lorrain and Salvator Rosa, who were indeed known, but of considerably less importance to major writers than were other painters, even other landscapists. It detaches Thomson from his proper environment and links him with tendencies to which his resemblances are fortuitous. And, finally, it credits the eighteenth century with discovering what had been an important element in Hellenistic pastoralism[11] and what in seventeenth-century England was already a widespread taste.[12] If we are to see the neoclassical image in its proper historical perspective, we must shake ourselves free from those connotations of "picturesque" for which Miss Manwaring and Mr. Hussey, perhaps far beyond their intention, are so largely responsible.

Viewed from the vantage point of the more than forty years that have elapsed since its publication in 1910, the once popular book of Irving Babbitt, *The New Laokoön*, must be judged somewhat harshly. I must risk saying that the single merit of its first portion—I do not wish now to comment on the analysis of the romantic confusion of the arts—is that its author saw the importance of *ut pictura poesis* to English neoclassicism and that he related it, although in too general a way, to the doctrine of imitation. Aside from this his essay is partisan and inaccurate; the argument proceeds by assertion and even at times by innuendo, not by the rules of scholarship and evidence. The author does not know that *ut pictura poesis* was almost as important to the seventeenth-century baroque as to what he calls "pseudo-classicism" and that one important link between the earlier and later periods lay in their pictorialism. He mistakes the nature and underestimates the contribution of neoclassicism, assuming that it is entirely characterized by stylistic ornamentalism, in which poetic devices are laid on like colors, and that its central preoccupation was the literal copying of objects. Although Babbitt vigorously attacked the romantics, his commentary on neoclassicism shares their prejudices about their eighteenth-century predecessors.

The pictorialism of English neoclassical poetry—the term "pictorial" is given preliminary definition toward the close of this introduction—has in the ensuing pages been studied in four related but separable ways. Since the chronological plan I have followed may

[11] Mario Praz, *The Romantic Agony* (London, 1951), pp. 18–19.

[12] Henry V. S. Ogden and Margaret S. Ogden, *English Taste in Landscape in the Seventeenth Century* (Ann Arbor, Mich., 1955).

obscure for a while these four ways of treating the theme, let me now bring them into the light.

1. I have looked closely at individual poems, studied intensively their pictorial images, and attempted to relate such images to the poet's total meaning and purpose. In analyzing particular poems I have come to believe that there is often an intimate relationship between pictorial visualization and total poetic structure. Dr. Johnson perceived that the order governing what he once called "many appearances subsisting all at once"[13] must necessarily differ from other poetic forms. Pictorial form was, in fact, along with narrative and didactic-logical form, one of the alternative methods of ordering his material that a neoclassical poet had at his disposal. Such considerations as these are in large part the preoccupation of Part II.

2. The neoclassical image can be illuminated by studying not only its position within a poem but also its relationship outside. I have frequently compared particular poems with particular works of visual art. I have also given considerable attention to the pictorialist comment that appears everywhere in neoclassical criticism. What the critic says enables us to understand better what the poet does. But the critic's comment also shows us that during the Restoration and eighteenth century poetic pictorialism was nourished by important philosophic insights and seems to have filled clamant psychological and intellectual needs.

3. Since I have attempted to provide relevant background for both the poetry and the criticism of the neoclassic period, I have considered what critics from Plato on have said about the relations of painting and poetry. I sketch the historical development of that persistent but ever changing strain in Western criticism that used Horace's phrase *ut pictura poesis* as its text.

4. I have also attempted to assess the neoclassical poet's use and modification of the pictorialist tradition inherited from earlier creative writers. That kind of criticism is manifestly impossible without knowledge of the relevant literary, as distinguished from critical and philosophical, background. This portion of my work—the survey of the pictorial in poetry antecedent to the eighteenth century—I present with considerable diffidence. How, in relatively brief compass, can one possibly say anything illuminating about a matter so complicated and so extensive as this? I was willing to make the attempt only

[13] "Life of Thomson," *Works of Johnson* (Oxford, 1825), VIII, 378.

because I became convinced that valid generalization did emerge from a concentration on one genre of poetry, the genre represented by Keats's "Ode on a Grecian Urn." That kind of verse—and closely related prose—in which a real or imagined work of visual art is the ostensible subject has had a long and various history, extending from Homer through Keats, Baudelaire, and Rilke to recent issues of the *Kenyon Review*[14] and the *Times Literary Supplement*.[15] I have dwelt on important moments in that long history in presenting the literary background of neoclassical pictorialism. So limited, the story is far from complete, but I hope it is full enough to enable us to see both continuity and change in the pictorialist tradition of Western culture. I also hope that the early background chapters will stimulate more intensive research than I have been able to pursue into the periods here treated synoptically and, I am afraid, somewhat superficially but not, I trust, unsuggestively or unhistorically.

Pictorialism is not, then, an isolated historical matter bounded by the frontiers of one epoch, nor is it an autotelic aesthetic structure bounded by the limits of a single work or, it may be added, of a single genre. In theory and practice it had been present long before its flowering in the seventeenth and eighteenth centuries—present, indeed, for so many centuries that it had acquired a set of well-defined conventions and forms that too often enabled the poet to be effortlessly dull.

Pictorialism has persisted, in spite of the attacks by Lessing and Burke, even up to the present day. But, I repeat, my concern is chiefly with the neoclassical pictorial image during its efflorescence and with its background. I have excluded Dr. Johnson and Goldsmith from intensive consideration in Part II partly because they come too late and partly because neither is pictorial in ways that cannot be better illustrated earlier.

Although this is not a work in aesthetics, I should expect the data here presented to be of some interest to philosophers. Mr. G. Giovannini, although writing an article that finds fault with investigators who have attempted in the past to study the relationship of the arts, says: "The effort at close analysis in the scholarship summarily discussed in this paper is not always discriminating, but the

[14] Harry C. Morris, "Stanzas To Be Placed under Fouquet's Madonna," *Kenyon Review*, XVIII (Winter, 1956), 123–24.

[15] Lawrence Durrell, "The Octagon Room National Gallery '55," *Times Literary Supplement*, Jan. 27, 1956.

examples cited in illustration of its limitations are not intended to discredit this scholarship; for only by such effort can general theory be furnished with empirical data for the formulation of workable definitions of the relations of literature to the other fine arts."[16] I believe that the investigation I have pursued bears some such relation to general aesthetics, and I hope that my book will in this sense be a useful document.

Although I am not a professional aesthetician, I believe it is my duty to state briefly what I conceive to be the essential principles upon which good pictorial poetry rests. However much lip service may be paid to the view that art imitates nature, good art also imitates other art, both in the same and in other media. This is especially true in a sophisticated age like the eighteenth century. Such a condition of artificiality and of generic interrelationship seems to me to be desirable in neoclassical poetry. It should not be difficult for an age that has been instructed by Croce, M. Malraux, and Mr. Eliot to accept the view that rich value often exists in the overlaying of art by art.

Pictorial imagery is most effective when it is in some way or other metaphorical rather than purely descriptive or purely imitative of visual reality. Professor Reuben A. Brower has said: "The failure of much eighteenth-century poetry . . . is not due to over-generality but to the lack of a metaphorical sense which connects and gives meaning to detail."[17] The comment is shrewd, but it can be applied to *much* of the poetry of any period. At its best, neoclassical imagery is metaphorical—sometimes directly and sometimes indirectly, sometimes within the framework of a single poem and sometimes in a wider context. Whatever the immediate condition, the pictorial is most effective when it is more than merely pictorial and when it serves some larger aesthetic or intellectual purpose. The achievement of the merely pictorial may be interesting as a stroke of technical virtuosity. But it must join with and support other values if it is to be fully satisfying.

In the arts technical virtuosity is, of course, important, and that consideration leads me to my last aesthetic assumption, one concerned with the materials (words, pigments) out of which a work of

[16] "Method in the Study of Literature in Its Relations to the Other Fine Arts," *Journal of Aesthetics & Art Criticism*, VIII (March, 1950), 194-95.

[17] *The Fields of Light* (New York, 1951), p. 37.

art is constructed. Henry Moore has said that "truth to material should not be a criterion of the value of a work."[18] Good pictorialism represents the operation of the old critical principle of the *difficulté vaincue*—that is, the achievement of value by overcoming handicap and mastering obstacle. Pictorial effects are admittedly not fully natural in verbal art. This is not necessarily a fault. The medium's extremity may be the poet's opportunity.[19]

Many of the engravings, statues, and paintings reproduced in this volume form a part of the neoclassical poet's visual tradition. They were not, however, selected to represent the best in the tradition but to illuminate a particular literary passage being analyzed or a particular point being argued. I do not wish the taste of the age or my own taste to be judged by these illustrations. It may do the prestige of neoclassical poetry, already very low in some quarters, little good to stress its relations to painters and schools now out of favor. But in these matters opinion changes and often changes very rapidly. The Bolognese painters of the seventeenth century, whom Pope and his contemporaries admired so greatly, did seem dead beyond all resuscitation until, so to speak, the day before yesterday. But recently the prices brought by the Carracci and their followers have risen spectacularly. Of the recent exhibit in Bologna of the works of the despised Guido Reni the *Burlington Magazine* says: "The exhibition has come as a revelation. The whole edifice of hostility has crumbled overnight."[20]

In the pages that follow, certain familiar words will be used in unfamiliar ways, and perhaps other words will be completely new to some readers. These words will be defined and their usage justified in the proper place. Even so, they will grate on sensitive ears; but a consistent use of technical terms may be better than an attempt to find elegant periphrases.

The most general term used of the phenomenon being studied is the one that appears in the subtitle: "pictorialism." What are its most basic meanings? Under what conditions may it be said to exist? (1) In order to be called "pictorial" a description or an image must

[18] Cited first by Rudolph Wittkower and then by the reviewer of his book on Bernini (*Times Literary Supplement*, Dec. 23, 1955).

[19] See below, pp. 21–22, 53.

[20] Gian Carlo Cavalli, *Mostra di Guido Reni* (Bologna, 1954); *Burlington Magazine*, XCVI (October, 1954), 301–2.

be, in its essentials, capable of translation into painting or some other visual art. It need not resemble a particular painting or even a school of painting. But its leading details and their manner and order of presentation must be imaginable as a painting or sculpture. (2) Visual detail constitutes the pictorial but is not, per se, the pictorial. Such detail must be ordered in a picturable way. It is therefore not fully legitimate to call what is merely visual in a poem pictorial. (3) The pictorial is, of course, not limited to one particular school or method of painting. Depending on what the poet knew or liked in visual art, it may bear relations with art that is imitative or abstract, representational or symbolic. (4) The pictorial in a verbal medium necessarily involves the reduction of motion to stasis or something suggesting such a reduction. It need not eliminate motion entirely, but the motion allowed to remain must be viewed against the basic motionlessness of the arrangement. (5) The pictorial implies some limitation of meaning. It does not, of course, involve the elimination of concept. Were that true, there would have been no pictorialism until the recent imagistic movement. But it does imply that meaning must seem to arise from the *visibilia* present. General didactic statement may appear, but in a pictorial context it must seem, like an inscription on a statue, to be subordinate to the visual presentation.

I have felt it desirable in these introductory pages frankly to state my disagreements with certain of my predecessors in this field. But I do not wish to seem ungrateful to the greater number who have helped me. To each of the following scholars—and of course to many others besides, whose contributions I hope are adequately acknowledged in the notes—I am indebted for insights and information. These scholars have, even though writing about other matters, perceived the importance of the pictorial in neoclassical verse and have understood something of its true nature. I am gratified to be surrounded in this particular matter by so great a cloud of witnesses and to be able to say that I have profited greatly by the background studies of Vitry, Lombard, Folkierski, Mâle, Praz, and Lee[21] and by the specific insights into eighteenth-century pictorialism expressed by M. H. Abrams, Chester F. Chapin, Donald Davie, Cicely Davies, Stephen A. Larrabee, Samuel H. Monk, Rachel Trickett, Earl R. Wasserman, and A. S. P. Woodhouse.

[21] Here I specify the work of only Rensselaer W. Lee, "*Ut Pictura Poesis:* The Humanistic Theory of Painting," *Art Bulletin*, XXII (December, 1940), 197–269, an excellent study of the doctrine and its effect upon painting.

PART ONE

The Tradition

CHAPTER I

Classical Antiquity

Men have often come to the material remains of classical antiquity as builders to a quarry, denuding forum and temple in order to decorate palace and church. Some students of human culture have been chiefly interested in the ruined temple—in restoring it to its original state in its original scene. But others have been most concerned with the church—with appreciating its inserted classical columns in their later setting. It is so in this book. We shall consider antiquity, not in order to undertake a full examination of the pictorialism of its literature—for that would be presumptuous—but in order to see what it contributed to the imagery of English neoclassical poetry and to the tradition of modern literary pictorialism.

CRITICISM: PLATO, ARISTOTLE, HORACE

The great critics of antiquity frequently associated poetry and painting. Plato said in the *Republic:* "The poet is like a painter."[1] Aristotle in the *Poetics* often turned to the sister art with some such expression as: "It is the same in painting."[2] And Horace is the author of the phrase *ut pictura poesis* ("as a painting, so a poem"),[3] which had by the eighteenth century become a critical proverb. Ancient criticism provided motto and epigraph—texts that were used as pretexts for riding critical hobbyhorses. It did not, however, provide lengthy theoretical consideration of the two arts in relationship, and its contribution consists rather of pregnant suggestions than of fully formulated argument.

Plato virtually ignored the art of sculpture and mentioned painting in only the most cursory fashion, linking it with weaving, interior decoration, and architecture. Although he seemed to admit that

[1] x. 605a.

[2] ὥσπερ οἱ γραφεῖς (1448a. 5.).   [3] *Ars poetica* 361.

painting and other visual arts can have limited value in providing a healthy moral atmosphere for the citizens of the Republic, he apparently felt that the visual arts possessed very little ethical or educative value. Music and rhythm, not painting and sculpture, were the pillars of *paideia*. Although Plato found it possible to admire the visual art that embodied proportion (συμμετρία), correct arrangement (τάξις), and pleasing shapes and colors (ἁρμονία), he clearly disliked the violent emotional realism of such contemporary art as that depicting the gigantomachies, and realistic artists were not admitted to his ideal state. Most of all, Plato seemed to dislike illusionistic painting (σκιαγραφία), in which perspective, shading, and color were all used to produce depth and achieve the effects of plasticity. Such art, he felt, was a deception; its practitioner, a trickster; its colors and shadows, false and fantastic.

It is in this context that Plato associated the two arts of painting and poetry. Poetry he compared to illusionistic painting, and "mimesis," a term of shifting significance, he often used to refer to the making of images and appearances—a process he opposed to the production of reality and the acquisition of true knowledge. When he thus associated painting and poetry, the purpose was severe censure. The lie of the poet was compared to the image of a painter; the analogy between the arts was designed to humiliate poetry. Plato unmistakably intended guilt by association. Both arts—but more especially and egregiously the art of painting—hold a mirror up to nature and reproduce appearance only. Both—but more palpably the art of painting—are thrice removed from true reality, the world of being (οὐσία), and can only copy what are themselves only copies (εἴδωλα) of ideal forms (παραδείγματα). Neither painter nor poet is capable of transmitting the highest knowledge; both mix falsehood with truth; both appeal to men in their lowest state of rationality; both are potentially dangerous to the young. And both must therefore be ultimately banished from the ideal commonwealth.

From a system of metaphysical idealism having as one of its chief tenets the existence of immaterial reality one would hardly expect to derive fruitful implications for an analogy between poetry and an art that has usually been considered very close to the realities of the physical world. Nevertheless, Plato's example has been of importance to those who have thought of poetry and painting together—even to those who have inverted his scheme of values. For Plato associated

4

painting and poetry even in banishing them. He gave to criticism one of its most persistent metaphors—that of the mirror—a metaphor that has been especially prominent whenever poetry has in any significant way been compared to painting. Visual, representable reality may have lurked behind even the most abstruse of his dialectical generalizations. The words *eidos* (εἶδος) and *idea* (ἰδέα), which Plato regularly used for supersensory forms, perhaps carried with them some of their original sense of visible shape. In Plato's Garden of Essences abstractions appear as feminine forms that could easily establish themselves—had, indeed, already established themselves— as the visual personifications of art and literature. The "picturesque" persona of eighteenth-century poetry may be indirectly indebted to the dialogues of Plato.[4]

Finally, Plato made one conceptual association that was most congenial to the rise of literary pictorialism in late antiquity, to its persistence in the Middle Ages, and to its flowering in the Counter Reformation of the seventeenth century. His striking analogy between light and beauty ennobled the sense of sight. Of all the senses, the eye had, for Plato, the closest kinship to spirit. He called it "sunlike," and his metaphor, "the eye of the mind," exalted both sense and intellect.[5]

Aristotle's association of painting and poetry differs from Plato's in two basic respects. The later critic rejected the pejorative meanings of "mimesis," thus removing the basic reason for censuring the two arts. And without ever giving us a developed argument on the subject, he indicated those areas in which a comparison between the arts is legitimate and those in which it is not. Therefore, to a far greater extent than Plato, he is related to the subsequent development of pictorialist theory.

There are in the *Poetics* five unmistakable references to painting.

[4] See below, p. 147.

[5] The passages in Plato referred to in this section are: *Republic* vi. 508; x. 596d, 596e, 508b, 586b; *Phaedo* 69b; *Laws* 889d; *Sophist* 234b; *Symposium* 219a; *Phaedrus* 250d. I have relied on the following commentary: Richard McKeon, "Literary Criticism and the Concept of Imitation in Antiquity," in R. S. Crane (ed.), *Critics and Criticism* (Chicago, 1952), pp. 147–75; Werner Jaeger, *Paideia*, trans. Gilbert Highet (New York, 1943), II, 227–29, 404, n. 115; T. B. L. Webster, *Art and Literature in Fourth Century Athens* (London, 1956), pp. 24, 28, 44–45; R. G. Stevens, "Plato and the Art of His Time," *Classical Quarterly*, XXVII (July–October, 1933), 149–55.

Four of these draw analogies between the arts. The other is concerned with qualities that differentiate one art from the other. We shall consider the distinction first.

The mimetic arts of painting and poetry are distinguished from each other by the *means* of imitation employed. Painting imitates by color and form; poetry, by language, rhythm, and harmony. This classification, which appears at the beginning of the treatise,[6] seems to deny the validity of associating painting and poetry in any special way. They are not sisters but cousins; and the sisters of poetry, when one considers the *means*—but only the *means*—of imitation employed are music and dancing (the arts of temporal movement) and not the visual or graphic arts (the arts of spatial stasis). Aristotle's classification also implies that the very means of imitation employed condition the kind of effect that can be achieved. Form and color, he says, can portray many but not all things.[7] And it is partly because language is what it is that proper form in verbal art consists of a sequential and logical arrangement of the actions of men. Each of the mimetic arts achieves its proper pleasure in its proper medium. Each must take into perpetual account its own peculiar limitations.

After this clear distinction it may seem inconsistent that later in the *Poetics* Aristotle should draw a parallel between form in poetry and form in painting. In section 6, after having restated the fundamental principle that in tragedy plot is the very soul of the art and character is secondary to it, he turns to painting for a parallel: there the "most beautiful colors laid on without order will not give one the same pleasure as a simple black-and-white sketch of a portrait."[8]

[6] 1447a. 15–25.

[7] 1447a. 19. Ingram Bywater (*Aristotle on the Art of Poetry* [Oxford, 1909], p. 102) sees in Aristotle's πολλά ("many things") an anticipation of Lessing's notion of the limits of the arts in the *Laokoön*. The limits of the arts were perceived with clarity in antiquity. Athenaeus (*ca.* A.D. 200), for example, tells this story: Sophocles once applied to a blushing boy the following line of poetry: "The light of love beams from his purple cheeks." A schoolmaster protested that "purple cheeks" was a poor expression because no painter could conceivably paint cheeks purple without making his picture ugly and ridiculous, and a poet meaning to describe beauty should not suggest ugliness. Sophocles replied that "purple cheeks" was fully as good as Homer's "golden-haired Apollo" or the "rosy-fingered Dawn." A painter could not paint hair golden, and hands with rosy fingers would look more like those of a dyer than those of a lovely lady. The point was that color in poetry was something different from color in painting. (*Deipnosophistiai* xiii. 603e.)

[8] 1450b. 1–3 (Ingram Bywater's translation); see also 1450b. 25–28.

Aristotle here compares plot in drama to design in painting and the portrayal of character in drama to color in painting. This comparison became the sanction in later centuries for many ingenious equivalences between the formal constituents of the two arts. But Aristotle is actually not establishing such equivalences at all. The emphasis is not upon color versus form or upon the equation of either or both with the formal elements of tragedy. The emphasis is, rather, upon the general notion of order. Aristotle says that character in tragedy is desirable but plot is more important and that if one must be sacrificed it should obviously be character. Similarly, in painting one finds design without color much more tolerable than even the most radiant colors without design. Aristotle turns to painting merely for an illustrative parallel. He has not equated any single element of painting with any single element of poetry, nor has he vitiated the important distinction made in his classification of the arts.

After the argument of the *Poetics* has moved from the means of imitation to the *objects* of imitation, the analogy with painting is more frequently made.[9] When the arts are classified according to the *means* of imitation, painting and poetry are further apart than comedy and tragedy. But when they are classified according to the kind of people represented, then a painting by Polygnotus is much closer to an epic poem than a comedy is. A comedy, in turn, is much closer to the unflattering caricatures of Pauson than it is to tragedy. Aristotle, by returning to this kind of analogy in considering the matter of idealistic, realistic, or satirical representation, seems to suggest that in such matters as these comparison between the arts can legitimately and fruitfully be made.

This is especially true of idealized representation. In section 5 of the *Poetics* Aristotle says that tragedy represents persons who are above the common level and that the tragic dramatist should follow the example of a good portrait painter who, without losing the likeness, yet makes a man handsomer than he really is.[10] This passage is of considerable importance. All critical systems that are basically

[9] 1448a. 5; 1454b. 10–11; 1460b. 8–11.

[10] 1454b. 10–11. Aristotle in the *Politics* (iii. 11) makes the point that men in association are often better than the individual. To illustrate the value of corporateness, he turns to the kind of reality that one finds in art, notably the art of painting: "Works of art differ from realities because in them the scattered elements are combined, although, if taken separately, the eye of one person or some other feature in another person would be fairer than in the picture."

7

realistic and therefore urge general fidelity to nature and experience but at the same time recommend the ennobling of reality must inevitably be concerned with adjudicating the claims of these two antithetical tendencies. To what extent does the artist imitate, and to what extent does he improve? One of the most attractive means of solving this problem has been not by argument but by analogy. And the analogy most frequently drawn has been the comparison with painting—most often with portrait painting. In good portraiture it is easy to see how nature can be elevated and yet remain nature still.

It was Aristotle who made this solution attractive to critics who subsequently faced the problem of reconciling ideal art with the demands of realism. He is responsible for the unshakable association that has existed between literary idealization and ideal form in the graphic arts. If the imagery of English neoclassical poetry tended to be pictorial and sculpturesque in its sublime moments, the reason is in part attributable to that line of analogical reasoning that finally goes back to the fifth section of the *Poetics*.

Aristotle's references to painting in the *Poetics*[11] do little more than adumbrate a theory of literary pictorialism. But in comparing poetry to painting at crucial points in the argument Aristotle provided his successors with a powerful example. He had implied that in the subjects treated there were profound affinities between the two arts, and it was later concluded by the Aristotelians that image and idea ought therefore to pass freely from one art to the other. He had, however, sharply distinguished painting from poetry with respect to the means of imitation employed. That distinction anticipated the emphasis upon the limits of the arts found not only in Lessing and the anti-pictorialists but also, as we shall see in chapter vi, among the pictorial theorists themselves.

Although Aristotle's use of the analogy between the two arts differs radically from Plato's, there is this basic similarity between them: in neither is the comparison of very great importance. The

[11] Among them I have not included 1450b. 34–36 or 1459a. 17–21, where Aristotle derives the principle of proper size and order (the famous conception of organic unity) from *zoon* (ζῷον), because the views of Bywater (*op. cit.* [n. 7], pp. 178–79), Butcher (*Aristotle's Theory of Poetry and Fine Art* [4th ed.; London, 1932], p. 188, n. 1), and Philip Wheelwright (*Aristotle* [New York, 1935], pp. 300–317) that *zoon* means "living organism" seem more convincing to me than the view of Susemihl (see Bywater, p. 179) and R. P. Hardie ("The *Poetics* of Aristotle," *Mind*, N.S., IV [July, 1895], 361–62) that it means a picture or a statue.

explanation may lie in the fact that in Greek culture "poetry and music, 'blest pair of Sirens,' were inseparable sisters," and that "no Greek ever thought of giving painting and sculpture and the enjoyment of visual art a place in paideia, whereas the educational ideals of Greece were always dominated by poetry, music, and rhythm."[12]

Horace has been more closely linked with our subject than any other critic largely because he gave to the world the memorable phrase *ut pictura poesis*. Nonetheless, he resembles his greater but less immediately relevant Greek predecessors in this respect: he ignores systematic argument about the relations of the arts and merely strikes out fortuitous and memorable parallels. In the passage in the *Ars poetica* (ll. 361 ff.) that provides the context of his famous phrase, Horace is saying that some poems please only once but that others can bear repeated readings and close critical examination. *Ut pictura poesis:* so it is with painting! Some pictures in a gallery please at a distance and in the shade; others survive intensive scrutiny in full daylight. This, and no more, is what the critic says in connection with his illustration from painting. Actually the phrase means less than what it says, which is, "As a painting, so also a poem." It really implies only this: "As sometimes in painting, so occasionally in poetry." There is no warrant whatever in Horace's text for the later interpretation: "Let a poem be like a painting."

And yet elsewhere in the treatise (ll. 1–9) there is implicit a doctrine that underlies the pictorialism of later literary criticism. In these famous opening lines Horace concedes to poet and painter alike the right of imaginative license but insists that it be exercised with restraint, in conformity with nature and good sense. He ridicules the unnatural and the grotesque in verse as "idle fancies shaped like a sick man's dream." Such images are fully as unacceptable in poetry as they would be in painting. For who would not laugh at a picture in which a human head appears on the neck of a horse or the tail of a black and ugly fish below the bust of a lovely lady? Here Horace is writing from an assumption about mimetic art that differs radically from the views of Plato and Aristotle. Imitation for Plato, in its highest sense, meant the imitation of the ideal form that exists eternally in the supersensory world. For Aristotle imitation meant doing

[12] Jaeger, *op. cit.* (n. 5), II, 224, 228.

in another realm what nature does in hers: the achievement in matter other than the original matter of a form that possesses unity of its own and that, when fully realized, achieves its own end and obeys its own laws. But for Horace imitation meant usually either imitation of other authors, imitation of the actual conditions and customs of life, or imitation of the object as it exists in nature.[13] The first kind of imitation—that of imitating literary models—is irrelevant here; but the others, the faithful rendition of life and of nature, are of the highest relevance. This aesthetic ideal—the vivid representation of reality—could be better achieved in painting than in poetry. Therefore, whenever in the history of criticism the phrase "imitation of nature" has been literally interpreted, the analogy with painting has been significantly present, and the notion that poetry must resemble painting has tended to be a critical dogma.

CRITICISM: A THEORY OF PICTORIALISM

The view of mimesis implicit in Horace's criticism was by no means confined to him. It was one of the most widespread conceptions of late Greek and of Roman antiquity. To it we owe the vogue of *ut pictura poesis*, both then and in the modern centuries.

This view of imitation was held by Plutarch, who would be important to our story if for no other reason than that he gave to the world one of the most influential comments ever uttered on the relations of the arts—the comment, which he attributed to Simonides of Ceos (*ca.* 556–467 B.C.), that painting is mute poetry and poetry a speaking picture.[14] But Plutarch is important also because he makes overt what must have been implicit in much ancient thought. For him the term "imitation" links art and reality. It is, in fact, the close relationship of art and reality that validates art; and that relationship is more prominently embodied in painting than in any other form of aesthetic expression. Painting therefore becomes exemplar and guide, possessing a moral force that other arts often lack. In discuss-

---

[13] See McKeon, *op. cit.* (n. 5), pp. 173–74. See also *Ars poetica* 317–18, 268–69, 310–11. My discussion is confined to Horace's criticism. I am not here concerned with his odes, where centaurs, chimeras, and other "unnatural" creatures often figure.

[14] τὴν μὲν ζωγραφίαν ποίησις σιωπῶσαν (προσαγορεύει) τὴν δὲ ποίησιν ζωγραφίαν λαλοῦσαν (*Moralia* 346 f). Laurence Binyon has said that "a precisely identical saying is proverbial among the Chinese" (*Proceedings of the British Academy 1917–1918*, p. 383).

ing a young man's study of poetry, Plutarch invokes the parallel with painting in his definition of the ends of poetic art: "We shall steady the young man still more if, at his first entrance into poetry, we give a general description of the poetic art as an imitative art and faculty analogous to painting."[15]

Plutarch does not confine the analogy with painting to poetry alone. In his life of Alexander the Great he compares his method as a biographer—his portrayal of "the signs and tokens" of the mind only—to the practice of the painter who copies the countenance, which reveals the manners and the disposition, and neglects the other parts of the body, which reveal little of the moral, psychological, and social life of man.[16] History, too, must achieve, through lifelike imitation of character, emotion, and the natural scene, the vividness of painting itself. Of Thucydides' description of an expedition Plutarch says: "Such a description is characterized by pictorial vividness both in its arrangement and in its power of description."[17]

The word in Plutarch's comment on Thucydides that Frank Cole Babbitt has rendered "pictorial vividness" is the Greek word *enargeia* (ἐνάργεια). When artistic imitation came to be understood as a rendering of natural objects, social details, and psychological effects, then *enargeia* became an important term in literary criticism. But it originated in rhetoric, where it was used to describe the power that verbal visual imagery possessed in setting before the hearer the very object or scene being described. It was one of the tendencies of later antiquity and of many modern centuries to blur the distinction between poetry and rhetoric and to adopt as critical terms words that had had their most intelligent uses in instructing orators, not poets. Not all critics, to be sure, confused the two disciplines. Longinus, for one, is careful to distinguish a rhetorical from a poetical image. The poetical image is intended to produce enthralment or astonishment (ἔκπληξις), but the rhetorical image is intended to achieve *enargeia*, or pictorial vividness.[18] And yet Longinus himself, in whose critical system it is important to make this distinction, is not always careful to observe it. Even he must admit the value in poetry of *enargeia*.

[15] *Moralia* 17f–18a.

[16] North's translation of *Plutarch's Lives* (Cambridge, 1676), p. 559.

[17] *Moralia* 347a, 347c in Frank Cole Babbitt (trans.), *Plutarch* ("Loeb Classical Library" [London, 1936]), IV, 501.

[18] *On the Sublime* xv. 2.

The scene in Simonides in which Achilles rises above his tomb to appear to the Greeks who are about to sail for home is memorable for its pictorial liveliness. Never, says Longinus, has a visual scene been verbally rendered with greater *enargeia*.[19]

The concept was not unknown to Aristotle, who recognized that a powerful rhetorical effect is achieved by the orator who is able, as it were, to set things before the eyes of the auditor by using words that signify actuality. But to describe that effect Aristotle uses not the word *enargeia* (ἐνάργεια) but the homonymous word *energeia* (ἐνέργεια).[20] The difference between the two is eloquent. *Enargeia* implies the achievement in verbal discourse of a natural quality or of a pictorial quality that is highly natural. *Energeia* refers to the actualization of potency, the realization of capacity or capability, the achievement in art and rhetoric of the dynamic and purposive life of nature. Poetry possesses *energeia* when it has achieved its final form and produces its proper pleasure, when it has achieved its own independent being quite apart from its analogies with nature or another art, and when it operates as an autonomous form with an effectual working power of its own. But Plutarch, Horace, and the later Hellenistic and Roman critics found poetry effective when it achieved verisimilitude—when it resembled nature or a pictorial representation of nature. For Plutarchian *enargeia*, the analogy with painting is important; for Aristotelian *energeia*, it is not.[21]

Along with the tendency in late antiquity to turn away from literature as an autonomous art to nature, to human character, and to an analogous art like that of painting for the validation of certain literary effects, there was also the habit of turning to psychology. Aristotle had said that imagination is impossible without sensation.[22] Theoretically, it could follow from this that literary *enargeia* could be achieved through any kind of image arising indifferently from any one or any combination of the senses. But *phantasia* (φαντασία),

---

[19] *Ibid.* xv. 7. The term appears everywhere in the rhetorical and literary criticism of antiquity. See *Three Literary Letters of Dionysius of Halicarnassus*, ed. W. Rhys Roberts (Cambridge, 1901), p. 190; *Demetrius on Style*, ed. W. Rhys Roberts (Cambridge, 1902), p. 279; Quintilian *Institutio Oratoria* iv. 2. 63; vi. 2. 32, 36; viii. 3. 61–62 (where *enargeia* is translated *illustratio* and *evidentia*); and Dio Chrysostom *Twelfth or Olympic Discourse* 25.

[20] *Rhetoric* iii. 111.1–2.

[21] See Wheelwright, *op. cit.* (n. 11), index under *energeia*.

[22] *De anima* 427b–429a.

the Greek word for imagination, comes ultimately from the word for light, *phaos* (φάος); and in Plato, as we have seen, and also in Aristotle, Cicero, and Horace, the sight is considered the most godlike of the five senses. From this type of evaluative and hierarchical psychology it follows that visual images and pictorial effects in words would be considered more desirable than any other kind. Of this widespread notion—and Sforza Pallavicino said in 1644 that Horace's statement of it had become proverbial[23]—Cicero has given us one of the clearest formulations: "Every metaphor is directed to the senses, but chiefly to the eye, which is the sharpest of all." Metaphors derived from the other senses are acceptable, but the most vivid arise from and appeal to the sight, which, compared with the other senses, is much keener—"multo acrior."[24]

In still another respect Roman antiquity provided an atmosphere congenial to the doctrine of *ut pictura poesis:* it made rational and empirical Plato's conception of ideal form by developing the hints concerning idealization that Aristotle had given in the *Poetics* and elsewhere. In Plato's and, more especially, in derivative systems of aesthetics, ideal beauty is given independent metaphysical status; it is ontologically real. From that belief diametrically opposed consequences arise: either artists are doomed to produce only the dimmest of dim copies of beauty and even actual falsifications of its true values; or they are exalted almost to the level of God Himself, since, like Him, they create by copying an immutable paradigm in which there is neither variableness nor shadow of turning. But this conception of ideal beauty was profoundly different from the ideal form that Cicero and Seneca conceived, even though there are many verbal echoes of Plato in the later writers.[25] For them ideal beauty arises not from the contemplation of an ontologically independent pattern in the heavens but from a process of generalization and synthesis

[23] *Del bene* iii. 2. 50. See also Antonio Possevino (*Tractatio de Poësi & Pictura* [Lyons, 1595]), who argues that one of the most cogent reasons for the tenacity of *ut pictura* was that the eye was considered superior to all other senses. He traces the idea back to Plato and Aristotle but, like Pallavicino, credits Horace (*Ars poetica* 464) with making it proverbial.

[24] *De oratore* iii. 161.

[25] Cicero *Orator* ii. 7–iii. 10; Seneca *Ad Lucilium epistulae morales* lxv. 4–8; lviii. 16 ff. For discussions of the difference between the idealism of Plato and that of Seneca and Cicero, see Edmondo Cione's Preface to the Italian translation of Erwin Panofsky's *Idea* (Florence, 1952), pp. viii–ix, and also Panofsky himself, pp. 13–17.

that selects and unites the scattered excellencies of nature. Nature may be corrected but never completely transcended. Beauty so selected and combined, so generalized and synthesized, is better and nobler than reality, but it arises directly from observing and experiencing reality itself. It is nature methodized but nature still— *la belle nature* of neoclassical thought (see Plate IV).

Plotinian idealism, in spite of the many verbal analogies it drew from the art of sculpture, was not congenial to any conception of the pictorial or the visual that resembles the one popular in late antiquity. It discouraged the artist from imitating nature and bade him turn his gaze inward to the immaterial reality that lies back of visible form. But the Ciceronian and Senecan conception of generalized beauty seemed everywhere to invoke the example of painting and to sanction the association of the two arts. Perhaps the reason for this lies not in any philosophical inevitability but rather in historical example. We have noted that when Aristotle wished to illustrate the kind of ideal beauty that can be achieved by improving upon nature without destroying the resemblance to nature, he turned to painting, chiefly portrait painting, for an illustration. There were others as well who gave currency to the notion. When the Xenophontic Socrates defended the type of ideal synthesis we are discussing, he was speaking to Parrhasius the painter and therefore drew most of his illustrations from that art.[26] But the most important illustration of how to achieve ideal beauty was the story of how Zeuxis painted Helen of Troy—a story retold countless times both in antiquity and in the modern world.

"Give me, then," said Zeuxis [in Cicero's version of the story] . . . "the most beautiful of these virgins, while I paint the picture which I promised you, so that the reality may be transferred from the breathing model to the mute likeness." Then the citizens of Crotona . . . collected the virgins into one place, and gave the painter the opportunity of selecting whom he chose. But he selected five. . . . For he did not think he could find all the component parts of perfect beauty in one person, because nature has made nothing of any class absolutely perfect in every part. Therefore, as if nature would not have enough to give everybody if it had given everything to one, it balances one advantage bestowed upon a person by another disadvantage.[27]

[26] Xenophon *Memorabilia* iii. 10. 1–5.

[27] *Second Treatise on Rhetorical Invention* II. 1 (C. D. Yonge [trans.], *Orations* [London, 1894], IV, 308).

The kind of idealization so frequently illustrated by this famous anecdote and so frequently recommended to both painter and poet suggests that one reason for the all too common interpretation of "mimesis" to mean the imitation of other literature and other art arose from the belief that antecedent artistic example was the best possible school for the achievement of ideal form. Imitate nature, to be sure; but also imitate nature already methodized. "Nature and Homer were, he found, the same." And in a period when distinctions between the arts were blurred, nature methodized could mean for a literary man not only antecedent literary works but also relevant works of graphic art. It is important that one contemplate nature methodized; it is of less concern whether it has been methodized by the pen, the chisel, or the brush. The material and method used are of little importance anyhow, since idealization takes place in the mind of the artist before he begins to work.

Such tendencies as these can be illustrated by a literary tour de force, in which painting and poetry alike contribute to an idealized verbal portrait. In Lucian's dialogue entitled *Eikones*, written in A.D. 162, one Lycinus reports that he has met an exceedingly lovely lady on the streets, who, like the Gorgon, had all but petrified him. His friend Polystratus asks for a description. Lycinus begins by levying a contribution from several famous artists of antiquity. The hair, forehead, and eyebrows he borrows from the Cnidian Venus of Praxiteles. Painters and poets alike are called in for color. Homer, called "the best of painters," colors the limbs as he had done those of Menelaus—in ivory tinged with red; and Pindar donates the brows of violet hue. When each of the sculptors, painters, and poets has offered his peculiar excellence, the lady is endowed with grace of motion, eloquence of speech, sweetness of voice, and the wisdom of the Milesian Aspasia.[28] And this inconceivable pastiche of marble, bronze, paint, and Greek adjectives is, like Pygmalion's image, supposed to come to life. Lucian's meaning and intention may be obscure. But if nothing else is clear from his verbal icon, this is: poetry and painting were intimately associated, and artistic idealization involved the collaboration of all the arts. Lucian's description is im-

[28] *Works of Lucian of Samosata*, ed. H. W. Fowler and F. G. Fowler (Oxford, 1905), III, 13–23. A. M. Harmon in his edition of Lucian considers this work an elaborate compliment to Panthea, the girl of Smyrna who became a favorite of the Emperor Verus (*Lucian* ["Loeb Classical Library" (London, 1925)], IV, 255). It is unlikely that the work has any satirical intention.

portant because it makes overt what may have been implicit in the idealized imagery of classical and neoclassical poetry.

In these opening pages I have not argued that the naturalism of pictorialist doctrine is the key to all classical aesthetics and art. Plutarch's theory can hardly be expected to account for everything in the imagery of Horace's odes and Vergil's epic, to say nothing of Pindar and the Greek drama. But my subject is neoclassical, not classical, pictorialism, and the criticism I have just described is the intellectual foundation of the neoclassical.

I do not wish to undertake a full-scale defense of the naturalistic doctrine I have commented on in connection with Plutarch, Horace, and other writers of late antiquity. And yet I find it desirable to say a passing word in its favor, if to do no more than deplore the contemporary notion that classical realism is always naïve and unsophisticated beyond belief.[29] Whenever it is encountered—not only in late antiquity but also in Shakespeare and in the eighteenth century—hands are raised in outrage or embarrassment. It must be admitted that the naturalism I have described is too simple to account for the triumphs of good realistic art, which, even at its most representational, must necessarily be more than the mere "reduplication of perceptible objects, whose value . . . is the same in kind as the value of the objects which it reduplicates."[30] But even so the notion does have general "orientative" value. And the extraordinarily rare power of achieving in a medium so unpromising as language the freshness and force of nature and life should not be undervalued merely because it is sometimes justified on the basis of a naïve illusionism.

Whatever the final verdict, at least this should be said. Naturalism in literary art, like naturalism in graphic design, is not an unsophisticated or primitive thing. It is the product of artistically ripe and intellectually mature civilizations. What the art historian has said of naturalistic design may be applied to poetry—more specifically, to poetry in its relation to painting.

---

[29] "Wie ausschlieszlich und oberflächlich beherrscht die Illusionswirkung die um laufenden Anekdoten von griechischen Künstler und ihren Werken !" (Karl Borinski, *Die Antike in Poetik und Kunsttheorie* [Leipzig, 1914], I, 1).

[30] R. G. Collingwood, "Plato's Philosophy of Art," *Mind*, XXXIV (April, 1925), 154.

The easiest and least true of these facile generalizations is that which regards naturalistic decoration . . . as the inevitable reflection of a rather primitive civilization in which . . . men lived close to nature. The exact opposite is in fact the case: such naturalistic decoration is produced in courtly civilizations in which men live in surroundings urban enough for distance to lend enchantment to their view of nature.[31]

ICONIC POETRY

To appreciate fully the association of the arts that modern European culture inherited from antiquity it is necessary to extend the discussion from criticism to literature. Undoubtedly the relation of Greek and Latin literature to the graphic arts was more productive than the world now realizes. Of the work of the great painters of antiquity—Polygnotus, Zeuxis, Parrhasius, Apelles—not a single undisputed example has survived, and we know about their works only what we read in encomiums written by literary men. The paintings of Pompeii, Herculaneum, and Stabiae, mercifully preserved by protective mud and ash, were created by artists whose names are unrecorded or, when recorded, elsewhere unknown; and the paintings, lovely though some of them assuredly are, have no place in literary discussion and therefore bear little direct, demonstrable relation to poetry.

It is therefore understandably difficult for us to learn very much about the indebtedness of specific poems to what must have been an important source of idea and image, the arts of both painting and sculpture. But there are several hints that the commerce between the arts was lively. One of the persistent legends of ancient times was that Phidias created his most famous statue (that of the king of the gods, which stood at Olympia and became for Greek, Roman, and Hellenistic culture the official and definitive representative of Zeus) from no living model but from an imagination stimulated by those verses in the *Iliad* in which the heavens tremble and Olympus quakes as Zeus speaks, bends his dark brows, shakes his ambrosial curls, and

[31] Joan Evans, *Nature in Design* (Oxford, 1933), p. 2. Gisela M. A. Richter has found that the art of Greeks in Italy moved from stylization to naturalism (*Ancient Italy* [Ann Arbor, Mich., 1955], p. 2). Arnold Hauser believes, however, that in the perennial conflict between geometrically ornamental art forms and naturalistically imitative forms, the naturalistic is the older (*Social History of Art* [London, 1951], I, 23).

nods the approval of fate.[32] In the imaginatively powerful series of landscapes discovered in 1848 in the arcade of a Roman house the inspiration is literary. All the eight sections illustrate episodes from the tenth and eleventh books of the *Odyssey*.[33] The influences must have been reciprocal. Literature could not have escaped shaping impulses from so distinguished an accomplishment as Greek and Roman painting, of which such a regrettably small proportion has actually survived.

Fortunately there has come down to us a kind of poetry that in its way strikingly illustrates the association of verbal and graphic art. This poetry, of which a work of graphic art is the subject, I shall in these pages call "iconic."[34] In such poetry the poet contemplates a real or imaginary work of art that he describes or responds to in some other way. Poetry of this kind may reveal not only the kind of

[32] i. 528–30. Phidias' Zeus sat on a throne of cedarwood and was surrounded with smaller statues. Its flesh was of ivory, its robe of beaten gold. In its right hand it bore a statue of victory in ivory and gold; in its left, a scepter mounted by an eagle. In A.D. 475 the statue was carried off to Constantinople by the Emperor Theodosius I, and it was there destroyed by fire (see Dio Chrysostom, *Discourses*, ed. J. W. Cohoon ["Loeb Classical Library" (London, 1939)], II, 28–29, n. 1). For some notion of what the original statue looked like see the coin reproduced as Plate II in Panofsky, *op. cit.* (n. 25).

[33] For a reproduction in color of one painting in this series, "Ulysses in the Land of the Laestrygonians," see Amedeo Maiuri, *Roman Painting*, trans. Stuart Gilbert (Geneva, 1953), p. 33. The painting is now in the Vatican Museum.

[34] I justify this usage of the word "iconic" to refer to literary descriptions of works of graphic art by the example of Lucian and Philostratus (see below, pp. 30, 31, and n. 65), who called their works in this genre *eikones* (εἰκώνες). They use it of their own prose; I have extended the usage to poetry. Julius Schlosser-Magnino in *La letteratura artistica* (Florence, 1935), an Italian enlargement, revision, and translation of the German original, places such poetry as this in the category of what he calls "la letteratura della 'ekphrasis'" (p. 12). His category is broad and includes the literal descriptions of Pliny and Pausanias. I use the noun "ecphrasis" and the adjective "ecphrastic" in a more limited sense to refer to that special quality of giving voice and language to the otherwise mute art object (see below, pp. 49–50, 53). My usage is etymologically sound since the Greek noun and adjective come from *ekphrazein* (ἐκφράζειν), which means "to speak out," "to tell in full." It should be clear that my usage is more limited than the usual one. The *OED* defines "ecphrasis" by citing an example from 1715: "a plain declaration or interpretation of a thing." The *Oxford Classical Dictionary* defines it as "the rhetorical description of a work of art." Saintsbury says it is "a set description intended to bring person, place, picture, &c., vividly before the mind's eye" (*A History of Criticism and Literary Taste in Europe* [New York, 1902], I, 491). For Saintsbury, if we confine ourselves to the vocabulary of the ancients, an *ekphrasis* is that which achieves *enargeia* (see below, pp. 35–36).

art that a given poet admires—that to us is of secondary importance—but also why he admires it, what posture he assumes before it, and how he interprets the role of language in relation to it. Iconic poetry, which antedates all recorded criticism, became a significant part of the classical heritage, greatly to the enrichment of the tradition of *ut pictura poesis.*

Such poetry has a long and impressive history that extends from Homer to Yeats and includes the Greek, Latin, and Byzantine anthologists, the rhapsodists of late antiquity, and distinguished poets of most modern European cultures. From this rich store we can select only a few examples: Homer, Alexandrian poetry, the great Latins, and miscellaneous works in late antiquity and the early centuries of the Christian era.

Perhaps the prototype of all such poetry is Homer's description, in Book XVIII of the *Iliad,* of the shield which Hephaestus is making for Achilles. This passage, extending to over 150 lines of Greek verse, is one of the longest and most substantial pieces of iconic poetry ever written. Although Hephaestus is introduced as making the work and although Homer keeps him before us with such phrases as "he wrought," "he fashioned," this is not, as Lessing believed, the presentation of an action or a process.[35] The reader's attention is made to concentrate on the object, which is described panel by panel, scene by scene, episode by episode. It is remarkable how the eye is held fast to the shield. Values other than the visual ones—and they are highly important—do arise, but they arise from the description itself, not from the action of making.

Those archeologists who have treated the shield as an artifact, those cultural historians who have speculated about the kind of object that Homer had before him and what it reveals about early Greek life, and especially those critics who have attempted to reproduce it to prove that Homer was a "painter" skilful in perspective and plastic arrangement have, though for different reasons, missed

---

[35] "Homer does not describe the shield as finished and complete, but as it is being wrought . . . thereby converting a tedious painting of a body into a vivid picture of an action" (*Laokoon* ["Bohn Library" (London, 1914)], p. 107 [chap. xviii]). Lessing seems to ignore precisely what happens in reading Homer's icon—that the reader moves from section to section, detail to detail, and the verbs referring to the process of making are secondary. Lessing disliked description on principle but admired Homer's and was forced to find grounds other than the visual and pictorial to explain his admiration.

the point as widely as did Lessing.[36] The passage remains faithful to the demands of verbal art and is by no means only an enumerative description. The shield becomes an emblem of the life of man: of nature and society, of the seasons of the year, and of cities at war and in peace; of agricultural scenes and the diversions of the rural day. There is obviously much that is non-pictorial: sound, motion, and sociological detail all "appear" on the surface of Hephaestus' masterpiece.

How, then, shall we interpret the description? We can see in it the finest flowering of Homer's love of the decorated object—of the thing useful in war or peace that the craftsman's art has made splendid and beautiful.[37] Or we can view it in the context of the epic action—in reference to what Goethe once called "the grand internal relations of the persons and the events." Homer has made great poetic virtue of the necessity that Achilles now be given a new shield to replace his old one, the one that Patroclus had worn into fateful battle and that Hector now proudly wears. The new armor, as Thetis says and as Hephaestus at once recognizes, is for a tragically doomed and short-lived mortal, for whom the only available immortality arises from military honor. Of that glory, so dear to men that die, the shield that Hephaestus has made is a radiant symbol.

The details that appear on the embossed surface are also profoundly relevant to the poem itself. The city at war and the city at peace are reminiscent of the tragic conflict that agitated the breast of more than one Homeric hero, chiefly Achilles himself—the conflict between the hard and destructive ways of war and the ways of peace that bring comfortable joys and the satisfactions of beauty and love. That conflict, one of the leitmotivs of the *Iliad*, appears on the shield in the murder and the ugly litigation that take place even in the peaceful city and in the descent of two ravening lions upon the peaceful pasture.

[36] See below, pp. 231–32. For a discussion of several interpretations of the shield see Samuel Eliot Bassett, *The Poetry of Homer* (Berkeley, Calif., 1938), pp. 94–99; for the form of the shield see F. Melian Stawell, *Homer & the Iliad* (London, 1909), pp. 199 ff., Frank Lowry Clark, *A Study of the Iliad in Translation* (Chicago, 1927), pp. 236 ff., and Walter Leaf, *A Companion to the Iliad* (London, 1892), pp. 298, 310–11.

[37] For other examples of Homer's love of the products of civilization see the houses built by Hephaestus (*Iliad* i), the lyre of Apollo (i), the corselet and shield of Agamemnon (xi), the shield of Hector (xii), the robe of Hera (xiv), and the sword of Neptune (xiv).

But these internal relationships must for us be subservient to the description of the shield as a work of art—a description that stands at the headwaters of iconic poetry. The verses are essentially, though indirectly, a celebration of the divine craftsman and the miracle of his art, even though Hephaestus himself remains shadowy in the background and his shield alone remains at the focus of attention. Viewed thus, the many non-visual details, which the pictorialist critics have overlooked, become peculiarly significant. For the rendering of such details in graphic art creates, a fortiori, admiration for what the artist can do with refractory and un-promising material. It is wonderful to reproduce visible form but more wonderful still to represent in tin and gold invisible moral qualities, the sound of music, the rhythms of the dance, the lives of men in society, and even the chiaroscuro and color of the painter:

> He made upon it a soft field, the pride of the tilled land,
> wide and triple-ploughed, with many ploughmen upon it.
> . . . .
> The earth darkened behind them and looked like earth that
> had been ploughed
> though it was gold.

Gold has achieved the blackness and texture of newly turned earth. "Such was the wonder of the shield's forging."[38]

And such was the meaning of Homer's icon—for both the poetic and the critical tradition that followed him: art can achieve lifelike vividness. Art may achieve form. The shield is cunningly fashioned and its circular rim is bounded by the ocean and at its center there are sun, moon, and stars. It may also achieve great beauty of surface (the gold gleams with brightness) and utility (it is great and strong, worthy of the hero who will wear it). But above all it is like life itself, and herein lies the miracle. Huge though it is, it is still a shield. Yet on it are the cities, the wars, the feasts, the industries, and the loves of men; the heavens, the sea, the seasons of the year, and the yield of the earth. *Multum in parvo.* And

[38] *Iliad* xviii. 541–42, 548–49. I quote Richmond Lattimore's translation (Chicago, 1951), pp. 389–90. For an interesting parallel to Homer's description see Hesiod's "The Shield of Hercules" (ll. 130 ff.), in *The Works of Hesiod, Callimachus, and Theognis,* trans. J. Banks (London, 1914), pp. 51–72. For an interpretation of the shield that, like mine, stresses the vivid naturalism of Homer's description see Jane E. Harrison, *Introductory Studies in Greek Art* (New York, 1892), pp. 141–42.

bronze, tin, gold, and silver have been able to represent the redness of blood, the glitter of polished stones, the blackness of soil, the color of fruit, and the gleam of oil on naked flesh. It is the miracle of the shield's rendering that it has imitated nature. In his use of poetry to describe, to celebrate, and perhaps even to vie with a work of graphic art Homer has created precisely the aesthetic situation that most frequently prevailed in antiquity when the verbal and the graphic arts collaborated.

The greatest single repository of iconic poems in antiquity was the *Greek Anthology*, which, when it was compiled in the tenth century A.D., was based on three older anthologies. Two of these came from classical antiquity: the *Garland of Meleager*, perhaps compiled—though the date is uncertain—in the first century B.C. and containing epigrams from the seventh to the third centuries B.C.; and the *Garland of Philippus*, perhaps compiled in the reign of Augustus and containing the Roman poets. Of the seven types of epigram that these collections include, one of the most prominent is the art epigram or the brief iconic poem. There are some thirty-nine epigrams extant on a statue of Aphrodite and some thirty-nine on Myron's famous cow.[39]

In considering these epigrams—indeed, in considering any poetry of this type in Part I of this study—we are not concerned with the popularity of particular works or styles of art or with whether poems were written about copies or originals, about real or imaginary pictures. We are concerned, rather, with the conventions and accomplishments of iconic poetry considered as poetry and with the critical and aesthetic presuppositions that such poetry reveals.

One of the most interesting and persistent of the conventions that clung to this genre can be introduced from our consideration of the art epigrams of the *Anthology*. The Greek word *epigramma* originally referred to an inscription in verse usually placed on a statue, tomb, or funerary column. Simple prose formulas appeared on Greek tombstones from the earliest times and may have been

---

[39] See the Preface to the *Greek Anthology*, trans. W. R. Paton ("Loeb Classical Library" [London, 1927]) and Paul Vitry, "Étude sur les épigrammes de l'anthologie palatine qui contiennent la description d'une œuvre d'art," *Revue archéologique*, XXIV (January–June, 1894), 315–64. Most of my material on the iconic epigram is drawn from Vitry's excellent study.

taken over from the Phoenicians along with the alphabet.[40] Verse inscriptions go back at least to the sixth century B.C. in Greece and up through those metrical extemporaries that were, in the best period of Latin literature, inscribed on statues sacred to Priapus. The poetical epigram never lost the marks of its origin. It was one of the oldest devices of the Greek epigrammatist to make the statue, the urn, the column, or the monument speak to the beholder or passer-by. A blackish-green boulder of Antibes, which may go back as far as 500 B.C., speaks as follows: "I am the Delighter, minister of the holy goddess Aphrodite; to those who have placed me here may Cypris render joy."[41] This habit persisted for many centuries. In the fifty epitaphs for Cecchino Bracci that Michelangelo wrote there are some three quatrains in which the tomb speaks: "la sepoltura," said Michelangelo, "parla a chi legge questi versi."[42] The flagstone on Shakespeare's grave in the Church of the Holy Trinity, Stratford, admonishes the passer-by: "Good frend, for Iesvs sake forbeare,/ To digg the dvst encloased heare"; and the inscription on his monument in the chancel begins: "Stay, passenger, why goest thou by so fast?"[43] Keats's urn, although we are told it is a silent form, speaks; and when it speaks it utters its baffling five-word epigram.

Simonides called painting mute poetry. But in the tradition we are studying, the mute statue was given a voice and the silent form was endowed with the power of speech.[44]

Apart from conventions such as the one just described, what do the iconic epigrams reveal? They again and again, with monotonous reiteration, proclaim the notion that the work of art is praiseworthy because it has created the illusion of reality. Such illusionism represented a popular response to art, and perhaps one reason that the naturalism of the ancients has seemed outrageously naïve to some is that it is often expressed in the hyperboles

[40] Paul Friedländer and Herbert B. Hoffleit, *Epigrammata: Greek Inscriptions in Verse* (Berkeley, Calif., 1948), p. 7.

[41] *Ibid.*, pp. 43–45. See also Simonides' "Epitaph of Cleobulus," trans. Richmond Lattimore, in *Greek Lyrics* (Chicago, 1955), p. 31.

[42] My attention was called to these epitaphs by Erwin Panofsky's reply to Werner Weisbach in *Gazette des beaux-arts*, ser. 6, XIX (May–June, 1938), 306.

[43] Tucker Brooke, *Shakespeare of Stratford* (New Haven, Conn., 1926), p. 87.

[44] This effect I shall call ecphrastic. See above, n. 34.

23

of the people. This is apparent in the fourth mime of the Alexandrian writer Herodas, where two women admire a statue in the temple of Aesculapius. One says, "Look at that child strangling the goose. If you did not see the marble before your very eyes, you would swear that he was going to speak. It's a sure thing that in time men will end up by making stone itself live."[45] In the *Greek Anthology* painters and sculptors are praised for having perpetrated a deception: the reality of their work is such that it becomes confused with nature itself. Calves low at the cow of Myron, and one creature dies vainly sucking the bronze udder.[46]

The vulgar illusionism of Herodas' women was not, however, confined to popular verse. In Pliny's survey of the history of painting the same aesthetic value is expressed frequently and is made the touchstone of greatness. Crows are deceived by the tiles of a brilliantly successful painting and fly down to settle on them. Birds peck at Zeuxis' grapes. So elated is the painter at this testimonial to his naturalness that he challenges his rival Parrhasius to display his picture that stands behind yonder linen curtain. When he discovers that the curtain is itself a painting by Parrhasius, Zeuxis surrenders the prize to his rival, admitting that though it required great skill to deceive the birds, it required even greater to deceive another painter.[47]

Such naïve naturalism is a common response to the visual arts in antiquity by the people and by the poet, by ordinary Greek women and by Homer: the work of art is more natural than nature itself, the material has been conquered to produce verisimilitude, art conceals itself, and nature has triumphed.

The *Greek Anthology* is useful in introducing important conventions associated with the iconic epigram and also in demonstrating how widely diffused in time and place were the habits of judging plastic art by the closeness of its approximation to reality. The task remains of considering, in more systematically chronological fashion, important moments in the history of ancient pictorialism. According to Andrew Lang, one of the three distinguishing characteristics

[45] Vitry, *op. cit.* (n. 39), pp. 346–47.

[46] ix. 604, 713–42, esp. 721, 735.

[47] C. Plinius Secundus *Historia Naturalis* xxv. 65–66 (trans. K. Jex-Blake, *The Elder Pliny's Chapters on the History of Art* [London, 1896], pp. 110–11).

of the Alexandrian age was the pictorialism of its poetry.[48] Such
pictorialism it of course did not create. Back of Alexandrian culture
lay centuries of development in literary pictorialism: the descriptions
of art objects in Homer and Hesiod; the earlier forms of the art
epigram; the iconic passages in the Greek drama, of which Euripides'
reproduction of details in a sculptured gigantomachy may be taken
as typical;[49] and the pictorially conceived songs of Anacreon.

Anacreon's lyrics require brief comment not only because of
their immediate impact on Hellenistic literature but also because
they established conventions for the shorter iconic lyric that were
to persist during many epochs in the subsequent history of Western
culture. The most important of such conventions is extremely simple.
It consists merely of the poet's addressing Hephaestus or some
human artisan and requesting him to create an art object according
to the specifications laid down by the poet in his poem. In one
lyric, which was brilliantly imitated during the late seventeenth century by the Earl of Rochester,[50] Anacreon commissions Hephaestus
to make him a drinking cup. In another he specifies in great detail
the scenes he wishes portrayed on its surface. In still another he
addresses a painter and requests him to paint the poet's mistress
according to the description that then follows.

The bare description of this Anacreontic device does not sound
promising, and there are innumerable abuses of the form by inferior
writers in the centuries that followed. These inferior poems should
not, however, be allowed to wither the freshness of lyrics created
by an Anacreon or a Rochester. The value of the convention of
summoning and instructing the painter lay in providing for an aural
form like the song a means of ordering visual detail. Looked at
from the perspective of the criticism we have already described,
these poems may be said to achieve the *enargeia* that ancient critics
and rhetoricians were almost unanimous in requiring.

Though Alexandrian culture did not invent poetic pictorialism,

---

[48] "Theocritus and His Age," in *Theocritus, Bion, and Moschus* (London, 1901),
pp. xi–xlii.

[49] *Ion* 184 ff.

[50] In the "Bowl," a poem beginning, "Contrive me, Vulcan, such a cup." For the
odes referred to, see Thomas Moore (trans.), *The Odes of Anacreon* (New York, n.d.),
pp. 46, 71 ff., 148, and Thomas Stanley (trans.) and A. H. Bullen (ed.), *The Odes of
Anacreon* (New York, 1901), pp. 52, 53, 62–63, 64–65, 95.

it certainly developed and sophisticated it. This may be owing in part to the fact that in this period splendid works of painting were produced, that knowledge of the art was widely diffused, that even private men collected paintings, that lesser artists copied masterpieces for the lower classes, and that the art of painting was not exclusively devoted to interior frescoes but could be shown to the multitudes in portable panels displayed on the public streets.

The masterpieces of Alexandrian painting have all disappeared, and one can therefore only conjecture about the exact nature of the relations of poetry to the sister art. Even so, it is possible to say that the relationship must have been intimate and fruitful. From those[51] who have compared Alexandrian poetry with the later but Hellenistically inspired frescoes of Pompeii and Herculaneum we learn that the principle of *ut pictura poesis* was operative centuries before Horace created the phrase. All the descriptive details, for example, of Moschus' famous "picture" of Europa riding the divine bull—so like Tennyson's rendition of the same mythic scene in the "Palace of Art"—appear in Pompeiian wall pictures. And the *amori* that appear everywhere in the imagery of Theocritus, Bion, and Moschus appear also in similar attitudes and situations on the walls of the Italian buried cities and were therefore also presumably the stock in trade of the fashionable mythological genre paintings of Alexandrian art. In painting and poem alike little *amori* ride on the backs of dolphins, are carried in cages and offered for sale, don the lion skin of Hercules, flutter about baskets laden with roses, perch on the heads of men and maidens, and break their bows and arrows in petulant grief.

Even where it is impossible to detect close correspondences between poem and painting, the effect of much Alexandrian verse imagery is pictorial. Its adornments are those of pencil and pallet and of the antecedent iconic tradition. Aphrodite combs her hair; Eros plays with Ganymede at dice; Aphrodite gives Eros a ball;[52] two wealthy ladies view tapestries and admire the lifelikeness of the figures;[53] Adonis and Venus appear disposed on couches that are

[51] See J. P. Mahaffy, *Greek Life and Thought from the Age of Alexander to the Roman Conquest* (London, 1887), Andrew Lang, *op. cit.* (n. 48), and J. W. Mackail, *Lectures on Greek Poetry* (London, 1911).

[52] This and the preceding two examples I owe to Terrot Reaveley Glover, *Studies in Virgil* (London, 1904), p. 54.

[53] Theocritus *Idyll* xv. 80–86.

described in detail and constitute a tableau that interrupts a hymn;[54] the cup of victory in a pastoral singing match is fully "rendered" in the iconic manner;[55] and Jason's cloak, given him by Pallas Athene, is splendidly described—its reds and purples dwelt on, its sheen compared to the rising sun, and its representation of the Cyclopes (who are in the very act of adding a thunderbolt to the embroidery) admired for its breath-taking verisimilitude.[56]

In Alexandrian poetry the iconic traditions that go back to Homer and Hesiod are united with impulses from a gifted school of painters who were decorating wall and canvas with artfully and dramatically disposed details from Greek mythology. As the painters, so also the poets, who characteristically presented mythic legend pictorially.

Many of the Latin poets, including Vergil, Propertius, and Ovid, went to school to the Alexandrian masters and proclaimed themselves indebted to such poets as Callimachus and Philetas.[57] Indeed, in some of the Roman poets there is the same combination of iconic conventions and the traditions of mythological genre-painting that so strikingly characterized the late Greek masters. Vergil describes the shield of Aeneas and paintings in the temple of Juno. Petronius Arbiter visits a public gallery and describes paintings by Zeuxis, Protogenes, and Apelles in the manner of the Greek anthologists, saying of an Apelles that " 'twas finished to the life, you'd have sworn it an image of the soul too." Ovid, long considered the most pictorial of poets, describes the temple of Sol soaring aloft on pillars of bronze and gold, its doors made of fine metal, of which the figured panels, engraved by Mulciber, show the skill of a master, for they represent sea, land, and sky. These doors lead to an interior where the god himself sits in high state surrounded with statuesque personifications—youthful garlanded Spring; lightly clad Summer, crowned with harvest chaplets; Autumn stained with trampled grapes; and icy Winter with long, white hair. In such

[54] *Ibid*. xv. 100 ff.

[55] *Ibid*. i. 29 ff. For a diagram of this cup see *Theocritus*, ed. A. S. F. Gow (Cambridge, 1952), II, 14.

[56] Apollonius Rhodius *Argonautica* I. 721 ff.

[57] See Gaston Boissier, *Promenades archéologiques: Rome et Pompéi* (new ed.; Paris, 1919) and Glover, *op. cit.* (n. 52).

passages as these the Roman poet looks back to Homer's shield and ahead to Pope and Keats.[58]

They also resemble the frescoes of Pompeii, Herculaneum, and Stabiae, for their pictorial images surely derive not only from the iconic tradition already centuries old but also from the nurturing of contemporary and immediately precedent schools of painting. Catullus' presentation of Ariadne by the sea, abandoned by Theseus and consoled by Bacchus; Propertius' mistress asleep, her head supported on her arm; his Ariadne stretched out on the shore of Naxos; his bacchante sleeping the sleep of utter exhaustion on the plains of Thessaly; Ovid's Paris, who writes the name of Oenone on the bark of trees; his Europa, who holds the horn of the bull with one hand and places the other on his back while the wind flutters and fills her robe—these and many other pictorial details and scenes appear on the walls of once buried cities.[59] One cannot, of course, prove direct relations between particular paintings and particular poems; but the correspondences in theme and detail are striking and permit the assumption that the poet had been in close touch with pictorial representation.

Alexandrian pictorialism was refined by the Roman poets. It

[58] *Aeneid* i. 446 ff.; *Satyricon* 83, 88, 89; *Metamorphoses* ii. 1–30. Vergil has other iconic passages than the two mentioned in passing: the description of the temple of Apollo (*Aeneid* vi); the personification of the Tiber (viii); the embroidered coverlets and engraved silver of Dido's palace (i); the golden cloaks with myths woven into the purple borders—cloaks given to the captains in the boat races (v). The description of the Temple of Juno at Carthage in Book I is Vergil's fullest iconic passage. Unlike Homer, he is interested in the effects of pictures rather than in the pictures themselves. Vergil's description of the shield of Aeneas (viii. 608–731) is, I believe, less effective as an icon than Homer's description of the shield of Achilles, to which it is indebted for many details. Vergil's concluding touch is, however, extraordinarily effective: Aeneas lifts the shield and goes to his destiny without comprehending the prophetic meaning of the design that it bears.

The influence of Ovid upon subsequent pictorialism was enormous, and I regret that I can give him so little space. For commentary on the passage cited see L. P. Wilkinson, *Ovid Recalled* (Cambridge, 1955), pp. 155–59, and Herman Fränkel, *Ovid: A Poet between Two Worlds* (Berkeley, Calif., 1945), pp. 86–87. For other pictorial passages in Ovid, see *Tristia* iii. 1. 60; ii. 525–28; *Fasti* v. 551–68; *Metamorphoses* vi. 1–145; xv. 654–57; *Heroides* xiii. 152–58. For an assembly of all the passages in Ovid that describe works of visual art see Maude Beamer, *Greek Art in Ovid's Poems* (published abstract of University of Missouri dissertation, 1936).

[59] These examples I owe to Boissier, *op. cit.* (n. 57), pp. 372–79, who believes that the pictorialism of Roman poetry did not come directly from contemporary paintings but from Alexandrian models.

was similarly refined during the European Renaissance and in English neoclassicism. In all these mythologically decorated verbal pictures, with their sophisticated combination of plastic stasis and the grace of animated movement, the literary heritage of the classical iconic tradition is enriched by impulses from a known and cherished tradition of painting.

ICONIC PROSE

All the passages of iconic poetry we have so far discussed or alluded to and the many more we have ignored would have been considered by ancient critics expressions of *enargeia*. In prose such effects are also prominently present. Since *enargeia* was a quality originally associated with rhetoric and oratory, we should expect it to occupy the important place in various forms of prose expression that it in fact does.

The attempts to achieve *enargeia* in language must have been voluminous. The skill to create set descriptions, intended to bring visual reality before the mind's eye by means of words, was taught in the schools. Ecphrasis, in this its broadest sense,[60] was an admired and fully approved trick of the rhetorician's trade and as such was a regular scholastic exercise. Pictorialism of this sort was bred in the very bone of the Roman boy. The ability to achieve it he assiduously cultivated, and he was fully prepared to admire it in the work of others. It is not surprising, therefore, that Plutarch attempted to achieve *enargeia* even in history and biography; that Marcus Terentius Varro called his seven hundred prose biographies of Greek and Roman celebrities *imagines* and is said to have illustrated each with a portrait; that Pausanias in his description of Greece often stopped to describe at great length the art objects that he recommended to the traveler's attention; and that Pliny described his Tuscan estate in the greatest detail and said of its setting, in words that anticipate the taste of an eighteenth-century gentleman trained to appreciate picturesque effects in his garden: "You would think it not a real but a painted landscape, drawn with exquisite beauty."[61]

[60] See above, n. 34.
[61] Cited by Rose Macaulay, *Pleasure of Ruins* (London, 1953), p. 8. Varro, whom Quintilian called "the most learned of the Romans" (*Institutio* x. 1. 95), lived from 116 to 27 B.C. See Pausanias *Description of Greece* v. 17. 5–19. 10, trans. W. H. S. Jones and H. A. Ormerod ("Loeb Classical Library" [London, 1926]).

Of all these expressions of pictorialism in prose there are none so impressive and influential as those produced in late antiquity by Philostratus the Elder, Philostratus the Younger, and Callistratus.[62] All three of these writers produced lengthy prose descriptions and celebrations of real or imaginary paintings in sufficient quantity to form collections. There are some differences between them. Philostratus the Younger is less rhetorical and rhapsodic and his descriptions are less subjective and more detailed and particularized than those of the others. Callistratus, who wrote even later and clearly knew the work of both his predecessors, is concerned with sculpture rather than with painting and therefore also with the difficulty of achieving verisimilitude in such resistant and potentially forbidding materials as bronze and stone.

But the three writers, in spite of these differences, are basically alike and may be considered together, using the most influential of them, Philostratus the Elder, as their representative. He was born in A.D. 190 and was one of three or four successful Sophists who traveled from place to place and bore the name of Philostratus.

In the *imagines* of these men, which are devoted exclusively to describing real or imaginary works of graphic art, the ancient iconic tradition reaches its culmination. "How I have been deceived!" says Philostratus in one of the *imagines:* the achievement of absolute verisimilitude is a basic and recurring theme. Because his form of utterance permits him to express himself at greater length than was possible in epigram, lyric, or even epic, he dwells lushly on the sensuousness of the representation before him: on the dewy look of roses and their painted fragrance; on purple figs dripping with juice; on heaps of fragrant and golden fruit; on curdled and quivering cheese.[63] But his full purpose is not exhausted by supposing that he was interested only in describing and praising paintings. He also wishes to vie with them, to achieve the lifelike freshness of painted reality, and perhaps even to supersede them, for it would be a greater triumph to achieve full sensuous reality in so unnatural a medium as words.[64]

[62] These three authors may be conveniently studied in *Imagines*, ed. and trans. Arthur Fairbanks ("Loeb Classical Library" [London, 1931]).

[63] *Ibid.*, I, 2, 28, 31.

[64] In this Philostratus may have been anticipated by Xenocrates of Sicyon, a sculptor who is thought to have written works of iconic prose on art objects in

Philostratus looks upon verbal expression as painterly, but he also considers paintings literary. Such criticism may be one inevitable result of associating the arts. Philostratus reads paintings as though they were dramas. He reconstructs their fables, myths, and even geographical details; he makes them speak and even act. For him one of the most important elements in a picture is the effective delineation of human character and the expression of human emotion.[65] Such a view undoubtedly derives from the doctrine that art imitates nature, for human psychology is as natural as physical form, the human soul as natural as a landscape. The doctrine of art as expression was implicit in the doctrine of art as imitation, an insight known to thinkers long before Philostratus.[66] But none before and few since have so strikingly exploited the doctrine of expression as a means of making graphic value available to literary art. Philostratus treated visual art *as* literature; and that is a first step absolutely requisite to the second, that of using graphic art *in* literature.

The example of Philostratus remained for many centuries a powerful one, and we shall in later pages encounter signs of his influence. But his was not the only expression in prose of the iconic tradition; it also was manifest in two other literary forms, the prose romance and the prose moral allegory.

It may have been the Greek romance, to a greater extent than any other literary form, that carried classical pictorialism into the Christian era. From Antonius Diogenes, who may have written near the end of the first century after Christ, to Achilles Tatius, who may have flourished as late as the beginning of the sixth cen-

---

which he attempted to outdo in verbal form what had been achieved in graphic form in his subjects. See Sellers' introduction to Jex-Blake, *op. cit.* (n. 47) and Lionello Venturi, *Storia della critica d'arte* (2d ed.; Florence, 1948), pp. 53, 496.

[65] With Philostratus' view may be compared that of Lucian, who, in a comment cited by Vitry (*op. cit.* [n. 39], p. 317), said that there are three ways of judging art: that of the crowd, which seeks novelty; that of the artist, who looks for technical skill; and that of the literary man, who is interested in character and expression. Lucian's *Eikones* are, in fact, among the important influences upon Philostratus.

[66] The Xenophontic Socrates, in the conversation with the painter Parrhasius already alluded to (above, n. 26), gets the painter to admit the truth of the proposition that painting can indeed represent emotions and states of mind since it can represent features, lineaments, and postures, which do represent such emotions and states.

tury, prose romances were produced in considerable quantity.[67] One of their hallmarks was the set description, too often a sophistical tour de force of word painting, that attempted to set the show and shine of things before the eyes of the reader. Many such passages deserve the censure they have received: they interrupt the action, to which they are frequently irrelevant, and they often display signs of being little more than rhetorical tricks. But they were at their best much better than this, and even when mediocre they did keep alive an appreciation of the sensuous powers of language in the midst of encroaching didacticism. They deserve brief consideration in this survey chiefly because they stand squarely in the tradition of iconic writing.

One of their most prominent characteristics is that their descriptions are pictorial, not natural, even when nature is the subject. When Achilles Tatius describes the real garden that adjoins Clitophon's house, he uses the same detail, presented in largely the same order, that he had used in describing the painting of a meadow at the outset of the story: the crystal fountains, the cloistered wall, the foliage that filters the sunlight to the grass beneath. The romancer was usually as much interested in "rendering" an artifact, an *objet d'art*, a painting, or a statue as he was in "rendering" a natural scene. The narrative pages abound in descriptions of crystal wine cups, purple robes, necklaces, statues of Zeus, and paintings that hang in the temples of the gods.

The prose romances, to a greater degree than any other form we have encountered, enable us to see a potentially intimate relationship between pictorial description and total structure. In Achilles Tatius' *Clitophon and Leucippe* the narrator is introduced at the outset gazing at a picture of Europa placed in a temple of Venus in Sidon. That picture is described in some detail, and from it the author derives the theme that is then developed independently.[68] But in Longus' *Daphnis and Chloe* the introductory contemplation of a picture is viewed as more integrally related

---

[67] My information regarding the Greek romances comes chiefly from Samuel Lee Wolff, *The Greek Romances in Elizabethan Prose Fiction* (New York, 1912) and John Colin Dunlop, *History of Prose Fiction*, ed. Henry Wilson (London, 1888).

[68] For other descriptions of paintings and statues in this romance, see iii. 6 ff.; iii. 8 ff.; v. 3.

to the ensuing story. The narrator begins his account by telling how, while hunting in Lesbos, he encountered in a grove sacred to the nymphs a beautiful picture of a tale of love, a famous work that drew many visitors from distant places.

In it were represented women in childbed, and others fitting swaddling clothes upon infants. There were sheep nursing them and shepherds taking them up; there were young lovers pledging faith to one another, an incursion of pirates, an attack by invaders. All these scenes spoke of love, and as I looked upon and admired them I conceived a strong desire to compose a literary pendant to that painted picture. Upon inquiry I found an interpreter of the picture, and I have carefully set the story out in four books.

This passage is highly significant, even though the author does not always rigorously follow the method of narration that it implies. *Daphnis and Chloe* is not always an obvious "literary pendant to the picture." But it often is. Men and gods are pictorially presented. The three nymphs that appear to the sorrowing Daphnis "seemed to stand over him, tall and handsome women, half nude and barefoot with loose-flowing hair, *very like the statues.*" Gardens are presented in precise and symmetrical patterns, and "nature itself seemed a work of art." Human characters sometimes assume statuesque poses that remind one of the appearance of a god. "If ever Apollo served Laomedon as cowherd he must have looked as Daphnis now appeared."[69]

But beyond such pictorial particulars as these that keep reminding one of the analogy with painting drawn in the opening paragraphs, there is present the strong suggestion that narrative form is conceived of in an un-Aristotelian way. It is not viewed as a primarily temporal sequence that presents a logically motivated action. It is viewed as a series of tableaux. Reading a story would therefore be like going through a gallery of paintings and statues. We move from scene to scene, from image to image, from one plastic arrangement to another (see Plate I).

Similar pictorial elements appear in one of the most influential moral allegories ever written, the famous *Tablet* of Cebes of Thebes.[70]

[69] *Three Greek Romances*, trans. Moses Hadas (Garden City, N.Y., 1953), pp. 17, 48, 78, 79, 84–85. Italics mine.

[70] Because I hope to deal elsewhere with the influence of this allegory, I shall do little more here than refer to the edition of C. S. Jerram (Oxford, 1878). Cebes was

In the eighteenth century, the last period in which this work was intensively studied in the schools, Cebes was praised as the first who had achieved an alliance of philosophy and picture. The *Tablet*, it was believed, was a moral painting, whose entire ordonnance was conceived in the manner of a picture.[71]

The eighteenth-century view of the Pilgrim's Progress of antiquity is essentially correct, as we can see if we consider the form in which it is presented. Cebes, like Longus and Achilles Tatius, finds himself in a temple, where he sees a large painting. Its meaning eludes him. As he stands before it baffled, a stranger approaches him and offers an explanation, which he says he had from the artist himself. The allegory that follows is presented as an explanation, interrupted now and again by the speaker's pointing to the picture with his cane, of what the two men see represented on the canvas. The meaning is unfolded emblematically. The subject, which concerns the entire moral life of man and is almost universal in scope, is presented as though it were fully expressed on a single canvas. Cebes' *Tablet* is more rigorously governed by the pictorial analogy than any other verbally presented moral allegory. Its example was not lost upon the didactic art of subsequent centuries.

These are the chief ingredients of the literary pictorialism of classical antiquity relevant to neoclassical poetry. If Plutarch is right, it was given proverbial expression as early as the fifth or sixth century B.C. by Simonides of Ceos. It was later formulated into the concept of literary *enargeia*, first as a rhetorical and then as a poetical principle. Long before its critical formulation it had been expressed in belles-lettres. Extending from Homer to Achilles Tatius, the iconic in verbal art crossed the generic boundaries and appeared in epic, drama, epigram, lyric, romance, and allegory. In so rich and varied an expression of literary pictorialism, the seeds of future development are virtually all present. Some writers,

---

a disciple of Philolaus the Pythagorean and became a friend of Socrates, appearing in the celebrated conversation in the *Phaedo* on the immortality of the soul. Few believe that the historical Cebes wrote the *Pinax*, or *Tablet*. It may have been produced under the influence of the Roman stoicism of the early imperial period or of the moral thought, not untinged with Christian influence, of the early centuries after Christ.

[71] James Moor, *Essays Read to a Literary Society* (Glasgow, 1759), pp. 40, 50–51.

including Homer, suggest the value of the *difficulté vaincue*, which arises whenever the frontiers that separate the arts are knowingly and intentionally crossed. Others introduce considerations of total form and structure. Still others suggest that poetry has derived theme and technique from the contemplation of visual art. All proclaim the values of verbal sensuousness.[72]

In this chapter I have attempted no more than to provide the background in classical literature and criticism for the pictorialism of Restoration and eighteenth-century poets. I did not select the writers discussed; later writers selected them for me. My comments up to this point are therefore intended only to introduce those conventions of pictorial imagery and those notions of literary criticism that were in some way relevant to the poetry of Alexander Pope, his contemporaries, and his immediate predecessors.

For these reasons I have stressed criticism and poetry that tended to be naturalistic and have neglected the great religious expressions of Greek civilization—the epiphenomenal poetry of Pindar and Aeschylus; the moral and religious canvases of Polygnotus, who, like Aescyhlus, apparently attempted to penetrate the mysteries of the spiritual world;[73] and the images of primitive magic that survived into classical times, including the Palladium, the aegis, the cult object, and the charm. Pictorial imagery related to such icons as these was certainly present in classical poetry, but I have conceived it to lie outside the scope of this survey.

This chapter has not therefore been concerned with the Heliconian muse of Pindar, the muse of oracular inspiration, but with the muse of fact, truth, nature, and *enargeia*—the muse that said to Hesiod: "We can utter many a fiction and make it seem true; and when we will we can voice the truth"; the muse that taught

---

[72] For further discussion of the kind of verse and prose discussed in this chapter see the Introduction to Paul Friedländer, *Johannes von Gaza und Paulus Silentiarius: Kunstbeschreibungen Justinianischer Zeit* (Leipzig, 1912), which contains a valuable survey of what he calls ecphrastic and what I have called iconic poetry and prose. Neither its title nor the references to it that I have seen would lead one to suppose it contained material of this nature. A survey of iconic literature that is more complete and extensive than mine, it covers such expression in all the ancient literary forms, but it does not relate the ecphrasis to literary criticism. Since it is an introduction to two Byzantine texts, it is not intended to prepare one for the reading of English poetry.

[73] G. Meautis, *Les chefs-d'œuvre de la peinture grecque* (Paris, 1939), p. 47.

Demodocus, who sings, as Odysseus tells him, of the Achaeans "as if you were present yourself, or have heard the tale from an eyewitness."[74]

The fact that this chapter emphasizes naturalism should not be interpreted to mean that later pictorialism was never religious. It often was, as the chapter on the seventeenth century will demonstrate. But such religious pictorialism came from—or at least by way of—Christianity, a fact that gives peculiar relevance to the subject of the next chapter.

[74] Bassett, *op. cit.* (n. 36), pp. 29–30.

CHAPTER II

The Christian Era

It is the purpose of this chapter to notice the persistence in medieval literature of classical pictorialism; to confront a new type of literary image that is prominently, though not uniquely, characteristic of Christian expression; to relate that image to Christian aesthetic theory; and to examine the embodiment of both types of image in the poetry of Dante, whose *Divine Comedy* will serve as a summary illustration of what we have learned from both pagan antiquity and the Christian Middle Ages.

THE PERSISTENCE OF CLASSICAL PICTORIALISM

In 1637 Franciscus Junius, during the seventeenth century the leading authority on ancient art, named both the pagan Cicero and the Christian Tertullian as witnesses to the truth of *ut pictura poesis*.[1] Cicero had used the metaphor of a consanguinity to express the relationship of the arts: "For all arts that belong to humanity possess a kind of common connection; they are bound together as though by a blood relationship."[2] Tertullian, using the same metaphor, said, "There is no art which is not either the mother or a very close kinsman of another art."[3] The two statements, however, in spite of their surface similarities, are separated by an intellectual and moral revolution. Cicero, arguing in typical Roman fashion that oratory and poetry are intimately related, seeks to exalt them both by finding their common source in human nature. But Tertullian, who also traces the several arts back to human nature, does so in order to discredit them. He says, in the sentence following the one quoted, that "the veins of the arts are as many as the concupiscences of men."

[1] Franciscus Junius, *De pictura veterum* (Rotterdam, 1694), p. 22. The first edition was published in Amsterdam in 1637.

[2] *Pro archia poeta* i. 2. [3] *De idolatria* 8.

The gulf that divides classical humanist and Christian moralist is also apparent in appraisals and definitions of painting alone. Philostratus opened his *Eikones* by saying: "Whoever scorns painting is unjust to truth; and he is also unjust to all the wisdom that has been bestowed upon poets—for poets and painters make equal contribution to our knowledge of the deeds and the looks of heroes."[4] But Isidore of Seville, the encyclopedist and codifier of Christian opinion, defines painting as follows: "*Pictura* is a representation expressing the appearance of anything, which when it is beheld makes the mind remember. *Pictura* is, moreover, pronounced almost *fictura*. For it is a feigned representation, not the truth. Hence it is also counterfeited, that is, it is smeared over with a fabricated color and possesses nothing of credibility or truth."[5] The classical criticism studied in chapter i had pointed to painting as the associate and sometimes even the exemplar of poetry because it was superior in representing truth and nature. But in Christian definition painting is itself a counterfeit, and the very color it must use is a sign of its falsity and unreality.[6]

Fortunately for art, however, the anticlassical spirit of the early Christian moral resistance did not entirely prevail during the millennium that ensued. That spirit was not entirely characteristic even of patristic opinion, which was itself deeply divided in its attitude toward the pagan past. Arnobius and Lactantius zealously upheld the conventional values of classical style, and Augustine, Jerome, and Basil of Caesarea shared the ambivalent feelings entertained by most early Christians about the Roman world and its culture. Isidore himself, although he forbade his monks to read any classical writers except the grammarians, was entirely conversant with pagan literature; and his encyclopedia, besides expressing Christian thought, gathered up much of the learning of the ancient world and transmitted it to the Christian centuries that followed.[7] It would be idle to speculate what would have happened had the

[4] i. 1.

[5] *Etymologiarum* xix. 16. 1–2, in J. P. Migne (ed.), *Patrologiae cursus completus*, Latin ser., Vol. IV, col. 436.

[6] This view of color persisted and was used by the eighteenth-century satirists. See below, pp. 240, 271.

[7] R. R. Bolgar, *The Classical Heritage and Its Beneficiaries* (Cambridge, 1954), pp. 45–58; John Edwin Sandys, *A History of Classical Scholarship* (Cambridge, 1903), I, 442–44.

"stark Christianity"[8] of the iconoclastic controversies everywhere prevailed in unmitigated severity. It did not so prevail in actual practice, and it is therefore possible to view the Middle Ages as in some ways the continuation and regeneration of classical culture, as a complicated cultural epoch which, in spite of its many deformations of ancient art and thought, often did keep the classical heritage intact and adapt it to its peculiar needs and conditions.[9]

In appropriating classical pictorialism, the Middle Ages retained many of its most essential elements. Love of external and visible nature, so basic to any notion of rhetorical and poetic *enargeia*, did not die out during the Christian epoch; on the contrary, it flourished at certain times and in certain places—notably in the France of the late medieval renaissance, where men perceived and portrayed the loveliness of flower and leaf, bird and beast.[10] St. Bernard says of the green banks, the shady bowers, and the herbs, trees, flowers, and bird songs of his monastery, "Good God! what a company of pleasures thou hast made for man."[11] Certain of those materially conceived personifications, without which pagan pictorialism would have been vastly different from what it was, continued to be reproduced. The classical representation of Love was so frequently repeated in the Middle Ages that the nude winged boy placed on a column and holding a bow became utterly banal.[12] The famous pictorial allegory of Cebes of Thebes was early Christianized—Tertullian is said to have had a kinsman who paraphrased the *Tablet* in hexameter verse—and apparently a stone-relief fragment of the early Christian era was directly inspired by the words of Cebes' *Tablet*.[13]

[8] The phrase is F. P. Chambers' and is cited in Katherine Everett Gilbert and Helmut Kuhn, *A History of Esthetics* (New York, 1939), p. 119.

[9] See Eugenio Garin, *Medioevo e rinascimento* (Bari, Italy, 1955).

[10] See Joan Evans, *Pattern: A Study of Ornament in Western Europe from 1180 to 1900* (Oxford, 1931), I, 39. "It is from the French naturalism of the Middle Ages, and not from any fresh source whether of antiquity or of their own time, that the artists of the Renaissance derived their scenes of courtly and peasant life" (*ibid.*, p. 70).

[11] Burton's translation in the *Anatomy of Melancholy* ii. 2. 4.

[12] Raimond Van Marles, *Iconographie et l'art profane au Moyen-Âge et à la Renaissance* (The Hague, 1932), II, 415–16.

[13] See Cebes, *Tablet*, ed. C. S. Jerram (Oxford, 1878), p. ix; E. K. Müller, "Relieffragment mit Darstellungen aus dem πιναξ des Kebes," *Archäologische Zeitung*, XLII (1884), 115–27.

The medieval appropriation of classical pictorialism must have been directly related to the rising and falling reputation of the pagan literary classics. It may have gone out of sight during their temporary eclipse in the early Middle Ages; it apparently became prominent again in the Carolingian and Ottonian revivals of learning in the ninth and tenth centuries and in the "proto-renaissance" of the high Middle Ages. In these periods of classical renaissance the *Ars poetica* of Horace was known and studied,[14] the phrase *ut pictura poesis* commented and reflected upon.[15] The achievement of *enargeia* in rhetorical ecphrasis and poetic icon remained an alluring literary goal.[16] Although the evidence is far from overwhelming, it is possible to say that, when classical scholarship was active, classical pictorialism was present—that Simonides and Horace were quoted and that the complex of ideas associated with the classical *ut pictura poesis* was in some manner operative.[17]

Horace's critical dictum may have been less influential than Ovid's pictorial practice. The greatest of the classical pictorialists in verse was fervently admired during the periods of classic revival. Isidore of Seville's warning that he of all pagan poets was most to be avoided went largely unregarded even by Isidore himself, who quoted the poet on some twenty separate occasions in his encyclopedia. Fulgentius at the end of the fifth century used the *Fasti* and the *Metamorphoses* as the bases for allegories in the *Mythologiae*. The scholars at the court of Charlemagne imitated Ovid and helped inaugurate the *aetas Ovidiana;* the troubadours and minnesingers echoed him, and he was the favorite poet of the

[14] Charles Homer Haskins, *The Renaissance of the Twelfth Century* (Cambridge, Mass., 1939), pp. 93–95, 110. In the late Middle Ages there were many *arts poétiques* produced under the influence of Horace by Matthieu de Vendôme, Geoffroi de Vinsauf, and others. See Édmond Faral, *Les arts poétiques du XIIe et du XIIIe siècle* (Paris, 1924), *passim.* Manutius prepared a table of references to Horace during the Middle Ages with these results for the *Ars poetica:* to the end of the eighth century, 23 references; ninth and tenth centuries, 21 references; eleventh century, 25 references; twelfth century, 138 references; thirteenth century, 75 references (cited by Edward Moore, *Studies in Dante* [1st ser.; Oxford, 1896], p. 201). Dante seems have copied from, alluded to, or adapted the *Ars* on many occasions (*ibid.*, pp. 197–200).

[15] See Karl Borinski, *Die Antike in Poetik und Kunsttheorie* (Leipzig, 1914), I, 97–98.

[16] Faral, *op. cit.* (n. 14), pp. 75–84.

[17] See chapter entitled "Imago" in Borinski, *op. cit.* (n. 15), I, 67–98.

Goliards; Vincent of Beauvais quoted him more frequently than any other ancient writer; Dante viewed him as a model of style; and Chaucer, who, as Dryden observed in the "Preface to the Fables," was related to him by deep affinities of spirit, must have known much of him by heart.[18]

Other signs, besides the knowledge of Horace's dictum and Ovid's practice, betray the presence of the pictorial ideal in the mind of the medieval writer. Philostratus continued to be read, East and West, and was widely imitated in epigram, ecphrasis, and iconic poem. Although such poetry became, as we shall see, one of the most characteristic forms of Byzantine expression that was nowhere in the West matched in quantity or quality, nevertheless the titulus, itself an adaptation of the art epigram, was Christianized and everywhere produced in considerable quantity.[19] Even the association of epigram and object, an association on whose great antiquity we remarked in the first chapter, continued in the Middle Ages: English medieval craft produced mazers, jugs, and bells that bore inscriptions in verse and prose.[20]

Perhaps the most prominent—or at least to us the most easily available—manifestation of persisting classical pictorialism was the medieval habit of telling stories by means of describing wall pictures and of expressing allegories by means of describing temples or palaces and their artistic appointments. It may be impossible to say why this un-Aristotelian notion of narrative and allegorical form, on which we have commented in connection with the Greek romances and Cebes' *Tablet*, had so firm a hold on the medieval mind. But there is no denying the tenacity of its grip and the fact that its ultimate inspiration was classical. The castle of Boccaccio's *Amorosa visione*, with its portraits and its scenic and symbolic paintings;

[18] Sandys, *op. cit.* (n. 7), I, 614–17; Edgar Finley Shannon, *Chaucer and the Roman Poets* (Cambridge, Mass., 1929), pp. xvi, 371; L. P. Wilkinson, *Ovid Recalled* (Cambridge, 1955), chap. xi.

[19] Schlosser-Magnino defines the "titulus" as a versified inscription explaining an image. Unlike the epigram, which has greater literary independence, the titulus is inseparably connected with the work of art it describes and explains. Paulinus of Nola wrote tituli in great quantity. See Julius Schlosser-Magnino, *La letteratura artistica* (Florence, 1935), p. 28. On the transmission of epigrams to the Middle Ages by authors who quoted them see James Hutton, *The Greek Anthology in Italy to the Year 1800* (Ithaca, N.Y., 1935), pp. 2–10.

[20] Joan Evans, *English Art: 1307–1461* (Oxford, 1949), p. 90.

the walls of Guillaume de Lorris' orchards—all painted, like those of *Floire et blanchefloir,* "a or e a azur"; Chaucer's House of Fame and his several temples, in the "Knight's Tale" and elsewhere, of Venus, Mars, and Diana—all these allegorical and romantic structures derive from the palaces of Vergil, Ovid, Statius, Apuleius, and Claudian. Classical and medieval writers alike gave their gods and godlike personae habitations and dwellings that were fully described.[21]

It must be admitted that the verbal "pictures" of medieval poetry are often nothing more than repeated convention. In such cases they are inferior to their originals. If we compare Guillaume's Envye, as it appears in Chaucer's translation, with Ovid's Invidia, we find the pagan figure pictorially precise, fresh, and dramatic and the Christian vague and general, its details often lost in moral aphorism and exhortation.[22] The medieval poet keeps saying that he sees—it is, for example, an essential part of Chaucer's and others' manner to insert at frequent intervals "I saugh," "then I saugh"—without always giving evidence that he actually has seen. But this is by no means always true. At their best these medieval word pictures are admirable as descriptions, quite apart from their metaphorical relevance to total meaning. They often possess the aureate otherworldliness, characteristic of the early Sienese masters, that transcends the sensuous without eliminating it.

We have seen that the pictorialism of Alexandrian and Roman poetry represented a fusion of the iconic literary tradition that stemmed from Homer with impulses from the graphic arts currently being produced. Something like this was true in medieval culture. Chaucer, for example, often used the pictorial conventions provided him by Vergil and Ovid and at the same time reproduced what he had seen and responded to firsthand. It has been suggested that such correspondences as the following exist between Chaucer's verse and the visual arts and crafts that he assuredly had seen and remembered: between his House of Fame, a palace of gold and glass, and the miniature palaces of crystal and gold that adorned the royal tables of Louis of Anjou; between the interior of Chaucer's

---

[21] See William Allan Neilson, *The Origin and Sources of the Court of Love* (Boston, 1899), pp. 11, 52–53, 116; Ernest Langlois (ed.), *Le roman de la rose* (Paris, 1920), II, 296, n. on l. 132 of the poem.

[22] Cf. *Romaunt of the Rose,* ll. 247–300, and *Metamorphoses* ii. 760–86.

House of Fame, with its sculpturesque figures of Venus, Cupid, and Vulcan, and the chalcedony vessels for sweetmeats with their twelve carved figures at the foot; between the exterior of Chaucer's House of Fame and the "Maison des musiciens" in Reims; between his Troy stories on painted glass and the Troy stories of enameled gold work; between his "walles with colours fyne," on which

> Were peynted, bothe text and glose,
> Of al the Romaunce of the Rose,

and Philip the Bold's gold tapestries on which were represented scenes from the *Roman de la rose;* and between his statues standing on symmetrically arranged pillars that themselves stood

> on eyther syde,
> Streight doun to the dores wide,

and the courts and halls of Renaissance palaces that he saw in Tuscany.[23]

Some of the correspondences between Chaucer's poetry and contemporary graphic art that have been suggested are unquestionably overingenious. Yet the belief that Chaucer saw with his own eyes and brought some of the forms and colors and stuffs of fourteenth-century art to his page is surely well founded. In his treatment of the Temple of Venus in the *House of Fame* the general notion ultimately derives from Vergil, and the glass of which Chaucer constructs it comes from innumerable palaces of love in contemporary courtly verse.[24] But, beyond that, purely literary convention ceases, and what seems like firsthand observation of art takes over. For where the classical poets and their imitators would have put a statue, Chaucer puts a painting. And in that "curiouse portreyture" he creates a form that anticipates Botticelli and takes us to *trecento*

[23] See Joan Evans, "Chaucer and the Decorative Arts," *Review of English Studies*, VI (October, 1930), 408–12; George G. Williams, "The Hous of Fame and the House of the Musicians," *Modern Language Notes*, LXXII (January, 1957), 6–9; Karl Brunner, "Chaucer's 'House of Fame,'" *Actes du Cinquième Congrès International des Langues et Littératures Modernes* (Florence, 1955), pp. 55–62. The quotations from Chaucer come from the *Book of the Duchess*, ll. 332–34, and the *House of Fame*, ll. 1419–20. For Chaucer's use of the verbal portrait, or *effictio*—a descriptive device authorized by the rhetoricians—see Louis A. Haselmayer, "The Portraits in *Troilus and Criseyde*," *Philological Quarterly*, XVII (1938), 220–23.

[24] Brunner, *op. cit.* (n. 23), p. 58. Chaucer's use of contemporary arts was typical of his age. See Marvin Alpheus Owings, *The Arts in the Middle English Romances* (New York, 1952).

Tuscany, where medieval and classical motifs had already creatively met.

> Hyt was of Venus redely,
> The temple; for in portreyture,
> I sawgh anoon-ryght hir figure
> Naked fletynge in a see.
> And also on hir hed, pardee,
> Hir rose garlond whit and red,
> And hir comb to kembe hyr hed,
> Hir dowves, and daun Cupido,
> Hir blynde sone, and Vulcano,
> That in his face was ful broun [i. 130–39].

CRITICISM: THE NEW SIMILITUDE

In Chaucer the classically oriented pictorialism of the Middle Ages comes to its fruition, not only because he borrowed time-honored devices and motifs from the classical authors he knew and admired but also because he, like his Greek and Roman predecessors, created verbal pictures that added to conventional form the freshness of firsthand observation and response. But to dwell exclusively on the persistence of classical form and example would be to tell only a part of the story. The Middle Ages may not have broken with the past so sharply as the early Christian apologists would have wished. But modify the pagan past—even its literary pictorialism—it most certainly did. How that alteration took place, what elements of pagan antiquity (the Neoplatonic and other religious elements) now took over and replaced naturalism, what the effect was of biblical imagery upon classical poetic imagery—such considerations as these are too complicated and technical to explore here. The purpose of the ensuing discussion must be much simpler: to consider only the most essential differences between the naturalistic pictorialism discussed in the first chapter and the Christian pictorialism of the high Middle Ages. But though these differences are great, the example of Dante, soon to be considered in some detail, shows that the Christian did not entirely drive out the naturalistic.

C. S. Lewis has distinguished between allegory and symbolism. In writing allegory the poet starts with something immaterial that he wishes to say and invents *visibilia* with which to express his meaning.[25] In symbolism—or sacramentalism—the material em-

[25] *Allegory of Love* (Oxford, 1936), p. 45.

bodiment is a revelation of ontological reality and involves, in a sense that simple allegory does not, the whole structure of super-sensuous reality and its entire relation to material phenomena. Mr. Lewis is concerned with allegory; we are now concerned with what may be called "sacramental pictorialism."[26] But before considering its poetic manifestations we must examine the theory that lay behind it.

Augustine again and again confesses to the allurements of the eye. He reveals, from the way in which he dwells on "fair and varied forms and bright and pleasing colors" and on light, that "queen of colors" that insinuates itself into the very heart of our being, that he fully understood the emotional power of classical *enargeia*.[27] Classical pictorialism and the climate that had surrounded it in late antiquity must have been naturally congenial to him. Although he looks upon the eye as a source of temptation and the *objets d'art* that appeal to it as contemptible when not useful, he does not reject them outright. There is another way, and that way lies in the complete reorientation of aesthetic thought. If art is merely sensuous and if aesthetic value is thought to lie in verisimilitude, then art is either vicious or superfluous. If art is only an imitation of nature, why not go directly to nature itself?[28] But if it is realized that all "beautiful patterns emanate from that Beauty that is above our souls but mediated through our souls" or, as Plato put it, that beautiful things are made beautiful by Beauty,[29] then art is acceptable. This Christianized Neoplatonism rescued art for the Middle Ages and gave it a quality not present in the naturalism of pagan antiquity.

To the greatest philosophers of the Middle Ages the analogy between painting and poetry, as it was understood in antiquity,

---

[26] The phrase is suggested by Mr. Lewis' discussion. "Sacramental pictorialism" is to be distinguished from merely using sacred or biblical instead of pagan imagery and allusion. It is profounder than the primitive magic that appears everywhere in the other-world landscapes of Celtic and Old French romance (see Arthur C. L. Brown, *Iwain: A Study in the Origins of Arthurian Romance* [Boston, 1903], pp. 63, 64, 85, 93, 133 ff.).

[27] *Confessions* x. 34.

[28] *De doctrina christiana* ii. 25.

[29] τῷ καλῷ τὰ καλὰ καλά (*Phaedo* 100e). This is an epigrammatic way of saying what Plato discusses more fully elsewhere (*ibid.* 100c, 100d). See also *Timaeus* 28a, 29a; Plotinus *Enneads* v. 8. 1; i. 6. 6, 7, 8, 9; and Philo *De opificio mundi* 4.

was largely irrelevant. The medieval mind seldom judged a work of art solely or even chiefly by the classical canon of its truth to nature. Thomas Aquinas had indeed said that "art imitates nature," but he added the phrase "in its operation," and that addition seems to deny the validity of the mirror analogy.[30] For there is a vast difference between (1) copying nature in order to enjoy her particulars or in order to generalize from them and (2) responding to the vital impulses and meanings of nature in order to do in another realm what she does in hers. But it is not only in the *relation* of art to nature that Aquinas differs from, say, Plutarch. It is also in the notion of what nature is. Nature was not for Aquinas merely the objective world, from which a Plutarch might derive the literary and pictorial value of *enargeia*, or vivid lifelikeness. It was, rather, a vast allegorical embodiment that reveals meaning. So conceived, it could not be appropriated by the eye, nor could it be thought of primarily as a subject for painting. It could only be appropriated by the mind.

For the medieval thinker exemplary form is not in nature but in the mind of the artist. Such form—immediately psychological but ultimately ontological—is substantial and essential: it exists now in the mind of the artist, but it was planted there by God. This inner, spiritual form is the cause of and therefore must take precedence over the actual material form.[31]

If truth resides primarily in the mind and only secondarily in external nature, fidelity to nature cannot usually be a fundamental artistic requirement. Similitude is important in medieval aesthetics, but we must remember with what it is concerned. Art is compared not with external reality but with pre-existing psychological and on-tological form. Verisimilitude, as it had been understood in antiquity and as it was to be understood once more in the Renaissance, was radically reinterpreted in the Christian centuries. Dante believed that there were three crucial moments in the production of art; not one of them is concerned with outside reality. "Art exists in three stages: in the mind of the artist, in his instrument, and in the material formed by art."[32]

[30] *Summa* i. q. 117. a. 1. c. See Amanda K. Coomaraswamy, "Medieval Aesthet-ics," *Art Bulletin*, XVII (March, 1935), 31–47.

[31] *Summa* i. q. 5. a. 4; i. q. 16. a. 1; Coomaraswamy, *op. cit.* (n. 30), pp. 31, 36–37, n. 9.

[32] *De monarchia* ii. 2. 11–15.

Within the framework of such theory as this the anaology between painting and poetry tended to lose its ancient meaning, and it was in fact not often drawn by such normative philosophers as Aquinas. Music and architecture, the least representional of the arts, seem to have usurped the place of painting; and Augustine's clear preference for architecture remained widely influential in the ensuing centuries.[33] Nevertheless, in practice the association of poetry with the graphic arts was by no means destroyed. In the persisting classical pictorialism of medieval poetry that we have already examined, the old values lingered on. In the sacramental pictorialism we shall now examine they were radically modified to accord with the new similitude of Christian aesthetics.

CHRISTIAN ICONIC POETRY

Sacramental pictorialism must have been present in the poetry of pagan antiquity. Platonism and Neoplatonism, the magical symbolism of ancient religions, the widespread pantheism that gave a sense of living being to nature, and the habits of religious and philosophical personification—all these tendencies must have been congenial to it. The epigram of Philippus on the Zeus of Phidias at Olympia, a statue that for centuries had been considered an example of divine inspiration, is certainly an anticipation of the Christian iconic epigram: "Either God came from Heaven to Earth to show his image, Phidias, or thou didst go to see God."[34] But such expressions are seldom encountered—at least in the pages of the *Anthology;* much more frequent are celebrations of the lifelikeness of Myron's cow. It was quite natural, therefore, that to the Renaissance and post-Renaissance man pagan antiquity should come to stand for naturalistic imagery and that religious imagery should be primarily associated with the immediate Christian past. There is historical justification for examining sacramental pictorialism in a Christian rather than a pagan context.

Within Christianity Byzantium provides the best example of the several arts in intimate and fruitful collaboration. Iconic poetry was, as we have seen, produced in the West. But such poetry tended to be classical in form and concept. For the literary icon that arose in response to Christian thought we must turn to the East.

[33] Lionello Venturi, *Storia della critica d'arte* (2d ed.; Florence, 1948), p. 99.

[34] *Greek Anthology*, trans. W. R. Paton ("Loeb Classical Library" [London, 1918]), V, 203, Planudean Appendix, No. 81.

Upon Byzantine culture, even though it differed profoundly from the pagan past, the example of antiquity had not been lost: the *Greek Anthology*, the descriptions of Lucian, the prose of Philostratus and his followers, and the descriptions of paintings in the Greek romances were studied and copied.[35] Byzantium provides a great variety of iconic literature, both brief and extended, both in poetry and in prose.[36] In almost every instance such literature is intended to be much more than a footnote to the work of art that is its subject. When Procopius describes in prose the buildings of Justinian, he is not satisfied merely to provide a catalogue or guide; he writes a rhetorical panegyric that is intended to convey an emotional response and, like the pagan masters of ecphrastic rhetoric, he apparently strives to reproduce in a verbal medium the beauties of plastic form. In the elaborate description of the church of St. Sophia, which the author, Paulus Silentiarius, a nobly born gentleman who preserved silence in the palace of Justinian, may have read at the consecration of the church, there are eloquent passages on the effects of space, light, and color and on the miraculous embodiment in plastic form of supersensory realities and meanings. Even in the brief epigrams we see clearly that the association of the arts was not fortuitous or merely conventional but was a manifestation of aesthetic meaning and experience.

Such epigrams continued to be written from the introduction of Christianity until the decadence of the fifteenth century by a variety of writers, including Paulus Silentiarius, who contributed eighty epigrams to the *Anthology*, of which twenty are poetic fancies inspired by painting. The Byzantine epigrammatists were fully conscious of the differences between the pagan and the Christian epigram. "Let the pious and godly Christian epigrams take precedence even if the pagans are displeased."[37] These differences lay not only in the use of new subjects—the lives and deeds of patriarch, prophet, apostle, saint, and Christ himself—or in the greater severity of Christian morality which prohibited many of the licentious fancies

[35] Schlosser-Magnino, *op. cit.* (n. 19), p. 28.

[36] See Antonio Muñoz, "Descrizioni di opere d'arte in un poeta bizantino del secolo XIV (Manuel Philes), " *Repertorium für Kunstwissenschaft*, XXVII (Berlin, 1904), 390–400.

[37] Epigraph for Book I of the Christian epigrams in the *Greek Anthology* (n. 34), I, 1.

that paganism had encouraged in contemplating art. The real novelty lay in the posture assumed before an object of visual art. In that posture we can see the effects of the new critical similitude. Agathias, a contemporary of Paulus, who lived during the sixth century under Justinian, illustrates it notably:

Greatly daring was the wax that formed the image of the invisible Prince of the Angels, incorporeal in the essence of his form. But yet it is not without grace; for a man looking at the image directs his mind to a higher contemplation. No longer has he a confused veneration, but imprinting the image in himself he fears him as if he were present. The eyes stir up the depths of the spirit, and Art can convey by colors the prayers of the soul.[38]

In this epigram prayer and art are associated. The object creates the religious emotion of fear and is itself closely associated with the theological quality of grace. Here the wonder is not the one Homer celebrated—the shaping of intractable stone and metal into the likeness of reality—but the introduction of the unseen, the supernatural, into the material. Veiled in stone the Godhead see! Such a conception tends to reduce the distance between object and beholder, as in Yeats's "Sailing to Byzantium":

O sages standing in God's holy fire
As in the gold mosaic of a wall,
Come from the holy fire, perne in a gyre,
And be the singing-masters of my soul.[39]

The desire, fostered by Christian art, to speak to the object, to implore it, and to induce it to respond, is seen clearly in the art epigrams of Manuel Philes, a contemporary of Dante, who lived in Constantinople. A highly sophisticated man whose interests ranged widely and whose literary manner varied greatly, he usually adopted a Christian posture before works of art with religious meaning. Sometimes he addresses the picture as though he were praying to it or expostulating with it. Sometimes he makes the figure speak. We have noticed this as an ancient habit of the epigrammatist, arising, as Philes is aware, from the very nature of plastic art: "It is the very law of art to portray us silent." But

[38] *Ibid.*, p. 34.

[39] William Butler Yeats, *Collected Poems* (rev. ed.; New York: Macmillan Co., 1956). Quoted with permission of the publisher.

Philes keeps recurring to this theme: he addresses the silent Virgin of a picture and reflects that painting does not know how to represent the voice. In an epigram on St. George he says that art can reproduce only the image of the body but cannot portray that which is in the mind—a fact in which he finds justification for the poetic response to art in epigram and iconic poem.[40]

The desire to make the art object speak—although it is present in pagan antiquity and arises from the obvious fact that painting is, as Simonides had said, mute—becomes more insistent in Christian iconic poetry. The reason is, I think, obvious. The statue or painting has, in spite of official pronouncements against idolatry and in spite of powerful iconoclastic movements, become a kind of intermediary between the divine and the human. Spoken to, entreated, implored, it speaks in return. Therefore, a Christian poet like Philes believed that a mixed form is more satisfactory than verbal art alone or plastic art alone. In iconic art the silent form will speak, and in the combination there will be united the peculiar excellencies of each medium.

Another striking result of the religious view of art is that emphasis upon beauty of form is in part replaced by emphasis upon beauty of light. This would seem to be an almost inevitable result when likeness to natural form has been supplanted by likeness to inner reality. When the mirror is the ruling metaphor, shape and line, form and design, are basic; when the lamp is the ruling metaphor, light is of understandably greater importance.[41] For Aquinas *claritas*—illumination or luminousness—was one of the basic qualities of beauty,[42] deriving ultimately from the Platonic analogy between light and beauty but also from the religious and mystical view that God is light ("the light that lighteth every man coming into the world") and that all truth is light ("a light to lighten the Gentiles and to be the glory of thy people Israel"). Light and fire are images basic to the Christian and Hebrew tradition, prominent in the biblical literature of both the Hebrew and the Christian church.

[40] Muñoz, *op. cit.* (n. 36), p. 400.

[41] I borrow the metaphor from M. H. Abrams, *The Mirror and the Lamp* (New York, 1953).

[42] *Summa* i. q. 39. a. 8. c. Aquinas' *claritas* seems also to include brightness of color. For a modification of James Joyce's view that *claritas* is *quidditas* see Robert E. Brennan (ed.), *Essays in Thomism* (New York, 1942), p. 341.

Such views were translated directly into art and its appreciation. One of the few surviving medieval tracts on painting—the one written by the priest Theophilus who lived in the thirteenth century —says nothing at all about nature or about design. Its great concern is with mixing colors to achieve not natural but artistic effects.[43] Paulus Silentiarius, in contemplating St. Sophia, responds to space, form, and size but chiefly to color and light: the gleam of gold and marble, of mosaics and silver candlesticks. Gold is precious in and of itself and therefore possesses symbolic value. But its chief glory is that it reflects light throughout the immense spaces of the church. The gold and gem of altar and column are even more splendid at night, when they reflect light in such a way that one imagines a kind of nocturnal sun: smiling, roseate, resplendent.[44]

DANTE

Dante Alighieri embodies both strains in medieval pictorialism— the peculiarly Christian, which we have just discussed, and the classical, which we discussed at the opening of this chapter.[45] We begin by considering the classical.

In Book X of the *Purgatorio* Dante and Vergil, behind whom the gate of Purgatory has just closed, ascend a narrow cleft of rock for some three hours of harrowing endeavor. When their struggles have ended, they come to a terrace, the first of seven that rise above one another on the mountainside. Each, representing one of the Seven Deadly Sins, is presided over by an angel. On each are presented both the vice that is being punished and its corresponding virtue. There are therefore two kinds of example for each level—one to admonish against the vice and the other to recommend the requisite virtue. The symmetry is maintained

[43] Venturi, *op. cit.* (n. 33), p. 105.

[44] *Descriptio ecclesiae Sanctae Sophiae*, ll. 279 ff., 378 ff., in J. P. Migne (ed.), *Patrologiae cursus completus*, Greek Ser., Vol. LXXXVI bis, cols. 2119–58. See also Paul Friedländer, *Johannes von Gaza und Paulus Silentiarius* (Leipzig, 1912), pp. 291–94. Friedländer summarizes the text in German and provides full annotation and discussion of the backgrounds.

[45] For a bibliography of works on Dante's relations to the fine arts, see Reto Roedel, "Il sussidio delle arti figurative nella interpretazione dei velami della Divina Commedia," *Actes du Cinquième Congrès International des Langues et Littératures Modernes* (Florence, 1955), p. 47, n. See especially the brilliant but not fully substantiated article by Adolfo Venturi, "Dante e Giotto," *Nuova antologia*, CLXIX (February 16, 1900), 659–73.

even in details. The first example of the virtue on each terrace is always the Virgin. On this, the first of the terraces, pride is the vice and humility the virtue. Humility is represented by sculptures, which adorn the precipitous encircling bank—a bank resembling the back wall of a stage. Against it three scenes are presented in sculptured marble: the Virgin and the angel of the Annunciation, David dancing before the Ark of the Covenant, and the Emperor Trajan accosted by the suppliant widow. Each of three sources of ethical wisdom are used: the New Testament, the Old Testament, and pagan antiquity.[46]

The sculptures appear appropriately in that portion of Dante's masterpiece that is the most symmetrical and spatially harmonious of any, for the beauty of plastic art was felt to consist largely of these very qualities of proportion and balance. But the presence of classical iconic poetry in Christian purgatory cannot be accounted for solely on the basis of aesthetic appropriateness. De Sanctis, in a memorable passage of criticism, has perceived the basic reason and given it effective statement.

Reality has ceased to be actually present; reality has become imagination —no longer action, representative or dramatic, but an image of the spirit, just as we paint and reproduce in our minds the image of things not present. That painted reality is shown on the walls and in the bas-reliefs of Purgatory. There are no paintings in Hell and Paradise, because Nature and reality are there; they are the original, of which Purgatory is the portrait. Both Hell and Paradise are found in Purgatory, but contingently; they exist in the past, and in the future of the souls, are seen not with the eye but with the mind. These pictures are the souls' memento, the spectacle of what they were, and of what they will be. . . .

Life is external. Passions appear to the souls, but are no longer their passions; they are outside of them. . . . Passions, whether good or bad, are not living passions, but are visions of the spirit, figured as in painting and sculpture.[47]

Although his subjects in this passage are figures of plastic art, Dante yet remains a poet. With exquisite sense of form and of the

---

[46] *Purgatorio* x. 28–99. On a lunette in the cathedral at Orvieto, Luca Signorelli has painted these scenes, showing Dante and Vergil admiring the reliefs. For a reproduction see *Signorelli* ("Des Meisters Gemälde" [New York, 1927]), Plates 116, 117.

[47] Francesco De Sanctis, *History of Italian Literature*, trans. Joan Redfern (New York, 1931), I, 220–21.

limitations of his medium, he describes and interprets but does not, like some of the Sophists of late antiquity, attempt to compete with his plastic models. Like Homer before him, he celebrates the artist, who, in the contest with Nature, has outwitted and shamed her. Again like his predecessor—for this is a recurring theme in iconic verse—he admires the *difficulté vaincue*, the transformation of intractable material into expressive form: hard stone represents eagles moving in the wind. Above all, truth to nature has been achieved, and Dante most appropriately invokes the example of the Greek sculptor Polyclitus, the ancient master of minute physical realism. Nowhere even in classical antiquity had there been so eloquent a celebration of the power of verisimilitude, the power to draw the lines and create the shadows of reality—the dead are actually dead and the living alive ("morti li morti, e i vivi parean vivi").

Fully as striking as Dante's embodiment of the main elements of the classical iconic tradition is his use of that motif present in all iconic verse but especially prominent in his Byzantine contemporary, Philes, who continually confronts the paradox that sculptures and painted forms, though "living," are speechless until they speak with the poet's voice. The angel of the Annunciation is so real (*verace*) that Dante cannot accept the fact of his silence: how can he be merely "un imagine che tace," for one would have sworn that he said "Ave"? The same is true of Mary, who, unlike the statues in Thomson that are "forever silent and forever sad," virtually speaks in her very physical attitude. Finally—and most prominently, for this is a kind of crescendo—in contemplating the last statue, which tells the story of Trajan and the suppliant widow who requests revenge for her dead son, Dante actually endows the graven figures with speech: first the woman, then the emperor, then the woman again, and then once more Trajan are quoted directly. In silent plastic art Dante has discovered visible speech ("visibile parlare")—a paradoxical comment which is at once a tribute to the verisimilitude of the object and also a justification of the poet's addition of language.

Into the medieval Purgatory, itself a world of imaged reality, Dante has brought the whole panoply of the classical iconic tradition. God had created these statues and reliefs, as Dante distinctly says, but in so doing He has created "imitations of Nature," and His triumph is, essentially, the triumph of Homer's Hephaestus.

In the *Purgatorio* Dante embodies the verbal icon of the classical tradition; in the *Paradiso* he creates verbal icons of the more especially religious variety. If Chaucer may be said to exemplify classical pictorialism alone, one would have to say that Dante's more capacious imagination had been able to encompass both. From some points of view the iconic achievement of Dante in the *Paradiso* is subtler and more intense than anything produced in either ancient or medieval literature. Dante's final vision is compounded of a radiance that achieves Aquinas' requirement of *claritas* in art.[48] A transcendence of natural reality, it is in part a design of abstract and geometrical motion, astronomically sublime and beyond the compass of all bounding human forms. Nevertheless, the light and motion do not annihilate, though they transcend, recognizable form and personality. Dante's meaning is conveyed by light *and* love—light that transforms and ennobles familiar form and reality and love that paradoxically keeps them intact and familiar as they move from time and space into the timeless and the spaceless.

The *Paradiso* presents us with the music of singing, burning suns; with light that sparkles like the rays of the sun on clear water; with a river of light glowing tawny ("fulvido di fulgore") between its banks, painted in all the radiance of spring, from which issue living sparks like rubies set in gold—an image that suggests Byzantine interiors. These luminous shapes sometimes assume the form of a cross and sometimes wheel in circles of flame, purer and more intense at the center than at the periphery, circle within circle of flame and light. Finally, at the climax, intense, primal, and cosmic light overpowers all the senses: "pura luce," "luce intelletuale," and "luce viva."

But even at this moment, so dazzling that "nulla m'appariva," Dante's language reveals that he has kept his other theme before him: the pure intellectual light is "piena d'amore." Light and love are joined; and love, as fully as light, has had its progression throughout the vision. Beatrice is presented in the opening canto standing with all the longing of a mother bird awaiting the coming dawn so that she may look after her young. In Mary's ascent as a flame crowned with celestial light, the other flames stretch themselves up

[48] Murray Wright Bundy (*The Theory of Imagination in Classical and Mediaeval Thought* [Urbana, Ill., 1927], p. 239, n. 43) has counted 160 specific references to light in the *Divine Comedy*, of which only nine are in the *Inferno* and only thirteen in *Purgatorio* i–viii.

after her, as an infant reaches his arms toward his nursing mother. As the blinding center is approached, Dante's guide—his last guide, who leads him to the place of ultimate meaning—is St. Bernard, whom Dante presents with the tenderness of a father. When at last Dante looks into the light itself, he remembers our human likeness painted in its own colors. Within the depths of fathomless light, he sees, bound by love into one volume, all the scattered leaves of the universe.[49]

The imagery of the *Paradiso* is in one sense the culmination of the medieval icon. But in another sense—and this we learn from the union of love with light—natural form persists even here to the very end. For mystical light, however intense or sublime, is not allowed to dissolve the familiar and natural forms of love. The prodigious imagination of Dante unites, as though they were primal archetypes, natural and abstract form, the world of nature and the world of supernature, the classical and the medieval genius.

Less than a century after Dante's death there lived a painter, a pupil of Agnolo Gaddi, who made a comparison between painting and poetry that can serve to summarize some of the main concerns of these first two chapters. He was Cennino Cennini. He ranks both painting and poetry below knowledge (*scienzia*), but immediately next to knowledge comes painting. Painting is worthy to be honored by poetry, for the two are intimately related. What unites them? It is here that Cennini differs so considerably from Horace, of whose comparison between the two arts in the *Ars poetica* he may, indeed, have been thinking. Horace admits that both poet and painter can claim freedom of imagination—but always within the bounds of natural probability. Cennini asserts the common imaginative freedom without such qualification: the poet may compose as he sees fit—"secondo suo voluta" (*sic*); the painter may create with equal freedom—"secondo suo fantasia" (*sic*). Nature and probability place no restrictions on him. The medieval artist may paint half man and half horse it it pleases him—"si chome gli piace."[50]

Cennini's assertion of an imaginative freedom greater than Horace

---

[49] *Paradiso* xxx. 19–66; xiv. 100–105; xxviii. 13–39; xxiii. 118–26; xxxi. 58–63; xxxiii. 85–87, 130–33.

[50] Cennino d'Andrea Cennini, *Il libro dell'arte*, ed. Daniel V. Thompson, Jr. (New Haven, Conn., 1932), pp. 1–2.

would have permitted and Dante's creative use of both natural form and mystical light, of icons that are at once representational and symbolic, invite an evaluative comparison of the two kinds of pictorialism hitherto confronted—the naturalistic and the religious. If it was appropriate in the first chapter to stress the virtues of natural pictorialism, it is perhaps equally appropriate here to call attention to its limitations. Classical naturalism, for all its congeniality to the association of the sister arts, sometimes created stultifying conditions by insisting that the real world appear in art. Such conditions, obviously capable of limiting the poet's imagination, produced that kind of dull enumeration of unrelated but "real" particulars that was sometimes the bane of neoclassical descriptive poetry. Medieval thought, on the other hand, although in theory indifferent to drawing the analogy between painting and poetry, was able to create conditions that favor the development and sophistication of the visual icon. This the example of Dante demonstrates powerfully. Why should it be so? It may be that color and light (aesthetic values stressed in medieval aesthetic doctrine) are essentially more amenable to verbal rendering than the natural shapes and forms admired in classical times. But it may also be that medieval thought stimulated artistic achievement by creating a rich and complex relationship between verbal and plastic form, a relationship in which vision takes the place of observation and in which subservience to reality is supplanted by the boldest imaginative freedom.

CHAPTER III

The Renaissance

"UT PICTURA POESIS": ITALIAN AND ENGLISH CRITICISM

The coming of the Renaissance, first to Italy and later to England, revived the ancient tradition of *ut pictura poesis*, and very soon classical comment acquired the force of sacred text and example.[1] When Petrarch called Homer "primo pintor delle memorie antiche,"[2] he was perhaps the first in a long line of modern Western writers to refer to poets as painters and to echo Cicero's famous comment that, although Homer was reputedly blind, he produced what is virtually painting, not poetry: whatever his subject—a natural scene, a battle, the movement of men or animals—he described it so vividly that we see as we read.[3] In 1435 Leon Battista Alberti revealed that he was fully acquainted with classical teaching and example on the subject of pictorialism. He argued theoretically that poets and painters have many ideas and ornaments in common. He illustrated his point by citing Lucian's description of Apelles' allegorical painting "Calum-

---

[1] On the general importance of the revival of ancient texts see Hans Baron, *The Crisis of the Early Italian Renaissance* (Princeton, N.J., 1955): "Students of the Renaissance, if asked to indicate the most conspicuous factor in the change, will point without hesitation to the new relationship of artists as well as humanists to antiquity" (p. 3).

[2] *Trionfo della fama* iii. 15. For a brief account of the habit in antiquity and the Renaissance of calling poets painters see Karl Borinski, *Die Antike in Poetik und Kunsttheorie* (Leipzig, 1914), I, 183–84.

[3] *Tusculan Disputations* v. 39. 114. Cicero is arguing that the pleasure of a wise man, even the pleasure of seeing, exists independently of the operation of the organ of sight. Though Cicero does not use the word, the passage is a clear expression of the doctrine of *enargeia* in literary art (see above, pp. 11–12). This passage was associated early in the Renaissance with Horace's *ut pictura poesis* and often quoted as a manifestation of it. See, for example, *In epistolam Q. Horatii Flacci de arte poetica Iasonis de Nores Ciprii ex quotidianis Tryphonis Gabrielii sermonibus interpretatio* (Venice, 1553), pp. 128–29.

ny" (a passage which inspired Botticelli's painting on the subject at the Uffizi) and by remembering that Phidias was inspired to create his famous Zeus by reading Homer.[4]

The comments of Petrarch and Alberti show that the rediscovery of ancient texts included the rediscovery of ancient pictorialist doctrine and example. The greatest critics of antiquity, Plato, Aristotle, and Horace, were invoked as though they had created a full-blown dogma of pictorialism rather than uttered only pregnant hints and suggestions. Julius Caesar Scaliger said that "every oration consists of image, idea, and imitation, *just like painting*,"[5] and then added, "id quod et ab Aristotele et a Platone declaratum est."

The founders of the pictorialist tradition were now quoted and approved. In 1586, in Hoby's translation of Coignet entitled *Politique Discourses*, Simonides' famous sentence came to England: "For as Simonides saide: Painting is a dumme Poesie, and a Poesie is a speaking picture; & the actions which the Painters set out with visible colours and figures the Poets recken with wordes, as though they had in deede been perfourmed."[6] Even where Simonides is not named, the influence of his proverb is obvious. Camoëns in Portugal defined painting as "muda poesia," and in Italy Leonardo, in defining the two arts, said,

Painting is poetry which is seen and not heard, and poetry is a painting which is heard but not seen. These two arts (you may call them both either poetry or painting) have here interchanged the senses by which they penetrate to the intellect.[7]

But it was not Simonides alone who rode into modern times on the wave of renascent pictorialism. Lucian appeared in *editio princeps* in 1496; Philostratus' *Eikones* in 1498; Achilles Tatius in 1601.[8]

It is not surprising, therefore, that in 1587 Jacopo Mazzoni, in defending the *Divine Comedy*, should reveal that he is a pictorialist critic who believes that imitation necessarily and always involves the creation of "idol" and "image" and that he defends his faith by turning to Horace and Plutarch, to Cicero's evaluation of Homer

---

[4] *Della pittura*, ed. Luigi Mallè (Florence, 1950), pp. 103–5.

[5] *Poetices* (Heidelberg, 1617), p. 401 (italics mine).

[6] *Elizabethan Critical Essays*, ed. G. Gregory Smith (Oxford, 1904), I, 342.

[7] Camoëns is quoted *ibid.*; Leonardo, in Wylie Sypher, *Four Stages of Renaissance Style* (Garden City, N.Y., 1955), p. 98.

[8] John Edwin Sandys, *A History of Classical Scholarship* (Cambridge, 1908), II, 103–5 and index.

in pictorialist terms, to the *eikones* of Philostratus, and to Lucian's comments on Homer's imagery.[9] Nor is it surprising that we find parallels between the sister arts everywhere enforced and recommended by the Italian critics: by Castelvetro, Daniello, Capriano, Fracastoro, J. C. Scaliger, Possevino, Pontano, Minturno, Benedetto Varchi, Robortello, Gelli, and doubtless others besides.[10]

But pictorialist theory in the Renaissance reverted to the spirit and letter of neither Plato, Aristotle, nor Horace, even though it paid these critics handsome lip service. It apparently began where Plutarch and the critics of Hellenistic and late Roman antiquity had left off. Influenced by their theory and practice, it built the already partially codified doctrine of Plutarch and Philostratus into a dogma. This process may perhaps be best observed if we examine Horace's famous phrase *ut pictura poesis* as it appeared in the modern world and as it began the long career that was to make it, in the ensuing centuries, one of the most frequently cited texts of ancient criticism.

The *Ars poetica* has had a continuous history from antiquity to modern times, and the earliest surviving comment on the phrase *ut pictura poesis* has come down under the name of a scholar named Acron, who lived in the third century A.D. The comment attributed to him, however, is believed to go back only to the fifth century.[11] That comment, which is of some significance since it appears in many of the earliest printed editions of Horace, begins as follows:

> Vt pictura poesis erit. i. non erit dissimilis
> poetica ars picturae.[12]

When this sentence was first written in the fifth century, it may have served no purpose other than to introduce the example that followed it, but it contains features that become important in later developments. Horace's line is punctuated to read "ut pictura poesis

[9] See Allan H. Gilbert, *Literary Criticism: Plato to Dryden* (New York, 1940), pp. 362–63.

[10] Paul Oskar Kristeller, "The Modern System of the Arts," *Journal of the History of Ideas*, XII (October, 1951), 511–17. I have benefited from reading Bernard Weinberg's analysis of painting and poetry in an article that will be published in a collection by the Società Editrice Internazionale of Turin.

[11] Horace, *Satires, Epistles and Ars poetica*, ed. H. Rushton Fairclough ("Loeb Classical Library" [London, 1932]), p. xxvii; Martin Schanz, *Geschichte der römischen Literatur* (Munich, 1922), sec. 601.

[12] I quote this passage from Landino's edition (*Horatius cum quattuor commentariis* [Venice, 1498]).

erit": the verb, that is, is placed with the first clause. In the reading of most modern authorities the verb is placed with the second part of the sentence after a colon: "Ut pictura poesis: erit quae . . . ," etc.[13] When read with the first clause, the verb makes Horace's meaning seem more dogmatic than it actually is: "a poem *will be* like a painting." When read with the second clause, the verb says merely, "it will sometimes happen that." It is of some historical importance that in the editions of Horace that appeared during the fifteenth and up to the middle of the sixteenth century the verb was placed with the first phrase.[14]

The only other noteworthy features of the fifth-century gloss is that for Horace's *poesis* the commentator substitutes *ars poetica* in the paraphrase. In and of itself that is innocent enough and may be perfectly just. But in view of the fact that Horace's offhand comment, made, as we have seen, by way of casual illustration, was later erected into critical dogma, it may be ominous that the first scholiast, whose comment was repeated in edition after Renaissance edition, should make this interpretation.[15]

[13] Otto Keller, in *Epilegomena zu Horaz* (Leipzig, 1879), quarrels with the modern punctuation: "Hinsichtlich der Interpunction nach *poesis* sind die bedeutendsten Herausgeber so ziemlich einig: Lambin, Bentley, Fea, Peerlkamp, Haupt, Zambra, u.v.a. Dagegen sind aber sämmtliche überhaupt interpungierende Codices und Porphyr. und wahrscheinlich mit Recht. Denn die Interpunction zwischen *poesis* und *erit* sieht doch ziemlich gekünstelt aus, und unsrem allgemeinen oft bewährten Grundsatze nach ist die einfachste Interpunction bei Horaz regelmässig auch die wahrscheinlichste. Ich würde also heute vorziehen so zu lesen:

Ut pictura poesis erit quae, si propius stes,
Te capiat magis, etc." (p. 766).

[14] Of the editions consulted, the following place *erit* with the first clause: Landino (Venice, 1483); Aldus (Venice, 1509); Gürninger (Strassburg, 1498); Grifolus (Florence, 1550); Cruqius (Antwerp, 1579). The following separate *ut pictura poesis* from *erit* by a comma, point, or colon: Lambinus (Verona, 1567); Chabot (Basel, 1587); Manutius (Venice, 1576); Rodellius (London, 1690); Talbot (Cambridge, 1699); Bentley (Cambridge, 1711). From then on, the prestige of Bentley's text led almost all subsequent English editors to follow his punctuation.

[15] The scholiast of the Parisian codices (λφψ) of the tenth century comments on the phrase *pictoribus atque poetis* (*Ars poetica*, l. 9): "Ab hoc incipit generalia praecepta dare, quibus instituit bonos poetas; et dicit pictoribus atque poetis legem unam esse, videlicet ut mentiantur in suo opere tantum ut veri simile sit." The *verum* to which both the arts should be faithful may have been conceived of in the medieval sense (see above, pp. 46–47). But it is clear that in the Middle Ages Horace's comments on the two arts were read as a general precept and interpreted as a law governing both arts. Thus the Renaissance continued what apparently had begun in the Middle Ages. There is no comment in these MSS on *ut pictura poesis*. See H. J. Botschuyver (ed.), *Scholia in Horatium*, λφψ *Codicum Parisinorum Latinorum 7972, 7974, 7971* (Amsterdam, 1935), p. 423.

So interpreted, Horace's text came into the modern world. Until the middle of the sixteenth century commentators did little more than repeat or slightly expand the comment of the Pseudo-Acron. At that time the punctuation began to be changed; the verb was detached from *ut pictura poesis* and placed with the example that followed. But this had no immediate effect upon the reading of the lines, and the comment—doubtless because the cumulative effects of Renaissance cultural history were much weightier than the position of a colon—became more, not less, dogmatic; more, not less, theoretical. The lines are read as a kind of universal principle applicable to all allegory; one commentator has Cicero say that Homer's poems must be esteemed as painting rather than poetry; and Aristotle's analogies of the two arts are referred to as previous discoveries of the same pictorialist insight.[16] Where the Pseudo-Acron had said modestly that the art of poetry is not unlike (*non dissimilis*) that of painting, Luisinus in 1554 called the two arts highly similar (*simillimas*).[17] Robortello argued in 1548 that it was highly appropriate in criticism to move freely from one art to the other, so similar were the aesthetic problems raised.[18] In 1541 Pomponius Gauricus stated flatly, "Poetry ought to resemble painting."[19] So frequently was Horace's dictum repeated that a literary historian

[16] "Hoc est allegoria ex similitudine sumpta. prius enim poesim picturae comparat, deinde ex ea re sumens allegoriam: cum de poesi loqueretur allegorice rem totam explicat. sumit autem a pictoribus ad artem referens similitudinem: cum poetice ars, & pictura inter se ita respondeant." The commentator then quotes Simonides without mentioning him by name and also the passage in Cicero on Homer as painter (see above, n. 3). In this text the line is punctuated "ut pictura poesis erit: ..." (*In epistolam Q. Horatii Flacci* ... [n. 3], pp. 128–29).

[17] "Picturam, et poesim ubique simillimas indicari reperies" (*Francisci Luisini commentarius* [Venice], p. 70). He quotes Aristotle's comparison of plot to design (see above, p. 7) and continues: "Nos oportet bonos pictores imitari, qui dum proprias, verisq; similes imagines referre student, pulchriores depingunt. & alibi in eodem libro."

[18] *Francisci Robortelli Vtinensis, in librum Aristotelis de arte poëtica, explicationes* ... (Basel, 1555), p. 55a (the first edition was published at Florence, 1548). See his paraphrase of Horace, p. 15a, usually bound at the end of the commentary on Aristotle.

[19] *Pomponius Gauricus super arte poetica Horatii* (Rome), D ii (recto). It should not be assumed that all critics of the Renaissance uncritically accepted the analogy between the arts. Castelvetro finds both similarities and dissimilarities between them, and the latter outweigh the former. For an analysis see Bernard Weinberg, "Castelvetro's Theory of Poetics," in R. S. Crane (ed.), *Critics and Criticism* (Chicago, 1952), p. 369. See also Weinberg, *op. cit.* (n. 10).

has said that *ut pictura poesis* may be considered "almost the keynote of Renaissance criticism."[20]

For this dogmatic intensification of critical theory no simple explanation that does not take into account the many diverse and contradictory aspects of Renaissance culture can possibly be considered acceptable. Yet the chief, if not sole, reason for the importance of *ut pictura poesis* in Renaissance criticism was that it somehow served the purposes of artistic naturalism. Filippo Villani in the early fifteenth century viewed the revival of the arts as not so much a reversion to antiquity for its own sake as a reversion to nature. Leonardo in the sixteenth century believed that there was no actual conflict between nature and the classical rules and that to repossess these rules was to take a step toward regaining the grasp that antiquity had upon reality.[21] If this is true in general of the revival of ancient text and ancient theory, it is more particularly true of the resurrection of *ut pictura poesis*. For that critical doctrine had originally arisen in connection with the notion of *enargeia*, the vivid and lifelike reproduction in verbal art of natural detail. Once more, in intensified form, this was to be its philosophical and cultural context. *Ut pictura poesis* was not a principle of art for art's sake, even though Shakespeare's and Spenser's use of it that we shall consider later may seem to suggest that it was. It was a reminder to the poet that the example of painting proved that art could achieve power only to the extent that it was in the closest possible contact with visible reality.

In the earliest important "defense of poetry" Boccaccio stated the notion as follows:

> The epithet [ape of nature] might be less irritating [than ape of philosophers], since the poet tries with all his powers to set forth in noble verse the effects, either of Nature herself, or of her eternal and unalterable operation ... the forms, habits, discourse, and actions of all animate things, the courses of heaven and the stars, the shattering force of the winds, the roar and crackling of flames, the thunder of the waves, high mountains and

---

[20] Joel E. Spingarn, *A History of Literary Criticism in the Renaissance* (New York, 1920), p. 42.

[21] See Erwin Panofsky, "Renaissance and Renascences," *Kenyon Review*, VI (Spring, 1944), 203.

shady groves, and rivers in their course . . . so vividly set forth that the very objects will seem actually present in . . . the written poem.[22]

Were the words "poet," "verse," "writing" not used, we might be persuaded that we heard here the voice of Leonardo explaining the highest powers of the painter. And if we did not know that these were the words of a fourteenth-century Italian standing on the threshold of the Renaissance, we could easily believe that we heard the voice of Cicero or Plutarch explaining the poetical *enargeia* of Homer's *Odyssey*.

The same sentiments and the same association with relevant critics of antiquity echo through the criticism of the English Renaissance and its immediate aftermath. Ben Jonson translates Philostratus (*"Whosoever* loves not *Picture* is injurious to Truth and all the wisdom of Poetry"), and then adds: "Picture is the invention of Heaven, the most ancient and most a kinne to Nature."[23] Ascham defines poetry as "a fair lively painted picture of the life of every degree of man." George Puttenham recommends *enargeia* as a quality that "giveth a glorious lustre and light"—the light and luster of reality itself, however stylized.[24] Spenser, without using the word *enargeia*, invokes the principle: in the "argument" to the February eclogue the old man's tale of the oak and the briar is described as being told "so liuely and so feelingly as if the thing were set for in some Picture before our eyes." Perhaps the most eloquent statement of the ancient association between poetry, painting, and reality is made by Chapman:

That, *Enargeia*, or cleernes of representation, requird in absolute Poems is not the perspicuous deliuery of a lowe inuention; but high, and harty inuention exprest in most significant, and vnaffected phrase; it serues not a skilfull Painters turne, to draw the figure of a face only to make knowne who it represents; but hee must lymn, giue luster, shaddow, and heighten-

[22] Cited in Katherine Everett Gilbert and Helmut Kuhn, *A History of Esthetics* (New York, 1939), pp. 180–81. For Shakespeare's use of "ape of nature" see below, p. 87.

[23] "Timber, or Discoveries," in Joel E. Spingarn (ed.), *Critical Essays of the Seventeenth Century* (Oxford, 1908), I, 29.

[24] *The Arte of English Poesie* iii. 3; iii. 10. 9. Ascham's phrase is quoted in Guy Andrew Robinson, *Elizabethan Criticism of Poetry* (Menasha, Wis., 1914), p. 94.

ing; which though ignorants will esteeme spic'd, and too curious, yet such as haue the iudiciall perspectiue, will see it hath, motion, spirit and life.[25]

Chapman's vigorous phrases show that he is concerned with reality and its clear, perspicuous rendition in verbal art. But they also show that he is concerned with the heightening and intensification of reality, which, as we saw in discussing Aristotle and the example of Zeuxis, was an important aspect of the analogy with painting. It is everywhere present in the sixteenth century. Spenser in his dedicatory sonnet to the *Faerie Queene* invokes the example of Zeuxis:

> The Chian Peincter, when he was requirde
> To pourtraict Venus in her perfect hew,
> To make his worke more absolute, desird
> Of all the fairest Maides to have the vew.

Marlowe uses the mirror image not to suggest, as Leonardo had, that art should imitate the very relief and contour of nature itself but to symbolize "the heavenly quintessence" distilled by poets from the "immortal flowers of poesy"

> Wherein, as in a mirror, we perceive
> The highest reaches of a human wit.[26]

Ut pictura poesis often encouraged the improvement as well as the imitation of nature, and it sometimes sanctioned poetic ornament. Scaliger spoke of *pigmenta dictionum* and Puttenham of "exornations"—"the pearl or passements of gold upon the stuff of princely garment" or "the rich orient colors laid upon a portrait."[27]

[25] Phyllis Brooks Bartlett (ed.), *The Poems of George Chapman* (New York, 1941), p. 49. The word "liveliness" is usually a synonym for *enargeia*. Many contexts make clear the association with painting. Thus Sidney defines poetry as "mimesis," "that is to say, a representing, counterfeiting, or figuring forth; to speak metaphorically [and here he turns to Simonides' proverb without saying so] a speaking picture" (see A. S. Cook [ed.], *The Defense of Poesy* [Boston, 1890], p. 9). Sidney not only adopted pictorialist language in his formal definition, but he was also in the habit of referring to poetry as painting. The "peerless poet" gives a "perfect picture" of what he recommends (*ibid.*, p. 15). Philosophy lies dark unless "illuminated or figured forth by the speaking picture of poesy" (*ibid.*, p. 16). The use of "lively" in connection with *enargeia* and the analogy with painting persisted at least up to the time of Dr. Johnson. See Jean H. Hagstrum, *Samuel Johnson's Literary Criticism* (Minneapolis, Minn., 1952), pp. 62–63, 99, 188.

[26] *I Tamburlaine the Great*, Act V, Sc. 2, ll. 103–5. For "mirror" in other senses, see below, pp. 135–36, 138–39.

[27] J. C. Scaliger, *Poetices* (4th ed.; Heidelberg, 1607), p. 125. George Puttenham is quoted in Madeleine Doran, *Endeavors of Art* (Madison, Wis., 1954). p. 44.

But such strains in Renaissance pictorialism did not vitiate the basic naturalism of pictorialist theory. They only suggested a way in which reality could be made more attractive. For when we have said that both the ancient and the sixteenth-century analogies between painting and poetry depended on the notion of *enargeia* and on the desire to approximate in verbal art the beauty and vivacity of the real world, we have made the essential comparison and laid bare the foundations. "Imitation," a term that had bound the verbal and graphic arts together in antiquity but had been replaced in official medieval philosophy by the new similitude between the work of art and unseen, unseeable reality, became in the Renaissance a crucially important term of critical meaning, not in the Aristotelian sense but in the more literal sense of late antiquity.

The truth of this the example of Julius Caesar Scaliger amply demonstrates. His notion of imitation is not, to be sure, crudely naturalistic. Poets, he believes, create an idealized second nature. Poetry, as the noblest of the arts, must appeal to the intellect and, as a verbal art, must recognize the limits of its medium. Even so, verisimilitude remains important and the analogy with painting highly relevant. For both pictures and words are "images of appearance"; the "forms" of words, statues, and paintings are natural and terrestrial objects. Words are *images* of things and acquire significance only as they arise from and remain related to things. Similarly, in Minturno's criticism the belief that painting and poetry are so intimately related as to be virtually indistinguishable rests upon a firm faith in literal verisimilitude. "For the poet must above all things behold the truth, so that he may, in undertaking to represent individual things, be as close as possible to truth; he should imitate it in such a way that not only the very form and spirit of a thing appear but that the very thing itself . . . appear in full lucidity."[28] Such aesthetic naturalism as this bound poetry and painting together during the Renaissance. That naturalism rested on the ancient foundations of rhetorical and poetical *enargeia*.

[28] See Scaliger, *op. cit.* (n. 27), p. 6, and Bernard Weinberg, "Scaliger versus Aristotle on Poetics," *Modern Philology*, XXXIX (May, 1942), 337–60. Minturno's comment comes from his *De poeta* (Venice, 1559), p. 26. For similar views of Castelvetro and other Renaissance critics see H. B. Charlton, *Castelvetro's Theory of Poetry* (Manchester, 1913), pp. 17, 36–37, 41 ff., 45, 62. See also Spingarn, *op. cit.* (n. 20), chap. ii.

THE "PARAGONE": PAINTER VERSUS POET

Stated in its most elementary but essential form, pictorialist doctrine can account for the many elaborations—sometimes dully enumerative, sometimes glowingly fresh and attractive—of physical and sensuous detail that appear everywhere in the poets of Renaissance Italy and England: in Poliziano, Tasso, Ariosto; in Sidney, Spenser, and Shakespeare. But for the sophistication of the critics' theory and the complication of the poets' imagistic practice we must go beyond the classical heritage to the history and sociology of interart relations during the Renaissance.

Leonardo died in 1519; Raphael in 1520. Michelangelo lived on until 1564; Titian until 1576. When, therefore, Pomponius Gauricus said in 1541 that poetry ought to resemble painting, the great work of the Italian Renaissance in painting had in part been already accomplished, and the art enjoyed a prestige that it had perhaps never before been accorded. The victory had not been achieved without a struggle that included rivalry even with the sister art of poetry, a struggle that was expressed in the famous *paragone* (or contest) of Renaissance critical comment. This tendency to view various occupations and even ideas and philosophies as competitive is one of the distinguishing marks of Renaissance thought. *Paragoni* existed not only between painting and poetry but also between sculpture and painting, between Florentine design and Venetian color, between nature and art.

The *paragone* involving painting and poetry is explainable not so much philosophically, on the basis of a theoretical distinction between these arts, as sociologically: painters and sculptors were now successful enough to reject the inferior social and educational position they had occupied since antiquity and to strive for recognition of their pursuits as liberal disciplines. In a tract on painting published in 1609 the personified *Pittura* says: "You know that what displeased me above all else was that I was not placed among the seven liberal arts and that I was born in ignorance."[29] Sculpture and painting had been considered mechanical, not liberal, arts, and

[29] *Tractato di pictura composto per Francesco Lancilotti fiorentino pictore* (Rome, 1509), p. 2.

hence worthy neither of a freeborn citizen's practice nor of a place in the trivium or quadrivium.[30]

Poetry had not always won approval either, and some Renaissance critics found it necessary to defend the art as morally and intellectually respectable. But if it proved desirable to defend poetry, which had after all come into the curriculum through the door of rhetoric and logic and had never suffered from the stigma that its practitioner dirtied his hands in physical labor, it was even more necessary to defend painting. In an age of supreme achievement in painting and sculpture it was inevitable that the tradition of treating its practitioners as social and intellectual inferiors should be roundly challenged and finally destroyed. Alberti in 1436 proclaimed painting as the mother art.[31] Raphael in 1508–11 placed painting among the liberal arts that surround Plato and Aristotle in the "School of Athens." The speakers in Francisco D'Olanda's dialogues, including Michelangelo himself, all assert the superiority of painting, and one of them says that the poets have no other aim than to illustrate the principles of painting and to imitate a good picture.[32]

Among the many defenders that painting won to her cause during the Renaissance, Leonardo da Vinci was the supreme apologist. He boldly asserts her sovereign claims and her superiority even to her sister poetry. His argument, though not particularly subtle, differs in the power of its conviction from the many textbookish *paragoni* that later become fashionable. Some elements are, of course, derivative, but even these acquire new life in a new context. He revives the ancient notion that of the five senses the noblest is sight, the peculiar possession of the painter. He repeats the Neoplatonic notion that the painter resembles, more closely than any other artist, the Creator, and he claims high sanction in the fact that in religious thought God has often been viewed as the greatest artificer of all, the supreme

[30] See Jean Paul Richter and Irma A. Richter, *The Literary Works of Leonardo da Vinci* (Oxford, 1939), I, 3–48; Anthony Blunt, *Artistic Theory in Italy 1450–1600* (Oxford, 1940), pp. 48–57; Arnold Hauser, *The Social History of Art* (London, 1951), I, 124–25; St. Isidore of Seville, *Etymologiarum* i. 1. 1–3; i. 2. 103 (J. P. Migne, *Patrologia latina*, III, 1–3).

[31] *Op. cit.* (n. 4), pp. 54–55.

[32] Antonietta Maria Bessone Aureli (ed.), *I dialoghi Michelangioleschi di Francisco D'Olanda* (4th ed.; Rome, 1953), p. 96.

painter. Paintings have even been worshiped by the people, so close have they at times come to representing divine reality and touching our deepest instincts of awe. And that, says Leonardo, revealing himself to be the son of the Southern Renaissance, far removed from the thought of the Northern Reformation, could never be asserted of any book ever written.[33]

Leonardo's argument achieves its greatest force when he associates the art of painting with the scientific investigation of the natural world and the experimental acquisition of knowledge, forming an alliance with one of the most stimulating forces of the modern world. Painting was related to science in two ways. Like science it explored, rendered, and in its rendering explained nature, the source of all truth. And in the very process it developed those powers of sense and mind most intimately associated with scientific investigation: honest, disciplined observation and its subsequent and consequent certitudes. Thus the painter, who deals with things, is superior to the poet, who deals with words. The painter is the lord of reality. Painting need not speak (here Leonardo glances at an important element in the iconic tradition); it possesses a superior language, that of fact and reality.[34]

This argument is effective less because of its own dialectical force than because it was supported by the exciting advances in the art of painting made by Leonardo himself and his contemporaries. Painting was in fact superior to poetry during the Renaissance in Italy, and it is understandable that a poet should be urged to look to it as the exemplary art. The Horatian dictum was launched on its career in modern Europe with the prestige of Renaissance painting behind it. It went forth under the banner of an art that had discovered perspective and had taken great strides in producing brilliance and

[33] Richter and Richter, *op. cit.* (n. 30), I, 24–25, 26, 41–48, 52–56.

[34] *Ibid.*, pp. 54, 311. On Leonardo and science see Ludwig H. Heydenreich's Introduction to Leonardo da Vinci, *Treatise on Painting*, ed. A. Philip McMahon (Princeton, N.J., 1956), I, xxxiii–xxxvii. Leonardo's use of the term "experience" strikingly anticipates the views of some of the British empirical philosophers, like Locke, and critics of the empirical stamp, like Dr. Johnson: "Experience [is] the interpreter between formative nature and the human race." "Wisdom is the daughter of experience." "Experience never errs; it is only your judgments that err by promising themselves effects such as are not caused by your experiments" (*ibid.*, II, 240). This may explain why Leonardo was studied and admired in England during the eighteenth century. See below, p. 163.

permanence of color. No other art could surpass painting in obeying the ancient command to imitate nature.

An argument so fundamental in concept and so forceful in presentation was bound to arouse echoes, even in faraway England. Shakespeare, for one, seems somehow to have encountered the Italian *paragone*. A poet and a painter in *Timon of Athens* discuss their respective arts; and after the poet has summarized an allegorical poem he has written on Fortune, the painter says, with obvious reference to the competitive superiority of his art to that of poetry:

> A thousand moral paintings I can show
> That shall demonstrate these quick blows of Fortune's
> More pregnantly than words.[35]

The rivalry of painting and poetry is glanced at in Kyd's *Spanish Tragedy*—and surely in many plays besides—when the distraught Hieronomo asks a painter who has also lost a son: "Art a painter? Canst paint me a tear, or a wound, A groan or a sigh?"[36] The theme of a recently discovered entertainment, probably written by John Lyly, is the contest between painter and poet, in which, as one might expect, poetry gets the better of the argument.[37] Spenser refers to the

> ... Poets wit, that passeth Painter farre
> In picturing the parts of beautie daint.[38]

The competition between painter and poet achieved philosophic and artistic status during the Renaissance largely because it repre-

[35] Act I, Sc. 1. Dr. Johnson was aware that a competition of some kind was involved here but does not relate it to the Italian *paragone*, of which he may have been ignorant: "Shakespeare seems to intend in this dialogue to express some competition between the two great arts of imitation" (Samuel Johnson and George Steevens [eds.], *Shakespeare* [London, 1793], XI, 474). For a correct interpretation of the passage and its historical relationship see Anthony Blunt, "An Echo of the 'Paragone' in Shakespeare," *Journal of the Warburg Institute*, II (1938–39), 260–62.

[36] Act III, Sc. 12, ll. 107–8.

[37] Leslie Hotson (ed.), *Queen Elizabeth's Entertainment at Mitcham* (New Haven, Conn., 1953). Hotson calls this a "contention" or "dispute" and relates it to the Italian *contrasto*, failing to see that his text concerns the Leonardesque *paragone* (p. 12). For a correction see D. J. Gordon's review in *Modern Language Review*, L (April, 1955), 195–96.

[38] *Faerie Queene* iii, Proem. 2. Spenser is confronting the difficulty of representing Chastity. He has just mentioned the "life-resembling pencill" of Zeuxis and Praxiteles.

sented a profound and far-reaching conflict of interest and idea, a conflict that itself may be said to have had a part in the making of the modern world. For poetry, the newly won position of painting carried a challenge; it, like painting, must seek to render the wholesome and vivacious realities of life and nature. But the prestige of painting also implied something subtler and more profound. The greatest power of painting, as it was understood by the Renaissance mind, was the power of making the visible intelligible by using only visible means, the power of making physical detail—and physical detail only—express order, character, meaning, morality, and purpose.[39] The poet in *Timon of Athens* says of the painting before him that it is "livelier than life"; that is, it possesses the *enargeia* desired by ancient and Renaissance critics alike. But he also says of particular physical details:

> Admirable: how this grace
> Speaks his own standing! what a mental power
> This eye shoots forth! how big imagination
> Moves in this lip! [Act I, Sc. 1].

Here is a fully developed doctrine of pictorial expression. Posture reveals grace, an eye expresses mental power, a lip suggests the power of mental conceiving.[40]

This too the poet can learn from the painter. Although his medium has greater range of expression than the painter's and goes beyond the use of sensuous detail and visible image, he can derive from the sister art the power of expressing meaning through *visibilia* alone. The *paragone* forced him to consider the claims of painting, an art that during the Renaissance had learned the full scope of its own peculiar genius.

ICONIC POETRY: PAINTER AND POET

The triumphant achievements of painting from Giotto through Tintoretto and the vigorous polemic of Leonardo on its behalf increased the prestige of painting, but they did not lower the prestige of poetry. Although Leonardo had insulted the art of poetry and although the *paragone* often aroused envious rivalry, painters and

[39] See Rosemond Tuve, *Elizabethan and Metaphysical Imagery* (Chicago, 1947), chap. iii.

[40] See above, p. 31, and below, pp. 121-23.

their spokesmen continued to look to poets for themes and inspiration—at least to poets of a certain kind. The eloquent defender of the Venetian school against the Florentines, Lodovico Dolce, is principally a panegyrist of painting and painters. Nevertheless, he looks upon Ariosto as a great example to the graphic artist. "If painters wish to find, without travail, a perfect example of a beautiful woman, let them read those verses of Ariosto in which he marvellously describes the beauty of the enchantress Alcina."[41] Giovanni Paolo Lomazzo, another apologist for painting, advised painters to turn to poetry not only for subject matter but also to learn such technical matters as the proper characteristics and motions of animals.[42]

Such advice from the art critics did not go unheeded. The Renaissance provides many examples of association between painter and poet in which the painter, in spite of his newly felt strength and his newly won prestige, looks to the poet for guidance and inspiration. There were countless opportunities for artists to meet in the princely courts and discuss their respective aims. Often painting and poetry were practiced by the same person. Brunelleschi, Andrea Orcagna, Leonardo, Cellini, Bronzino, Donato Bramante, and especially Michelangelo all wrote verses.[43] Stories were repeated of the association of painter and poet. Alberti's retelling of Lucian's description of Apelles suggested to Botticelli the subject for his "Calumnia," now at the Uffizi. Poliziano is believed to have inspired both the "Primavera" and the "Nascita di Venere" as well as Raphael's "Galatea" in the Palazzo Farnesina in Rome.[44] It was said that Raphael turned to Ariosto for advice about the personages to intro-

[41] D. Ciàmpoli (ed.), *L'Aretino: Dialogo della pittura di Lodovico Dolce* (Lanciano, Italy, 1913), p. 44.

[42] *Trattato dell'arte della pittura scultura ed architettura* (Rome, 1844), I, 302–4. The date of the *Trattato* is 1584–85. It was translated into English in 1598 by Haydocke. Lomazzo is convinced that a good painting is literary: "non possa essere pittore, che insieme anco non abbia qualche spirito di poesia" (II, 67). He devotes some fifty-three pages to citations from poets to whom painters ought to turn for examples of the proper expression of emotion. Of the poets cited, Ariosto seems regularly to predominate (II, 469 ff.).

[43] *Ibid.*, II, 68–69; Enrico Panzacchi, *Il Libro degli artisti* (Milan, 1902), pp. 69–71, 39–41, 272–76, 182–84.

[44] Panzacchi, *op. cit.* (n. 43), pp. 90–93. For the relations of Botticelli and Poliziano and the relations of both to Ficino see Arnolfo B. Ferruolo, "Botticelli's Mythologies," *Art Bulletin*, XXXVII (March, 1955), 17–25.

duce into his Vatican fresco "La Disputa."[45] Benedetto Varchi believed that two of Michelangelo's greatest works were accomplished with Dante's poem open before him: the "Last Judgment," which is Dantean in subject and manner; and the allegorical tombs in the Medici chapel, where the antithetical position of Dawn and Day, directly opposite the parallel but contrasting Night and Evening, reflects, as he thought, the passage in the *Paradiso* in which Dante gazes at the sun, which has reached its' equinoctial point, causing midday in Purgatory and midnight at Jerusalem.

> Fatto avea di là mane e di qua sera
> Tal foce quasi; e tutto era là bianco
> Quello emisperio, e l'altra parte nera.[46]

The association of the arts was also manifested in the continuation, during the Renaissance, of the uninterrupted tradition of iconic poetry, which had been present in Western culture since the writing of the *Iliad*. Such poetry, although voluminous in the Renaissance, was largely, as its closest student has observed, artificial and insincere.[47] It might have been otherwise had poets been able to participate more extensively in the exciting achievements of painting and science. They did perceive the relevance of the ancient notion of verisimilitude, but not in its full and creative association with the new naturalism of science and art. They kept saying that the aim of painting, as of all art, was *naturam vincere*. But they seldom rose, as Leonardo had risen, to the importance of the theme. It was ironic that so many poetic celebrations of naturalness in graphic art should themselves be overlaid with a heavy crust of convention.

Although many of these poets do no more than repeat without conviction and with little skill the hoary themes of iconic poetry, there are some who achieve ingenuity if not inspiration. Iconic elements entered the fashionable Petrarchism of the period. Painter, subject (usually a lady), and poet are often worked into witty relationship. The iconic situation may be exploited to praise or lament

[45] Vincenzo Golzio, *Raffaello nei documenti nelle testimonianze dei contemporanei e nella letteratura del suo secolo* (Vatican, 1936), p. 188. Golzio cites the English painter Richardson as the source of the information that Raphael wrote to Ariosto. This does not increase one's belief in its reliability.

[46] *Paradiso* i. 43–45. *Lezzioni di M. Benedetto Varchi* (Florence, 1590), pp. 228–29.

[47] Arduino Colosanti, "Gli Artisti nella Poesia del Rinascimento: Fonti poetiche per la storia dell'arte Italiana," *Repertorium für Kunstwissenschaft*, XXVII (Berlin, 1904), 194–207, esp. p. 194.

the lady, sometimes by complaining that the picture is only a dull version of the original; sometimes by saying that it is necessarily so, since the picture must be viewed by weak mortal eyes, which would be dazzled blind by the original; and sometimes by asserting that the lady on the canvas is kindlier than the cruel She of reality. As one would expect from certain of the intellectual tendencies of the period, Neoplatonic ideas appear frequently in poems on the graphic arts. If such poetry remained only derivative and conventional in poets like Varchi, it did achieve great beauty in Petrarch and Michelangelo.[48]

Renaissance iconic poetry also revived, in both its Neoplatonic and its naturalistic manifestations, the ancient notion that the material of art—stone or pigment—has in successful art been transcended and overcome. Painter and sculptor are praised for the *difficulté vaincue*. The iconic poet may present himself as the voice of the statue or picture. Back of the conceits of more than one such poem lies Simonides' proverb that painting is mute poetry and poetry a speaking picture. One of them strikingly anticipates Keats's "Ode on a Grecian Urn": Aretino, in a sonnet praising Titian's portrait of Diego di Mendoz, calls the painter a modern Apelles, who creates both "silent nature" and "speaking likeness"—"una tacita natura" that "nel silenzio suo par che favelli."[49]

Towering above both the flats of conventional literary exercise and the bogs of mere ingenuity are a few peaks of genuine iconic achievement. If Poliziano's celebration of Giotto, Seraphino Aqua-

---

[48] For Michelangelo see below, pp. 74–75. For Varchi see *De sonetti di M. Benedetto Varchi*, Part I (Florence, 1555). The second part appeared in 1557. Varchi's poetry, written in his old age, is fairly lively on patriotic Tuscan themes, but on Neoplator : subjects and on paintings it tends to be derivative. Usually addressed in the Anacreontic manner (see above, p. 25) to a painter, it seldom reveals close observation of a particular work. Petrarch's fine sonnets (*In vita di M. Laura*, Nos. 77, 78) beginning "Per mirar Policleto" and "Quando giunse a Simon" were analyzed by Gelli in the sixteenth century as an elaboration of Dante's simpler iconic verse in the *Purgatorio* (see above, pp. 51–53). In fact, Gelli, in an interesting passage that reveals a keen sense of historical continuity in the matter of iconic verse, believes Petrarch had the tenth book of the *Purgatorio* in mind when he wrote these sonnets. Gelli finds the first Platonic, the second Aristotelian. See *Tutte le lettioni di Giovanni Battista Gelli, fatte da lui nella Accademia Fiorentina* (Florence, 1551), pp. 372–73.

[49] Letter No. 532 (to Marcantonio d'Urbino, Aug. 16, 1540), in Fausto Nicolini (ed.), *Pietro Aretino* (Bari, Italy, 1916), II, 262.

lino's of Pinturicchio, Bembo's of Giovanni Bellini, Aretino's and Della Casa's of Titian, Molza's of Giulio Romano, and Varchi's of Bronzino are of interest only on the grounds of historical continuity, surely Petrarch's poems on Simone Martini's paintings, Michelangelo's iconic sonnets, and certain luminous painterly passages in Ariosto and Tasso represent literary achievements of permanent and independent value. Of these, the art poems of Michelangelo are both the most conventional and the most original. Some of his themes come directly and without change from Neoplatonic thought: Dante came from heaven, was robed in earthly clay, and returned, in his poetic visions, to see God. Other themes are purely naturalistic: Vasari's art is itself the purest nature. But such ideas as these have been refined and elevated by a superior artist.

Michelangelo's creative use of the iconic tradition may be illustrated by his reply in verse to a highly conventional poem written by G. B. Strozzi in praise of Michelangelo's allegorical figure of Night in the Medici chapel. Strozzi displays the witty ingenuity often characteristic of this type of poetry. The convention forces him to praise the statue as living, breathing reality; but since it represents the figure of a *sleeping* woman, the poet—and here he achieves some subtlety—alludes to the scene in the Gospel when Jesus, about to raise from the dead the ruler's daughter, says: "The maid is not dead, but sleepeth" (Matt. 9:24).

Night, whom you see in a pose of sweet sleep, was carved in this stone by an angel [Angelo]. Because it sleeps, it has life. If you don't believe this, awaken her and she will speak to you.[50]

To this poem Michelangelo responded with one of his own. His statue speaks.

It is sweet to sleep but even sweeter to be of stone. While evil and dishonor last, it is my blessing not to see, not to feel. Therefore, do not awaken me. Hush! speak softly.[51]

[50] La Notte, che tu vedi in sì dolci atti
    Dormire, fu da un Angelo scolpita
    In questo sasso: e, perchè dorme, ha vita:
    Destala, se no'l credi, e parleratti
(Panzacchi, *op. cit.* [n. 43], p. 221).

[51] Caro mi è il sonno, e più l'esser di sasso:
    Mentre che il danno e la vergogna dura,
    Non vedere, non sentire, m'è gran ventura;
    Però non mi destar; deh! parla basso
(*ibid.*, p. 221). For a verse translation see John A. Symonds (trans.), *The Sonnets of Michelangelo* (London, 1950), p. 176.

Michelangelo's lines are recognizably and in some respects conventionally iconic. Like many of those in the *Greek Anthology*, they are typically epigrammatic and paradoxical. In these verses, as in Keats's ode, the silent marble speaks. But the speech is more than paradoxical. It achieves both dramatic originality and moral profundity. In reminding the beholder that Night sleeps the sleep not of men but of statues, Michelangelo reverses the usual comment about lifelike art. He also invokes the theme of Ecclesiastes and rises far above the level of witty conceit to the universal human condition. The final intense whisper ("deh! parla basso!") reconciles the spectator to the inevitable and eternal silence of the stone, broken only momentarily by the poem itself.

Laurence Binyon once said that, though Elizabethan poetry was "exuberant, sensuous, and teeming with splendid imagery," it had no corresponding pictorial counterpart: "We have nothing but the delicate small portraiture of a Hilliard" to set against the sensuous achievements of a Shakespeare, Spenser, or Sidney. The comment is an exaggeration. Sidney, whose portrait Veronese painted, must have known something about Italian art. Shakespeare seems to have been highly conscious of the claims and achievements of painting, judging by the frequency with which he compares it to poetry and uses the technical language of graphic art. It has been suggested that he saw with his own eyes the great Holbeins at the Guildhall. Italian painters and artisans worked in England; some Englishmen visited Italy and talked and wrote about their travels. Italian art criticism was fairly early translated into English.[52] There are several critics besides Jonson who respected painting and remarked on "the secret friendship" of the two arts and their "affinity with one another."[53] And there is at least one critical principle applied to poetry that seems to have been derived from the study of painting. E. K., in discussing the use of harsh dialectal terms in poetry, says:

But all as in most exquisite pictures they vse to blaze and portraict not onely the daintie lineaments of beautye, but also rounde about it to shadow the rude thickets and craggy clifts, that by the basenesse of such

[52] See above, n. 42. Binyon's comment appears in the *Proceedings of the British Academy 1917–1918*, p. 387. On Shakespeare and the fine arts see Arthur H. R. Fairchild, *Shakespeare and the Arts of Design* ("University of Missouri Studies," Vol. XII [Columbia, Mo., 1937]), pp. 104, 109 ff.

[53] Lodowick Lloyd, *The Pilgrimage of Princes* (1586), cited by Samuel C. Chew in *The Virtues Reconciled: An Iconographic Study* (Toronto, 1947), pp. 6, 131.

parts, more excellency may accrew to the principall; for oftimes we fynde ourselues, I knowe not how, singularly delighted with the shewe of such naturall rudenesse, and take great pleasure in that disorderly order.[54]

The passage is memorable. Although conceding that thickets and cliffs are "base," E. K. takes delight in them. The value of antithetical contrast was recognized in ancient and Renaissance criticism, but not the beauty of natural wildness and disorderly order. It was, however, a practice of Renaissance painters, noticed and sanctioned by Vasari,[55] to use a background of crag and thicket, of rock and natural growth, to achieve the effect of startling natural contrast. From painting the practice passed to poetry, notably that of Ariosto, who, in a noteworthy passage, describes a beautiful castle— "a maraviglia bella"—its beauty clearly heightened by its desolate position on a lonely rock surrounded by the Alpine wildness of crag and cliff.[56]

The example of Ariosto suggests that poets as well as critics seem to have learned something by observing paintings. Some of their images and scenes seem to have been derived from the graphic arts. Spenser has in this sense long been considered one of the most pictorial of poets. A woman who had heard Pope read a canto of the *Faerie Queene* commented that she had been conducted through a picture gallery. Leigh Hunt's criticism of the same poem consisted largely of comparing each of its great descriptions to a particular painting that was thought to embody its peculiar excellence. A recent scholar has seen the *Epithalamion*, in part at least, as "a series of processional pictures."[57] Such criticism of Spenser, which from the eighteenth century to the present has been the reigning orthodoxy, has of late come under attack,[58] and we must concede that it has

[54] Preface to the *Shepheardes Calendar.* For the diffusion of E. K.'s notion in the seventeenth century see Frederick Hard, "E. K.'s Reference to Painting: Some Seventeenth Century Adaptations," *Journal of English Literary History,* VII (June, 1950), 121–29.

[55] *Lives* ("Everyman's Library" [London, 1950]), I, 70; see also Hard, *op. cit.* (n. 54).

[56] *Orlando Furioso* ii. 41; see also i. 37, 52; ii. 34, 35; vii. 11; xii. 8–10, 68; xxxiii. 104; xlvi. 3–19, 76–101; and below, pp. 152–54.

[57] Douglas Bush, *Classical Influences in Renaissance Literature* (Cambridge, Mass., 1952), p. 46.

[58] Rudolf Gottfried, "The Pictorial Element in Spenser's Poetry," *Journal of English Literary History,* XIX (September, 1952), 203–13; Lyle Glazier, "The Na-

often suffered from impressionistic subjectivity. But the fact remains that, if we compare him with Donne or Milton, Chaucer or Shakespeare, Spenser does strike us as a painterly poet. His draftsmanship is often visual and plastic to the extreme. Sometimes the scene is consciously limited to what can be represented on canvas. His colors, crude like those of the Florentine masters, are often used to achieve contrast. His descriptions, often almost to the point of physical seductiveness, achieve the tactile values Mr. Berenson has found so pre-eminent in Renaissance painting. He sometimes works in chiaroscuro. Many of his pages shine with the lavish spendor of the Renaissance scene, rendered for its own luminous sake. He often treats his allegorical personifications as one who has seen and remembered illuminated manuscripts, tapestries, wall paintings, sculptures, reliefs, architectural motifs, and even some versions, perhaps provincial, of the masque.[59] It is probably true, though not susceptible of full proof, that Spenser's imaginative appropriation of the available visual arts was profound, more profound than the present summary treatment can possibly demonstrate.

For these reasons Binyon's disparagement of the Elizabethan poets' knowledge of the visual arts seems to be excessive. Yet it must be conceded that the road on which we have taken a few steps can admittedly be followed too far—in fact, to its inevitable dead end. Few of the correspondences between particular poems and particular paintings that have been suggested are very convincing or illuminat-

---

ture of Spenser's Imagery," *Modern Language Quarterly*, XVI (December, 1955), 300–310. Both these studies are valuable correctives and contribute shrewd insights into the nature of Spenser's allegory and imagery. Neither of them sees that pictorialism is a literary convention. It does not prove that Spenser was unpictorial and stood in no close relation to any visual art to prove that he was often "heedless" in his descriptions, that he did not know Renaissance paintings, that he uses few colors, that he seems to have rated poet above painter. All this can be true; yet he *is* pictorial. There were other sources of pictorial theory and practice. We shall see later that he uses iconic convention to denigrate art and praise nature (below, pp. 82–85).

[59] Comment on the painterly qualities in Spenser is already voluminous. For a good summary see Gottfried, *op. cit.* (n. 58); see also Frederick Hard, "Spenser's 'Clothes of Arras and of Toure,' " *Studies in Philology*, XXVII (April, 1930), 162–85; "Princelie Pallaces," *Sewanee Review*, XLII (July–September, 1934), 293–310; Jefferson B. Fletcher, "The Painter of the Poets," *Studies in Philology*, XIV (April, 1917), 153–66; B. E. C. Davis, *Edmund Spenser* (Cambridge, 1933), chap. vii; Rosemond Tuve, "Spenser and Some Pictorial Conventions," *Studies in Philology*, XXXVII (April, 1940), 149–76; Enid Welsford, *The Court Masque* (Cambridge, 1927), pp. 302–7.

ing. We come much nearer understanding Renaissance pictorialism if we consider it essentially a literary matter, related to the iconic tradition in poetry, to the ideals of the critics, to antecedent poetic pictorialism—to the type of visual effect that derives from these areas of predominantly literary concern. For although the English graphic arts may indeed be said to have been more vigorous than was formerly thought, they can by no stretch of the fancy be compared to the Italian. Yet poetic pictorialism was a sturdy and flourishing growth. It derived its nourishment from sources other than the contemporary graphic arts.

From the considerable body of Elizabethan literature directly or indirectly related to the ancient and medieval tradition of iconic poetry, examples from the prose of Sir Philip Sidney, from the nondramatic poetry of Shakespeare, and from the *Amoretti* of Spenser will serve to delineate the main features of Renaissance pictorialism in English letters.

In the *Arcadia* Sidney reveals unmistakably that he has absorbed the tradition of ecphrastic or iconic description, which may have come to him through reading Greek romances, notably those of Achilles Tatius. He describes in the house of Kalendar a gallery of pictures created by the "most excellent workeman of Greece"—a description that clearly arises from believing the graphic arts to be capable both of imitative realism and of emotional and intellectual expression. Moreover, Sidney also reflects the influence of Greek romance by presenting human beings in picturesque or statuesque postures. Here, as elsewhere, the descriptive habit suggests that his imagination had been carefully trained to render visual values in a pictorial way. Sidney, like his contemporaries, wanted formal beauty in his imagery, and that aim was in part achieved through the pictorialization of natural fact. In the *Arcadia* Musidorus comes upon Pyrocles in female disguise and looks at him in amazement "as Apollo is painted when he saw Daphne sodainly turned into a Laurell." Later Basilius falls down on his knees before Zelmane, "holding up his hands, as the old governesse of Danae is painted, when she sodainly saw the goldẽ shoure." When Plangus makes Erona's acquaintance in captivity, he perceives "the shape of lovelinesse more perfectly in wo, then in joyfulnesse (as [and here Sidney reflects clearly that he perceives the aesthetic principle expressed by E. K.] in a picture which receives greater life by the darknesse of shadowes, then by more glittering colours)." And when Amphialus enters Philoclea's room and finds her sitting on the side of the bed away from the window, he sees that this casts "such a shadow upon her, as a good Painter would bestowe uppon Venus, when under the trees she bewayled the murther of Adonis."[60]

Sidney's prose pictorialism is of some historical interest because it links Renaissance style with the style of Hellenistic and late Roman antiquity and keeps alive the kind of formalism in imagery that was to reappear in later poetry. But as art it is now dead. The same cannot, however, be said of Shakespeare's description in the *Rape of Lucrece* of a huge historical tapestry or painting on the Fall of Troy. If Sidney's effects are reminiscent of those of Greek romance, Shakespeare's spring from the central tradition that begins with Homer's shield of Achilles and includes the wall paintings of Chaucer's "Knight's Tale." Shakespeare's description, in fact, recalls the Temple of Venus in the *Aeneid* and the tapestries of Minerva and Arachne in Ovid.[61] But Shakespeare's aim was not merely to describe (as in much ancient iconic poetry) or to draw a moral (as in much medieval iconic poetry) but dramatically to relate the paintings to the human being who confronts them. Lucrece, after the departure of her ravisher Tarquin but before the return of her husband, turns to the painting to find relief from her great grief. Almost frantically she searches the canvas for images of her own condition. In the "thousand lamentable objects there," which "in scorn of Nature Art gave lifeless life" (ll. 1373–74), she finds one that displays distress and dolor sufficient to match her own. It is the figure of "despairing Hecuba," in whom the painter had expressed "Time's ruin, beauty's wreck, and grim care's reign." To the sorrows of Hecuba, Lucrece shapes her own and finds the painted figure fully adequate but for lack of words.

> The Painter was no God, to lend her those;
> And therefore Lucrece swears he did her wrong,
> To give her so much grief and not a tongue.
> "Poor instrument," quoth she, "without a sound,
> I'll tune thy woes with my lamenting tongue" [ll. 1461–65].

[60] My examples come from R. W. Zandvoort, *Sidney's Arcadia: A Comparison between the Two Versions* (Amsterdam, 1929), pp. 135–43. Zandvoort is one of the few scholars who have perceived the literary nature of pictorialism.

[61] *Rape of Lucrece*, ll. 1366–1568; *Aeneid* i. 446 ff.; *Metamorphoses* vi. 1–145. For a list of studies on the sources of this passage and on the arguments of whether

Shakespeare, like Dante and the Byzantine Philes before him, confronts the fact of silent but lifelike art; yet seldom in a long tradition has the relationship between the inarticulate but expressive object and the responsive beholder been more dramatically exploited than in these lines, where Lucrece

> . . . sad tales doth tell
> To pencill'd pensiveness and colour'd sorrow;
> She lends them words, and she their looks doth borrow [ll. 1496–98].

Words like these last are a bit showy in their attempt to find elegant periphrases for the word "painting." Nevertheless, the passage in *Lucrece* quickens to new life many of the dry bones of the venerable iconic tradition.

Spenser wrote many passages of iconic poetry, describing paintings, wall hangings, "the clothes of Arras and of Tours," the needlework of Arachne.[62] But in the sixty-seventh sonnet of the *Amoretti*, which he adapted out of Tasso, his whole manner of seeing and of proceeding is pictorial rather than directly iconic. Though no tapestry or painting is in view, the scene is plastically conceived; and the concluding couplet is like nothing so much as the kind of epigram that in antiquity was placed under a statue, a painting, or an urn.

> Lyke as a huntsman after weary chace,
>   Seeing the game from him escapt away,
>   sits downe to rest him in some shady place,
>   with panting hounds beguiled of their pray:
> So after long pursuit and vaine assay,
>   when I all weary had the chace forsooke,
>   the gentle deare returned the selfe-same way,
>   thinking to quench her thirst at the next brooke.
> There she beholding me with mylder looke,
>   sought not to fly, but fearlesse still did bide:
>   till I in hand her yet halfe trembling tooke,
>   and with her owne goodwill hir fyrmely tyde.
> Strange thing me seemd to see a beast so wyld,
>   so goodly wonne with her owne will beguyld.

Shakespeare had a painting or tapestry in mind see Fairchild, *op. cit.* (n. 52), who argues that Shakespeare described a Troy tapestry. The iconic elements are present, however, whatever the exact nature of the object described.

[62] *Faerie Queene* iii. 1. 34 ff.; iii. 11. 28 ff. *Muiopotmos*, ll. 27 ff.

This poem is not pictorial in any obvious way. Without color and richness, without iconographic or visual sign, it is yet a graphically etched scene, from which almost all motion is gone. The weary hunter rests; the game has escaped. The dogs do no more than pant. The returned deer does not run but, half trembling, stays to be tied. The poem is successful, however, not merely because the pictorial finesse of the delineation has been rigorously sustained but because the hunting scene has been made so perfectly symbolic of the love chase that even the pun on the word "deare" does not seem absolutely necessary. Such poetry is pictorial in the highest sense. The visible has been made intelligible. A paintable scene has, by the addition of what is very little more than epigraph or motto, become a metaphor of human experience.

NATURE VERSUS ART

One of the most popular *paragoni* of the Renaissance was the contest between nature and art.[63] It appeared frequently in aesthetic philosophy and literary criticism. Genius and inspiration (on the side of nature) often opposed nurture and education (on the side of art). But the contrast most relevant to Renaissance pictorialism opposed nature and art in the following manner: the artist and Nature herself are in friendly contest, and the successful artist has defeated nature by surpassing her. Of the thousand examples of this conceit, which was a cliché of the iconic poetry of the period, Cardinal Bembo's influential epitaph on Raphael may be considered typical: "Nature feared that she would be conquered while he lived, and would die when he died."[64]

Perhaps one reason for the popularity of this epitaph is that it condensed into brilliant epigram the whole notion of ancient and Renaissance artistic naturalism. In discussing the naturalistic illusionism often attributed to successful art by the ancients, we noticed how hyperbolically the elder Pliny illustrated the power of art to imi-

[63] See above, p. 66, and Doran, *op. cit.* (n. 27), pp. 70–71.

[64] Hic ille est Raphael, timuit, quo sospite vinci
Rerum magna parens, & moriente mori.

This epitaph was known to Dr. Johnson, who used it to illustrate the contest between the artist and nature in connection with Shakespeare (Johnson and Steevens, *op. cit.* [n. 35], p. 469). See also the brief discussion in Frank P. Chambers, *The History of Taste* (New York, 1932), p. 59.

tate reality. His anecdotes were widely read and admired in the Renaissance. Vasari often tells the same kind of story in unqualified seriousness. Bramante painted a horse in a stable near Milan which deceived a real horse into kicking it. Bernazzano painted in an outdoor fresco a strawberry bed that possessed such fidelity to reality that it was pecked at by the peacocks and thus finally destroyed. A real dog attacked Francesco Monsignori's painted dog. Living birds tried to fly through a tree painted by Girolamo of Verona. And so on.[65]

Such comment as this would not be worth quoting again were it not for the fact that during the Renaissance the new tools of perspective and anatomy with which the graphic artist rendered the real world had made Vasari's illustrations of the power of painting to create illusion much less hyperbolic than those of Pliny. The painter was now all but able *naturam vincere*. He could produce the mirrorlike image that Leonardo had called for—the appearance of relief on a perfectly flat, painted surface. He was able, as Shakespeare said, to "tutor nature," because, as Shakespeare also said, "perspective it is best painter's art."[66]

It is therefore not inconceivable that art can be more natural than nature without being nature, more true than truth without being truth. What then? Have not the wholesome lines that morality had set up between appearance and reality, between falsehood and truth, come dangerously near being obliterated? Is it after all true, as had been said immemorially, that art does deceive and the truth is not in her?

Such conclusions as these questions suggest were, as every student of the Renaissance knows, actually drawn. But how was the iconic tradition affected by this strain of iconoclasm in Renaissance thought? Pictorialism was obviously not wiped out completely or even weakened. But its uses were affected, as we shall now see in considering some of the best pages of Spenser and Shakespeare.

Spenser, who appropriated the visual arts available to him and used the conventions of iconic poetry, also accepted the Renaissance notion of verisimilitude as a desirable artistic quality. He says of the tapestry that Arachne wove and that he describes in a highly iconic

---

[65] Cited in *ibid.*, pp. 62–63.

[66] *Timon of Athens*, Act I, sc. 1; Sonnet XXIV. For Leonardo, see above, pp. 67–68.

passage deeply indebted to Moschus, Ovid, and Achilles Tatius (writers all prominent in the pictorial tradition):

> *Arachne* figur'd how *Ioue* did abuse
> *Europa* like a Bull, and on his backe
> Her through the sea did beare; so liuely seene,
> That it true Sea, and true Bull ye would weene.[67]

The notion of artistic verisimilitude also appears in the description of the Bower of Bliss in the *Faerie Queene*. This place of physical allurement demands descriptions as sensuously real as it is possible for verbal style to achieve. Art must strive with nature, for the bower was located in

> A place pickt out by choice of best aliue,
> That natures worke by art can imitate [ii. 12. 42].

But however natural it may seem to be, the bower is a work of art, an imitation only. This fact about it—that it seems natural but actually is not—suggests that, if any conventions would be appropriate to its description, they would be those of iconic poetry. These are the conventions that Spenser chose to use. On the gates of the bower, "a worke of admirable wit" (ii. 12. 44), are represented stories of Jason, Medea, and the Golden Fleece, which stand unmistakably in the tradition that produced Achilles' shield, the sculptures in Purgatory, the *padiglione* of the Cardinal Ippolito d'Este and Merlin's fountain in Ariosto, and Armida's bower in Tasso.[68] Like his predecessors Spenser comments on the marvels of the artistic achievement and commends the ability to achieve realistic effects in a medium ill suited to express them:

> Ye might haue seene the frothy billowes fry
> Vnder the ship, as thorough them she went,
> That seemd the waues were into yuory
> Or yuory into the waues were sent [ii. 12. 45].

The bower becomes more alluring as Guyon penetrates into it, and the pictorial and iconic effects become correspondingly more sensuous. Excess is presented as though in a painting by Rubens; to reach her one must pass through a gate—not a real but an artistic

---

[67] *Muiopotmos*, ll. 277–80. See Ovid *Metamorphoses* vi. 1–145.

[68] *Orlando Furioso* xxvi. 30; xxxiii. 1–58; xlvi. 76–98. *Gerusalemme Liberata* xv. 53–66; xvi. 1–6. For a discussion of pictorial effects in Tasso see E. K. Waterhouse, "Tasso and the Visual Arts," *Italian Studies*, III (1947–48), 146–62.

gate made of boughs and branches that dilate their clasping arms "in wanton wreathings intricate" (ii. 12. 53). Excess reclines on a porch under a roof, made by a vine which is temptingly studded with grapes:

> Some deepe empurpled as the *Hyacine*,
> Some as the Rubine, laughing sweetly red,
> Some like faire Emeraudes, not well ripened.

> And them amongst, some were of burnisht gold,
> So made by art, to beautifie the rest [ii. 12. 54–55].

The fountain, another iconically treated *objet d'art*, is surrounded with images of wanton boys, and over them hangs a trail of ivy made of purest gold but suggesting the native green. In the crystal streams that flow from the fountain wanton maidens bathe—flesh-colored Titians all, animated into seductive motion by the poet.[69] Their allurements are surpassed only by those of the Enchantress herself, presented, as in Giorgione, Tintoretto, or Veronese,[70] reclining upon a bed of roses.

> Vpon a bed of Roses she was layd,
>   As faint through heat, or dight to pleasant sin,
>   And was arayd, or rather disarayd,
>   All in a vele of silke and siluer thin,
>   That hid no whit her alabaster skin,
>   But rather shewd more white, if more might bee:
>   More subtile web *Arachne* can not spin,
>   Nor the fine nets, which oft we wouen see
> Of scorched deaw, do not in th'aire more lightly flee.

> Her snowy brest was bare to readie spoyle
>   Of hungry eies, which n'ote therewith be fild,
>   And yet through languour of her late sweet toyle,
>   Few drops, more cleare then Nectar, forth distild,
>   That like pure Orient perles adowne it trild,
>   And her faire eyes sweet smyling in delight,
>   Moystened their fierie beames, with which she thrild
>   Fraile harts, yet quenched not; like starry light
> Which sparckling on the silent waues, does seeme more bright
>   [ii. 12. 77–78].

---

[69] The parallel with Tasso is close: cf. *Faerie Queene* ii. 12. 66–68 with *Gerusalemme Liberata* xv. 58–59.

[70] In spite of the modern tendency to disparage the kind of criticism he represented (see above, n. 58) I find that James Russell Lowell revealed a just sensi-

Perhaps the most important point about Spenser's gorgeous description is not that it represents one of the freshest responses to the iconic tradition ever made but that it uses the tradition in a special way and for a special purpose. C. S. Lewis has said that the Bower of Bliss is artificial and therefore evil.[71] The bower is evil, however, not because all art is evil but because a work of art has here deceptively replaced nature. The land of the enchantress is a land where many of the epigrammatic hyperboles of the poets about the deceptive naturalness of painting have actually been embodied. Here motherhood has been transferred from nature to art. In that perversion Mother Art has scorned niggard Nature and lavished upon the scene all the adornments and allurements of fleshly and worldly pomposity (ii. 12. 50).

Spenser apparently found it fully conceivable that, in the words of the critical commonplace, art can defeat and supplant nature. But however alluring such an imaginative and unnatural construction may temporarily be, one is ultimately supposed to be appalled that the ivy is painted, that the waves are waves of ivory. It is the direct antithesis of the garden of Adonis, which is "So faire a place, as Nature can devize" (iii. 6. 29). The bower is the product of Mother Art alone. It begins in deceit and ends in death.

Shakespeare's appreciation of the power of graphic art seems to be expressed by Bassanio in the *Merchant of Venice* when he discovers Portia's miniature inside the leaden casket.

> What find I here?
> Fair Portia's counterfeit! What demi-god
> Hath come so near creation? Move these eyes?
> Or whether, riding on the balls of mine,
> Seem they in motion? Here are sever'd lips,
> Parted with sugar breath; so sweet a bar
> Should sunder such sweet friends. Here in her hairs
> The painter plays the spider, and hath woven
> A golden mesh t'entrap the hearts of men
> Faster than gnats in cobwebs: but her eyes!—

---

bility when he compared Spenser and the Venetian masters. See the quotations in Fletcher, *op. cit.* (n. 59). I grant that some of these effects—perhaps most of them—derive immediately from Tasso and Ariosto.

[71] *Allegory of Love* (Oxford, 1936), pp. 324–32. For a corrective of Lewis' view see N. S. Brooke, "C. S. Lewis and Spenser: Nature, Art and the Power of Bliss," *Cambridge Journal*, II (April, 1949), 420–34.

> How could he see to do them? Having made one,
> Methinks it should have power to steal both his
> And leave itself unfurnished. Yet look, how far
> The substance of my praise doth wrong this shadow
> In underprizing it, so far this shadow
> Doth limp behind the substance [Act III, Sc. 2, ll. 115 ff.].

This speech contains in brief the aesthetic theory of the Renaissance. Art is a "counterfeit," an imitation, that comes "near creation." It deceives the senses: "Move these eyes?" It has allurements that can trap the heart of man. And yet it is a shadow that halts far behind the substance of reality.

In Bassanio's speech the ideas are stated; in the *Winter's Tale* they are embodied. This play represents Shakespeare's use of contemporary art theory and the entire iconic tradition not to exalt art but, as Spenser had done, to exalt nature at the expense of art.

The entire last act of the *Winter's Tale* is compounded of themes intimately associated with the tradition of *ut pictura poesis* and iconic poetry. It opens with Paulina's idealization of Hermione in terms reminiscent of Zeuxis' selection of the best features of the loveliest maidens of Crotona:

> If, one by one, you wedded all the world,
> Or, from the all that are, took something good,
> To make a perfect woman, she you kill'd
> Would be unparallel'd.[72]

The second scene of the last act consists of a series of verbal tableaux. Three gentlemen describe the reactions to the discovery of Perdita's identity. So amazing are the revelations that those who receive them are, by the operation of an old conceit, frozen into statues. But they are expressive statues and can be described in terms one would use of successful graphic representations.

> To the dumbness of the gesture
> One might interpret,

said the poet of a painting in *Timon of Athens* (Act I, Sc. 1). "There was speech in their dumbness, language in their very gesture," says

[72] Act V, Sc. 1, ll. 13–16. See above, p. 14. The story of Zeuxis was well known in Renaissance England. Lyly (Hotson, *op. cit.* [n. 37], p. 24), says: "One paynter by the view of 1: virgins shadowed one Venus." Spenser makes at least two references to this story: *Faerie Queene*, iv. 5. 12 and the dedicatory sonnet.

the first gentleman in the *Winter's Tale* of those who heard the truth about Perdita.

The notion of resemblance, so crucial to the final identification of Hermione, is kept before the reader. The third gentleman comments on "the majesty of [Perdita] in the resemblance of the mother." But it is the resemblance of art to reality that is even more crucial. "As like Hermione as is her picture," Paulina had said. And before the final revelation, when the statue is discussed and attributed to Giulio Romano (the only graphic artist Shakespeare ever mentioned by name), he follows the tradition that goes back to Homer's description of the shield of Achilles and eulogizes the artist who is able to achieve verisimilitude. Of the statue and its creator he says: "a piece many years in doing and now newly performed by that rare Italian master, Julio Romano, who, had he himself eternity and could put breath into his work, would beguile Nature of her custom, so perfectly is he her ape." In calling the artist the ape of nature, Shakespeare uses the traditional iconographic symbol of painting and the painter, *simia naturae*, which for centuries had appeared in poetry, painting, emblem, and criticism.[73]

The iconic strain continues in crescendo through the final scene of restoration while the spectators in Paulina's gallery gaze upon what they imagine to be only a statue. The speech of each of the admiring characters becomes a kind of iconic utterance on the time-honored themes of such poetry. They all amplify Paulina's remark that here life is "as lively mock'd as ever / Still sleep mock'd death."

But Hermione is not a statue. She only seems to be one. A living being, she steps down from her niche in the gallery and is restored to her husband. Shakespeare has reversed the situation that usually prevails in the art epigram. Art has not defeated nature; nature has defeated art. For this triumph of nature, the imagery of the entire play has prepared us. That imagery expresses the idea that natural life flows through all things, including man himself, binding humanity to the fundamental rhythms of nature itself.[74] By means of such imagery Shakespeare in earlier acts enforces the notion of the beauty and power of nature, just as in the final act he uses the iconic tradition to praise art. But the two motifs are not allowed to hang in balance. For when Hermione, in that bold *coup de théâtre* that closes

[73] Erwin Panofsky, *Idea* (Leipzig, 1924), p. 89.

[74] Caroline F. E. Spurgeon, *Shakespeare's Imagery* (Cambridge, 1935), pp. 305–6.

the play, steps down from her niche, nature triumphs. The Shakespeare of this play, unlike the Keats of the "Urn" or the Yeats of the Byzantium poems, finds only temporary and limited value in art. It is nature and reality that finally satisfy. The joy of the final restoration comes from the fact that the ideal creature is not a statue after all but a woman of living flesh and blood, restored to her natural position as wife and mother. Shakespeare said of Giulio Romano that he had come close to beguiling nature of her custom. In this play Shakespeare has beguiled art of its custom. The *Winter's Tale* is a negation of one element in the pictorialist and iconic tradition. The birds in the trees, even though they are dying generations, are preferable to the birds of hammered gold and gold enameling set upon a golden bough to keep an emperor awake.

THE MASQUE

It has been suggested that the Renaissance mind in its frequent moments of melancholy chose the court masque as a symbol of evanescent beauty and impermanent splendor. Is it possible that when Prospero dismisses his airy wraiths and makes his famous speech, his mind is filled with the imagery of its insubstantial fabrics? Are

> The cloud-capped towers, the gorgeous palaces,
> The solemn temples, the great globe itself

details from the sudden creations and the sudden disappearances of these courtly pageants? Did Shakespeare's contemporaries look upon the splendid erections of the masquing hall as baseless fabrics which vanished suddenly into air, leaving not a rack behind?[75]

If for the Elizabethans the masque was a symbol of the transitoriness of art in contrast to the permanence of nature, then it would be possible to account for Shakespeare's and Spenser's use of the iconic and pictorialist conventions to denigrate art and exalt nature. For it was as clear to the people of the sixteenth and early seventeenth century as it is obscure to us that the masque was a supreme embodiment of the pictorial and the iconic.

[75] Allardyce Nicoll, *Stuart Masques and the Renaissance Stage* (New York, 1938), pp. 19–22. In the ensuing discussion I have relied upon the following studies, in addition to those specifically noted: E. K. Chambers, *The Medieval Stage* (Oxford, 1923), Vol. I, chaps. v, vi; Welsford, *op. cit.* (n. 59); Don Cameron Allen, "Ben Jonson and the Hieroglyphics," *Philological Quarterly*, XVIII (July, 1939), 290–300.

The ultimate origins of the masque lie elsewhere than in the tradition we are studying: in the indoor revel of dancing, in disguising and mumming, and in the unexpected arrival of visored persons as a compliment to the host and the principal guests whom they often honored in the presentation of gifts. But these historical views of the origins of the masque simple in no way vitiate the view that the masque spectacular was in the days of its greatest sophistication and power intimately related to the pictorialist tradition.

It was so related in its very essence. In the hands of Ben Jonson and Inigo Jones it was primarily a union of image and word. Men and women danced to music, made courtly gestures of compliment, and exchanged favors. But the chief producers were always the painter and the poet, and of these the painter was supreme because the scene predominated. The words, even when written by Ben Jonson, were subordinate to the spectacle. The masque is in actuality what Simonides of Ceos had said a poem was: a speaking picture. The picture is substantive and essential, the word adjectival and ancillary.

In spite of its gorgeous and courtly settings, the Elizabethan and Jacobean masque represents the return to a somewhat primitive condition in the relation of verbal and graphic art. In its essentials it is not unlike the classical column, urn, or statue that bore a verse inscription; the medieval titulus that explained the work of art to which it was attached; or the many examples of similar associations of the arts that continued to be produced everywhere in Europe during the Renaissance. In France, for example, one M. Baude prepared a work called *Dicts moraux pour mettre en tapisserie*. In the *camposanto* of Pisa beneath the fresco of the creation attributed to Buffalmacco there is inscribed a sonnet that relates to the painted scene. And on the walls of the Piccolomini library in the cathedral at Siena the sentences of the humanist Campano interpret the frescoes of Pinturicchio.[76]

But though in this respect the masque may suggest a reversion to simpler and earlier forms of interart collaboration, from another point of view it represents the fulfilment of a widely held Renaissance ideal that the highest possible effect was achieved when several arts worked together to create a harmonious whole and that simultaneous

[76] André Chastel, "Arts et littérature au XVe siècle," *Actes du Cinquième Congrès International des Langues et Littératures Modernes* (Florence, 1955), pp. 67–68.

appeals to several of the senses were more effective than temporally separated appeals to one sense after another. Reality was best imitated if we saw, heard, and felt all at once and received one instantaneous and powerful impression. Leonardo said: "Our spirit is composed of harmony, and harmony is not produced except in instants of time, in which the proportions of objects are presented to the eye, or to the ear."[77]

When those two successful collaborators, Ben Jonson and Inigo Jones, quarreled, the poet revived the ancient prejudices against the mechanical and physical arts. "Painting and Carpentry," he exclaimed, "are the soule of Masque."[78] But even before he had fallen out with his collaborator, Jonson used to compare the spectacle of the masque to the body and its poetry to the mind—the very terms that Castelvetro and many other critics had used in exalting poetry and that, though in inverted application, Leonardo and Michelangelo had used in exalting painting. (Michelangelo had said that "one paints with the mind and not the hands.") And so it was when the collaborators quarreled: they continued to view their disintegrated relations and the art they had served in the light of traditional pictorialism.[79]

Jonson's own practice betrays the essential falseness of his analysis of the relation of poetry and painting in the masque. It is not true that the soul of the masque was verbal, even when the words were as eloquent as the art of Ben Jonson at its best could make them. The fact that his lyrics often achieved their own independent beauty and can still be read at many removes from their original settings in the royal masquing hall is accidental. They were originally related to the graphic representation that unfolded before the spectator. Reason in the *Hymenaei* recalls the interpreter in the *Tablet* of Cebes of Thebes, who constantly points to the picture before him and interprets it detail by detail. At one point in the masque

[77] *Ibid.*, p. 72.

[78] Nicoll, *op. cit.* (n. 75), p. 24.

[79] *Ibid.*; Kristeller, *op. cit.* (n. 10), p. 511, n.; *Ben Jonson*, ed. C. H. Herford, Percy Simpson, and Evelyn Simpson, X (Oxford, 1950), 420, 689–92 (Appendix on quarrel between Jonson and Jones); Michelangelo to Marco Vigerio, Bishop of Sinigaglia, October, 1542, in *Lettere e rime*, ed. Guido Vitaletti (Turin, Italy, 1925), p. 186. For a full account of the intellectual setting of the Jonson-Jones quarrel see D. J Gordon, "Poet and Architect . . . ," *Journal of the Warburg and Courtauld Institutes*, XII (London, 1949), 152–78.

the clouds of the upper scene open, disclosing Juno upon a throne, supported by two beautiful peacocks, wearing a white diadem on her head, from which there flowed a veil, bound with a "fascia" of several colored silks, set with jewels, lilies, and roses. "*All which* . . . Reason *made narration of.*"

> And see, where Ivno, whose great name
> Is VNIO in the *anagram*,
> Displayes her glistering state, and chaire,
> As she enlightened all the *ayre.*[80]

Words are unmistakably the pendants of the visual scene.

Ben Jonson's practice reveals in other perhaps more convincing ways that the masque stands in the pictorialist tradition. The masque looks very much like Ovid pictorialized—Ovid translated into visual symbol and scene. Other writers, who also stand in the ancient pictorialist tradition, are frequently drawn upon for iconic motifs. Ben Jonson often turns—with great appropriateness if we have been right about the essential orientation of the masque—to the verbal icons of Philostratus the Elder, Lucian, and Achilles Tatius.[81]

He also turns, and far more frequently, to that influential collection of visual symbols assembled by Cesare Ripa chiefly from ancient literary sources and presented in the successive editions of his *Iconologia*, which first appeared in 1593 and of which Jonson owned a copy as early as 1604.[82] A page of Ripa is, of course, far from resembling a masque, consisting as it does of a single figure, usually female, wearing her iconic symbols and representing an emotion like love, melancholy, or anger, an idea like perfection or literary mimesis, an art like poetry or music, a city like Rome, or a river like the Tiber (see Plate II). But taken all in all the collection is a highly suggestive one for a form like the masque, and we can easily see why Jonson and Jones made it one of their chief sources. Text and image are brought together. Each engraving is accompanied by a verbal explanation. The fact that the masque is so indebted to this com-

---

[80] Herford and Simpson, *op. cit.* (n. 79), VII (1941), 217.

[81] *Ibid.*, VII, 187, margin; X (1950), 587.

[82] Allan H. Gilbert, *The Symbolic Persons in the Masques of Ben Jonson* (Durham, 1948), p. 4 and *passim*; D. J. Gordon, "The Imagery of Ben Jonson's *The Masque of Blacknesse* and *The Masque of Beauty,*" *Journal of the Warburg and Courtauld Institutes*, VI (London, 1943), 122–41.

pendium of literary and graphic symbols attests strongly to its affiliation with the line of iconic literature.

The masque became so intimately involved in pictorialism that it
may have been one of the chief transmitters of the tradition to the
seventeenth and eighteenth centuries. It is certainly impossible now
to disentangle the web of pictorial influence and say that a particular
imagistic effect in Milton or Pope derives from the masque, or from
Ripa, or from Achilles Tatius, Ovid, or Philostratus. Nor is it of great
importance that we isolate every strand in that web. What is important is that we see that certain details in subsequent poetry are
pictorial in a peculiarly masquelike way. Milton's, Collins', and
sometimes Gray's allegorical figures with their quality of processional picturesqueness; the moral and natural icons of Pope, with
their symbolic signa; Dryden's peculiar type of emblematic political
compliment; and even the stately progresses of Thomson's natural
personifications—all these may reveal the direct or indirect influence
of the "unsubstantial pageants" of Ben Jonson and Inigo Jones.

But this is only one contribution among several that the Renaissance made to the development of literary pictorialism. It redis-
covered and diffused the ancient texts and the ancient meanings. It
energized the old naturalism with impulses from the new science and
gave *ut pictura poesis* a philosophical and intellectual context of
dignity and power. In its *paragone* between poet and painter it not
only won social and intellectual prestige for what had formerly been
considered only a manual art. It also alerted the poet and the literary
critic to what was the essential power of painting: the power to
make intelligible the visible. The Renaissance not only imitated the
ancient iconic poetry but it sophisticated the genre and in the poetry
of the masters created a pictorialism of such sensuous richness and
power that it has seldom been equaled. And, as the example of
Spenser and Shakespeare reveal, it put iconic conventions to uses
undreamed of and made them serve the ends of a kind of naturalistic
iconoclasm. In such moments it demonstrated that the iconic tradition was capable of highly original application, an example that was
not lost upon succeeding generations of poets.

CHAPTER IV

The "Baroque" Century

Our century has demonstrated its profound sense of affinity with the seventeenth by the formidable amount of scholarship it has devoted to the "baroque" in art and literature. That scholarship we cannot now undertake to survey but must confine our attention, as we have done in these early chapters, to the perpetuation and modification of the pictorialist tradition. It is now more important to stress modification than to observe mere historical continuity, since for our purpose the most important development of the century was the transformation of the classical icon into the baroque. The seventeenth century of these pages is therefore that of Italy and England and not of neoclassical France; of certain Counter-Reformation tendencies important to the relations of the arts; of poetic imagery peculiarly related to the baroque images of the visual arts; of Marino and Bellori; of Herbert, Crashaw, and Marvell.[1]

[1] For an excellent summary of recent work on the baroque in its relations to literature see Giuliano Pellegrini, *Barocco inglese* (Messina-Florence, 1953), chap. i. As an example of the continuation of the ancient and Renaissance conception of *enargeia* (above, pp. 11, 62, and 65) see Sir William Sanderson, *Graphice: The Use of the Pen and Pencil* (London, 1658), in which the range of pleasure afforded by the eyes, "the looking-glasses of Nature," is commented on. Sanderson is convinced that poetic descriptions are as effective as pictures. He cites a verbal description of the sea, which he calls "a challenge in the name of Apollo to the art of Apelles" (see Cicely Davies, "*Ut pictura poesis,*" *Modern Language Review,* XXX [April, 1935], 160). For examples of the continuation of sensuously descriptive poetry modified by the landscapes that became popular in the seventeenth century see Henry V. S. Ogden and Margaret S. Ogden, *English Taste in Landscape in the Seventeenth Century* (Ann Arbor, Mich., 1955), pp. 26 ff. I have, with one important exception, excluded France from the discussion, not because I am unaware that French classicism is now perceived to be related to the baroque tendencies everywhere else present but because the problem is much too complex for treatment in a background survey (see Imbrie Buffum, *Studies in the Baroque from Montaigne to Rotrou* [New Haven, Conn., 1957], and Odette de Mourges, *Metaphysical Baroque and Précieux Poetry* [Oxford, 1953]).

THE EMBLEM AND EMBLEMATIC POETRY

One of the most widely discussed critical comments of our day is Mr. Eliot's demand for poetry that embodies the "quality of sensuous thought, or of thinking through the senses, or of the senses thinking"—a quality he felt to be peculiarly characteristic of seventeenth-century English poetry.[2] The seventeenth century itself consciously desired the union of sense and thought in art. One reason for the emphasis, perhaps stronger than ever before in literary history, upon the association of the arts—"There are no two things in the World that have a nearer affinity and resemblance than Poetry and Painting," said Robert Wolseley in a typical comment made in 1685[3]—was the belief that in association the two arts achieved a desirable fusion of the sensuous and the intellectual. Giambattista Marino, it has been said, "was the intellect of the century—in fact, was the century itself, in its greatest force and clearness of expression."[4] He begins a discussion of poetry and painting by quoting the proverb of Simonides—poetry is a speaking picture, a picture a silent poem—which he interprets in a highly subtle, metaphysical, and almost scholastic way. The peculiar property of painting is silent eloquence; of poetry, an eloquent silence.

The latter is silent in the former; and the former speaks in the latter, from whence it happens that, occasionally exchanging with one another the quality proper to each, poetry is said to paint and painting to describe. Both are dedicated to the same end, that is, to nourish pleasingly the human spirit and with the highest pleasure to console it. Nor is there any other difference between them than this, that one imitates with colors, the other with words; that one imitates chiefly the external, that is the features of the body, the other the internal, that is, the affections of the soul. One causes us almost to understand with the senses, the other to feel with the intellect.[5]

[2] "Tradition and the Individual Talent," *The Sacred Wood* (London, 1928), p. 23. The essay first appeared in 1920.

[3] "Preface to *Valentinian*, a Tragedy . . . ," in *Critical Essays of the Seventeenth Century*, ed. Joel E. Spingarn (Oxford, 1909), III, 16.

[4] Francesco de Sanctis, *History of Italian Literature*, trans. Joan Redfern (New York, 1931) II, 696.

[5] *Dicerie sacre del Cavalier Marino* (Vicenza, 1622), Essay I, Part ii, pp. 52 verso–53 recto. The comment just translated appeared, with slight modifications but no acknowledgment, in Cesare Ripa, *Iconologia* (Padua, 1618), p. 416.

The last sentence—"L'una fa quasi intendere co' sensi, l'altra sentire cõ l'intelletto"—is extremely close to the very phraseology of Eliot, and Ezra Pound[6] as well.

We are less interested in Marino's echoes in the twentieth century than in the way in which his statement is related to the emblem we are now to consider and the way in which it links the emblem itself to the last topic of the last chapter, the courtly masque. The masque united scene and word in settings of courtly magnificence. The emblem book, too, united the visual and the verbal, though in a vastly different way: on its pages the poem appeared as a pendant to an austerely and sometimes naïvely engraved allegorical scene, person, or design (see Plate VI). But the same terms ("body" for the picture, "soul" for the word) that Ben Jonson and Inigo Jones had used of the masque Marino and others now used of the emblem.

The emblem, like the masque, belongs squarely in the pictorialist tradition, of which it was believed to embody several important elements. Francis Quarles, in an unmistakable echo of Simonides, defined the emblem as a "silent Parable."[7] Tasso defined the *impresa* as a "mutola comparatione dello stato, e del pensiero"—a "specie d'una muta poesia."[8] François Menestrier, in his *L'art des emblemes*, calls painting "une parleuse muette, qui s'explique sans dire mot."[9] The French translator of Lucan's *Pharsalia* says that the emblem is "un art ingénieux / De peindre la parole, & de parler aux yeux."[10] Le Moyne, in his *De l'art des devises*, says of the device: "C'est une Poësie: mais une Poësie qui ne chante point; qui n'est composèe que d'une Figure muette, & d'un Mot qui parle pour elle à la veuë."[11] In 1695 there appeared in Amsterdam a book of heroic classical and mythological emblems bearing the title *Pictura loquens*. Horace was

[6] Pound, in an essay on Remy de Gourmont, published in 1920, calls De Gourmont the embodiment of the "civilized mind from 1885 to 1915" because he perceived that feeling was a mode of thought and that ideas are of little significance separated from sensibility (*Literary Essays*, ed. T. S. Eliot [London, 1954], p. 344).

[7] *Emblems, Divine and Moral* (London, 1736), "To the Reader."

[8] *Dialogo dell'imprese* (Naples, n.d.), p. 19.

[9] (Lyons, 1662), p. 1.

[10] This fact is noted by Menestrier on page 6 of another work that bears the same title (*L'art des emblemes*) as the Lyons, 1662, imprint but was published in Paris in 1684.

[11] (Paris, 1666), p. iii recto. For a discussion of another work by Le Moyne, see below, pp. 104–6.

invoked and quoted as well as Simonides. The emblem was felt in a peculiar way to achieve the union of the *utile* with the *dulce*.[12] It was also felt to achieve the requirement of *ut pictura poesis*. Menestrier refers to painting as that art which Horace requires poetry to imitate.[13] As early as 1552, in Lyons, a book of religious, moral, social, and political emblems was entitled *Picta poesis* and bore on its title page the Horatian dictum *ut pictura poesis erit*.

The epigram, as we noted in the first chapter, first arose as an inscription engraved upon statue, tomb, or urn; and in its long subsequent history, even when separated from the art object itself, it continued to bear evidence of its origin. The emblem and device may be considered as a kind of reunion on the printed page of the art object and the epigram. The partners have of course been changed by their long separation. The design usually lacks the simplicity of the ancient sculpture, and the accompanying poetry is often correspondingly more complicated and subtle. And yet the verse, usually short, witty, or commemorative, unmistakably retains many of the qualities of the epigram.

The Jesuit Possevino, whose tract on painting and poetry has been called "insignificant but widely read,"[14] said that the rationale of the emblem lay in its uniting poetry and painting in a form that maintained the values of each art, permitting one to be the interpreter of the other.[15] To some the emblem seemed to be the completest and most satisfying form of expression imaginable, since body (the picture) and soul (the verse) were vitally connected. There were, of course, emblems of many kinds—heroic, social, political, religious, amatory—expressing various views—Plato's, Aristotle's, Plotinus'. Some were directed to public questions, others were private. Some were ethical and classical, like Vaenius' Horatian emblems; others

[12] Mario Praz, *Studies in Seventeenth-Century Imagery* (London, 1939), I, 155 ff. "The true vse heereof from time to time onely hath beene, *Vtile dulci miscere*, to feede at once both the minde, and eie . . ." (Henry Peacham, *Minerva Britanna or a Garden of Heroical Deuises* [London, 1612], p. A3 verso). F. Filippo Picinelli's *Mondo simbolico* (Milan, 1653), has, on one section of its elaborately engraved title page, the motto *utile dulci* over a garden scene with a beehive in the center, toward which bees in a swarm are flying.

[13] *Op. cit.* (n. 10) (Paris, 1684), p. 1.

[14] Julius Schlosser-Magnino, *La letteratura artistica* (Florence, 1935), p. 347.

[15] Antonio Possevino, *Tractatio de poësi & pictura ethica, humana, & fabulosa* (Lyons, 1595), p. 279.

were private and esoteric. Some emblematists, like Giarda, felt that the emblem was a hieroglyph of divine reality, an instrument of cosmological religious meaning; others, like Ripa, felt that graphic images represented Aristotelian essences and were important chiefly in defining reality.[16] But to whatever end they were directed and from whatever philosophy they sprang, they had this in common, that they associated the arts, brought together both the sensuous and the intellectual, and fulfilled an ancient dream that somehow the sister arts of painting and poetry would profit by formal union.

These reflections arise in attempting to see what the emblem, with its combination of graphic design and word, actually is. Similar reflections arose in attempting to define the masque spectacular in the days of its glory under James I. But one element that is new, or at least that received greater emphasis in the century of the baroque than in the Renaissance, is the notion that in the union of body and soul, picture and word, sense and intellect, there was some kind of interpenetration. Each art, as Marino said, exchanges with the other its own proper quality—"scambiandosi alle volte reciprocamente la proprietà delle voci."[17] Poetry would therefore derive special excellence by assuming the voice and air of her sister. It would attempt to understand with the senses, to feel with the intellect.

The relationship of word and image was not always intended to be so complex or sophisticated. The emblem was a popular as well as an esoteric art, enormously influential during the sixteenth and seventeenth centuries all over Europe. The degree and nature of the relationship between the graphic and the verbal varied. In the device, or *impresa*, a cryptic and almost occult graphic representation was usually accompanied by an equally cryptic *mot* or posy. Word and design were complementary and quite inseparable; both were expressions of a private conceit, a private wish, or a private line of

[16] See E. H. Gombrich, "*Icones Symbolicae:* The Visual Image in Neo-Platonic Thought," *Journal of the Warburg and Courtauld Institutes*, XI (1948), 164, 184. On the emblem and related forms see Praz, *op. cit.* (n. 12); Rosemary Freeman, *English Emblem Books* (London, 1948); Henri Stegemeier, "Problems in Emblem Literature," *Journal of English and Germanic Philology*, XLV (January, 1946), 26–37 (containing a list of studies); Robert J. Clement, "The Cult of the Poet in Renaissance Emblem Literature," *Publications of the Modern Language Association*, LIX (September, 1944), 672–85; Elbert N. S. Thompson, "Emblem Books," in his *Literary Bypaths of the Renaissance* (New Haven, Conn., 1924), pp. 29–67.

[17] *Op. cit.* (n. 5), p. 52 verso.

conduct. In the emblem, addressed as it was to a larger audience with the obvious purpose of instruction, design and verse could often exist independently of one another. Although much of the effect is lost, the poems of Francis Quarles often have been printed separately from the design that originally accompanied them.

We have observed that the epigram early became detached from the sculpture on which it was written but that it nevertheless often remained iconic in being concerned with an imagined art object. Similarly, the poetry of the seventeenth century, the century of emblems, can be hieroglyphic and emblematic even when not accompanied by an emblematic design. It then verbally creates or implies its own design. The title of the poem or the metaphorical words of its text may bring an image to mind, which then becomes the emblem of the poem, the "visual" embodiment of its abstract meaning.

The poetry of George Herbert is fully emblematic without being accompanied by literal emblems.[18] His titles are graphic in an emblematic way and seem almost to take the place of engraved design. The "Collar," the "Pulley," the "Windows," the "Church-floor," "Church Monuments," "Joseph's Coat," the "Bunch of Grapes," may be considered surrogate emblems. In the "Posie" Herbert even uses the technical language of the device or *impresa*. The title-word "posy" was a synonym for *mot* or motto. Such mottoes were found not only in books of devices or shields and on coats of arms but also on rings and on windowpanes, wherever, in fact, the *impresa* might be represented.

THE POSIE

Let wits contest,
    And with their words and posies windows fill:
    Lesse then the least
Of all thy mercies, is my posie still.

This on my ring,
    This by my picture, in my book I write:
    Whether I sing,
Or say, or dictate, this is my delight.

[18] On Herbert see Joseph H. Summer, *George Herbert* (London, 1954), pp. 123–46; Rosemond Tuve, *A Reading of George Herbert* (Chicago, 1952), excellent in explaining Herbert's meaning through the reproduction and discussion of visual symbols; and Freeman, *op. cit.* (n. 16), pp. 148 ff.

Invention rest,
Comparisons go play, wit use thy will:
Lesse then the least
Of all Gods mercies, is my posie still.[19]

Not all the poems in the *Temple*, which was published in 1633, so directly suggest the emblem or the *impresa*. Some are almost exclusively concerned with abstract moral qualities, with virtues and vices, with the seasons and days of the church year. But even in this respect the *Temple* resembles a book of *imagini*, like Cesare Ripa's *Iconologia*, the common source of many of the recurring iconological motifs that appear everywhere in the art and literature of the Counter Reformation.[20] In this influential work, as we have previously observed in connection with the masque, the engraved figure, usually a human figure in full length, wearing or bearing the necessary iconographical symbols, is accompanied by a long commentary, consisting of explanation and quotation—an essay, in other words, on the meaning, origin, and diffusion of the symbol (see Plate II). Ripa represents and explains not only abstract intellectual, moral, and psychological qualities—like virtue, truth, anger, mercy—but also cities, rivers, the seasons of the year, the arts and occupations of man. Herbert's collection of poems represents the same kind of subject, limited of course to the church, its symbols and its seasons, its feasts and its fasts.[21]

Herbert's poetry is not descriptive but emblematic. It differs radically from Homer's description of Achilles' shield or from Spenser's description of the tapestries in the House of Busyrane. Herbert does not contemplate and describe the object; he alludes to it and quickly draws an analogy. His mind spins off into verbal paradox, intellectual subtlety, and witty comparison. The object it-

[19] *Works*, ed. F. E. Hutchinson (Oxford, 1941), pp. 182–83.

[20] On Ripa see above, p. 91; Praz, *op. cit.* (n. 12), I, 184; Émile Mâle, *L'art religieux après le Concile de Trente* (Paris, 1932), chap. ix.

[21] I have been describing fairly subtle and indirect ways of suggesting the emblematic and pictorialist tradition. Occasionally Herbert is cruder and more direct. The forms on the printed page of the "Altar" and "Easter Wings," for example, resemble the objects of their titles. Summer, *op. cit.* (n. 18), calls such pattern poems "visual hieroglyphs" and argues that they were fully serious instruments of meaning (p. 145). Addison, who scorned such wit as "false," evidently believed that Herbert and others of his school were attempting to follow Horace's dictum: he used as the motto of his essay on false wit *ut pictura poesis erit* (*Spectator*, No. 58).

self—its beauty, its fulness, the craft that designed it—is not so important as its relationship to man and God, its symbolic meanings, its revelation of correspondences. The "Church-floor" is really not about the floor of the church at all but about the human heart that it exemplifies. And the "Windows" is concerned less with the object than with its metaphorical meaning. Like all iconic poetry it contemplates the material, but not to suggest how skilfully it has been used or how miraculously it represents reality. What matters is that the glass, although fragile, has a lofty and important place in the church, that upon it has been pictured the life of Christ, and that through it shines the light of the day. These facts symbolize the frailty of the priest as a man but his dignity as an imitator of Christ's life and as a transmitter of divine grace.

The iconic poetry of Drayton, like the tapestries it describes, contents the eye;[22] Herbert's contents the mind. The light of day shining through a stained window is a lovely thing in and of itself. That loveliness Herbert does not exploit. He is content if one sees that color represents doctrine preached from the pulpit and that the light of the sun represents the life of Christ relived by the dedicated priest. And yet Herbert, though in a vastly different way from a poet like Drayton and the Elizabethans we have studied, also belongs to the iconic and pictorialist tradition. For if the emblem itself belongs, the most emblematic of poets cannot fairly be excluded. But even apart from that, it is clear that the graphically conceived icon in Herbert's verse often provides its organizing form.

MARINO, LE MOYNE, AND BELLORI

In antiquity and the Renaissance painting and poetry were intimately united by their common ability to achieve verisimilitude. But the association was extremely close in the age of the baroque also—closer perhaps than during any previous period—and at that time the requirement of fidelity to reality, though present, was not a prominent critical demand. What, then, accounts for the intimacy of association? The most obvious reason appears in the didactic and religious aims of the baroque art of the Counter Reformation. We may be sure that the doctrine of *ut pictura poesis* was included in the articles of the creed of the Jesuit cultural missionaries because it served some purpose. In a Kulturkampf of such proportions the ultimate aim

[22] *The Barons' Wars* vi. 38.

was not autonomous aesthetic pleasure but religious and political commitment. On one level the Counter Reformation preached propaganda, and on another it attempted to encourage the confrontation of supernatural reality. The form of expression—color, line, word— was therefore necessarily less important than its meaning or the experience to which it could lead. As the literature of the emblem makes very clear, picture is the sugar-coating on the pill of instruction. Professor Praz has said that the emblem was a kind of *biblia pauperum*.[23]

But there is also something in the very nature of baroque expression that seems to make highly congenial the association of the arts and, if we remember Marino, their very interpenetration. Such well-known baroque characteristics as the depreciation of the separating, defining line; the development of an open form that is not a self-contained unity; the sacrifice of clarity and explicitness to pervasive, disturbing, and disrupting emotions; the tendency to merge the figure with its environment; the use of light not to construct but to dissolve form—all these seem to encourage a literary, moral, and philosophical approach to represented form. It might be said of a Renaissance painting that it is autotelic, that it has no other end than to "content the eye." A baroque painting, however, invites the beholder to look beyond the canvas—the very line and movement challenge the limitation of frame and border—to other realities. To a painting that is full of restless, challenging movement the most appropriate response may not be a purely aesthetic or formal appreciation but a total human response, religious, ethical, emotional. Once again, as in the popular art of the Counter Reformation, the barriers separating form and art would tend to break down. Painting would be encouraged to be literary; poetry, to be painterly. The end —the response—is all.[24]

These baroque values appear, along with a persistent emphasis upon the need for associating the arts, in the work of three writers typical of the seventeenth century outside England: a poet, a Jesuit moralist, and an art critic close to the official doctrine and policy of the Counter Reformation. The three deserve special consideration

---

[23] *Op. cit.* (n. 12), I, 155.

[24] See the analysis of the baroque in Denis Mahon, *Studies in Seicento Art and Theory* (London, 1947), pp. 11–31; Heinrich Wölfflin, *Principles of Art History*, trans. M. D. Hottinger, pp. 18–29.

because in them we can see a combination of traditional pictorialist convention and baroque value. What we now know of the iconic tradition will set in relief the original and peculiarly *seicentesco* contributions of these writers.

We begin with the poet because his work comes first in order of time. Giambattista Marino, whose prose comment on the relations of the arts was quoted at the beginning of this chapter, also revealed in his poetry that he was dedicated to strengthening the ties that bound poetry and painting together. Marino's interest in painting appears prominently in so consciously a pictorial work as the *Adone*, with its panegyrical naming of painters and its languorous and voluptuous descriptions. It also appears in the undeniable influence that his critical doctrine and his poetry both exerted upon the paintings of Nicolas Poussin.[25] But the most obvious, if not the most excellent, expression of this interest was a collection of iconic poetry that appeared in Venice in 1620 under the title *La galeria del Cavalier Marino: Distinta in pitture & sculture*. Marino, stimulated to emulation by the splendid galleries a man of his social and literary position inevitably saw in the noble houses and royal palaces of Italy and France, made it an ambition of his life to create a princely collection of his own. He wrote to many of his artist friends, requesting paintings, suggesting subjects, freely giving instruction and advice. How well he succeeded is not known. What happened to the pictures he must have received is also unknown. But it is fairly certain that a man who was on such familiar terms with both the political and artistic great, whose influence crossed national and artistic boundaries alike, who was hailed by Lope de Vega as a literary Rubens, superior as a poet to Tasso, did not entirely fail of his aim.

The *Galeria* is the literary expression of Marino's great ambition. Many of the paintings and sculptures on which he wrote poems

[25] A. Moschetti, *Dell'influsso del Marino sulla formazione artistica di N. Poussin* (Rome, 1913); Jane Costello, "Poussin's Drawings for Marino and the New Classicism," *Journal of the Warburg and Courtauld Institutes*, XVIII (July–December, 1955), 296–317. See *Adone* vi. 54, 58. For Marino see the following: *Opere scelte di . . . Marino*, ed. Giovanni Getto (Turin, 1949), I, 251 ff.; Carlo Culcasi, *G. B. Marino* (Turin, 1932); Marino, *Epistolario*, ed. Angelo Borzelli and Fausto Nicolini (Bari, 1911), I, 131, 134–41, 219–20, 233–39, 267 ff., 281 ff.; Mario Menghini, *La vita e le opere di Marino* (Rome, 1888); Angelo Borzelli, *Il Cavalier Marino con gli artisti e la "Galeria"* (Naples, 1891); Luigi Panarese, *Lope de Vega e Marino* (Maglie, 1925); Marino, *Poesie e prose varie*, ed. Carlo Culcasi (Milan, 1930), esp. pp. 224 ff.; *La Galeria del Cavalier Marino*, ed. G. Batelli (Lanciano, 1926).

Marino did not himself possess—he uses as subjects, for example, the grand-ducal "Madonna" of Raphael and Titian's "Maddalena"; others unquestionably formed a part of his own private collection in Naples. As the title page suggests, the work is divided into two main sections, one devoted to painting, the other to sculpture. The section on painting, by far the larger, comprising some nine-tenths of the volume, is much the more important and is itself divided into (1) *favole*, on mythological subjects; (2) *historie*, consisting chiefly of episodes from scriptural or ecclesiastical history; (3) *ritratti*, or portraits of all sorts and conditions of men and women, and (4) *capricci* or *bizzarrie*, which seem to have been imagined paintings of a more fanciful variety.

In a sense the title of the last section, *capricci*, is applicable to the entire collection. In the Preface Marino says that his aim was not to create a universal museum, to celebrate famous artists living and dead, to write a history of painting, or even to vie with painting and attempt a competitive *Wortmalerei*. His aim was, rather, to "scherzare intorno ad alcune poche, secondo i motivi Poetici, che alla giornata gli son venuti in fantasia"—"to let the mind play about certain few [works of art] in accordance with the poetic ideas which are produced in the fancy."[26] That is, he wishes to write *capricci* or *bizzarrie*. These verses may be better examples of Marino and the *seicento* than they are of independently valuable poetry—"assai più bizzarra che geniale," in the words of one Italian critic[27]—but the intentions are perfectly clear. Marino wished to write poetry that was stimulated by the art object but independent of it. As such, it is still iconic poetry, but iconic poetry of a kind somewhat different from that which celebrates the artist or closely describes the object itself. Marino's conception gives to the poet a greater imaginative freedom and encourages the fancy to play around the object. Marino, like Mr. Eliot, was "moved by fancies that are curled / Around these images, and cling. . . ."[28]

In an interesting passage from his first *diceria*, the subject of which is painting, Marino discusses the ways in which one ought to respond to those works of painting and sculpture that are not only "nobili e

[26] *Galeria* (3d impression corrected; Venice, 1636), leaves A5 verso–A6 recto.

[27] Culcasi, *Marino* (Turin, 1932), p. 47.

[28] T. S. Eliot, "Preludes," *Collected Poems, 1909–1935* (New York: Harcourt, Brace & Co., 1936).

degne [noble and excellent] ma rare e mostruose [singular and extraordinary]."[29] He then goes on to say that they are able almost to work miracles among the people because they serve to arouse the memory—that storehouse of the intellect—and aid in the production of phantasms. A painting stimulates mental and imaginative activity, piques the mind with ingenious artifice, and helps arouse remembrance of things past. The effects of painting, thus psychologically defined, are quite inevitably amenable to literary response. An advanced position congenial to the twentieth-century mind, such a view as Marino's does not confine art to regular and symmetrical beauty but admits the eccentric and the grotesque. It also implies that there can be a strong correspondence between the wit of a painter and the wit of a poet. Marino has provided a theoretical foundation for his own practice of responding verbally—and imaginatively—to graphic expression.

The notable fact about Marino's poems on art is not, therefore, that they constitute a body of memorable verse but that they make a contribution to the genre they represent by revealing a new kind of relationship between poet and art object. It is true that what Marino calls for in his prose criticism he himself did not always fully attain. All too often he relies on the cliché of lifelikeness to describe the effect and merit of a painting. At times, when he is obviously bent on creating the independent literary effects his criticism required, he stoops to farfetched comparisons, to the mechanical exercise of that *arguzia* which for generations blackened the reputation of seventeenth-century Italy in the eyes of French and English neoclassicists. Nevertheless, the example of Marino is important. He conceived of the icon as a kind of objective correlative for the emotion he was expressing poetically. The poem should never be allowed to become subservient to description. It should be autonomous, held together by the bone of its own meaning and the sinew of its own wit.

The contribution of the French moralist Pierre le Moyne to the iconic conventions is less immediately striking and suggestive than that of Marino. But in its relations to the didactic poetry of the eighteenth century it may be of even greater importance. His work, the *Peintures morales*,[30] appeared in 1640–43.

[29] *Op. cit.* (n. 5), leaf 1, verso and recto.

[30] I have used the second edition, Paris, 1643–45.

We noticed in our survey of antiquity that pictorialism had entered the field of morality in the famous *Tablet* of Cebes of Thebes. By virtue of the enormous influence that this "moral picture" exerted on the modern centuries, the association it made between graphic representation and moral philosophy persisted in the post-Renaissance world. One sees the force of its example in a work like the *Peintures morales*. Strangely enough, however, its author does not name Cebes (perhaps that relationship was obvious enough to the seventeenth-century reader), but he does take care to relate himself to the ancient pictorialist tradition, mentioning by name Philostratus, Achilles Tatius, Lucian, Callistratus. He selects the authors of romances and sensuous pagan descriptions, probably in order to suggest to his audience that by transferring to morality the blandishments of sense he has made the morality more attractive. Cebes, his more direct ancestor, may have appeared too dour and forbidding.

Le Moyne's pictorialism is revealed not only by his antecedents but also by the very language he uses. He refers to Philostratus' "tableaux illustres & durables" in ink; he believes the statues in paper of a Callistratus are more durable than the originals in stone and bronze. He says that he himself has "ajousté la Poësie à la Peinture"; he calls his prose delineations of character (*caractères*) "peintures sans couleur."[31]

The structure and appearance of the work further reveal that Le Moyne is a pictorialist, closely related to the peculiarly seventeenth-century manifestations of the tradition. Like Marino before him— and perhaps under the influence of the Italian poet—he presents his work as a gallery of paintings. That analogy is drawn everywhere, beginning with the engraved title page, on which a baroque colonnade, standing in a magnificently stylized garden with long walks and vistas, takes the eye off into the distance, but not before it has observed on the inner wall two handsomely framed paintings that represent the first two in the series of "peintures morales" that constitute the work itself (see Plate I). What the design on the title page suggests is everywhere maintained. The work is a "gallery"—the word itself is used several times—that contains "pictures" of the virtues and the passions. A particular virtue or passion is presented in four related ways in the course of the discussion. Purity, for example, is first discussed in prose according to the scholastic method.

[31] *Ibid.*, "Advertissement," leaf ō ij, recto and verso.

It is then illustrated by an elaborate engraving entitled "L'isle de pureté." It is then further illustrated by an iconic poem that describes and elaborates on the engraving just presented. It is finally enforced by a *caractère*, delineated under the analogy to portrait painting and bearing some resemblance to the books of characters that appeared in seventeenth-century England.

Peintures morales is obviously related to the books of emblems, but in many ways its morality is subtler and more intellectual. The designs are history paintings in natural perspective, based on classical myth and history, and not hieroglyphic symbols of the rather crude variety that we see in the popular emblem. This is a type of work that would not fall under the eighteenth-century strictures on the emblem and the related conceit. In fact, it seems directly related in spirit to the pictorialism one finds in eighteenth-century morality.[32]

The extent of Le Moyne's influence in England I have not determined. But Giovanni Pietro Bellori (*ca.* 1615–96) was certainly known and some of his ideas may have been influential.[33] A fervent Neoplatonist and a devoted son of the Counter Reformation, he expressed his ideas chiefly in *Le vite de' pittori, scultori et architetti moderni*, published in Rome in 1672.[34] Perhaps the nature of Bellori's contribution will be clearer if we say a word about the commentary on art made during and shortly before his lifetime.

If we compare the *Lives* of Vasari, who died in 1574, with those seventeenth-century commentaries that represented the dominant tendencies of their epoch, the following differences become apparent. Vasari very seldom relies upon poetry to explain or recommend a painting under discussion. He discusses the themes of particular works rather perfunctorily. He is usually content to explain the mythological references, define the subject clearly, and identify the historical or contemporary personages represented. Beyond that his chief interest is in the craft displayed in the painting, the skill of the painter, the lessons of the atelier, and the relations of styles. But

[32] Maynard Mack, ed. (Pope, *Essay on Man* [Twickenham ed.; London, 1950], p. 68, n.), cites *Peintures morales* in connection with Pope's discussion of the passions. In the foregoing paragraphs I have referred specifically to Le Moyne's dedication to Henry de Mesme, *op. cit.* (n. 30), "Advertissement"; I, 91 ff.; II, 321 ff.

[33] See below, pp. 184–85.

[34] Bellori's philosophical ideas are most conveniently found in the Preface.

there is a decided change of emphasis in the art criticism that followed Vasari in the seventeenth century. In a handsome book that appeared in Venice in 1648, *Le maraviglie dell'arte*, Carlo Ridolfi moves constantly back and forth from painting to poetry. He frequently quotes iconic verse specifically dedicated to the painting under consideration, and draws upon Ovid, Marino, Aretino, Tasso, Seneca, Catullus, and Guarini to praise the art of painting, to explain a particular picture, to quicken appreciation, or to illustrate the diffusion of a theme. The Florentine Filippo Baldinucci, in the earlier biographies of his *Notizie de' professori del disegno da Cimabue in qua*, which he began to publish in 1681, is fairly close to Vasari; but in the later lives, notably that of Bernini, the author is greatly concerned with literary relations, and his use of poetry reminds one of Ridolfi.

Of them all the aristocratic and religious Bellori is the most influential, perhaps because he most centrally expressed the reaction of religious idealism to both the naturalism of the Renaissance and the morbid exaggerations of later mannerism. Bellori tended to "read" paintings as moral, literary, and philosophical texts. It is therefore not surprising that he was profoundly interested in the association of poetry with painting. His critical aim is everywhere to get back of the particular work to the idea that lay behind it—to view the picture or writing as only a single external manifestation of supersensory meaning. He was consequently indifferent to unique expression in a particular medium and juxtaposed verbal and graphic expression in order better to perceive the supersensory meaning that lay back of both.

There is something in Bellori's descriptions of paintings that recalls Philostratus the Elder, Philostratus the Younger, and Callistratus. Bellori quotes Philostratus the Younger approvingly in the Proem to the *Vite* of 1672. He opens the prefatory comment of his *Descrizione delle imagini dipinte da Rafaelle d'Urbino* (Rome, 1695) by quoting Philostratus the Elder—the encomium on painting paraphrased by Ben Jonson. His many descriptions of paintings—the very heart and soul of his biographies—are passages of iconic prose, highly reminiscent of the rhapsodic orations that Philostratus devoted to real and imaginary works of art.

The three authors we have discussed in this section have these qualities in common: they were intimately related to the aesthetic tendencies of baroque Europe; they consciously strove to perpetuate the ancient and Renaissance pictorialist tradition, which they adapted to their particular purposes; and they illuminate the imagery of English poetry during the seventeenth and eighteenth centuries. They have earned a place in the story of neoclassical pictorialism.

THE PICTORIAL PANTHEON

A typical poet of the eighteenth century was likely to be an intimate friend of painters, to be surrounded with rather intense artistic activity, to have seen at first hand the masterpieces of Italy, to be himself a collector of prints and sometimes of original oils, and to have read a sufficient amount of art history and criticism to make him familiar with the leading schools and the most important critical clichés. By the time of Pope a national taste had been formed, a pantheon of pictorial excellence established. That pantheon was created in the seventeenth century after the death of Shakespeare.

We have noted that Shakespeare mentions by name only one painter, Giulio Romano. His silence is typical of the English—though not, of course, of the Italian—Renaissance. There were, to be sure, a few scattered references. "Aretine's pictures"—undoubtedly Giulio's licentious illustrations of Aretino's poems—are mentioned by Donne, Burton, Jonson, and Middleton. But the lack of knowledge and sophistication reflects the relatively retarded condition of the plastic arts in England. It was not until the accession of Charles I that painting was much encouraged and that the taste of the nation and its writers began to be formed. It was then that Van Dyck returned to England for his triumphal stay and achieved the brilliant work in portraiture that became almost a part of the indigenous British movement. Through the king himself and his courtiers the work of the Venetian school, to which the English ever since have shown great partiality, became more widely known. Rubens executed his commission to paint the ceiling of the Banqueting Hall at Whitehall and introduced to England some of the grandiose features of the Continental baroque.[35] The route of the Grand Tour was now being established. The peace treaties of 1598 and 1604 had relaxed tension in Italy, and the traveler could now see without much danger the Renaissance and baroque splendors of Rome and Naples. It became

[35] Ellis Waterhouse, *Painting in Britain, 1530 to 1790* (London, 1953), chaps. v, vi.

papal policy to invite the visitor, and the highly uncertain state of affairs encountered by Fynes Moryson had been so remarkably altered that the Puritan John Milton became a friend not only of Italian poets but also of the Vatican librarian himself, the scholar Holstenius.[36]

These new conditions, favorable to a literary man's knowledge and appreciation of painting, were coupled with the influence of classical example, always potent in England when circumstances were propitious. A reader of the classics was aware that at least from the time of the elder Pliny ancient Rome had had an artistic pantheon. The fact that a history of painting had been written, that schools had been defined, that excellencies had been discriminated, and that critical judgments, however tentative and crude, had been made was of general cultural importance to poet as well as painter. Propertius drew upon it to illustrate the diversity of excellence in human life, and Quintilian devoted a long section of the *Institutio* to the history and criticism of the graphic arts.[37]

In Italy and France the history and criticism of painting continued vigorous and flourishing. As we have noted, it was quite usual for poets like Ariosto in the sixteenth and Marino in the seventeenth centuries to refer to painters with the greatest familiarity and with that sense of easy generalization and facile classification that comes only after a critical and historical tradition has been established.

In seventeenth-century England classical, Italian, and French examples of pictorialism were not only known but influential. Pliny and Philostratus were quoted; Marino was imitated; Bellori and Vasari were translated or in part parapharased; Dufresnoy and De Piles were introduced under powerful auspices during the Restoration. Poets paid attention to prominent and successful painters and often mingled with them on terms of intimate friendship. Charles Cotton addressed verses "To my Friend Mr. Lely,"[38] and Lovelace wrote two long and notable poems to the same artist, a personal friend. Lovelace referred to the "great Vasari and Vermander."[39]

[36] John Walter Stoye, *English Travellers Abroad, 1604–1667* (London, 1952), pp. 111–12; James Holly Hanford, *John Milton, Englishman* (New York, 1949), pp. 83, 92, 96.

[37] Propertius *Elegies* iii. 9; i. 2. 22; Quintilian xii. 10. 3 ff.

[38] *Poems*, ed. John Beresford (New York, n.d.), pp. 275–76.

[39] "Vermander" is Karel van Mander, author of the *Het Schilder-Boeck* (Haarlem, 1604), an important work on Flemish and Dutch art.

Waller celebrated Van Dyck in an intelligent and discriminating panegyric.[40] Herrick, in a poem addressed to his nephew, a painter, drew up a list of painters.

> On, as thou has begunne, brave youth, and get
> The Palme from *Urbin, Titian, Tintarret.*
> *Brugel* and *Coxu*,[41] and the workes out-doe,
> Of *Holben*, and That mighty *Ruben* too.
> So draw, and paint, as none may do the like,
> No, not the glory of the World, *Vandike.*[42]

The pantheon was obviously in process of being created.

Before mid-century, more precisely in 1644 and 1645, John Evelyn saw and admired, in the course of his Italian travels, the paintings of Guido Reni, the Carracci, Arpino, Michelangelo, Raphael, Leonardo, Tintoretto, Titian, and Bellini.[43] Michelangelo's reputation was to decline somewhat in the Restoration and early eighteenth century and to revive powerfully during the age of Reynolds.[44] Bellini's fame was to come later, and Arpino's was only temporary. Others, like Domenichino, Parmigianino, and Correggio were greatly admired for special qualities. But Raphael, Leonardo, Titian, and Tintoretto were to remain consistently the greatest of masters until the late nineteenth century, and the Carracci and Guido were to enjoy enormous popularity, at least until the time of Hazlitt.

Evelyn's and his contemporaries' taste in painting unquestionably owed much to Vasari's *Lives*, which brought to polite Europe the view that the painting of the high Renaissance in Italy represented the greatest achievement of the human spirit in graphic art. Known to many in Italian and French versions during the earlier seventeenth century, Vasari was in 1685, through the work of William Aglionby, to become known in English, although in abbreviated and unsatisfactory form.[45] Vasari's principles, codified and refined in

[40] *Poems*, ed. G. Thorn Drury (London, 1901), II, 44–45.

[41] Gillis van Coninxloo, the Flemish landscapist.

[42] *Poetical Works*, ed. George Saintsbury (London, 1900), I, 194.

[43] *Diary*, ed. William Bray (London, 1906), I, 118, 125, 152, 158, 162, 164, 170, 220, 252; II, 45, 119–20, 134; III, 131.

[44] See Giorgio Melchiori, *Michelangleo nel settecento inglese* (Rome, 1950).

[45] *Painting Illustrated in Three Dialogues, Containing Some Choice Observations upon the Art. Together with the Lives of the Most Eminent Painters* . . . (London). It is only the *Lives* that are translated from Vasari.

French academies, were widely diffused by French critics of art. Along with many other French confections, the Restoration brought to England the art criticism of Monier, Dufresnoy, Félibien, Chambray, and De Piles.[46] Frenchmen became the teachers of Italian art to English gentlemen, and Italian light was filtered through French glass.

This may have lost Italian light some of its brilliance, but French teachers in no way underrated the Italian masters. Monier gives credit to Raphael for raising "Painting . . . to its highest degree of perfection," and to the high Renaissance for having discovered "the true and regular Way and Manner."[47] Similarly, Gailhard finds that the Italians have brought art to the height of its perfection,[48] and Perrault ranks the age of Apelles much below the age of Raphael.[49] Dufresnoy brings to England under the auspices and in the English dress of the greatest poet of the Restoration the doctrine of the high Italian Renaissance as interpreted by French classicism.[50]

Dufresnoy's formulation of *ut pictura poesis*—a more dogmatic one than even the Italian Renaissance had known—fell into congenial soil in England. The ground had been prepared by seventeenth-century developments, notably the creation of the pantheon. Now that there was something to resemble, the renewed demand that poetry follow the example of painting had greater point to Englishmen than ever before. Poets could now be referred not only to single, isolated works of art but to whole schools of excellence, unequaled even in antiquity.

By the last two decades of the century the pantheon was established. In defending the poetry of Rochester, Robert Wolseley appeals to the sister art and reveals knowledge of such paintings as Perino del Vaga's "Hercules," Annibale Carracci's "Venus and

[46] For a brief account of these critics see William Guild Howard, *"Ut Pictura Poesis," Publications of the Modern Language Association*, n.s. XVII (1909), 40–123, esp. pp. 69–97; Luigi Salerno, "Seventeenth-Century English Literature on Painting," *Journal of the Warburg and Courtauld Institutes*, XIV (1951), 234–58.

[47] *History of Painting, Architecture, Sculpture, Graving* (London, 1699), p. 118.

[48] *The Present State of the Princes and Republicks of Italy* (London, 1668), p. 164.

[49] He also, in a burst of not untypical Louis Quatorze fervor, ranks the age of Raphael much below his own (*Parallele des anciens et des modernes* [Paris, 1693], I, 136, 145–47).

[50] See below, pp. 175–76.

Cupid," Parmigianino's "Leda," Titian's "Diana and Andromeda," Correggio's "Sleeping Venus," Raphael's "Paris," and Michelangelo's "Leda."[51] In Henry Wright's *Country Conversations* (London, 1694) one Lisander and his two friends go to see Eugenius, who lives in the country and who, since his retirement, "imploy'd himself much after the Italian Fashion in Building." Eugenius has a large gallery of French and Italian paintings, and also "some of the best of the Flemings, and Plenty of Vandikes Portraits. He also had some Excellent Sculptures of Cavalier Bernini, and our own Mr. Gibbon."[52] During the Restoration the royal collections, which had first assumed importance under Charles I, grew apace, and the amount of private collecting has been characterized as "immense."[53] Pictures were being purchased in increasingly impressive quantity by nobles like the dukes of Buckingham, Devonshire, Grafton, and Lauderdale and the earls of Essex, Arlington, Rutland, and Sunderland; by commoners like William Cartwright, Dr. Walter Charleton, Sir Francis Child, Sir William Coventry, Roger North, and Sir William Temple; and by painters like Sir Peter Lely and Prosper Henry Lankrinck.

ENGLISH ICONIC POETRY: THE METAPHYSICAL MANNER

One striking characteristic of the poetry of the English Renaissance was its delight in long and sensuous descriptions of works of art, in which the poet vied with the painter in creating pictorial vividness and verbal color. That literary habit, though it did not disappear, was not prominent in the English seventeenth century. From metaphysical poetry it is almost entirely absent in its old form. Thomas Flatman wrote the following lines—obviously a paraphrase of Simonides' proverb:

> For pictures are dumb Poems; they that write
> Best Poems, do but paint in Black and white.[54]

---

[51] Spingarn, *op. cit.* (n. 3), III, 18–19. I have not tried to give the accepted modern titles of the paintings or to locate or otherwise identify them. Some of these attributions are undoubtedly dubious.

[52] Pp. 53, 58. The Yale catalogue attributes this work to Henry Wright.

[53] Ogden and Ogden, *op. cit.* (n. 1), p. 86.

[54] *Life and Uncollected Poems*, ed. Frederic Anthony Child (Philadelphia, 1921), p. 26.

But very few poets of the period, including Flatman himself, strove for the pictorial effects of long description or extended simile. Painting in black and white must have meant something else.

Iconic poetry continued to be written. There is scarcely a poet during this century in whose collected works there do not appear at least a few poems on paintings or other art objects. There was no disposition to deny the close relationship of the arts, but that relationship was interpreted—at least by the school of Donne—in a new way. The metaphysical poet prefers being witty to being visual; and even when he is contemplating a work of graphic art, he remains psychological and fanciful: he assumes new postures, strikes out new motifs, and encourages subtle implications. One result is that the metaphysical poet wishes to seem as independent of the painter as possible. The two arts are often quarreling sisters, a fact that may be no more than a later manifestation of the Renaissance contest between the arts but seems rather to arise from a tendency latent in this type of verse, a tendency to be unpictorial, conversational, and witty.

The unpictorial and undescriptive qualities of seventeenth-century verse are everywhere apparent. William Strode knows of "no paynt of poetry" that can compete with the "colourd Imag'ry" of stained glass windows.[55] When he is writing poetry, such color is precisely the effect that he does *not* try to achieve. Donne, who very seldom uses images from painting or sculpture, wrote a few iconic poems; in one the picture is not on the wall but in the heart, a typical bit of seventeenth-century subjectivism. Donne appears less interested in portraits as works of art than in the way they appear to stare at you from the wall wherever you stand.[56] George Wither, in a Neoplatonic fit, found that even the exactest painting is "nothing but the Shadow of a Shade,"[57] a view sharply at variance with the Renaissance habit of undiscriminatingly praising the verisimilitude of painting. Thomas Carew somewhat scornfully challenges the painter to "paint a virtue" and to distinguish the blush of virtue

[55] "On Fayrford Windowes," *Poetical Works*, ed. Bertram Dobell (London, 1907), p. 25.

[56] Milton Allan Rugoff, *Donne's Imagery* (New York, 1939), pp. 108–9.

[57] *A Collection of Emblemes* (London, 1635), p. A4 recto.

from the blush of shame, the pallor of innocence from the pallor of sickness.[58]

In its own way metaphysical poetry could be more pictorial than these comments suggest. In such moments one of the most formative influences upon it was contributed by Marino. That famous poet was widely known in England. Between 1623, when there appeared a poem of his that Samuel Daniel had translated, and 1685, when Philip Ayres included a translation of Marino in his collection, such writers as Sherburne, Thomas Stanley, Drummond of Hawthornden, Donne, Crashaw, and "R. T." had translated, adapted, or been influenced by the Italian poet. One of Drummond's sonnets, entitled "Upon a Portrait," is indebted to Marino's sonnet "La dea, che'n Cipro e'n Amatunta impera," which is an iconic poem on the "Venere ignuda" attributed to Phidias. That poem appeared in Marino's *Galeria*, which we have already discussed.[59]

Marino's *Galeria* is responsible for the form of two excellent English poems, directly for one by Marvell and indirectly, perhaps through the intermediary of Marvell, for one by Pope. Marvell's "Gallery," much superior to its Italian model, is one example among many of Marino's ability to attract English imitators who surpassed him. To Marino, Marvell is indebted for the title and for the basic idea of writing a poem on a gallery; but he is indebted to his own genius for the freshness, compactness, and subtlety of the verse. Marino's sprawling and amorphous work has been compressed into seven stanzas, all of which, except for the first and last, present in alternation an impressive series of parallel contrasts. Marino's largely literal gallery has been subtilized into a psychological metaphor; Marvell's gallery is in the soul. But however psychological in basic conception, Marvell has retained much of the objectivity of the iconic tradition. He has hung in the gallery of his soul several

[58] "To the Painter," *Poems*, ed. Arthur Vincent (London, 1899), p. 147. For other iconic poems see William Browne of Tavistock, *Poems*, ed. Gordon Goodwin (London, n.d.), II, 284; Sir John Harington, "Of a Painted Lady," Book IV, No. 58, in Norman Egbert McClure (ed.), *The Epigrams of Sir John Harington* (Philadelphia, 1926), p. 183; William Drummond, *Poetical Works*, ed. L. E. Kastner (Manchester, 1913), I, 107.

[59] *Complete Works of Samuel Daniel*, ed. Alexander B. Grosart (London, 1885), I, 263–66; Drummond, *op. cit.* (n. 58), I, 110, 128–30; Austin Warren, *Richard Crashaw* (Baton Rouge, La., 1939), pp. 118–32; Mario Praz, *Secentismo e Marinismo in Inghilterra* (Florence, 1925), pp. 93, 238 ff.

striking verbal scenes that remind one of paintings in the contemporary Italian tradition.

I.

Clora come view my Soul, and tell
Whether I have contriv'd it well.
Now all its several lodgings lye
Compos'd into one Gallery;
And the great Arras-hangings, made
Of various Faces, by are laid:
That, for all furniture, you'l find
Only your Picture in my Mind.

II.

Here Thou are painted in the Dress
Of an Inhumane Murtheress;
Examining upon our Hearts
Thy fertile Shop of cruel Arts;
Engines more keen than ever yet
Adorned Tyrants Cabinet;
Of which the most tormenting are
Black eyes, red Lips, and curled Hair.

III.

But, on the other side, th'art drawn
Like to *Aurora* in the Dawn
When in the East she slumbr'ing lyes.
And stretches out her milky Thighs;
While all the morning Quire does sing
And Manna falls, and Roses spring;
And, at thy Feet, the wooing Doves
Sit perfecting their harmless Loves.

IV.

Like an Enchantress here thou show'st,
Vexing thy restless Lover's Ghost;
And, by a Light, obscure, dost rave
Over his Entrails, in the Cave;
Divining thence, with horrid Care,
How long thou shalt continue fair;
And (when inform'd) them throw'st away,
To be the greedy Vultur's prey.

V.

But, against that, thou sit'st a float
Like *Venus* in her pearly Boat.
The *Halcyons*, calming all that's nigh,
Betwixt the Air and Water fly.
Or, if some rowling Wave appears,
A Mass of Amergris it bears.
Nor blows more Wind than what may well
Convey the Perfume to the Smell.

VI.

These Pictures and a thousand more,
Of Thee, my Gallery do store;
In all the Forms thou can'st invent
Either to please me, or torment:
For thou alone to people me,
Art grown a num'rous Colony;
And a Collection choicer far
Then or *White-hall's* or *Mantua's* were.

VII.

But, of these Pictures and the rest,
That at the Entrance likes me best:
Where the same Posture, and the Look
Remains, with which I first was took.
A tender Shepherdess, whose Hair
Hangs loosely playing in the Air,
Transplanting Flow'rs from the green Hill,
To crown her head, and Bosome fill.[60]

Marvell's poem is an original and satisfying combination of the psychological and the pictorial. It suggests that the analogy with painting can, by a sensitive mind of metaphysical bent, be exploited to yield considerable poetical value. The third and fifth stanzas achieve satisfying pictorial qualities that are not unrelated to the Renaissance and its aftermath: a pervading and alluring sensuousness of flesh and flower, color and light, is presented in a mythological "history" that seems inconceivable apart from the pictorial masterpieces of the Renaissance and the seventeenth century in their

[60] *Poems and Letters of Andrew Marvell*, ed. H. M. Margoliouth (Oxford, 1952), I, 29–30. Neither Margoliouth nor Pierre Legouis (*André Marvell* [Paris-Oxford, 1928], p. 71) seems to have seen Marvell's relation to Marino.

secular and Ovidian moods. The second and the fourth stanzas, pictorial in another way, point to the more peculiarly baroque quality of mysteriously obscure and brooding light that one finds in Rembrandt, Rubens, Caravaggio, and occasionally in the Bolognese eclectics. In fact, these stanzas, especially the fourth, have a quality that seems to look ahead to Alessandro Magnasco, the creator of gypsy scenes set in caves, dark valleys, and forests, by blasted and gnarled trees. In the very combination of Renaissance and baroque that appears in this poem Marvell illustrates one of the characteristic ambivalences of the English seventeenth century that is not entirely absent from the greater poetry of John Milton.

Marvell's poem introduces one other consideration. It is an example of what we may now call the picture-gallery manner of ordering the details of a poem (see Plate I). We have, in our discussion of Greek romance, Cebes' *Tablet*, and Le Moyne's *Peintures Morales*, already confronted the type of formal organization that leads the reader from scene to scene, from tableau to tableau. The "Gallery" is an excellent example of just such formal organization as that. It was to remain important through much of the eighteenth century.

If Marvell's poem may be taken as typical of the seventeenth century in its secular mood, Crashaw's impossibly titled poem, "The Flaming Heart vpon the Book and Picture of the Seraphicall Saint Theresa (As She Is Vsvally Expressed with a Seraphim biside Her)," is typical of the dominant religious preoccupations of the Continental baroque. The poem, as its title reveals, is iconic. It has the hieroglyphic and emblematic quality that we have noticed in Herbert and that runs through all the arts of the period. But it also illustrates another persistent seventeenth-century tendency, that of addressing the painter—advising, instructing, or challenging him. This, as we remember from the first chapter, is ultimately derived from Anacreon, who describes his lady by summoning a painter and specifying what he wishes to be represented. At no previous period did Anacreon's pictorial formula receive such extended and daring modification. Crashaw's poem represents one such modification, intimately related to others that in the seventeenth century anticipated or accompanied it.

The drama of the earlier seventeenth century often included the device of addressing a painter directly. Oddly enough, this occurs sometimes at moments of high emotion: a suffering character addresses a painter or some other artist and challenges him to express, if he can, the emotion that has overpowered the speaker. We have already cited the moving passage in Kyd.[61] In Beaumont's and Fletcher's *Maid's Tragedy* the grieving Aspatia asks to see the needlework of her maids. She says that the woman whom the cozening Theseus had deserted is ill represented: let me be the model for that wretched creature; let your graphic skill reproduce me if it can.

> I stand upon the sea-breach now, and think
> Mine arms thus, and mine hair blown with the wind,
> Wild as that desert; and let all about me
> Tell that I am forsaken. Do my face
> (If thou hadst ever feeling of a sorrow)
> Thus, thus, Antiphila; strive to make me look
> Like Sorrow's monument; and the trees about me,
> Let them be dry and leafless; let the rocks
> Groan with continual surges; and, behind me,
> Make all a desolation. Look, look wenches,
> A miserable life of this poor picture [Act II, Sc. 2, ll. 68 ff.].

Implicit in this moving passage is the reason a dramatic character in a moment of emotional anxiety might be made to use the iconic formula. It had become conventional to say that a person in great grief, admiration, or any other overwhelming emotion had been so drained of vital power that he was like a statue, a monument, or some other graphic representation of reality.[62] If so, nothing could illustrate the quality of excessive emotion any more powerfully than to summon the artist and ask him to try to capture this condition of lifeless lifelikeness. But, besides reflecting a convention that had wide contemporary currency, the passage from Beaumont and Fletcher is itself highly baroque: figure and landscape merge, the posture of grief suggests a symbol in Ripa, and in the energetic physical movement and posture one senses the powerful theatricality of seventeenth-century art.

The Anacreontic device used by the dramatists appeared else-

---

[61] See above, p. 69. Cf. *Arden of Feversham*, the conclusion of Act I, Sc. 1.

[62] Cf. Milton's "On Shakespear, 1630": "Then thou our fancy of it self bereaving, / Dost make us Marble with too much conceaving." The comparison may go back to the ancient myth of Niobe, who, stricken with grief for the loss of her children slain by Apollo and Artemis, was turned to stone. Cf. Dryden's "Threnodia Augustalis," ll. 7–8: "Like Niobe we marble grow, / And petrify with grief." These conceits go back to Ovid *Metamorphoses* vi. 298 ff.

where in the seventeenth century: in Bussnello, Waller, and Marino.[63] But nowhere else is the painter so vigorously expostulated with as in Crashaw's poem. Such expostulation was characteristic of the metaphysical poet, who liked to adopt the tone of witty, animated, and at times angry conversation. This quality, so generally prominent in Donne, Crashaw has made specifically iconic.

> Painter, what didst thou vnderstand
> To put her dart into his [the seraph's] hand!

The poet contemplates a graphic representation of the saint's transverberation and quarrels with the usual method of representing the coming of the angel with the flame-tipped spear, of which Bernini's famous statue is the most celebrated example.[64] She, the saint and not the seraph, should be given the flaming dart. Hers is the mistress flame, not his. He has caused or created nothing and has come merely to observe her "happy fireworks." The angry expostulation continues: "Cold Pencil!" (Another feature of this kind of iconic verse was an address to the art itself or the material of the art; it was not by accident that Keats addressed the urn as a "cold pastoral.") The faint shade you have here drawn cannot be the true saint, who is a living flame of fire. Therefore, "Resume & rectify thy rude design; / . . . Giue Him the vail, giue her the dart." But if this cannot be done—if the tradition proves to be unbreakable—"If all's præscription"—then, "leave Her alone The Flaming Heart."

The poem then moves to a climax of Counter Reformation art,

---

[63] Giovanni Francesco Bussnello, *A Prospective of the Naval Triumph of the Venetians over the Turk: To Signor Pietro Liberi* . . . (London, 1658); Waller, "Instructions to a Painter for the Drawing of the Posture and Progress of His Majesty's Forces at Sea, under the Command of His Highness-Royal: Together with the Battle and Victory Obtained over the Dutch, June 3, 1665," Drury (ed.), *op. cit.* (n. 40), II, 48–60; Borzelli and Nicolini (eds.), *op. cit.* (n. 25). It is most likely that Waller's poem was inspired by Bussnello's, which Waller knew and for whose translator ("Mr. Higgons") he wrote the commendatory verses that appeared in the translation of 1658. This ancient poetic habit of instructing the painter may have received additional impetus during the Renaissance and seventeenth century from the fact that men of letters delivered the already devised *libretto* or program to the painter, who then translated it to the fresco of wall or ceiling (see John Rupert Martin, "Immagini della virtù: The Paintings of the Camerino Farnese," *Art Bulletin*, XXXVIII [June, 1956], esp. pp. 103–4).

[64] For the text of this poem, see *Poems*, ed. L. C. Martin (Oxford, 1927), pp. 324–27. I must call attention once more to Professor Praz's justly celebrated juxtaposition of Bernini's statue of the saint and Crashaw's poetry (*op. cit.* [n. 59], pp. 145 ff.).

where love and desire, death and ecstasy, all meet and are essentially interpenetrated. The poem concludes with a magnificent litany, addressed to the saint—a litany that possesses great cumulative power. In spite of some tasteless and ridiculous ingenuity, the poem in its revised form[65] is one of the most intense iconic poems in the language and also an impressive embodiment in verse of the qualities that prevailed in baroque art after the Council of Trent.

RECOLLECTION AND ANTICIPATION

We have so far in this chapter attempted to isolate those elements that constitute the peculiar contribution of the seventeenth century to the pictorialist tradition. We now consider those features of seventeenth-century pictorialism that seem especially relevant to the Restoration and eighteenth century.

These may appear if we examine one modification of the ancient Anacreontic device of addressing the painter that we have not as yet considered: its use for satirical purposes. Satirical iconic poems had existed in antiquity. Ausonius wrote three epigrams entitled "In statuam Rufi," in which the poet expressed his irremediable hatred of the *rhetor* whose statue he is contemplating. For Ausonius—and this is itself an interesting adaptation of the famous convention of contemplating the material of the object—the stone of the statue typified his victim: insensible, mute, witless.[66] During the Renaissance in Italy, some time before 1535, Francesco Berni wrote a *ritratto* ("portrait") in which he burlesqued the colors that appear so often in Petrarchan love poetry—the red of lips, the white of skin, the gold of hair—by misplacing them and endowing his *donna* with silver hair, golden skin, black teeth, and bluish-white lips.[67]

Marino also provides a relevant example, for he used iconic verse for invective as well as panegyric. In the section of the *Galeria* devoted to portraits there are several poems of the most direct and violent denunciation, occasioned by the portraits of, for example,

---

[65] The version of 1652 is some 24 lines longer than that of 1648 (see Warren, *op. cit.* [n. 59], pp. 141–42).

[66] Cited by Arduino Colosanti, "Gli artisti nella poesia del Rinascimento," *Repertorium für Kunstwissenschaft*, XXVII (Berlin, 1904), 197.

[67] For both the Italian original and a translation see L. R. Lind, *Lyric Poetry of the Italian Renaissance* (New Haven, Conn., 1954), pp. 292–93.

Luther, Erasmus, and Queen Elizabeth.[68] The Virgin Queen of innumerable English poetical compliments is addressed by the Italian as an English Jezebel, a tigress, a serpent, a she-dragon, a viper, a chimera, and a homicidal fury.

Such is the background of the late seventeenth-century English poet's habit of adapting the device of instructing the painter to the purpose of political satire. In 1667 Marvell wrote his "Last Instructions to a Painter," in which he addresses a painter who is "limning" the portrait of "Lady State." The poem is satirical throughout, as is the same poet's shorter and subsequent "Further Advice to a Painter," written in 1670 or 1671.[69] The form so used was extremely popular in the Restoration. In the archives of Florence, for example, there is a collection of pamphlets relating to the Popish Plot sent by the Tuscan minister back to his grand-ducal master. Among these printed ephemera is a catalogue of books and pamphlets on the plot. Four titles in the year 1679 alone reveal that this device of instructing a painter was used in the political controversy.[70]

Why did this particular form, so intimately related to the tradition of love poetry and of the arts in association, become so frequently attached to verse satire? The analogy with painting was useful to the satirist for the same reason it had been useful to ancient and Renaissance poets and critics. It suggested that the poet had been faithful to the truth, had held a mirror up to actuality, had striven to achieve *enargeia*. The satirist wanted to say by means of this device that his verbal accusations were so real that they could be painted by a portraitist: mine is a portrait, lifelike even though unflattering.

Another important strain in the English literary pictorialism of this period is related to the doctrine of expression—the belief that painting, though confined to *visibilia*, yet has the power to portray psychological and moral reality.[71] The poet had traditionally turned

[68] *Marino: Poesie Varie*, ed. Benedetto Croce (Bari, Italy, 1913), pp. 256, 257, 258.

[69] Margoliouth (ed.), *op. cit.* (n. 60), I, 267 ff.

[70] Archivio di stato, Florence: file 4250–52. This collection contains the pamphlets. The catalogue referred to is in file 4252 and bears this title page: *A Compleat Catalogue of All the Stitch'd Books and Single Sheets Printed Since the First Discovery of the Popish Plot (September 1678) to January 1679/80. . . .*

[71] See above, pp. 31, 70. For an excellent discussion of the doctrine of expression, particularly as applied to painting, see Rensselaer W. Lee, "Ut Pictura Poesis: The Humanistic Theory of Painting," *Art Bulletin*, XXII (December, 1940), esp. pp. 217–26.

to the painter for guidance in undertaking to represent vividly the qualities of *physical* reality. It was now widely acknowledged that the painter could also penetrate into the recesses of the heart and mind. It became highly stimulating to the literary artist to think that impalpable qualities could be represented instantaneously and economically, as in painting, by universally understood material signs.

The increasing respect for pictorial expressiveness may have been related to the development in England of an indigenous school of portrait painting that was at once skilfully realistic and psychologically sophisticated. The presence in their midst of portraits by Van Dyck and Lely led poets to appreciate representations of the inner man on the canvas. Waller hailed Van Dyck as one who creates

> Not the form alone, and grace,
> But act and power of a face.[72]

Richard Lovelace was moved by his friend Peter Lely to state wittily and maturely the doctrine with which we are concerned. Inspired by the painter, the poet seems to have taken large strides toward rejecting the metaphysically hieroglyphic and recommending the naturally symbolic. To him painting is an art

> That contemplation into matter brought,
> Body'd *Idaea's*, and could form a thought.

He hails "Sacred Peincture" as

> Thou that in frames eternity dost bind,
> And art a written and a body'd mind.[73]

Even as early as 1649 Lovelace thought very significant Lely's ability to represent mental states through means that remain fully naturalistic. He rejected the crude hieroglyphical form of symbolic representation, where an unformed color, a simple device, or an abstract line was a conventional sign of an idea.

> Not as of old, when a rough hand did speake
> A strong Aspect, and a faire face, a weake;
> When only a black beard cried Villaine, and
> By *Hieroglyphicks* we could understand;

[72] Drury (ed.), *op. cit.* (n. 40), II, 44–45.

[73] These lines come from "Peinture: A Panegyrick to the Best Picture of Friendship Mr. Pet. Lilly," which appeared in *Lucasta: Posthume Poems* (1659–60) (*Poems of Richard Lovelace*, ed. C. H. Wilkinson [Oxford, 1930], pp. 180–83).

When Chrystall typified in a white spot,
And the bright Ruby was but one red blot;
Thou dost the things *Orientally* the same,
Not only paintst its colour but its Flame:
Thou sorrow canst design without a teare,
And with the Man his very *Hope* or *Feare;*
So that th'amazed world shall henceforth finde
None but my *Lilly* ever drew a *Minde.*[74]

Lovelace's verses are extremely important in considering the transition from seventeenth- to eighteenth-century verbal icons. The last line awoke echoes everywhere in eighteenth-century iconic poems, largely because Lovelace had interpreted the symbol in a way highly congenial to the neoclassical poet. The older and cruder form of hieroglyphic symbol at which Lovelace scornfully glances back is the symbolism Shaftesbury was to call "the emblem kind" and to characterize as "magical, mystical, monkish and Gothic."[75] Lovelace, inspired by the naturalistic paintings of Lely, looks ahead to the "true, natural and simple" type of neoclassic icon that can, without destroying natural resemblance—on the contrary, by exploiting and refining natural resemblance—nevertheless convey sophisticated moral and psychological truth.[76] Lovelace measured the distance between the enigmatic emblem of the seventeenth century and the natural-seeming, neoclassical icon of the eighteenth.

We have delayed discussing John Milton until the very end because he cannot be said to belong, in his moments of visual rendition, to any one of the tendencies we have considered. His early verse has been said to be suffused with the "warm colours that suggest Italy," and he has been often viewed as a belated son of the Renaissance.[77] He has more recently been described as a great baroque artist, who, in spite of his religious and political partisanship, fully participated

[74] "To My Worthy Friend Mr. Peter Lilly: on That Excellent Picture of His Majesty, and the Duke of Yorke, Drawne by Him at Hampton-Court," from *Lucasta* (1649) (*ibid.*, pp. 57–58).

[75] Cited by Freeman, *op. cit.* (n. 16), p. 10.

[76] *Ibid.*, p. 17.

[77] E. M. W. Tillyard, *Milton* (London, 1946), p. 35. Tillyard is specifically referring to the ode "On the Morning of Christ's Nativity." For a discussion of the visual (but not the pictorial) in Milton's verse see Tillyard, *The Miltonic Setting* (New York, 1949), pp. 90–104.

in the stirring aesthetic life of his own time. And Mr. Eliot and other influential critics of our day not long ago considered him a bookish poet of withered sensuous power, by whom sharpness of visual imagery had been sacrificed to the monotony of pure sound.[78] Perhaps no one who has considered the imagery of Milton in all its complex relations can be satisfied with any of these points of view.

Coleridge does not make Milton's ability as a poet coterminous with his powers of visualization. "Milton is not," he said, "a picturesque, but a musical poet," and he finds it "very remarkable that in no part of his writings does Milton take any notice of the great painters of Italy, nor, indeed of painting as an art; while every other page breathes his love and taste for music."[79] The truth of that comment has been verified by modern research.

Yet Coleridge believes that Milton did occasionally refer to or suggest a painting. He sees, for example, the "tawny lion, pawing to get free" as a copy of "the fresco of the creation in the Sistine chapel at Rome."[80] Other such correspondences have been suggested. Professor Praz, in a sensitive comparison, has seen a resemblance between the figure of "meek-eyed Peace"

> With Turtle wings the amorous clouds dividing
> And waving wide her mirtle wand

and a female figure of Correggio.[81] When Satan orders his standards raised and

> All in a moment through the gloom were seen
> Ten thousand Banners rise into the Air
> With Orient Colours waving: with them rose
> A Forrest huge of Spears: and thronging Helms
> Appear'd, and serried Shields in thick array
> Of depth immeasurable [i. 544 ff.],

I see a reflection of the spears and banners of Piero della Francesca's "Battle of Constantine" in Arezzo, Italy, or of Paolo Uccello's "Rout

[78] "Note on the Verse of John Milton," *Essays and Studies by Members of the English Association*, XXI (Oxford, 1936), 32–40.

[79] *Literary Reminiscences*, I, 169; *Table Talk*, Aug. 7, 1832, in *Complete Works*, ed. W. G. T. Shedd (New York, 1853), VI, 409–10. See also Ida Langdon, *Milton's Theory of Poetry and Fine Art* (New Haven, Conn., 1924), pp. 32–34.

[80] *Table Talk*, Aug. 7, 1832. Coleridge finds the image in *Paradise Lost* vii. 463–64 appropriate to the painter but "wholly unworthy" of the poet.

[81] "Milton and Poussin," in *Seventeenth Century Studies Presented to Sir Herbert Grierson* (Oxford, 1938), p. 198.

of San Romano" in the National Gallery, London. Milton had been to Italy and had seen Renaissance art, and the diligent investigator will doubtless find more than one reflection. But they will remain few,[82] and the search for correspondences promises little to the student of Milton's imagery.

More promising in recent criticism is the search for an equivalence between the mind and art of Milton and the mind and art of baroque Europe, in spite of the speculation and the assumptions about the relations of the arts that this criticism encourages. A recent essay has suggested that Milton's art reveals five essential qualities of baroque art.[83] Of these, two are so general and vague—Milton is said to show audacity of enterprise and sublimity of effort and to enjoy displaying the enormous virtuosity of which he was capable—as to be useless. But the other three—that there is rich amplitude in his description, that he often achieves a synesthetic interpenetration of the senses in his imagery, and that he loves to present figures hurtling through space, struggling in aerial warfare, and dazzled by rays of light—suggest fruitful lines of inquiry and comparison. Their investigation, however, should be preceded by an attempt to relate Milton to the iconic and pictorialist tradition. It is here impossible to undertake full exploration of this relation. I can make only preliminary and tentative suggestions about a few of Milton's iconic passages.

Pandemonium was created by a stroke of masquelike magic: it "rose like an Exhalation." Yet it was "built like a Temple," solidly. We see its pilasters, its Doric pillars, golden architrave, cornice, frieze, and fretted roof. But actually we do not see very much. We are told that the frieze is "with bossy sculpture grav'n," but where Dante, Spenser, or even Chaucer would have at that point elaborated the details, Milton goes on at once to the doors with "brazen foulds" and the "smooth and level" pavement. Milton does achieve a sensuous effect of power and richness, but it is not the kind of effect that we usually encounter in classical, Western medieval, or Renaissance literature. It is only partially visual, and those visual

---

[82] I do not find Professor Merritt Y. Hughes's assimilation of *Paradise Lost* vii. 374 ff., to Guido Reni's "Aurora" (Plate XXIV) convincing because there are no exact details repeated (see his edition of *Paradise Lost* [New York, 1935], p. 233, n.).

[83] Margaret Bottrall, "The Baroque Element in Milton," *English Miscellany* (ed. Mario Praz), I (Rome, 1950), 31–42.

details are swallowed up in a kinesthetic feeling of space and light in space. In this respect Milton's icon seems more Byzantine than Western, more medieval than ancient, and reminds one more of Paulus Silentiarius' contemplation of the lighted magnificence of St. Sophia than of the interiors of Vergil or Ovid:[84]

> . . . and strait the dores
> Op'ning their brazen foulds discover wide
> Within, her ample spaces, o're the smooth
> And level pavement: from the arched roof
> Pendant by suttle Magic many a row
> Of Starry Lamps and blazing Cressets fed
> With *Naphtha* and *Asphaltus* yeilded light
> As from a sky [i. 723–30].

The qualities present in this passage are fully characteristic of Milton's iconic moments. Heaven, with its pendent golden stairs, and the "bright Sea" of jasper or of liquid pearl underneath, on which sail the blessed in chariots drawn by fiery steeds (*PL* iii, 516–22), is compounded of visual ingredients but is not picturable in any naturalistic way. Rome, when viewed through Satan's optics, is presented not so much as a scene—although the Capitol raises her stately head above the rest—as a roll call of chanted nouns. Towers and temples, statues and gardens, porches and theaters are intoned (*PR* iv. 33–79), but none of them is visually particularized.

Eden comes closer to being a visual scene than any other of Milton's potentially paintable descriptions. Called a "Lantskip," a "Silvan Scene" (*PL* iv. 153, 140), it does embody certain purely plastic values. The shaggy and forbidding sides of the outside present a contrast, in E. K.'s manner, to the inside. There the fruit produces a golden hue with "gay enameled colours mixt." But, once more, nothing is sharply visualized. Milton is more intent on having us feel in a kind of kinesthetic sensation the full opulence of nature itself than in having us see its particulars. The fresh water, the orient pearl, the sands of gold, the purple grapes, the "flours of all hue"—all create an idea streaked with sensuous recollection, in a sense the antithesis of a visual scene that implies an idea.[85]

---

[84] It should be noted, however, that in some of Ovid's descriptions of architectural interiors there is often a kind of lavish, baroque magnificence. For a discussion of this point, see L. P. Wilkinson, *Ovid Recalled* (Cambridge, 1955), pp. 155–59.

[85] See above, pp. 121–22.

It is in such intellectual, emotional, and musical structures as these that Milton's visual touches are to be seen. Touches and strokes they remain, serving other larger aims. The iconic and pictorialist conventions do appear, but they are soon absorbed in intellectual conceits, musical resonances, or sublime epic movements. The "meek-eyd Peace" of the ode "On the Morning of Christ's Nativity" is a visual persona, crowned with "Olive Green," who descends in masquelike fashion through the "turning sphear." Her central "gesture," however, is to "strike a universall Peace through Sea and Land"—a most welcome action but hardly a picturable one. Some of the personifications in "L'Allegro" are pictorially conceived— Bacchus is "Ivy-crowned" and Laughter holds both her sides—but most are not. The "storied windows richly dight" of "Il Penseroso" are almost at once blurred and shadowed by the "dimm religious light." And so it is everywhere in Milton. One of the most characteristic motions of his imagination is to approach the pictorialist conventions and then to withdraw into other forms of expression. This habit seems almost to be conscious. Satan in *Paradise Lost* sees the gate of heaven, an object that would have invited a poet more centrally in the iconic tradition to loving and detailed visual elaboration. But Milton's gate, compounded exclusively of light and general splendor, with a

> Frontispice of Diamond and Gold
> Imbellisht, thick with sparkling orient Gemmes,

is not a picturable object. Milton says as much:

> The Portal shon, inimitable on Earth
> By Model, or by shading Pencil drawn [iii. 506–9].

These words may provide a key to Milton's imagery. It is obviously not the product of the Renaissance conviction of a Leonardo that visual splendors *are* imitable by the shadowing pencil and the modeled clay. Milton's basic iconic affiliations lie elsewhere: with Paulus Silentiarius, the Byzantine poet of light, color, and general splendor. Although Milton's hell is much less specifically described than Dante's Inferno, the English poet does recall the light of Paradiso and Thomas Aquinas' *claritas*.

Like the medieval philosopher and poet, he has a conception of outer form as an expression of spirit—a form that sin can mar and ultimately destroy. The unseen exists in the seen, and the unseen is the essential subject.

> Beyond compare the Son of God was seen
> Most glorious, in him all his Father shon
> Substantially express'd, and in his face
> Divine compassion visibly appeerd [iii. 138–41].

For Milton the visual is valuable chiefly because it sacramentally—if one may use that word of a Puritan poet—reveals the intellectual, the moral, the religious. It is not dwelt on for its own sake, nor is it allowed to speak its implications and meanings for itself without assisting comment. It is conceptually related to the inner reality being contemplated.

Milton's immediate affiliation in his use of the iconic is not, of course, medieval. He had absorbed the pictorialism of the Italian and English Renaissance. But, as the poet of religious and metaphysical meaning, he, like the baroque century in which he lived, revived some of the essential elements of what we have called sacramental pictorialism. Milton had been exposed to the entire pictorialist tradition of antiquity and the Renaissance. But, like Dante before him, who had also absorbed classical pictorialism, he found it inadequate for his larger purposes. For Milton, as for Dante but not for poets standing in the central tradition of antiquity and the Renaissance, the pictorial was a gate that opened not primarily upon visible nature but upon transcendent and invisible reality.

CHAPTER V

English Neoclassicism (I)

Literary pictorialism is a continuous tradition, extending without serious interruption from early antiquity into modern times, but it has proved possible for poets standing in that tradition to create radically different poetic icons. Of the many modifications that the art of making verbal images has undergone during the long history of poetry, two have been profoundly antithetical. These have alternated in response to the great rhythms of intellectual and moral history. One of them, the roots of which lay in the naturalism of antiquity and the Renaissance, may be exemplified by the rhetorical and critical notion of *enargeia*, or lifelike vividness. The other, peculiarly characteristic of the medieval centuries and of the baroque seventeenth century, tended to remove the pictorial from the external and natural and associate it with the internal and supernatural.

If the imagery of English neoclassical poetry is viewed against this background, two of its most eminent characteristics appear with great clarity. It was positively related to the pictorialist traditions of antiquity and the Renaissance. And, embarrassed as it always was by what we have called sacramental pictorialism,[1] it was in open revolt against the emblematic expression of the seventeenth century, which it considered barbarously unnatural and inelegant.

The eighteenth century, like the Renaissance, turned its gaze outward. Instructed by its philosophers and scientists, it contemplated nature with an enthusiasm matched only by the masters of Italian graphic art during the sixteenth century. It translated Leonardo and enthusiastically applied the mirror image to literary art. In its idealization of nature as well as in its essential realism, the eighteenth century was profoundly related to Plutarch, Cicero, and the humanists. Like the Renaissance, it established an intimate relationship

---

[1] See above, pp. 44–45, 47, 128.

between painter and poet—a relationship more intimate than had previously been known in England and one that could now be described as "friendly emulation."[2]

And yet English neoclassical pictorialism was no mere copy of its Renaissance model. It had been powerfully affected by intervening cultural history, not least by baroque expression. Influenced both by what it accepted and by what it rejected, the English Enlightenment made its own peculiar and effective contribution to pictorial imagery.

THE ANALOGY BETWEEN THE ARTS

The eighteenth century saw the culmination of the literary man's increasing sophistication in the visual arts. In no previous age did writers to the same extent see and understand paintings, possess such considerable collections of prints and engravings, and read so widely in the criticism and theory of the graphic arts. And in no previous period in English literature could a poet assume knowledge of great painting and statuary in the audience he was addressing.

Many forces contributed to the sophistication of the age. The ever widening diffusion of prints; the growing independence of the English school, which later in the century led to the flowering of indigenous English painting; the notable increase in private collecting; the growing popularity of treatises on the arts; the excitement engendered by changing taste in architecture and gardening; the greatly increased amount of foreign travel and the innumerable guidebooks and manuals that travel always produces; the popularity of connoisseurship in many areas—all these and many other developments made possible initimate and extensive experience of the visual arts.

Concurrently, the habit of applying terms of painting to the criticism of poetry became more deeply ingrained than ever before. It was, of course, an old habit, characteristic of some ancient criticism and, as we have seen, deliberately revived by Petrarch.[3] But in the eighteenth century it was indulged by nearly everyone who wrote about poetry. Lord Chesterfield urged his son to read Ariosto because "his painting is excellent." Of Shakespeare, Gray said, "Every word in him is a picture." Uvedale Price found *Gulli-*

----

[2] "Ut Pictura Poesis, by Mr. Nourse, late of All-Souls College, Oxon, 1741," in *A Collection of Poems . . . by Several Hands* (London, 1758), p. 95.

[3] See above, p. 57, and below, p. 176, n. 10.

ver's *Travels* to be a picture. Boswell called his *Life of Johnson* a "Flemish picture" of his revered friend.[4]

Such phrases possess an air of seeming natural, inevitable, and unconscious. But the critics of the period were in fact deliberate in drawing analogies between the sister arts and urging upon poets *ut pictura poesis*. William Whitehead asserted that the "pencil" was the proper test of any "piece of poetry" whatever. George Turnbull said that there was no other way "of trying the Propriety, Force and Beauty of a poetical Image, but by considering the Picture it forms in the Imagination, as a Picture."[5] Joseph Warton, in analyzing Dryden's first song for St. Cecilia's day, which as a whole is much less pictorial than the later "Alexander's Feast," dwells on the one stanza that does have some pictorial suggestion:

> When Jubal struck the corded shell,
> His list'ning brethren stood around,
> And, wond'ring, on their faces fell.

Of that rather briefly and casually drawn pictorial outline, Warton says:

> This is so complete and engaging a history piece, that I knew a person of taste who was resolved to have it executed on one side of his saloon: "In which case, (said he,) the painter has nothing to do, but to substitute colours for words, the design being finished to his hands."[6]

One can only conclude that Joseph Warton saw more than we do and that a mere visual suggestion created in his mind a full-blown pictorial allegory or "history" capable of being rendered on a painted wall.

Such a response to verbal art did not happen accidentally. It is related to the tendencies we have mentioned and to the determination of poet and critic alike to act upon the Horatian phrase *ut pictura poesis* as though it were a command. Joseph Warton praises Thomson for achieving in one place the "wildness" of Salvator Rosa and in

[4] Chesterfield Feb. 8 (O.S.), 1750, in *Letters to His Son and Others* ("Everyman's Library" [London, 1929]), p. 159; Gray to West, Apr. 8, 1742, in *Correspondence*, ed. Paget Toynbee and Leonard Whibley (Oxford, 1935), I, 193; Price, *Essays on the Picturesque* (London, 1810), I, xiii. Boswell is quoted in a review of J. L. Clifford's *Young Sam Johnson*, in *Times Literary Supplement*, Nov. 24, 1955.

[5] This and the preceding reference I owe to Chester F. Chapin, *Personification in Eighteenth-Century English Poetry* (New York, 1955), p. 33.

[6] *An Essay on the Genius and Writings of Pope* (London, 1806), I, 51–52.

another a group so "particular and picturesque" that it was worthy the pencil of Giacomo da Bassano."[7] Of Milton's description of Raphael as an armed angel, Thomas Warton says that the poet must have been indebted to a painting seen in Italy and "particularly one by Raphael, where Michael, clad in celestial panoply, triumphs over Satan chained." Goldsmith compares the characters of Addison's *Cato* to the figures of Nicolas Poussin—all alike are faultlessly drawn from the antique. Nichols said of Fielding: "His works exhibit a series of pictures drawn with all the descriptive fidelity of a Hogarth." Webb said of a passage in the *Aeneid* (i. 590) that it contains "the finest effect of clear obscure that . . . ever entered into the imagination of either poet or painter. . . . I am persuaded the poet must have had in his eyes some celebrated picture in this style."[8] The Jonathan Richardsons included in the index to their *Explanatory Notes and Remarks on Milton's Paradise Lost* a topic entitled "Pictures." They refer to an impressively large number of passages in the poem, which they compare either to specific paintings or to the art of painting in general. Everywhere they suggest that the proper response to Milton's poetry is to form "a Well-Chosen Collection of Poetical Pictures." Hence such phrases as these: "The soil is admirably painted"; "a Wonderful picture"; "Here is an amazing Picture"; "I wish Raffaelle had attempted this"; "What a picture."[9]

Never before in England had the commerce between painting and poetry been brisker. Pope might have been speaking of his own age, rather than of ancient Rome, when he said that "Art reflected images to Art."[10] But though the relations between painting and poetry were usually considered the most intimate of all, the analogy between the arts was by no means confined to these two. Reynolds advised his students to take hints from the masters and employ them "in a situation totally different from that in which they were

[7] *Ibid.*, pp. 41, 43, 44.

[8] These references I owe to Cicely Davies, *"Ut Pictura Poesis," Modern Language Review*, XXX (April, 1935), 163–65.

[9] (London, 1734), pp. 544, 377, 522, 78–79, 99, 195, 249.

[10] "To Mr. Addison, Occasioned by His Dialogue on Medals," l. 52, in Norman Ault and John Butt (eds.), *Alexander Pope: Minor Poems* (Twickenham ed.; London, 1954), p. 204.

originally employed."[11] The statement is capable of infinite extension and was almost so extended in the eighteenth century. That first example of the *ferme ornée*, Philip Southcote's Woburn Farm near Chertsey in the Thames Valley, was said to have been directly inspired by Addison's essay on taste. Charles Hamilton's gardens, which, according to Walpole, were created in deliberate response to Pope's statement that "gardening is landscape painting," were intended to reproduce the canvases of Poussin, Salvator Rosa, and other pictorial masters.[12] Robert Adam found architecture, painting, and gardening similar. He liked "picturesqueness" of architectural composition and called for the same effects in a building that "hill and dale, foreground and distance, swelling and sinking have in landscape."[13]

Examples of the analogies drawn between the arts could be multiplied almost indefinitely by bringing together the novel and the engraving,[14] poetry and sculpture, play-acting and painting,[15] music and gardening. This summary discussion of the analogy may be concluded by considering Lord Chesterfield's habit of comparing life to art—a happy metaphor for one who wanted studied but natural-seeming elegance in manners and taste.

But if, upon the solid Tuscan foundation, the Doric, the Ionic, and the Corinthian Orders rise gradually with all their beauty, proportions, and ornaments, the fabric seizes the most incurious eye, and stops the most careless passenger, who solicits admission as a favour, nay, often purchases it. Just so will it fare with your little fabric, which, at present, I fear, has more

[11] Cited by E[dgar] W[ind], "The Maenad under the Cross," *Journal of the Warburg Institute*, I (July, 1937), 70.

[12] H. F. Clark, "Eighteenth Century Elysiums: The Role of 'Association' in the Landscape Movement," *Journal of the Warburg and Courtauld Institutes*, VI (1943), 171, 172.

[13] Bernard Fehr, "The Antagonism of Forms in the Eighteenth Century," *English Studies*, XVIII (June, 1936), 120.

[14] See Robert Etheridge Moore, *Hogarth's Literary Relationships* (Minneapolis, Minn., 1948).

[15] "Garrick's performance [was] an excellent imitation of the passions, which would give [Fuseli] a lesson essential to historical designs; he never missed the opportunity of seeing him act" (John Knowles, *The Life and Writings of Henry Fuseli* [London, 1831], I, 39). Fuseli's entire life, including his relations with Cowper, Alderman Boydell, Macklin, and the Milton Gallery, is itself an example of the relations of the arts in a later epoch.

of the Tuscan than of the Corinthian order. You must absolutely change the whole front, or nobody will knock at the door. The several parts, which must compose this new front, are elegant, easy, natural, superior good-breeding; an engaging address; genteel motions; an insinuating softness in your looks, words, and actions; a spruce, lively air; fashionable dress; and the glitter that a young fellow should have.[16]

Chesterfield reminds us that in a sophisticated age life imitates art. But that, too, may be only another example of the eighteenth-century habit of analogizing that brought art closer to art and made even Nature herself desert her ancient and uncivilized disorders.

NATURE, "ENARGEIA," AND JOSEPH ADDISON

All the poets whose work we shall examine in Part II—Dryden, Pope, Thomson, Collins, and Gray—were pictorialists, adhering to the dominant theory of the age. Not all of them made theoretical pronouncements, and none of them established a formal system of critical value. But they all reveal, most often indirectly, that they accepted as axiomatic the doctrine of *ut pictura poesis* and indulged with considerable satisfaction the habit of analogizing that we have just described. In imagery and pictorial relationship they all obviously belong to the same school. This essential consistency seems to reveal that poetic practice rested firmly on critical theory. But in attempting to reconstruct that theory we must turn to the critics, for the poets themselves do not usually discuss it.

In 1746 Abbé Batteux of the French Academy, annoyed at the patina of convention with which aesthetic matters had become incrusted and wishing to lay bare the true surfaces, published a book entitled *Les beaux arts réduits à un principe*. That one principle is the imitation of nature. "La Nature, c'est-a-dire tout ce qui est, ou que nous concevons aisément comme possible, voilà le prototype ou le modèle des Arts." Batteux's statement is interesting because it discriminates the two aspects of nature with which we shall be concerned: the particular (or visible) and the ideal (which he here calls "possible" and elsewhere, in the terminology of French neoclassicism, *la belle nature*). Batteux swiftly and decisively uses this analytical reduction to get to *ut pictura poesis*. All poetry, even the lyrical, must be "une image artificielle, un tableau, dont le vrai & unique mérite consiste dans le bon choix, la disposition, la ressemblance:

[16] *Op. cit.* (n. 4), pp. 130–31. This letter is undated but belongs to the year 1749.

ut Pictura Poesis." If both arts rest on the same foundation and render the same reality, it follows that virtually everything said of painting is applicable to poetry and vice versa: "Ces deux Arts ont entre eux une si grande conformité, qu'il ne s'agit, pour les avoir traités tous deux à la fois, que de changer les noms, & de mettre peinture, dessein, coloris à la place de poësie, de fable, de versification."[17]

Although it is present, this type of radical simplification is not very frequently found in England. We note only one of its more extreme manifestations, which is directly related to the Addisonian notions we shall presently confront. In the engraved frontispiece of the second edition of James Harris' *Three Treatises* of 1765 the grotesque central figure represents, ironically enough, Nature (Plate V B). She is obviously an imitation of an ancient statue, the fertile Diana of Ephesus, of which an example may be seen in the Naples museum (Plate V A). This statuesque emblem of Nature is, in the English engraving, being crowned by a Minerva-like representation of Virtue. Nature so honored is surrounded by the arts and sciences, each of which—for the meaning is obvious—derives its nourishment directly from her. Sculpture, Music, Architecture all appear, each identifiable by her own iconic symbol. Of these several subordinate figures, only two interest us here: Poetry, identified by the scroll, and Painting, by the tablet and stylus. These two are placed together, doubtless to illustrate their close relation to one another. But that relation depends in turn on the more fundamental one to the central figure, Nature. The two arts are sisters, daughters of one mother.

Anyone familiar with eighteenth-century uses of critical terms will see in the central figure of this engraving the two related but diverse aspects of the concept of nature that we encountered in Batteux: the visible and particular; the general and ideal. The nourishing mother with her many breasts symbolizes the first; the fact that she is an antique statue, the second.

The same two meanings emerge from the metaphor of the "mirror," which was once again widely used by the critics. Dr. Johnson, who relied on the term at crucial points in his criticism, defined "mirror" in two ways in his dictionary: (1) as a "looking-glass; any-

---

[17] References to *Les beaux arts* come from the text in *Principes de la littérature* (Paris, 1774), I, 33, 329, 330.

thing which exhibits objects by reflection"; (2) as a "pattern; for that on which the eye ought to be fixed; an exemplar; an archetype." In its first meaning "mirror" stands for the rendition of particular nature and is associated with the ancient notion of *enargeia*—that is, *evidentia*, force, vigor, strength, vividness, efficacy, palpability, for the notion appears under various synonyms in the eighteenth century.[18] In its second meaning "mirror" points to a generalized rendition of archetypal nature or to some kind of artistic idealization of the actual. Addison may be chosen to represent the first of these meanings, Reynolds the second.

The definitive statement in English of the doctrine of *enargeia* appears in the *Spectator* series on the "Pleasures of the Imagination." To the traditional doctrine of imitation of nature Addison has added the sanctions of Newtonian physics and Lockean epistemology—a combination of ancient aesthetic principle and modern scientific psychology that was exciting to the eighteenth century. The papers of Addison that embodied it greatly influenced poet and critic alike: Burke and the Scottish school, Thomson, Akenside, Young, Richard Jago, and many others.[19]

Addison repeats the ancient notion that sight is the greatest of the senses and expresses Hobbes's idea that imagination is the reflection of visible—and only visible—objects.[20] Like Locke, Addison believes that the imagination operates in a primary and secondary way. It is pleasingly stimulated when it *sees* nature and her works directly (the primary imagination). But it is also pleasingly stimulated when it is *reminded* of nature and her works by paintings, statues, and even verbal descriptions (the secondary imagination). Poetry is, by the necessity it is under of using non-representational signs, farther from nature than are the other arts. But this fact should move poets to learn from these other arts how to transcend their limitations and to get as close to nature as possible.[21]

On first consideration Addison's doctrine seems to place the emphasis upon original nature and to favor in poetry the faithful transcription of visual details. Aesthetic excellence, it would at first

[18] See above, pp. 11–12.

[19] See Marjorie Hope Nicolson, *Newton Demands the Muse* (Princeton, 1946), pp. 148 ff.

[20] *Leviathan*, Part I, chaps. 2–3, ed. A. R. Waller (Cambridge, 1904), pp. 3–13.

[21] *Spectator*, Nos. 411, 416.

seem, arises from the ability to reproduce direct visual experience. Addison praises the camera obscura and considers the most beautiful painting he ever saw one produced by Nature herself on the wall of a dark room. This—and other passages like it—would seem to say that *enargeia* consisted simply of achieving as accurate a reproduction of visible objects as possible so that the original excellence and vigor of the "new," the "great," and the "beautiful" can be transmitted to the work of art. The power of poetry would therefore closely resemble that of painting, since it would attempt above all else to place visible nature in mental view.[22]

But Addison's position, as his influence on Burke and Young would suggest, rests on something subtler than this direct naturalism. He makes it clear that the aesthetic value of the sublime object in nature is not exclusively visual but also psychological, because it can produce empathic effects. Such effects have potentially great mental, moral, and political value. Spacious horizons suggest liberty; great, rude, savage vistas create wholesome awe; small beautiful objects arouse our desires for physical union and companionship. And art can be even more ennobling than observation. Description adds to the pleasure of seeing the pleasure of comparing the rendered and the original, of enjoying even the ugly and disagreeable, of understanding moral meaning in allegory, and of admiring the inventive power expressed in persona and image ("the fairy way of writing").[23]

Our summary of Addison's position reveals that for him aesthetic value lay primarily in (1) nature and (2) the mind of man. These realms of reality cannot be separated, since the human mind is itself a most essential part of nature. But for purposes of exposition it is necessary to examine them separately and to attempt to define carefully the position of both the natural and the psychological in Addison's thought.

1. *The natural.*—Addison's aesthetic system retains the old association of literary *enargeia* with the rendition of particular, visible nature. It was of importance to the eighteenth century to remain firm to the notion that the power of art largely lay in its power to bring real nature into view. As Locke's censure of the "internal light" of the fanatics makes clear, the power of seeing must be interpreted

[22] *Ibid.*, Nos. 414, 412.
[23] *Ibid.*, Nos. 415, 416, 418, 419, 421.

literally. If not—and if "seeing" is allowed to become a metaphor for purely subjective mental operation apart from the empirical experience of reality—then it "imposes" on us, and we confound the objectively real and the subjectively fanciful, making empirical certitude impossible.[24] The widespread acceptance in the eighteenth century of this Lockean idea gave new importance to *ut pictura poesis*. Poetry, like painting, is closely related to the art of actual seeing: the poet too must have seen and must be able to cause others to see.

2. *The psychological.*—Addison goes beyond the traditional view that located *enargeia* in the verbal rendering of natural objects and scenes. Under impulses from the new psychology *enargeia* now arises from the process of seeing and no longer resides primarily in the thing seen. As one of Addison's followers, George Turnbull, put it, "Beauty signifies a satisfaction which certain visible objects are adapted to give to the sight."[25] An admirer of Addison, Hugh Blair, saw in description "the highest exertions of genius" and believed that the power of producing it lay in making us "*imagine* that we see [reality] before our eyes." The true poet "catches the distinguishing features; he gives [his description] the colours of life and reality; he places it in such a light, that a Painter could copy after him. This happy talent is chiefly owing to a strong *imagination*, which first receives a lively impression of the object; and then, by employing a proper selection of circumstances in describing it, transmits that impression in its full force to the *imagination* of others."[26] Such language is psychological. It emphasizes stimulation of the mind and the communication of that stimulation to others.

These statements of Addison and his followers permit us to draw a necessary distinction between the eighteenth-century conception of *enargeia* and the conceptions of antiquity and the Renaissance. According to Aristotle, Alcidamas called the *Odyssey* "a beautiful mirror" of human life.[27] Leonardo found that the work of art is itself a mirror: a painting is a flat, smooth surface on which both relief and chiaroscuro are nonetheless represented.[28] The function of the mirror

[24] *Essay concerning Human Understanding* iv. 19. 8–9.

[25] Cited by Cicely Davies, *op. cit.* (n. 8), p. 161.

[26] *Lectures on Rhetoric and Belles Lettres* (4th ed.; London, 1790), III, 159. Italics mine. For Blair's great admiration of Addison see I, 365.

[27] *Rhetoric* iii. 3. 3.

[28] *A Treatise of Painting* (London, 1721), pp. 139–40.

analogy seems, in passages like these from ancient and Renaissance critics, to suggest that the work of art itself was closely analogous to the reflection in a mirror.

But in the eighteenth century the locus has shifted from the work to the mind, from canvas and page to the imagination.[29] William Cowper's "mirror" is not the poem but the mind.

> There is a pleasure in poetic pains
> Which only poets know. The shifts and turns,
> The expedients and inventions multiform
> To which the mind resorts, in chase of terms
> Though apt, yet coy, and difficult to win,—
> To arrest the fleeting images that fill
> The mirror of the mind, and hold them fast,
> And force them sit, till he has pencilled off
> A faithful likeness of the forms he views.[30]

This important shift of focus in criticism from work to beholder seems to have been paralleled by a corresponding shift in descriptive technique. In the Renaissance, as Ariosto's famous description of Alcina reveals, the analogy with painting was felt to be realized if, somehow, you painted out to the corner of the verbal canvas and enumerated, often with breath-taking sensuous power, detail after exquisite detail. The verbal description itself was made to resemble, to the best of its ability, the canvas of a painting. It was static and complete: item followed item until the whole was drawn. Not all poetic description in the Renaissance can be so categorized, but our formula does fit one important tendency.

Eighteenth-century psychological criticism, however, encouraged the poet to achieve *ut pictura poesis* in another way, by making the reader "see" a picture in response to brief but precise verbal stimu-

---

[29] This shift may also be seen in the different attitudes toward the notion that art is deception. That view had been widely held in antiquity and the Renaissance (see above, pp. 23, 81). But, except for occasional repetitions of the cliché (see, for example, the anonymous poem entitled *"Ut Pictura Poesis,"* in *The Honey-Suckle* [London, 1734], 325–30, and the opening essay on *ut pictura* in *The Free-Thinker,* Oct. 27, 1718), the doctrine of art as deception is under serious attack. See the articles on Appelles and Zeuxis in Bayle's *General Dictionary* (1735); Dr. Johnson's attack on the unities in the *Preface to Shakespeare;* Reynolds' third Discourse, where he says that if "deceiving the eye were the only business of art," painting would not rank as a liberal art; and the thirteenth Discourse, where he severely limits the use of the mirror analogy.

[30] *Task* ii. 285–93.

lus. It is not necessary to paint out to the four corners of the "canvas." A carefully selected pictorial detail, a hint of painterly structure, or a central iconic reference can evoke a train of controlled pictorial sensations. The danger of uncontrolled response must of course have been apparent to an age that liked restraint. But restraint was imposed by using publicly accepted iconic detail, by establishing identity with a known and respected visual tradition, by suggesting particular paintings or schools of painting, and by resting safely on the assumption that the visual imagination of the age was not licentious but effectively disciplined.

If the eighteenth-century poet is psychologically suggestive in his imagery and if he differs from some of his Renaissance predecessors, who would have "painted" Venus to the last detail, how then does he differ from the metaphysical poet of the seventeenth century, who is also pictorially suggestive rather than pictorially imitative? The difference is one that we have anticipated in our discussion of the emblem and of Lovelace. The poet of the metaphysical and baroque seventeenth century tended to be emblematic and symbolic, to suggest the world of invisible reality, or to express private, esoteric, and individual meaning. The poet of the neoclassical eighteenth century tended to be pictorial and natural and to suggest, however briefly, the reality of nature and normative human experience.

To the extent that an eighteenth-century poet like Pope was suggestive and oblique, creating intellectual configurations rather than picturable physical details—to the extent, that is, that his icon was "witty"—he does remind us of his metaphysical rather than his Renaissance ancestors. Such reminiscences of the seventeenth century are important and cannot be overlooked. But they are not central. For eighteenth-century *enargeia*, although conceived of as part of a psychological process, retained intact the essential lines of ancient and Renaissance fidelity to nature. The mirror was, as Cowper suggests, held up to the mind; but the mind itself, as Locke and Addison strove to make clear, was in its turn held up to visible nature. Wit lay in the poet's ability to unite widely disparate details. But those details must all come from natural reality. The wit lay in combining, not in creating, them.[31]

[31] See the discussion in Jean H. Hagstrum, *Samuel Johnson's Literary Criticism* (Minneapolis, Minn., 1952), pp. 117–19.

We have noted that in his second definition of "mirror" Dr. Johnson used these synonyms: "pattern," "exemplar," "archetype." Such meanings, common in Western thought since Plato, had become especially prominent in the Middle Ages and the Renaissance. Spenser addresses the Faerie Queene, "O Goddesse, heauenly bright / Mirrour of grace and Maiestie diuine." Marlowe describes the "immortal flowers of poesy"

> Wherein, as in a mirror we perceive
> The highest reaches of a human wit.[32]

"Mirror" was used to suggest not only the exact rendition of reality in art but also the idealization of reality.

That double significance also appears if we remember the use of mirrors in the atelier. Giorgione, by setting up mirrors around his model, was able to win a wager that painting on a canvas could be as lifelike and multidimensional as a sculptured figure.[33] Such use of the mirror made reality more real. But when Dufresnoy, who called a looking glass the painter's "best master," urged that it be used in instructing the artist, he meant that it was useful in learning how to proceed in the direction of ideal generality.[34] The mirror gives distance to the reflected painting, shows the effect of the whole, emphasizes the main masses and contours, subordinates the less important details. The mirror, by heightening and lessening, can help to correct and universalize nature. Even the popular and somewhat ridiculous plano-convex mirror, which had curved glass tinted with two or three colors and mounted on a black foil—the so-called Claude glass carried by travelers and walking tourists like Gray—was used to

[32] *Faerie Queene* i. Proem. 4; *I Tamburlaine*, Act V, Sc. 2, ll. 103–5; above, pp. 135–36. For an excellent study of the mirror analogy in criticism see M. H. Abrams, *The Mirror and the Lamp* (New York, 1953), esp. chap. ii. See also Sister Ritamary Bradley, "Backgrounds of the Title *Speculum* in Mediaeval Literature,"*Speculum*, XXIX (January, 1954), 100–115, and Heinrich Schwarz, "The Mirror in Art," *Art Quarterly*, XV (Summer, 1952), 97–118.

[33] Vasari, *Lives* ("Everyman's Library" [London, 1927]), II, 171.

[34] "De Arte Graphica," l. 387: "Multa ex natura speculum praeclara docebit" (trans. in *Works of Dryden*, ed. Walter Scott and George Saintsbury [London, 1892], XVII, 376–77). See also De Piles' comment, *ibid.*, p. 471.

modify natural scenes, arranging them like an idealized landscape by Claude Lorrain on the soft-hued surface of the glass.[35]

Because the mirror suggests both faithful realism and stylized idealism (the two large aspects of nature and art in our period), it is a revealing symbol of contemporary aesthetic thought. In pictorialism it is a linking metaphor that brings the two sister arts together, and its use was often a sign of the presence of the pictorialist tradition in criticism and poetry. But the term is useful in still another way: it helps us detect not only the presence but also the nature of artistic idealization as the eighteenth century conceived it.

If art is said to hold a mirror up to nature, the metaphor cannot, even in a context of idealization, legitimately describe a Neoplatonic process. The Claude glass, for example, reproduced nature that was idealized and corrected but that remained nature still. In this respect neoclassical general nature differs from the Neoplatonic ideal. It is true that the Neoplatonic critic Bellori, whom we discussed in our last chapter, was widely read in the eighteenth century. Dryden, as we shall see, translated a long passage from him; Gray apparently carried the *Vite* along with him on his Italian travels.[36] Most eighteenth-century writers in England would have agreed with Bellori's disparagement of the Dutch and of Caravaggio[37] and his praise of Raphael, Guido Reni, and the Carracci. Nevertheless, his religious idealism was radically transformed.

Sir Joshua Reynolds' conception of general nature holds the key to what eighteenth-century idealism meant. Reynolds does sometimes suggest, in word and phrase, the Neoplatonic ideal. But nothing is actually further from his meaning than the notion of supernal reality mediated to the artist by inner vision, by mystical contemplation. For Reynolds the ideal does not descend to the artist or beholder from supersensory archetypes; it arises from continuously and vigorously pursued empirical observation and search.

[35] See Christopher Hussey, *The Picturesque* (London, 1927), p. 107.

[36] *Works of Gray*, ed. John Mitford (London, 1836), IV, 232. This is only one of several references in Gray's notes made during his tour of Italy. Evidently he had Bellori open before him when writing, for he refers to the *Vite* by page.

[37] "We appear a Nation of *Grotesque Thinkers*, whose Idea of our Writers Excellence, like the *Dutchmens* Taste of *Painting* seems to be Nature, in a Fit of Distortion, where *Grimace* is placed for *Dignity*" (*The Plain Dealer*, July 24, 1724). See Reynolds' Discourses, *passim*.

This great ideal perfection and beauty are not to be sought in the heavens, but upon the earth. They are about us, and upon every side of us. But the power of discovering what is deformed in nature, or in other words, what is particular and uncommon, can be acquired only by experience; and the whole beauty and grandeur of art consists . . . in being able to get above all singular forms, local customs, particularities, and details of every kind.[38]

For Reynolds, and for his friend Dr. Johnson, general nature is a synthesis of scattered excellencies, the abstraction of general form and species from particular manifestations. Such general forms are in nature; otherwise our search would be vain. General beauty is like scientific law: it is disclosed not by revelation but by research.[39]

Reynolds' views are not original. They represent the culmination in English criticism of tendencies that go back to the ancients, who made of the story of Zeuxis and the maidens a proverbial illustration of artistic idealization; to tendencies in the Renaissance that we have elsewhere specified; to Poussin in the seventeenth century, who believed that ideal beauty consisted of the union of minor beauties;[40] to Roger de Piles, for whom the ideal in all art is "the choice of various perfections";[41] and to the leading poets of Augustan England. Reynolds' views also look ahead—to the critical neoclassicism of Mengs and Winckelmann, the sculptures of Canova, Gérard, and Thorvaldsen, and the romantic Hellenism of Keats.[42] The view of the ideal embodied in Reynolds was the normative view of the eighteenth century. It received no distinguished full-scale refutation until Hazlitt placed the ideal not in abstraction from natural particulars but in the intensification of their natural forms and the revelation of their individuality.[43]

[38] Discourse III.

[39] For a development of this notion see Jean H. Hagstrum, review of W. R. Keast, "The Theoretical Foundations of Johnson's Criticism," in R. S. Crane (ed.), *Critics and Criticism* (Chicago, 1952), pp. 389–407, in *Philological Quarterly*, XXXII (July, 1953), 276–78.

[40] Beauty has "in se tutte le bellezze raccolte" (cited by Bellori, *Vite* [Pisa, 1821], II, 204).

[41] *Principles of Painting* (London, 1743), p. 19. This is a translation of the *Cours de Peintre*.

[42] *Opere di Antonio Raffaello Mengs* (Bassano, Italy, 1783), I, 169–71; Mario Praz, *Gusto neoclassico* (Florence, 1940).

[43] See *Complete Works of Hazlitt*, ed. P. P. Howe (London, 1930–34), VI, 145; VIII, 31–42, 111; XX, 302–6.

Such is the intellectual background for pictorial idealization. But how, specifically, did poets use the plastic arts in attempting to idealize reality? They appear to have used the sister arts in three ways that overlap but may be separated for purposes of exposition: (1) by suggesting the forms and attitudes of classical sculpture; (2) by imitating the heroic history and mythology of pictorial art; (3) by creating allegorical personifications reminiscent of the icons and images of the graphic arts.

1. *Idealization through the imitation of ancient statuary.*—Gay's Fable XVIII, "The Painter Who Pleased No Body and Every Body," tells the story of a realistic painter who lost his trade when

> He hit complexion, feature, air,
> So just, the life itself was there

but who became prosperous when he turned to idealization and flattery:

> Through all the town his art they prais'd
> His custom grew, his price was rais'd.

How was this achieved? By means of statuary.

> Two bustos, fraught with ev'ry grace,
> A *Venus'* and *Apollo's* face,
> He plac'd in view; resolv'd to please,
> Whoever sate, he drew from these,
> From these corrected ev'ry feature,
> And spirited each aukward creature.

This witty and satirical fable was not written to reveal the serious practice of painters in achieving ideal form. But it is nonetheless significant, for the use of statues in flattering strutting lords and flouncy ladies is not unrelated to the more grandiose flattery of human nature practiced by painter and poet alike. Poussin was praised by nearly everyone who mentioned him for having absorbed the spirit and forms of ancient sculpture. As Le Brun and many others after him said, Poussin was led into nature itself by his study of classical marbles. To that study he is supposed to have owed the serene grandeur of his faces and figures.[44] Painters and sculptors alike strove to achieve ideal nature by consulting the sculptured remains of Greece and Rome. Reynolds the critic intended general

[44] See Henri Jouin, *Conférences de l'Académie Royale de Peinture et de Sculpture* (Paris, 1883), p. 91.

nature to be visualized as sculptured reality. The beauty of class or species, which is superior to the beauty of the individual in nobility, austerity, and invariability, is essentially the beauty of the gladiators, of the Apollo Belvedere,[45] and of the Farnese Hercules (Plates XIX A, XVIII A). Each of these differs from the other, not as one individual differs from another, but as one type from another: as manly beauty differs from womanly beauty, as youthful beauty differs from aged dignity. For Reynolds such scuplture came closest to "representing perfect beauty." But not all sculpture did, and it is revealing that Reynolds regarded the "picturesque" sculptures of Bernini as renegade to the genius of his art. It was chiefly to ancient statuary that the artist must turn if he would achieve the grandeur of generality.[46]

Reynolds addressed the graphic artist. But what he said of ideal beauty and its relation to sculptured form was in some ways applicable to the poet, who also felt that *la belle nature* was essentially sculpturesque. Particular manifestations of this way of seeing and feeling we shall consider in Pope's "Temple of Fame," some of Thomson's garden scenes, and many of Collins' personifications. Here we shall say only an introductory word. It is clear that for Pope and Joseph Warton—to take two examples only, but two that represent differing and complementary tendencies—landscape statuary should properly express noble personification and exalted moral reflection. Pope says that his grotto at Twickenham requires "nothing to complete it but a good statue with an inscription." Such a statue he regarded as a personification that symbolized the "aquatic idea of the whole place." Joseph Warton compares the pleasure of landscape statuary to the moral reflection one often encounters in reading passages of scenic description. He says of one such insertion of general morality in Dyer's "Grongar Hill" that it "imparts to us the same pleasure that we feel, when in wandering through a wilderness or grove, we suddenly behold in the turning of the walk, a statue of some VIRTUE or MUSE."[47] Both these passages

---

[45] This statue was a great favorite of the eighteenth century. It is a good example of the theophany, the sudden appearance in the material universe of a hitherto invisible deity. See Wolfgang Helbig, *Guide to the Public Collections of Classical Antiquities in Rome* (Leipzig, 1895), I, 106.

[46] Discourses III and X.

[47] These references I owe to Chapin, *op. cit.* (n. 5), p. 56.

are significant. In one the poet reveals that for him a statue represents an idealizing symbol. In the other the critic compares the moral reflection of a poem to allegorical statuary.

2. *Idealization through the creation of pictorial "histories."*—During the seventeenth and eighteenth centuries in England the genre of painting that had the greatest prestige was the "history." That term included not only episodes in the lives of national heroes but also sacred and profane mythology. "History" invaded portraiture, and long before Reynolds' brilliant use of "borrowed attitudes" contemporary personages were presented in heroic, mythic, and historical stance. Sir Peter Lely drew the Duchess of Cleveland as Juno, Mrs. Middleton as Pomona, Jane Kelleway as Diana, the Duchess of Rutland as St. Agnes.[48] Godfrey Kneller drew Anne, Lady Middleton, and Mrs. Voss and her daughter as Arcadian shepherdesses bearing staffs in their hands and, on another occasion, the same Mrs. Voss as St. Agnes holding a prayer book in her hand and cuddling a lamb.[49]

Literature shares with painting this habit of presenting living people in attitudes taken from history and mythology. Dryden, in one of his finest lyrics, compares himself to Nisus and his subject, the poet Oldham, to Euryalus, an allusion to the *Aeneid* obviously made less for the purpose of clarifying the meaning than for exalting the tone. But neoclassical poets, as we shall see, often went beyond merely using the same sources that painters drew on. Poets sometimes tried to make their poetical histories resemble pictorial histories in total structure and central illusion. One notable example is Gray's "Bard." At other times poets allowed the pictorial to affect only particular lines and isolated scenes that decorate and idealize. This type of stylization is frequently one of the charms of neoclassical English verse, a charm that evaporates unless we respond to its casual, subtle, but unmistakable suggestions of the pictorial.

The second stanza of Rochester's lyric, beginning "My dear Mistress has a heart / Soft as those kind looks she gave me," reads:

> Melting joys about her move,
> Killing pleasures, wounding blisses,
> She can dress her eyes in love,

[48] R. B. Beckett, *Lely* (London, 1951), Plates CI, CII, CIV, CXIV.

[49] Lord Killanin, *Sir Godfrey Kneller and His Times, 1646–1723* (London, 1948), Plates XVI, XXVIII, LXI.

And her lips can arm with kisses;
Angels listen when she speaks,
She's my delight, all mankind's wonder,
But my jealous heart would break
Should we live one day asunder.

The description in this stanza is effective only if visualized, and it can be visualized only in a pictorial, not in a natural way. What are the "melting joys" that "move about" the lady if not the amoretti of the mythological canvas? Who are the listening angels, if not the angels of baroque and rococo art—angels that have been transferred from paintings above the altar to portraits of fashionable ladies in their drawing rooms? To be insensitive to these touches is to miss the decorative finesse with which Rochester has surrounded his lady.

Similarly, Prior sometimes introduces a pictorial touch so slight and evanescent as to elude the unalerted. He concludes his ode (beginning "The Merchant, to secure his Treasure, / Conveys it in a borrow'd Name") with the following stanza:

Fair Cloe blush'd: Euphelia frown'd:
I sung and gaz'd: I play'd and trembl'd:
And Venus to the Loves around
Remark'd how ill we all dissembl'd.

Who are the "Loves around" and where is Venus? We cannot possibly answer unless we conceive the scene pictorially. The gallantry has been played under a cloud of mythical beings. Venus is in the room above the heads of the gallants, and she turns to speak to the winged amoretti that constitute her train.

Such hints of pictorial idealization we encounter everywhere in eighteenth-century verse. Their function, whether peripherally decorative or centrally symbolic, is always to move the meaning and mood to some sort of idealized or decorated condition.

3. *Idealization in the creation of pictorial allegories.*—No age has been blamed more for its innumerable allegories than has eighteenth-century England. One reason is that this form of literary expression tends to be abstract and lifeless. Partly because he wished to counteract the natural tendency of allegory to become intellectually abstract, the critic of the period never wearied of insisting that moral personifications be "picturesque" and particular.[50] For allegory

[50] See Earl R. Wasserman, "The Inherent Values of Eighteenth-Century Personification," *Publications of the Modern Language Association*, LXV (June, 1950), 456–60.

can be rescued, if at all, only when its skeletal figures are clothed in visual particularity.

But the peculiar qualities of neoclassical allegory do not arise merely from a vague desire to make the general concrete. *Ut pictura poesis* has been operative, and an attempt has been made to endow the allegory with the quality of the "picturesque." Often the eye of the poet has been trained on the allegories of the graphic arts.

This state of affairs, of which abundant illustration will be provided in Part II, can be partly explained by the way in which ancient mythology was viewed. Long before the eighteenth century the gods and goddesses of Greece and Rome had been transformed to moral and natural abstractions. For Pope it was quite natural that Juno be considered an element of air and Jupiter ether. Mars stands for "mere martial Courage without Conduct"; Minerva, for "martial Courage with Wisdom." Minerva's descent to encounter Achilles represents "Prudence restraining Passion."[51] This habit of allegorizing mythology implies that with moral abstraction there was associated an easily visualized figure. If Minerva embodies wisdom and if you think of the goddess when you consider the abstract quality, you have added visual dimensions and concrete graphic traits to the abstraction. For Minerva had not only appeared in the pages of the poets; she had been *seen* again and again in statuary and painting.

The eighteenth century had inherited from Renaissance culture and its aftermath an entire pantheon of visually expressed moral abstractions. From Italy, France, and Holland had come thousands of moral engravings. In the icons of Cesare Ripa alone there were hundreds of examples of graphically rendered abstractions (see Plate II). The virtues, the vices, the mental faculties, natural phenomena, countries, provinces, and cities all appeared as visual figures bearing their appropriate insignia.

It is not, of course, necessary to believe that the poet who created visual iconic symbols had Ripa open before him, although he might have, since an English edition appeared in 1709 and Continental editions were not hard to come by. Ripa's icons had become so widely diffused throughout all Western culture by the time the Augustan poets wrote that the creation of verbal images in his man-

---

[51] *The Iliad of Homer*, trans. Alexander Pope (London, 1715–20). See "A Poetical Index," which appears at the end of Vol. VI, under "Fable," subhead "Allegorical Fables." See also I, 261; IV, 141.

ner was natural and almost inevitable. As William Melmoth said, "To represent natural, moral, or intellectual qualities and affections as persons, and appropriate to them those general emblems by which their powers and properties are usually typified in pagan theology, may be allowed as one of the most pleasing and graceful figures of poetical rhetoric."[52] Taste for such figures was widely diffused, and the appropriate and relevant iconography was easily available. For the eighteenth-century reader visualization of a full and proper picture was possible under the stimulus of a carefully selected detail. If this is true, the modern reader must learn the relevant iconographical context and respond to even slight visual stimulus.

Because of the full discussion that is to follow of particular poems that embody pictorially conceived allegorical personages, we need here do no more than call attention to the habit of expression that brings personification and picture together. That habit is fully revealed in the letters of Lord Chesterfield. He continually writes, not of grace or gracefulness, but of the Graces: "Charites, Charites!" "Remember the Graces!" "Join the Graces!" "Invoke the Graces!" To explain such apostrophes and imperatives as these it is of course not necessary to invoke pictorial example. But Chesterfield did in fact visualize his Graces and apparently wanted his reader to visualize them too. He refers his son expressly and often to a painting by Carlo Maratti entitled "Il [*sic*] Studio del Disegno," which he describes as follows:

An old man, supposed to be the master, points to his scholars, who are variously employed, in perspective, geometry, and the observation of the statues of antiquity. With regard to perspective, of which there are some little specimens, he has wrote, *tanto che basti*, that is, *as much as is sufficient;* with regard to geometry, *tanto che basti*, again; with regard to the contemplation of ancient statues, there is written, *non mai a bastanza,—there never can be enough*. But, in the clouds, at top of the piece, are represented the three Graces, with this just sentence written over them, *senza di noi ogni fatica è vana;* that is, *without us all labour is vain.*[53]

In this chapter we have been concerned with the historical and theoretical foundations of *ut pictura poesis* in the eighteenth century. A part of an almost universal tendency to analogize, the doctrine was nurtured by a hitherto unrivaled sophistication in the fine

[52] Cited by Chapin, *op. cit.* (n. 5), p. 60.
[53] Nov. 18 (O.S.), 1748, *op. cit.* (n. 4), p. 83.

arts that brought knowledge of painting and statue to virtually every poet. *Ut pictura poesis* also rested on English empiricism—on Lockean epistemology and the related aesthetic tradition that ran from Hobbes to Addison. This meant that poetical *enargeia* had become a more subjective phenomenon than ever before. But *enargeia* still arose from man's contact with living, objective nature. Its ancient association with the rendition of the freshness and vivacity of the real and particular world, though altered, was by no means weakened. Pictorialism was not confined, however, to literary realism. It also served the purposes of that kind of un-Platonic idealization characteristic of an age that wished to trim, dress, and elevate Nature without destroying her form and force (see Plate IV). One of the distinguishing features of eighteenth-century poetical imagery was that it borrowed heavily from ancient statuary, pictorial history, and graphic allegory. And when it did not borrow directly, its habits of expression and ordering were often directly parallel to dominant tendencies in the graphic arts.

CHAPTER VI

English Neoclassicism (II)

THE CRITICAL CHALLENGE TO PICTORIALISM

Literary pictorialism was challenged not by romantic idealists or their supposed forerunners but by empirical rationalists, whose thought lay well within the tolerant domain of English neoclassicism. The quarrel between pictorialist and antipictorialist was not owing to important change in taste and thought. Burke, in vigorously attacking pictorialist doctrine, used precisely the same empirical psychology that Addison had used in supporting it. Neoclassicist lifted his sword against neoclassicist, Lockean against Lockean. Nevertheless, the debate on the nature of visual imagery and language did break ground for the seedtime of later decades, and Burke and Lessing may have contributed to the virtual disappearance of *ut pictura poesis* in major romantic criticism and to the replacement of painting by music as the art most analogous to poetry.[1]

We are interested, however, not in the large effects of the critical challenge upon subsequent cultural history or even in the ultimate philosophical or logical merits of the attack itself. Our concern is, rather, to examine what in pictorialism survived the onslaught, what pictorialist values were accepted as axiomatic even by the attackers, and what light the challenge throws back upon pictorialism itself.

Lessing's awareness of the limits of the arts, which had been antici-

---

[1] "The use of painting to illuminate the essential character of poetry . . . almost disappears in the major criticism of the romantic period; . . . music becomes the art frequently pointed to as having a profound affinity with poetry" (M. H. Abrams, *The Mirror and the Lamp* [New York, 1953], p. 50). For a discussion of the breakdown of classical aesthetics during the eighteenth century see Rudolf Wittkower, "Principles of Palladio's Architecture," *Journal of the Warburg and Courtauld Institutes*, VII (1945), esp. pp. 100–103. We should not assume that pictorialism steadily declined after it had been vigorously attacked. The "picturesque" school arose after Burke and Lessing had written, and some of the greatest pictorial effects were achieved in the poetry of Keats.

pated time and time again even in antiquity,[2] was, ironically, shared by the very writers he attacked. In its barest essentials Lessing's distinction is so elementary that we must believe that even Abbé Batteux was capable of making it. But the insistence of the pictorialists themselves upon the distinction between poetry and painting suggests something more than the observation of an obvious fact. The influential French aesthetician, Abbé du Bos, did much to commend the analogy between the arts to the English: he printed the motto *ut pictura poesis* on the title page of his *Réflexions critiques sur la poésie et la peinture* (1719), and he considered both the arts imitative ones that presented images of sight to the mind. Yet he insisted on maintaining the limits of the arts. He observed that some subjects were appropriate to poetry, others to painting; that painting ought to be more circumstantial and detailed than poetry; and, most important of all, that the painter has but one moment of time but the poet an infinite extension of time.[3]

Why were such differences as these stressed by the pictorialists? Because poetry cannot logically be bidden to resemble an art from which it is virtually indistinguishable. *Ut pictura poesis* must of course assume that there exist significant interart resemblances. But it makes sense only if we believe that sharp differences nevertheless do exist between the arts, that each has peculiar qualities of its own, and that there is something uniquely pictorial for poetry to strive to achieve.

Of the many forerunners of Lessing none is more important than Edmund Burke, who, without naming the names of men or movements, directly challenged the values of pictorialism. Obscurity is of greater aesthetic value than clarity; the absence of detail is desirable in poetry. Though painting is and must be an imitative art in which objects are realistically represented, poetry is not; and the art most analogous to poetry is music, not painting. The terrible-sublime, one of the greatest achievements possible in poetry, would be ridiculous in painting. Language is a social, not a natural, sign; it

---

[2] See Pindar *Nemean* v. 1; Aristotle *Poetics* 1447 a. 19 (see above, p. 6, n. 7); Dio Chrysostom *Twelfth or Olympic Discourse*, secs. 51–77. See also Lessing, *Laokoön*, ed. William Guild Howard (New York, 1910), pp. l–xcviii; A. Lombard, *L'Abbé du Bos* (Paris, 1913), chap. ii, sec. ii; and Władyslaw Folkierski, *Entre le classicisme et le romantisme* (Paris, 1925), chap. v.

[3] Lombard, *op. cit.* (n. 2), *passim;* Folkierski, *op. cit.* (n. 2), pp. 175–81.

brings to us not the images of natural vision but the ideas of society and the emotions that attend them. Words are not onomatopoetic or imitative but emotionally and intellectually evocative. They operate with greatest emotional effect when unclogged by distracting visual particulars.[4] Dr. Johnson illustrates Burke's theory when he censures Edgar's speech to Gloucester (in which the view from the precipice near Dover is being described) for containing too many particulars that "dissipate" and "enfeeble" the central idea: "The enumeration of crows, the samphire-man and the fishers, counteracts the great effect of the prospect, as it peoples the desert of intermediate vacuity, and stops the mind in the rapidity of its descent through emptiness and horrour."[5] Such a theory as this, in which obscurity, darkness, and incompleteness have great value and in which undefined but powerful kinesthetic emotions can be aroused by words with no visual image, leaves little room for *ut pictura poesis*.

From a pictorialist's point of view Burke's absolute disjunction of words (which create emotional response) and images (which bring to the mental retina the objects of nature) is nothing short of revolutionary. This appears with great force if we compare Burke's definition of verbal *enargeia* with the classical conception. Joseph Warton, expressing the traditional view, wrote:

The use, the force, and the excellence of language, certainly consists in raising *clear*, *complete*, and *circumstantial* images, and in turning readers into *spectators*.[6]

But Burke said:

So little does poetry depend for its effect on the power of raising sensible images, that I am convinced it would lose a very considerable part of its *energy*, if this were the necessary result of all description. Because that union of affecting words, which is the most powerful of all poetical instru-

---

[4] "A Philosophical Inquiry into the Origin of Our Ideas of the Sublime and the Beautiful," *Works* ("Bohn Library" [London, 1876]), pp. 83, 89–93, 99, 105, 106. See also William Guild Howard, "Burke among the Forerunners of Lessing," *Publications of the Modern Language Association*, XXII (December, 1907), 608–32; Dixon Wecter, "Burke's Theory concerning Words, Images, and Emotion," *Publications of the Modern Language Association*, LV (March, 1940), 167–81.

[5] Walter Raleigh (ed.), *Johnson on Shakespeare* (Oxford, 1925), pp. 158–59.

[6] *An Essay on the Genius and Writings of Pope* (London, 1782), II, 165. Italics mine.

ments, would frequently lose its force, along with its propriety and consistency, if the sensible images were always excited.[7]

For the pictorialist from Plutarch to Addison, energy arises directly from the verbal rendition of the visual; for Burke language that contains sensible images loses "a very considerable part of its energy." This condition arises because "no real picture is formed" when words describe. Language is in its very nature uncongenial to the pictorial.

The truth is, all verbal description, merely as naked description, though never so exact, conveys so poor and insufficient an idea of the things described, that it could scarcely have the smallest effect, if the speaker did not call in to his aid those modes of speech that mark a strong and lively feeling in himself. . . . It may be observed, that very polished languages, and such as are praised for their superior clearness and perspicuity, are generally deficient in strength.[8]

To the extent that the pictorial was excessively descriptive and merely enumerative and to the extent that it neglected the values of emotional and imaginative suggestiveness, it richly deserved Burke's attack But some of the values he required were actually cultivated by pictorial poets and pictorialist critics. It would be mischievous if we allowed his argument to confuse the lengthy descriptions of the second-rate—a John Dyer, say—with the richly suggestive pictorialism of an Alexander Pope. Moreover, pictorial poets, though of course they must cherish the values of clarity and visual concreteness, do not always stand in "one clear, unchanged, and universal light" even in their pictorial moments. There is some room even in neoclassical pictorial imagery for Burke's values of obscurity and darkness, and we remember the effective images of Chaos, Darkness, and Old Night in the *Dunciad*, the shadowy suggestiveness of Collins' personifications, and the dimly lit Miltonic grandeur of some of the best images in Dryden's great odes. Pictures also often embodied these qualities; Rembrandt, Caravaggio, and Magnasco found it desirable to express Burkean qualities even on the canvas. Although the pictorial has most often been composed of clear and sharp detail, it should not be made coterminous with these qualities. You still *see* even when you see through a glass darkly.

[7] *Op. cit.* (n. 4), I, 175–76. Italics mine.

[8] *Ibid.*, pp. 176, 180.

In the Preface of the *Laokoön* Lessing quotes the famous proverb of Simonides, which he calls "the dazzling antithesis of the Greek Voltaire," and finds that though it has sanctioned error and created confusion, it does contain evident truth.[9] We shall examine first Lessing's attack upon the error and excess and then his concession of evident truth to the notion that poetry is a speaking picture and painting a silent poem.

Lessing opposed a condition in the arts in which painting had become excessively literary and poetry excessively pictorial. The plastic arts, he believed, were intended to express only the beauty of physical form and not the meanings of the mind and the emotions of the heart. In plastic art baroque motion and baroque allegory were unacceptable to Lessing, and only the austere, simple, nude beauties of ancient marbles were allowable. For poetry another condition was desirable: action should predominate—full-bodied, expressive, even violent action; the decorum of natural beauty should be eliminated and word-painting discouraged. Each art should live contentedly within its own borders. Painting, a spatial and visual art, should not strive to become a temporal and psychological art; and poetry, a temporal and intellectual art, should ignore the demands of line, space, color, and simultaneity of effect.

This side of Lessing's argument, persuasive though it is, has serious limitations, if not as philosophical discourse, then certainly as a tool of historical description and analysis. For, quite apart from whether it is theoretically justifiable to define painting in terms so austerely and classically formal as Lessing has done or to confine poetry so exclusively to temporal narration, this analysis will not help at all in understanding and appraising the poetry and art of the seventeenth and eighteenth centuries, to go no further afield. If, by some compelling fiat, Lessing's aesthetic law should universally prevail, the loss would be great: much of Spenser, some of Shakespeare, Homer's description of Achilles' shield,[10] the entire tradition of emblematic verse, some of the best images of Pope, much that is most enduringly characteristic of Venetian art, and the triumphs of baroque expression would be cast out of the pantheon. There would

[9] (London, 1914), p. 4.

[10] Lessing in chap. xviii attempts to exempt this passage from his strictures but, in my view, fails (see above, p. 19).

remain only classical marbles and the purely narrative sections of epics.

Even Lessing would not have allowed his polemical argument to be reduced to its logical conclusion. He himself admits that Simonides' proverb contains essential truth, and it is possible to read the *Laokoön* as an attack upon the abuses of pictorialism that nevertheless manages to recognize its legitimate values. Thus, though he laments that the word *picture* has crept into the critical discussion of *enargeia*, he enthusiastically concedes that the poet has the power to "set forth picturesquely the most unpicturable data."

To believe it to be otherwise is to suffer ourselves to be misled by the twofold meaning of a word. A poetical picture is not necessarily convertible into a material picture; but every feature, every combination of several features, by which the poet makes his object so palpable to us, that we become more conscious of this object than of his words, is picturesque, is a picture, because it brings us nearer to that degree of illusion of which the material picture is especially capable, and which is most quickly and easily called forth by the contemplation of the material picture.[11]

To that affirmation of belief in the achievement of *enargeia* through skilful response to *ut pictura poesis* the best neoclassical poets and critics would have heartily assented. They would have agreed that poetic pictures need not conform to all the specifications of actual pictures, and they would have disliked poems that consisted only of paintable details in paintable arrangements. They would have approvingly noted that Lessing grants high value to *enargeia* and recognizes that its literary manifestation bears strong resemblance to the visual illusion of painting. To say as much as this is to admit the validity of *ut pictura poesis*. The more one considers the essential elements of Lessing's treatise, the more one becomes convinced that his critical guns were trained at very minor writers indeed—perhaps the lesser German descriptive poets of the early eighteenth century—and not at the richly allusive, highly compressed, visually sharp, but emotionally evocative pictorialism of neoclassical poetic art at its best.

[11] *Op. cit.* (n. 9), pp. 88–89 (end of chap. xiv). In the original "poetical picture" is *poetisches Gemälde;* "picturesque" is *malerisch*. In note 2 on page 89 Lessing fully accepts the notion of *enargeia* (*die Energie*). He deplores the use of the word "picture" (*Gemälde*) instead of *enargeia* and "phantasia," since "picture" suggests that the poet's images should be so presented as to be fully paintable. This is convincing evidence that he accepts much that is central in the pictorialist tradition.

The word "pictorial," as it has been used in these pages, is a general term that includes the critical notion of *enargeia*, the genre of iconic verse, particular image, and total form—everything, in fact, that we have discussed from antiquity to the eighteenth century. The "picturesque," to be historically and critically useful, must be given a more restricted meaning.

Neoclassic critics, however, used "picturesque" much as we have used "pictorial." For some reason "pictorial" did not catch on during the eighteenth century. Johnson admits it to his dictionary, quoting Sir Thomas Browne to illustrate its meaning and sanction its usage. But, even though he calls it "elegant and useful," he describes it as "a word not adopted by other writers."[12] Of "picturesque" it is possible to distinguish four historical meanings:[13]

1. The oldest and in many ways most useful is simply "like a picture" or "capable of being represented in a picture."[14] This was the usual sense of the word in the time of Pope and Gray.

2. The term was also used of the visually particular.[15] Johnson made it synonymous with "graphic," the adverbial form of which he defined as "In a picturesque manner; with good description or delineation." Although the slightly pejorative sense of petty and minute appears in Reynolds' use of the word,[16] it usually in this sense referred to the highly desirable quality of *enargeia*.[17] For Hazlitt "the *picturesque* altogether depends on particular points or qualities of an

[12] 4th ed.; 1773.

[13] See Elizabeth Wheeler Manwaring, *Italian Landscape in Eighteenth Century England* (New York, 1925), chap. vii; Christopher Hussey, *The Picturesque* (London, 1927).

[14] The Accademia della Crusca in its *Vocabulario* (Florence, 1733) defines *pittoresco* as "di pittore." Francesco Milizia (*Dizionario delle belle arti del disegno* [Bassano, Italy, 1797]) says *pittoresco* " è quanto conviene alla pittura." William Gilpin (*An Essay upon Prints* [London, 1768], p. x) defines "picturesque" as a "term expressive of that peculiar kind of beauty, which is agreeable in a picture." See also *OED*, "picturesque."

[15] Thus Milizia (*op. cit.* [n. 14]) says that "poche cose in natura non saranno pittoresche."

[16] Discourse X.

[17] The Della Cruscans of the eighteenth century (n. 14) said the "pittoresco.... ha in se del portamento, del brio, ec. che usano i pittori dare.... all' opere loro."

object." It is "a sharper and bolder impression of reality." He uses it in opposition to the "ideal."[18]

3. Both Hazlitt and Reynolds suggest other meanings that make "picturesque" virtually synonymous with "fanciful," "capricious," "various," and "irregular." Reynolds so uses it in describing a quality that contrasts with the sober and regular effects of classical sculpture—a quality that exists in Bernini's stones, to their everlasting detriment.[19] The picturesque for Hazlitt tended toward the fantastic and the grotesque; it was associated with the portrayal of fairies and satyrs.[20] P. I. Charrin, the editor of Saint-Non, associated his subject's "picturesque" with both the beautiful and the sublime, with "idées agréables ou mélancoliques" and with "idées séduisantes ou terribles."[21] These associations have persisted to our own day. Geoffrey Scott has said that the "unexpected, wild, fantastic, accidental" constitute the picturesque. In a manner somewhat reminiscent of Reynolds' discussion of picturesque sculpture, he has denied its appropriateness to architecture.[22]

4. The most influential meaning—one closely related to the preceding—arose in connection with a school of taste that flourished in the late eighteenth century.[23] In that movement the term became associated with pleasing distortion or roughness in nature and rocks and cataracts, like those in a work of Salvator Rosa; with lonely ruins in rude but studied neglect, winding and whimsical paths of sheep, the vapory qualities of shimmering leaves and distant buildings, weather-stained moss, and loosened and tumbled stones. Thanks to Uvedale Price and his contemporaries, these may even today be the essential ingredients of the picturesque.[24]

---

[18] "On Certain Inconsistencies in Sir Joshua Reynolds's Discourses," *Complete Works*, ed. P. P. Howe (London, 1930–34), viii, 141. See also "On the Picturesque and Ideal," *ibid.*, pp. 317–20.

[19] Discourse X.   [20] *Op. cit.* (n. 18), VIII, 317.

[21] Jean Claude Richard de Saint-Non, *Voyage pittoresque à Naples et en Sicilie* (Paris, 1829). Saint-Non's work first appeared in 1777. For another and earlier example of the *voyage pittoresque* see Marco Boschini's *Carta del Navegar Pittoresco* (1660). The idea of the "picturesque tour" did not originate in eighteenth-century England.

[22] *The Architecture of Humanism* (Garden City, N.Y., 1954), p. 70. First published in 1914.

[23] See Manwaring (*op. cit.* [n. 13]) and Hussey (*op. cit.* [n. 13]).

[24] See Heinrich Wölfflin, "The 'Picturesque' and Its Opposite," in his *Principles of Art History*, trans. M. D. Hottinger (New York, n.d.), pp. 23–27.

But they were not its ingredients to Dryden, Pope, Thomson, Collins, or even Gray. To them, as we have said, "picturesque" meant simply "like a picture." But "like a picture" is not so simple as it may at first seem, for the phrase can mean either (1) like a particular painting, painter, or school[25] or (2) like painting considered as an art. The first of these justifies considering the relationship of poetry to the pantheon of known and approved art, for it was perhaps inevitable that the picturesque in poetry should resemble the paintings that the artist liked best. The second of these sub-meanings raises another kind of question. It suggests that the technique of poetry can resemble a peculiarly pictorial technique. We shall hereafter use "picturesque" in this last sense only.

The "picturesque" in neoclassic poetry may be elucidated if we inquire what the critic and aesthetician understood to be the most important characteristic of painting. It was simply this: painting was able to produce its effect all at once in a single pregnant moment. A truly imitative art, its physical details coexisted simultaneously, like those of nature. For the influential Du Bos, as for Leonardo, from whom emphasis on this idea may ultimately have derived, the picturesque is produced at a glance, at a stroke.[26] For Shaftesbury the test of painting was its ability to produce a "certain *Easiness of Sight*; a simple, clear, and *united View*."[27] Jonathan Richardson believed painting to be superior to other arts because it can convey meaning in an instant of time: paintings "pour ideas into our minds; words only drop them."[28] Reynolds said the painter "has but one sentence to utter, but one moment to exhibit."[29]

If this was looked upon as the unique pictorial quality, it would be logical to assume that the literary picturesque (meaning a technique "like the *art* of painting") would attempt to incorporate that quality. Neoclassical poetic imagery at its best does seem to be picturesque in this sense: it has achieved the economy and sugges-

[25] Boschini *op. cit.* (n. 21), associates *pittoresco* almost exclusively with effects peculiar to the Venetian school, especially Tintoretto.

[26] *Critical Reflexions on Poetry, Painting, and Music,* trans. Thomas Nugent (London, 1748), I, 221.

[27] "An Essay on the Freedom of Wit and Humour" (1709), *Characteristicks* (3d ed.; London, 1723), I, 142–43.

[28] Cited by Folkierski, *op. cit.* (n. 2), p. 174.

[29] Discourse IV.

tiveness of visual detail that we find in a good picture; it has reduced random motion to plastic fixity. Coleridge found that the desirable poetic image is not one with details faithfully copied from nature but one in which "succession [has been reduced] to an instant." Coleridge invokes the example of the painter in defining the poetic image: "With more than the power of the painter, the poet gives us the liveliest image of succession with the feeling of simultaneousness."[30] The comment is aesthetically sophisticated because it does not equate the two arts. It leaves with poetry its temporal quality but adds to it the painterly quality of spatial simultaneousness. In commenting on the *sonetti pittorici* of Cassiani, Minzoni, and Zappi—poems of the eighteenth century in which every word is "a sure stroke of the pencil"—Croce disputes Lessing's view that poetry requires temporal sequence and painting, spatial coexistence. What happens in reading a good poem—at least a *sonetto pittorico*—is essentially what happens in viewing a good painting: we begin by observing particulars, moving from detail to visual detail, and end by seeing the whole. We begin in "circumvision" and end in vision.[31]

Croce's and Coleridge's perceptions of stasis in poetry belong to later epochs, and it must be confessed that no English neoclassical critic developed the notion. Leonardo had adumbrated it, Continental aestheticians had insisted on it, and the practice of the English poets seems to indicate that they were aware of it. But in the absence of English commentary, we are forced to go abroad for a neoclassical formulation of the idea.

In the early eighteenth century the distinguished Italian neoclassical critic, Lodovico Antonio Muratori, analyzed a poetic effect that he called *viva dipintura* ("lively painting"). This he carefully distinguished from description, amplification, enumeration, all of which can be destructive of the beauty of this effect. *Viva dipintura* is a means poets use to bring fresh, natural, lifelike details into their poems. Muratori recognized that this was the ancient notion of *enargeia*, the achievement of which he considers a highly desirable poetic aim. Such effects have the dignity of being produced by "la prima operazione della fantasia," and they constitute one of the chief

[30] *Biographia litteraria* ("Everyman's Library" [London, 1906]), pp. 169, 171 (chap. xv).

[31] *La letteratura italiana del settecento* (Bari, Italy, 1949), p. 179.

graces of poetry. But if *viva dipintura* is not and cannot possibly be enumerative description, what is it? It is the economical use of revealing and relevant visual images that recall reality and suggest ideas. Poetry in such moments does resemble painting. But not because it overlays its design with ornamented speech as a painting lays colors on a design—the modern notion of what the pictorial meant to a neoclassic critic. It approaches the condition of good painting because selected details are presented in a united form that is intellectually cogent, emotionally effective, and at the same time essentially imagistic and visual.[32]

One value of Muratori's definition of *viva dipintura* is that it disabuses our minds of the unhappy notion, for which Lessing and others have been responsible, that the neoclassical picturesque is identical with enumerative description. If that were true, it would deserve to be treated with contempt. Although Keats, who said that mere description is "always bad," or Croce, who said it abounds in times of aridity or superficiality,[33] may have exaggerated, one can certainly understand their grievance. But that the neoclassical picturesque must be equated with that kind of description the best visual passages of the best neoclassical poets vigorously deny.

Illustrations of the neoclassical picturesque in Part II all come from the century that followed the Restoration. But examples may be found outside the Augustan age. Keats, who in the "Ode on the Grecian Urn" has provided the classical example of iconic verse, has in the second stanza of the "Ode to Autumn" embodied the essential qualities of the neoclassic picturesque.

[32] *Della perfetta poesia italiana* (2 vols.; Venice, 1770), I, 104, 105, 106, 110, 113–20, 123. The first edition appeared in 1706. To illustrate *viva dipintura* Muratori uses a scene from Martelli. A blind shepherd in Arcadia was asked by someone who did not know he was blind why he was sad in so lovely a country. He replied, " 'If you wish to know why I weep, look way up there. That is my hut.' The blind man pointed with his finger, but pointed in exactly the opposite direction." The scene is strikingly Wordsworthian. Muratori was known in England, but his influence has never been fully studied or his criticism rigorously analyzed in English. But see J. G. Robertson, *Studies in the Genesis of Romantic Theory in the Eighteenth Century* (Cambridge, 1923), pp. 67–95. Muratori was elected to the English Royal Society on the motion of Newton (see Giulio Bertoni, "Muratori e Newton" in *Spunti: Scorci e commenti* [Geneva, 1928]). For a refutation of Robertson's view that Muratori's criticism was "pre-romantic" see Victor M. Hamm, "Antonio Conti and English Aesthetics," *Comparative Literature*, VIII (Winter, 1956), 12–27.

[33] *La critica e la storia delle arti figurative* (Bari, Italy, 1946), pp. 242–43.

Who hath not seen thee oft amid thy store?
Sometimes whoever seeks abroad may find
Thee sitting careless on a granary floor,
Thy hair soft-lifted by the winnowing wind;
Or on a half-reap'd furrow sound asleep,
Drows'd with the fume of poppies, while thy hook
Spares the next swath and all its twined flowers:
And sometimes like a gleaner thou dost keep
Steady thy laden head across a brook;
Or by a cyder-press, with patient look,
Thou watchest the last oozings hours by hours.[34]

These lines are not without motion: Autumn's hair is "soft-lifted by the winnowing wind"; she slowly crosses a brook; and from the cider press the "last oozings" drop hour after patient hour. But these extremely delicate and slight movements do not disturb the plasticity of Autumn's *picturesque* poses. She is *seen*, she *sits* on the granary floor, she *sleeps*, she *watches* with patient observation. Such a poem is picturesque. The art of the poet resembles the art of the painter.

THE NEOCLASSICAL PANTHEON

We have suggested in earlier chapters that pictorial poetry can conceivably be nourished by antecedent literature alone. This may have been true of other epochs but not of the eighteenth century. The neoclassical image often resembled particular paintings.

The English poet of the eighteenth century carried about in his head what Malraux has called a *musée imaginaire*, composed of recollections of some of the leading masterpieces of European art. The English poet of no previous period had attained a similar sophistication in the graphic arts. There is some point to Shaftesbury's remark that the invention of prints was to English culture during the eighteenth century what the invention of printing had been earlier to the entire Republic of Letters.[35]

English taste from Dryden to Gray rested on the firm and uncomplicated acceptance of the Italian Renaissance as one of the four or five greatest ages in the history of mankind. The fact that the

---

[34] Reuben A. Brower's sensitive comment on Keats's "Autumn" made me see its relevance to my subject (*The Fields of Light* [New York, 1951], pp. 38–40).

[35] Cited in Isabel W. U. Chase, *Horace Walpole: Gardenist* (Princeton, N.J., 1943), p. 101.

Renaissance was an age of triumphal achievement by painters gave to painting a prestige in England that it had previously lacked but was now to enjoy abundantly in its relations with poetry. The Renaissance was also an example to posterity not so much of the triumph of a single art as of the fruitful intercourse and collaboration of all the arts, which, now awakened from their Gothic sleep, mutually stimulated one another. Such a reading of cultural history as this was characteristic of the major and minor poets of the period and of the leading critics and aestheticians, including Abbé du Bos, who called the Renaissance a "prodigy."[36] The Age of Anne sometimes flattered its own complacency by considering itself the direct inheritor of the intellectual and artistic splendors of Florence and Rome.

Of the painters of the high Renaissance Raphael commanded the greatest esteem. He was accorded almost universal adulation. The reputation of Michelangelo had not as yet been firmly established; for, although certain of his pieces were believed unsurpassed and some critics anticipated Reynolds in believing him the greatest of all artists, opinion was by no means unanimous. Michelangelo's taste was not considered impeccable: he often deserted the natural for the grotesque; his manner was strained; his realism, though skilful, was crude; and he was guilty of floridity and pomposity. Michelangelo's day was to come with the triumph in England of the Longinian sublime.[37]

The standard taste accepted only the masters of the high Renaissance; those of the early fifteenth century, if noticed at all, were usually considered the historical forerunners of the truly great. Leonardo was of course admired, but not chiefly as a painter. Because his writings were known and read in English translation and because the English had come to know something of the universality of his culture, he was considered a "most singular instance of an universal genius."[38] The English had an especial fondness for the

[36] *Op. cit.* (n. 26), II, 131. See Pope *Essay on Criticism*, Part III, ll. 138–45; Joseph Warton, *An Essay on the Genius and Writings of Pope* (London, 1806), I, 181–82; Walter Harte, "An Essay on Painting" in *Poems on Several Occasions* (London, 1727), pp. 3–39.

[37] See Giorgio Melchiori, *Michelangelo nel settecento inglese* (Rome, 1950).

[38] *Spectator*, No. 554, written by John Hughes. Except for direct quotations and other special matters, I shall not annotate all the information and opinions expressed here. My conclusions are based on my reading of De Piles, Félibien, Dufres-

Venetians, for Titian first and then Veronese and Tintoretto. Exact evaluation is of course impossible, but one feels that this school was rated higher by the English than by their French instructors. One can almost always count on a literary Englishman's admiration of Titian, although Tintoretto was occasionally criticized for the obscurity and complications of his allegory and the unnaturalness and strain displayed by some of his forms. What especially appealed to the English poet and connoisseur was that Titian and the Venetians had supremely achieved what criticism had taught him to look for in art: a realistic but at the same time vivacious rendition of reality—its colors, its motions, its sensuous allure.

Yet it is Raphael who won the highest acclaim.[39] This must in part be owing to his unchallenged position in French criticism as the fountainhead of all modern excellence; the English derived both theory and taste in large measure from the French. How much the English exaltation of Raphael was the result of genuine appreciation one cannot say with any degree of certainty. One suspects that some of it was derivative. At least this is true: in spite of the fact that lip service to his greatness was universally paid, there seems very little direct relation between his paintings and English literary production. Pope's, Collins', and Gray's vision now and then suggests Raphael's, but his direct influence upon poetry was much less than that of painters not rated so high. This may not necessarily mean that the adulation was purely conventional. It may mean merely that Raphael's art was not in itself easily available to literature. Ideal in its forms, regular in its harmonies, and somewhat remote in theme and style from someone living almost two centuries later, it provided the poet very few handles to grasp. The correspondences of his art with literature, if they exist to any significant extent, would have to to be stated in unspecific terms. Raphael's values did coincide with neoclassic literary values. But they were mediated to poetry not so

---

noy, Du Bos, Richardson, Batteux, Spence, the Wartons, James Harris, Hildebrand Jacob, Reynolds, and others. See also *Spectator*, Nos. 166, 226, 229, 244, 265, 292, 407; *Tatler*, No. 156.

[39] Joseph Warton says that the Vatican frescoes display the "beauty and sublimity of [Raphael's] genius"; we behold there "the first of his works that are worthy the great name he at present so deservedly possesses" (*op. cit.* [n. 36], I, 101). This is only one of hundreds of similar comments.

often by the master himself as by such Raphaelesque painters as Correggio, Giulio Romano, and Guido Reni.[40]

The well-known "Balance des Peintres," which a contemporary scholar has called "that regrettable blemish on the excellent record of Roger de Piles,"[41] ranks Raphael as the greatest of the painters, giving him not a perfect score but the highest as yet achieved. The same score is achieved by only one other painter, Rubens.[42] Rubens' high position leads us directly into the next major characteristic of the taste of English literary men: along with admiration for the Renaissance painters there existed an almost equally great admiration for the masters of the baroque and of seventeenth-century eclecticism.

The masters of the seventeenth century may have been much closer to the neoclassical writer than the esteemed masters of the high Renaissance. The English poet is more likely to be directly indebted to Domenichino, the Carracci, Guido Reni, and Nicolas Poussin than he is to Raphael, Titian, Veronese, and even Giulio Romano. This orientation of eighteenth-century taste is one of its most important features and deserves brief analysis.

English neoclassical culture was much more than a pale, silvery Renaissance created by respectable French influence in mild, gentlemanly reaction to seventeenth-century expression. It was, as we have seen, positively oriented to the Italian Renaissance, but in practical manifestation there were then, as there always are, com-

[40] One evidence that eighteenth-century taste considered these four painters closely similar is that poets and critics apply the same epithets to all of them indiscriminately. Thus, for example, Pope refers to Guido's "air" ("Epistle to Jervas," l. 36), and Walter Harte, *op. cit.* (n. 36), refers to Raphael's "air divine." Grace was usually associated with Correggio but also with Guido and Raphael (see Thomas Morrison, "A Pindarick Ode on Painting [1767]," ll. 11–12 [Augustan Reprint Society Publication No. 37 (Los Angeles, 1952)]).

[41] Denis Mahon, *Studies in Seicento Art and Theory* (London, 1947), p. 227, n. 84. For the "Balance" itself see the English translation of De Piles entitled *Principles of Painting* (London, 1743), pp. 297–300. See also John Steegman, "The 'Balance des Peintres,' " *Art Quarterly,* XVII (Autumn, 1954), 255–61. De Piles' "Balance" was widely discussed in the eighteenth century. "Musiphron" wrote a poem, "Ballance of Poets," in Dodsley's *Museum,* Dec. 6, 1746.

[42] Each received a score of 65, which is reached by adding the numerical rating in each of the four categories of excellence: composition, design, coloring, and expression. Raphael's scores in each category, in the order given, were: 17, 18, 12, 18; Rubens', 18, 13, 17, 17. The perfect score in each category was 20.

plicating elements. It will not do to quote the late eighteenth-century Milizia,[43] who defined *barocco* as the superlative of the bizarre, the excess of the ridiculous, and assume that this manifestation of a later neoclassicism in the visual arts corresponded to the view of the seventeenth century held by the English Augustans of an earlier generation. The Augustans did, it is true, revolt against the excesses of metaphysical wit in literature and of emblematic allegory in art. Rubens is sometimes criticized for being gross and unrefined and for mixing the real and the fanciful, the obvious and the obscure. English taste would not have rated him as high as that determined *Rubéniste*, De Piles, had done in his "Balance des Peintres." Nevertheless, English poets of the Enlightenment remained under strong seventeenth-century influence, chiefly emanating from the so-called eclectics of Bologna and their French followers, whose special contribution was to fuse high Renaissance classicism with those expressive energies we have come to call "baroque."

That very combination of values links the Bologna of the Carracci and the London of Dryden and Pope. Even while the classicism of Inigo Jones prevailed and the procession of classical and Palladian pillars began that was to extend through the eighteenth and into the nineteenth century, Grinling Gibbons carved his baroque choir stalls in St. Paul's, and Vanbrugh, the "English Michelangelo," the British Bernini, created his architectural movements in stone. Similarly, the poets themselves revealed the presence of the same antithetical tendencies. The classically oriented Dryden wrote odes that are Rubensian in their visual imagery; Pope, who admired Raphael as the prince of painters, "quoted" Domenichino and was often reminiscent of Annibale Carracci; Thomson, an admirer of the Renaissance, used Guido more often than Raphael; and Gray placed what he borrowed from Raphael and Parmigianino in wild nature and heroic story.

I am oversimplifying the contrast between the high Renaissance and the Italian masters of the seventeenth century in order to call attention to a significant but frequently neglected characteristic of eighteenth-century culture. I do, however, wish to make the tentative suggestion that the conflict of value, which almost every student of English neoclassicism has observed and which is usually described

[43] See above, n. 14.

as a tension between classic and preromantic, Horace and Longinus, French intellectuality and English emotion, may be better understood if we look back to the seventeenth century rather than forward to the nineteenth or all the way back to Rome and Greece. If we do that, we observe that this dichotomy was already present in seventeenth-century graphic art. Nicolas Poussin had both his classic and baroque sides, as did his masters, the Carracci. Of this antithesis within the seventeenth century itself the eighteenth seems to have been somewhat aware. Joseph Warton, writing as a literary critic and commenting on Pope, could find correspondences in seventeenth-century painting for the central critical antithesis of his own age: he seems to feel that the honorific beautiful-sublime contrast had been anticipated in the "rivalship and contention" of the graceful Guido and the noble Domenichino.[44]

There is perhaps nothing about the eighteenth-century English poet's devotion to seventeenth-century artists that baffles the modern man more than the hold of Guido Reni on the English imagination. That fascination can scarcely be exaggerated. The young but already learned and fastidious traveler Thomas Gray reflects the typical attitude when he fills his journal with such exclamations as these about the paintings of Guido: "The most lovely and Guidesco imaginable"; "in none of them all [the Raphaels and Titians of the Borghese Gallery] [is] that heavenly grace and beauty that Guido gave"; "the heads are exceedingly lovely"; "so angelical a beauty . . . as this master could only imagine"; "a divine Guido."[45] These very phrases, reserved at other times for Raphael alone,[46] are here applied to a painter who, until very recently,[47] seemed to modern taste to be meretricious in his emotions, hedonistic and sensual in his idealism—he created the *madonna voluttà!*[48]—and impossibly superficial and sweet in his transformation of tragic feeling to melting languor. But to the eighteenth century this artist represented a creative fusion of the ideal beauty of antique sculpture, the viva-

---

[44] *Op. cit.* (n. 36), I, 83–84.

[45] *Works of Gray*, ed. John Mitford (London, 1836), IV, 228, 231, 242.

[46] See above, n. 40.

[47] See above, p. xxi.

[48] Vincenzo Costantini, *Guido Reni* (Milan, 1928), p. 23.

cious and alluring naturalism of the Renaissance, and the emotional power of the baroque—at least in its less violent and less mystical manifestations.

The taste in painting shared by Dryden, Pope, Thomson, their contemporaries, and their immediate followers was indebted to travel (the tours of Addison, Thomson, and Gray are of considerable imtance);[49] to private collections (Prior, Burke, and Thomson had collections that contribute to our knowledge of their own taste and that of their age);[50] and to the widely diffused treatises on the fine arts, most of which were intended not to train the expert but, in the words of one of them, the influential André Félibien, "pour mieux donner connoissance de la Peinture aux Gens de Lettre."[51] In these ways was knowledge of painting spread abroad. But not alone mere knowledge: these treatises tirelessly supported the belief that the arts of poetry and painting were intimately related and ceaselessly propagated the doctrine of *ut pictura poesis*. It was not only young gentlemen or idle ladies who became connoisseurs; the poets themselves traveled, read treatises on the fine arts, collected prints, painted canvases, and went to school to contemporary painters, whom they frequently numbered among their closest friends. Thus the poets themselves participated fully in the connoisseurship and artistic sophistication of the times. All the roads, even those traveled by the poets, led to Rome—and Bologna.[52]

The pantheon not only supported the doctrine of *ut pictura poesis* and emphasized the orientation to the Renaissance and Roman

[49] William Edward Mead, *The Grand Tour in the Eighteenth Century* (Boston, 1914); Paul Franklin Kirby, *The Grand Tour in Italy (1700–1800)* (New York, 1952).

[50] Carl B. Cone, "Edmund Burke's Art Collection," *Art Bulletin*, XXIX (June, 1947), 126–31. H. Bunker Wright and Henry C. Montgomery, "The Art Collection of a Virtuoso [Prior] in Eighteenth Century England," *Art Bulletin*, XXVII (1945), 195–204. See below, pp. 244–45.

[51] *Entretiens sur les vies et sur les ouvrages des plus excellens peintres anciens et modernes* (Trévoux, France, 1725), I, 33. For a list of the Continental treatises on art most widely read in the eighteenth century see *Works of Jonathan Richardson* (London, 1792), p. 207.

[52] Reynolds, whose discourses reveal the same taste we have been describing, said: "Thus the Roman and Bolognian schools are reasonably preferred to the Venetian, Flemish, or Dutch schools, as they address themselves to our best and noblest faculties" (Discourse VII).

antiquity that characterized the period. It also supported those critical, philosophical, and aesthetic tendencies we have discussed in this and the preceding chapter in defining eighteenth-century naturalism and idealism. For Titian, Veronese, and the seventeenth-century landscapists displayed the values of *enargeia* in their gorgeously sensuous naturalism. And Raphael, Guido, Nicolas Poussin, and Annibale Carracci often exemplified that statuesque idealization so characteristic of the stylized imagery of neoclassical verse. To an extent that must surely have been greater than ever before in England the neoclassical eighteenth century fused the old critical tradition of *ut pictura poesis* and the even older tradition of iconic verse with impulses from the living art of Renaissance and post-Renaissance Europe. English neoclassical poetry takes its place with Alexandrian, Ovidian, and Renaissance poetry in the tradition of classical pictorialism—a pictorialism that is, however, not completely untouched by the version of the pictorial that we found present in the seventeenth century.

Perhaps the chief reason that the pictorial tradition described in these pages won the esteem of Englishmen of taste during the eighteenth century lay in the fact that it embodied the qualities of politeness and urbanity—of grace, to use a term very popular in neoclassical criticism. Raphael was himself regarded as a child of the Graces, who in both art and life expressed a *douceur, politesse,* and *civilité*[53] that made him a civilized being and a civilizing force. And Correggio, never since his own day so fervently admired as during the English eighteenth century, was the supreme embodiment of delicacy and grace. No one who has seen the original oils of this Parmesan master can fail to understand what the eighteenth century saw in him or why they called it "grace." No reproduction can do justice to the subtle plastic rhythm and the exquisite chromatic and formal motion that one sees in the "Madonna di S. Girolamo," the "Madonna della Scodella," and the "Deposition" at Parma or in the "Holy Family" and the "Repose on the Flight to Egypt" in Florence —to their gently suggestive "motion" of attitude, of curved limb, of flowing drapery; to their subtle alternations of gentle color and soft light (see Plate III). Correggio may not often have expressed tragic emotion or intellectual profundity. But he did express with supreme

[53] Félibien, *op. cit.* (n. 51), I, 291.

skill the pleasing grace of elegant motion that makes him peculiarly available to the literary mind. The eighteenth century owes an impressive debt to the art of Correggio, whose influence appears in the serpentine lines of both baroque and rococo, the S-curves and ogee arches of decorated interiors, the fluttering delicacy of putti and amoretti on canvases and of sylphs and gnomes in poems.[54] His work may justly be selected as an embodiment of those pictorial values most cherished by an English neoclassical poet.

[54] For examples of English admiration for Correggio see Hildebrand Jacob, *Works* (London, 1735), p. 391; Reynolds, Discourse IV; Hazlitt, *op. cit.* (n. 18), XX, 300.

PART TWO

The Neoclassical Poets

CHAPTER VII

John Dryden

In this and the ensuing chapters we shall study intensively the pictorial imagery of the leading English neoclassical poets. We shall consider the poet's use of the analogy between painting and poetry, his knowledge of *ut pictura poesis* in criticism and of iconic poetry, and the relations of his imagery to the paintings he knew and liked and to the pictorialist traditions available to him.

THE PICTORIALIST TRADITION

Dryden was an interested and reasonably well-informed student of painting. He lived in an age that brought to a higher level than ever before in England a knowledge and love of painting, and he associated, on terms of intimacy, with its leading practitioners. What he did not acquire by systematic study, of which there may have been relatively little, he managed to learn through personal conversation. As a student of the classics, he knew what antiquity had said about painting and its relations to poetry. He quoted Philostratus the Elder, whom he seems to have considered the Aristotle of the art of painting.[1] Understanding Italian, he may have known the literary works of Leonardo and Vasari at first hand. He had certainly read Bellori, from whom he translated a long passage; he was in contact with the art criticism of French classicism; and he was unquestionably influenced by the historical fact, discussed in our chapter on the seventeenth-century background, that a pantheon had been created in England. He assuredly had seen many original paintings, prints, and engravings. He mentions by name Raphael, Titian, Correggio, Michelangelo, Holbein, Rubens, and Van Dyck in his pages and

---

[1] *Works of Dryden*, ed. Walter Scott and George Saintsbury (London, 1892), XVII, 310 (hereafter in this chapter abbreviated *"Works"*; poetry references will be identified by title and in longer works by line).

singles out the "Last Supper" of Nicolas Poussin for enthusiastic mention and sympathetic, though brief, analysis.[2]

Perhaps the most important single document illustrating Dryden's relationship with the pictorialist tradition is his translation into English prose of Alphonse Dufresnoy's Latin poem "De arte graphica," which was composed in Rome in 1637, published posthumously in Paris in 1667, and introduced to the English public in the handsome edition of 1695. The translation was prefaced by Dryden's own "Parallel of Poetry and Painting" and was followed, in an appendix, by the notes of the influential Roger de Piles.[3] Dryden prepared the translation and wrote the Preface at the insistence of his painter friends and with the benefit of their assistance in defining technical terms. The document is therefore in part a product of the circle of Dryden's friends and of the ateliers of Restoration England. More important is the fact that the work brought to England knowledge of Italian art as interpreted by French criticism and established the basic pattern of influence from painting to poetry that was to prevail during the entire subsequent century.

Dufresnoy's poem embodies *ut pictura poesis* in a form more codified and doctrinaire than in earlier expressions. The English volume of 1695 bore on its title page the very phrase *ut pictura poesis erit*, punctuated in the manner of the early Renaissance;[4] and with the same phrase the poem itself begins. In his opening paragraph Dufresnoy quotes not only Horace but also the proverb of Simonides, bringing together the two most influential ancient texts on the relations of the arts. That fact in itself would be worth attention, but Dufresnoy interprets his texts in such a way as to go far beyond a mere general statement of affinity.

> Ut pictura poesis erit; similisque Poesi
> Sit pictura,

which, literally translated, reads: "As a picture, so a poem will be; likewise let a painting be similar to poetry."[5] The second clause,

[2] *Ibid.*, pp. 311–12, 290, 308.

[3] *Ibid.*, pp. 281–504.

[4] See above, pp. 59–60.

[5] *Works*, XVII, 342–43. Dryden's excessively free translation obscures the dogmatism of the original: "Painting and Poesy are two sisters, which are so alike in all things, that they mutually lend to each other, both their name and office."

which urges painting to resemble poetry, makes it clear that Dufresnoy interpreted the first clause (the words of Horace which, as we have seen, were extremely casual) to mean that poetry too should resemble painting. Dufresnoy brings to a climax the dogmatic intensification of Horace's meaning that had begun during the Italian Renaissance.

Dryden's association with Dufresnoy must have been an example of considerable importance. We know that it weighed heavily with Pope,[6] and it is a fair assumption that Dryden is in part responsible for the fact that Dufresnoy became popular during the Restoration and remained so for at least a hundred years. Knowledge and appreciation of Dufresnoy's poem became signs betraying the presence of pictorialist theory in eighteenth-century England, and the curve of Dufresnoy's popularity corresponded to the popularity of the views his opening lines express. It is quite remarkable how much attention the English paid the French critic. Dryden was only the first to translate his poem. Defoe also gave it English dress in 1720; Wright, in 1728; James Wells, in 1765, with a biography by Dr. Thomas Birch; and William Mason, in 1783, with notes by Joshua Reynolds. In addition to these translations and annotations, Shaftesbury, Pope, Gray, and Dr. Johnson admired the poem and were considerably concerned with it. Johnson, for example, used it frequently in illustrating definitions of the terms of painting in his dictionary.[7]

Dufresnoy was a cultivated amateur who had been a painter and had seen at first hand the art that aroused his enthusiasm. It was no handicap with his English audience, who had always treated Titian as a great favorite, that the French critic was an admirer of the Venetian school or that in the famous French academic quarrel between form and color he was on the side of color. In the first English version of Dufresnoy's poem the notes of Roger de Piles that were published with it brought to the English public the views of an art critic who, like Dufresnoy himself, was a friend of Mignard and therefore the enemy of Le Brun, an art critic who had some reserva-

---

[6] See below, p. 211.

[7] Władyslaw Folkierski, "*Ut pictura poesis* ou l'étrange fortune du *De arte graphica* de Du Fresnoy en Angleterre," *Revue de littérature comparée*, XXVII (October–December, 1953), 385–402; John W. Draper, *William Mason* (New York, 1924), pp. 92, 308–9; William K. Wimsatt, "Samuel Johnson and Dryden's *Du Fresnoy*," *Studies in Philology*, XLVIII (January, 1951), 26–39.

tions about the classical austerities of Nicolas Poussin and who, as a *Rubéniste*, tended to interpret the Renaissance in terms of color and expression rather than form and line. Dufresnoy, never a member of the French Academy, was classical without being "academic"; his spirit, although committed to the accepted tradition of the plastic arts, was nevertheless somewhat freer than that of French artistic officialdom. "De arte graphica" stood in the tradition of Horace, Vida, and Boileau, and its seed fell on receptive soil in neoclassical England. At the same time it was not excessively Gallic and austere and it made important concessions to the heart and the fancy, to freedom and spontaneity.[8]

This career in England Dryden helped to launch in 1695 by his translation and by his Preface, the "Parallel of Poetry and Painting." The "Parallel" is not, in its totality, a distinguished document. Its central points are made without the glow of conviction that usually characterized Dryden at his honest and perceptive best. His excessive reliance on quotation seems to indicate that the ideas of French and Italian criticism he felt called on to express were not fully his own. That derivative quality is especially notable in the close analogies he somewhat mechanically draws between the various kinds of painting and the various kinds of poetry; between the various parts of painting (invention, disposition, design, color) and the various parts of poetry. He gives dogmatic and not very persuasive expression to an idea only implicit in the writing of Horace and Scaliger, that expression in poetry (i.e., diction, versification, metaphor, and simile) is exactly parallel to color in painting.[9] The process involved in both applying color and creating verbal expression is considered similar. Expression in poetry is applied, like a pigment on design, after fable, moral, and plot have been constructed.

Much more important than these artificial correspondences is the fact that Dryden draws the general analogy between the arts, an analogy present in his poetry and prose from as early as 1658 to his last work. He used it as a fruitful source of comparison in his criticism and of metaphor and simile in his poetry and drama.[10] The compari-

[8] Louis Hourticq, *De Poussin à Watteau* (Paris, 1921), pp. 51, 82–83; William Guild Howard, "*Ut pictura poesis*," *Publications of the Modern Language Association*, N.S., XVII (1909), 92–112.

[9] *Works*, XVII, 329, where Horace's phrase *operum colores* is quoted.

[10] See, e.g., "Heroic Stanzas to Cromwell" (1658), ll. 59–60, 94–96; "Astraea

sons from painting came naturally and easily to Dryden, revealing a degree of intimacy and sympathy with the sister art that we do not find in any important poet before him.

The passages in which the analogy between the arts is drawn admittedly contain much that is purely conventional. When Dryden praises the naturalness of one of Kneller's female portraits, which "wants but words to speak her thoughts," and when he says that the painter of the decorations in the imaginary temple of Diana drew them with "such command / That Nature snatch'd the pencil from his hand," he is palely echoing a theme which had become stale even in antiquity.[11] But these echoes of the pictorialist tradition do show that it is operative. And alongside such passages as these there are others proving that traditional pictorialism has been energized by an able and interested mind.

Dryden accepted the view, which Lovelace had forcefully expressed in the earlier days of Lely, that painting was a humanistic art capable of expressing in natural symbols moral and psychological truth. To that doctrine of expression, important in separating the natural neoclassical symbol from the hieroglyphic emblem of the seventeenth century, Dryden now gave clarity of statement and the sanction of his prestige. He did rank painting below music and poetry, which he believed closer to the mind and soul and further removed from purely manual skill. "Yet," he added, "let it allwayes be acknowledgd, that painting and Statuary can express both our actions & our passions: that if they neither speake nor move, they seem to do both: and if they impose on the eye, yet they deceive nobly: when they make shadows pass for substances, and even animate the brass & marble."[12] Of Kneller's portraits he said, "Thy pic-

---

Redux" (1660), ll. 125–28; "Prologue to the University of Oxford" (1676), ll. 21–24; "Preface to the Fables." Mark Van Doren says that Dryden has drawn the parallel between painting and poetry no fewer than twenty times (*John Dryden* [3d ed.; New York, 1946], p. 52).

[11] "To Sir Godfrey Kneller" (1694), l. 10; "Palamon and Arcite," II, 655–56 (Dryden's additions, for which there is no warrant in Chaucer).

[12] These words come from the manuscript dedication to the music of Purcell's opera, the *Prophetesse*. The dedication was written by Dryden but published as Purcell's in 1691 along with the opera. The words quoted were deleted before publication. See Roswell G. Ham, "Dryden's Dedication for *The Music of the Prophetesse*, 1691," *Publications of the Modern Language Association*, L (December, 1935), 1070–71.

tures think, and we divine their thoughts" (l. 72), language that echoes Lovelace's witty tribute to Lely.

To have accepted Lovelace's notion of expression, which was itself intended to explain the power of Lely's realistic canvases, was quite understandable in the friend of Lely's successor, Godfrey Kneller, noted for his frank, direct manner as a portraitist. But beyond this, the father of English neoclassicism has spoken in favor of the visual symbol that remains faithful to the lineaments of physical reality even while it is illuminated by thought and emotion.

Dryden's unhesitating theoretical acceptance of the neoclassical image should not be allowed to obscure the complexity—even the ambivalence—of his poetic practice. For his poetic imagery is often highly reminiscent of the color, light, and chiaroscuro of baroque art, which blurred boundaries, created formally disrupting motion, and suggested the ineffable. The light of reason "dies" and "dissolves in supernatural light";[13] an aurora borealis appears during the Battle of Sedgemoor to "Gild the brown horror, and dispel the night";[14] and the light of God destroys natural light and creates mystical darkness:

> Thy throne is darkness in th' abyss of light
> A blaze of glory that forbids the sight.[15]

Such passages as these represent a counterclassical tendency of major proportions in Dryden's verse—a tendency that will be explored in the concluding section of this chapter. The leading poet of the Restoration and the father of English neoclassicism was also a younger contemporary of Milton and Marvell.

No account of Dryden can be satisfactory that does not consider both the classical-Renaissance and the Counter Reformation–baroque[16] in his poetic genius. These antithetical elements existed in his mind and art from the beginning. Which one predominated depended, as we shall presently see, on the genre of poetry he was writing and also on the events of his outer and the convictions of his inner life.

DESCRIPTION AND SATIRE

Dryden, unlike many poets of the Renaissance, was not a descriptive poet, painting sensuous details out to the corner of his verbal

---

[13] *Religio laici*, ll. 11, 12.

[14] "Hind and the Panther," Part II, l. 1231.

[15] *Ibid.*, Part I, ll. 66–67.

[16] See below, n. 44.

canvas. He preferred creating the *viva dipintura* of Muratori's criticism, and that, as we have seen, excluded enumerative and detailed description. His metaphors and similes are often pictorial, his symbols resemble the emblem and Ripa's *imagines*, the position of his characters often suggest allegory or "history." But he is seldom descriptive.

The way to test this generalization is to examine a poem that he intended to be in part descriptive, the "Annus mirabilis" published in 1667. This work, subtitled "An Historical Poem," contains an account of the war with Holland and "describes the fire of London." It is certainly true that Dryden intended more than description, and it seems plausible that his aim was to celebrate the city's rise through trials to victorious strength. He wished in this manner to challenge the Puritans' reading of recent history by interpreting the disastrous events not as a judgment for sin but as a visitation of suffering sent to inspire civil and Christian virtue.[17] The fires of London were not those of hell but of the fiery furnace in the Book of Daniel. Nevertheless, the fact remains that subsidiary to such an aim but as a means of realizing it was the desire to make the theme graphic and vivid. In order to make us understand, Dryden wanted first to make us see.

This aim is supported not only by the subtitle but also by Dryden's prefatory "account of the poem." In it he defines wit as "the delightful imaging of persons, actions, passions, or things," a definition not intended to be valid for all times and circumstances but surely for this type of poem. Dryden's aim is not to create epigram, conceit, antithesis, or argument or to express moral sentence. It is, rather, to achieve "some lively and apt description, dress'd in such colours of speech that it sets before your eyes the absent object as perfectly and more delightfully than nature." In other words, Dryden wanted to achieve the aesthetic value of classical *enargeia* and produce an image of reality. Dr. Johnson was fully justified in evaluating "Annus mirabilis" as a descriptive piece.

But judged by those standards, how well does it come off? Johnson said that Dryden "affords more sentiment than description, and does not so much impress scenes upon the fancy, as deduce consequences and make comparisons."[18] The justice of the comment is in-

[17] Edward N. Hooker, "The Purpose of Dryden's 'Annus Mirabilis,' " *Huntington Library Quarterly*, X (1946), 49–67.

[18] "Life of Dryden," *Works of Samuel Johnson* (Oxford, 1825), VII, 317.

escapable. Again and again we see in Dryden a tendency to invoke classical pictorialist and iconic ideas in his criticism but in his practice to look elsewhere. Instead of vividly drawn scenes, Dryden has given us metaphysical conceits and visual images that do not come directly from nature but from the canvases of baroque artists and emblematists. Instead of describing the fleet, Dryden introduces the decorative motifs of a pompous history piece:

> To see this fleet upon the ocean move
> Angels drew wide the curtains of the skies.

In one vignette the moon shines clear on the calm scene and silvers the deck, chiefly, we judge from the emphasis and arrangement, to illuminate the spot where "our careful general stood" deep in heroic thought. Elsewhere Neptune appears with a trident, Father Thames raises his head from his oozy bed, and a cherub with a flaming sword drives the fire away from the naval magazines.[19]

Dryden makes it clear from his prefatory account of "Annus mirabilis" that he attempted to follow classical example. The same desire underlay his satires, and we are therefore justified in inquiring to what extent these poems embody the main features of classical pictorialism. We should also observe that in drawing the analogy between painting and satire, Dryden followed the example of Marvell and other seventeenth-century satirists, who had used this parallel frequently enough to make it a convention.[20]

The motto of "Absalom and Achitophel" is inadvertently significant. The sentence "Si propius stes, / Te capiat magis" immediately follows the famous words *ut pictura poesis* in the *Ars poetica* and begins Horace's famous comparison of painting and poetry. The motto also suggests strongly that one is to view this poem as one views a picture in a gallery. Dryden in the Preface invokes the comparison more directly: "The frame of [this poem] was cut out but for a picture to the waist, and if the draught be so far true, 'tis as much as I designed."

[19] Ll. 61–62, 393–96, 733–36, 925–28, 1081–82. It may have been quite easy for Dryden to adopt painterly rather than natural forms in treating a subject like this. Bussnello and Waller (see above, p. 119, n. 63) had most obviously suggested the art of painting in their poems on related themes. At this time naval painting was considered very important. See the comments on the career of Willem van de Velde in Ellis K. Waterhouse, *Painting in Britain: 1530 to 1790* (London, 1953), p. 111.

[20] See above, p. 121.

What does the analogy imply? Principally, what the motto suggests: that the poem, taken as a whole, should be viewed as a painting.[21] We have already seen that the pictorialist tradition contained implications for poetic form and that in antiquity there was created and in the seventeenth century there was further developed what we have called the picture-gallery type of structure, in which we move from scene to scene, tableau to tableau[22] (see Plate I). "Absalom and Achitophel" stands in precisely that tradition. Neither a narrative sequence of Aristotelian complication, development, and resolution nor an argument moving deductively from general thesis to exemplum or inductively from premise to conclusion, the poem is a *display* of personages whose mental and physical measure is being taken and who reveal their character in what they are seen to be and heard to say.

The massing of particulars on this crowded canvas is more dramatically conceived than the comments have so far revealed. It is not only that the eye and mind move from one individual to another. Opposing groups that include the individual figures are arrayed against each other and are portrayed in separate and contradictory motion: the downward motion of conspiracy, which could bring destruction to the whole fabric of society, and the ennobling and socially redemptive motion of loyal men looking upward to their divinely appointed ruler. Dryden has given us a "Last Judgment," or at least a "Judgment." He distributes reward and punishment. In Achitophel we see Satan and in David, Christ; and Christ stands over the people forgiving when he can, condemning when he must. Unlike Milton's epic, which he everywhere echoes, Dryden's is not a narrative with supporting visual particulars; it is a pageant with interpretative comment.

Dryden himself draws the analogy with painting only for the poem as a whole. But others before him had compared the individual satirical "characters" to portraits, a comparison that had already become conventional and that has persisted to our own day. But are these portraits in the seventeenth-century meaning? That is, are they, as both Lovelace and Dryden had conceived portraits, the expression of moral and intellectual qualities by means of physical

[21] I am not the first to make this suggestion. See Ian Jack, *Augustan Satire* (Oxford, 1952), p. 73, and Ruth Wallerstein, "To Madness Near Allied," *Huntington Library Quarterly*, VI (August, 1943), 448–49.

[22] See above, pp. 33, 105–6, 114, 117.

features and bodily postures? In general they are not. Dryden's shorter pieces do not suggest the limitations of visual art, even though the total structure of which they are a part often does. They are, rather, statements of great rhetorical force about the character of the victim. They may here and there be illuminated by an image, but they do not unfold an organic and consistent relationship to that image. They express intellectual and moral insights in striking phrases and in carefully chosen abstract words that obey the laws of persuasive logic. These condensed statements are intellectually, not visually, conceived biographies of the mind and soul. They resemble paintings only in the way in which they are inserted, like set descriptive passages, into the frame of the poem.

Some "portraits," like the highly effective one of Zimri, are entirely free of pictorial detail. That of Achitophel has only one paintable stroke, the reference to the rebel's pigmy body, which, however, is designed not to make us see the body but to make us respond to the fact that this body is warped because a powerful mind has worn it out.

There is an occasional use of visual detail. Shimei is presented with a vare of justice in his hand and a chain of gold about his neck, the emblems of his office that are appropriate to the kind of economic and sociological analysis that Dryden has here presented. Corah is compared to a serpent in order to debase him and to ridicule his illusion that he is the serpent that Moses lifted up in the wilderness for the healing of Israel. The repulsive Og, drunkenly reeling behind the linkboy through the streets of London, is viewed as a "goodly and great" ship sailing behind its bowsprit lantern. The midwife with her hand on Og's infant skull is a statue with an inscription: "Be thou dull." Of the "bristling Baptist boar," to turn to the "Hind and the Panther" for an illustration, all we see is the "white foam of sanctity"; but the Presbyterian wolf is presented in full pictorial detail, except that it is difficult to visualize "predestinating ears." Such visual details are effective. But they are occasional and seldom organic and organizing.

There is one notable exception: the opening lines of the "Medal." Dryden seized upon the fact that the supporters of Shaftesbury had struck a medal in honor of their hero, and he therefore devoted the first twenty-five lines of the poem exclusively to viewing this medal and its details. These lines comprise an iconic satirical poem distinguished by the skill with which the conventions of that genre have been accommodated to the purpose of invective. In expressing the conventional contest between art and nature—the hallmark of all iconic verse—Dryden attempts what has not been done before, unless the notion is implicit in Spenser's "Bower of Bliss": he makes the art object an idol.

> Never did art so well with nature strive
> Nor ever idol seem'd so much alive.

There is the usual contemplation of the material of the work:

> So like the man; so golden to the sight,
> So base within, so counterfeit and light.

The details of the medal are emblematically interpreted:

> One side is fill'd with title and with face;
> And, lest the king should want a regal place,
> On the reverse, a tow'r the town surveys;
> O'er which our mounting sun his beam displays.

Like ancient statue, urn, or monument and like the seventeenth-century *impresa* or device, this work has an inscription or a posy:

> The word, pronounc'd aloud by shrieval voice,
> *Laetamur*, which in Polish, is *rejoice*.

It had early become customary to praise the artist and describe the process of creation:

> Five days he sate for every cast and look;
> Four more than God to finish Adam took.
> But who can tell what essence angels are,
> Or how long Heav'n was making Lucifer.

Dryden uses the convention of considering the disparity between subject and material employed:

> O could the style that copied every grace,
> And plow'd such furrows for an eunuch face,
> Could it have form'd his ever-changing will,
> The various piece had tir'd the graver's skill!

For these lines Dryden had precedents in Ausonius and the satirical portraits that Marino included in his *Galeria*.[23] Dryden's adaptation of these precedents—of iconic conventions going back to Homer and of a few emblematic motifs peculiar to the seventeenth century—is moderately effective. He has realized satirical intention by inverting a form of which the traditional use had been panegyrical.

From our discussion of Dryden up to this point it is clear that pictorialism was part of his classical inheritance; there are unmistakable signs of it in the verse we have considered and in the criticism that attempted to justify it. But an obviously competing strain, derived from Milton and the seventeenth century, modifies the classic icon and image. Both these tendencies persisted through Dryden's entire career. We shall observe the culmination of the first in the drama we are now to consider and of the second in the great odes of Dryden's middle and late career.

IDEAL FORM IN "ALL FOR LOVE"

In the discussion of literary idealization in Part I the following points were made: (1) literary idealization is intimately related to statues and allegorical pictures; (2) it has immemorially existed in two varieties, (*a*) the Platonic-Christian, in which ideal form descends from on high and is mediated first through the mind in inspiration and (*b*) the Aristotelian-humanist of antiquity and the Renaissance, in which ideal form arises from below, from particular experience, and is mediated first through the senses. All these elements are present in Dryden's greatest play and in his relevant criticism.

The Platonic-Christian conception of idealization enters Dryden's pages most prominently in the long quotation in the "Parallel" from Bellori, who asserts that the Idea emanates from the divine Maker and then "descends upon the marble and the cloth, and becomes the original of those arts." Is Bellori's Neoplatonism adopted by Dryden? It seems not. Dryden concedes that the Italian is "a most ingenious author" and that "there is somewhat in the matter." But he objects to the pompous, smoky style and turns, with obvious relief, to Philostratus, the ancient pictorialist par excellence, whom he quotes

[23] See above, pp. 120–21.

in a passage that is completely free of Bellori's metaphysical trappings and that states the "plainer"—the word is Dryden's—views of classical generalization. It seems fair to assume, in view of the main tendency of Dryden's thought—though, it must be conceded, of only a portion of his poetic practice—that what the Englishman quarrels with in the Italian is not only the language but the idea. Dryden seems to accept the doctrine of ideal form but is made uncomfortable when it appears in the dress of Platonic or Plotinian metaphysics. He was too skeptical to see much of an analogy between the artistic process and the creation of the cosmos, between artistic and religious inspiration. A conception of ideal form he most certainly possessed; but he derived it, like Cicero, Seneca, and the Italian humanists, from the generalizing mind operating upon empirical reality. *La belle nature* results from methodizing nature into *la forma cogitata.*[24]

Such ideal nature Dryden did not find relevant to all literary genres. In comedy, burlesque, and satire the poet sought to portray life with its flecks and blemishes. But in the epic and tragedy he sought to produce ideal form that had corrected nature and was superior to reality.[25] If we wish to examine Dryden's ideal general nature, we must, since he wrote no epic, turn to *All for Love*, the work that he said he wrote for himself alone.[26]

In a subtle passage in the "Parallel of Poetry and Painting" Dryden compares this play to the *Oedipus*, to which he contributed only two acts. In the *Oedipus* he had improved upon nature, following Sophocles in drawing men as they ought to be. But in *All for Love*, the idealization, though present, was less extreme; it had "nothing of outrageous panegyrick." The passions of the hero and heroine

were their own, and such as were given them by history; only the deformities of them were cast into shadows, that they might be the objects of compassion: whereas if I had chosen a noon-day light for them, somewhat must have been discovered, which would rather have moved our hatred than our pity.[27]

We are not now interested in the exact degree of idealization present in this play. We are interested in the analogy with painting, here

[24] See above, pp. 14–16.
[25] *Works*, XVII, 302–8.
[26] *Ibid.*, p. 333.   [27] *Ibid.*, p. 327.

only implied by the metaphor of light and shade but elsewhere obviously drawn and clearly applied to the art of tragedy.

In fact, of the many correspondences that exist between poetry and painting, none is closer, Dryden believed, than that between a tragedy and a historical painting. Both share the problem of ennobling the form without destroying the resemblance to history. And a disciplined tragedy like *All for Love*, which attempts to respect the three dramatic unities, strives to attain the simultaneousness and instantaneousness of painting. The author of a tragedy and the painter of a historical scene both face the difficult task of imposing severe formal economy upon grand and heroic action. The parallel with painting is valid, Dryden conceded, also for the epic, but it is "more complete in tragedy." This is because "Tragedy and Picture are more narrowly circumscrib'd by the mechanic rules of time and place, than the epic poem." So smitten was Dryden with the closeness of this parallel that he gave extreme statement to the pictorialist ideal. Since economy is an artistic desideratum, "I must give the advantage of painting, even above tragedy, that what this last represents in the space of so many hours, the former shews us in one moment." Of Poussin's "Institution of the Blessed Sacrament" he said:

Here is but one indivisible point of time observed; but one action performed by so many persons in one room, and at the same table; yet the eye cannot comprehend at once the whole object, nor the mind follow it so fast; it is considered at leisure, and seen by intervals. Such are the subjects of noble pictures; and such are only to be undertaken by noble hands.[28]

Dryden has in this passage clearly stated the ideal of the neo-classical picturesque. That ideal, as we saw in chapter vi, exalted the "single moment" of painting and invited literary art to strive to achieve it. This notion of the close parallel between the tragic drama and historical painting, between pictorial economy and the rules of drama, did not, of course, begin or end with Dryden.[29]

[28] *Ibid.*, pp. 306–8. Dryden's comparison of economy in poetry to economy in painting is a version of the notion of the *difficulté vaincue* (see above, pp. 35, 53, 73). It was not natural for the drama to assume such disciplines, but it was desirable, since they could confer aesthetic benefit.

[29] Testelin, Dufresnoy, Boileau, Coypel, Webb, Jouin, and Jonathan Richardson all stressed the especial closeness of tragedy and painting and the relation of the unities to painting (see *Laokoön: Lessing, Herder, Goethe*, ed. William Guild Howard [New York, 1910], pp. lx ff.).

But he seems to have been greatly attracted by the neoclassical picturesque,[30] a fact that alerts us to the striking pictorial quality of *All for Love*, which arises in part from a stricter adherence to the dramatic unities than, as Dryden said in the Preface, is required for the English stage. This quality appears not absolutely but relatively. One must consider what a play can be, what other plays on this very theme have been—restlessly varied by changing scenes, warring characters, melodramatic actions, and innumerable personages—to appreciate how pictorially static Dryden's play actually is. The characters tend to be fixed in poses. Antony turns to the right; he turns to the left; he turns finally to death and Cleopatra. The actions may be significant, but they are extremely slight. The speeches of the characters resemble noble inscriptions or mottoes—an effect that Shakespeare achieves in his final death scene but that is present all through Dryden's play. The speeches in *All for Love* are often iconic. One character describes another as if he were a work of art and not a living being. Ventidius says of—and to— Antony:

> But you, ere love misled your wandering eyes,
> Were sure the chief and best of human race,
> Framed in the very pride and boast of nature;
> So perfect, that the gods, who formed you, wondered
> At their own skill, and cried—A lucky hit
> Has mended our design. Their envy hindered,
> Else you had been immortal, and a pattern,
> When Heaven would work for ostentation's sake
> To copy out again [Act I, Sc. 1].

The words "framed," "perfect," "skill," "hit," "design," "pattern," and "copy" all are signs that a graphic metaphor is operative, that Antony is being viewed as a work of ideal art. We attempted to demonstrate in our last chapter that the analogy with statuary

[30] Dryden states it elsewhere, in "To Sir Godfrey Kneller," thus: If you were not occupied with portraits, we should
> ". . . see your noble pencil trace
> Our unities of action time, and place;
> A whole compos'd of parts, and those the best,
> With ev'ry various character express'd;
> Heroes at large, and at a nearer view;
> Less, and at distance, an ignobler crew;
> While all the figures in one action join,
> As tending to complete the main design" (ll. 166–73).

was often present when a neoclassical poet sought to idealize his forms. The point is illustrated here.

It is so important in Dryden and in the neoclassical poetry that followed him that it must be more fully developed. In the "Parallel" Dryden sees a close correspondence between pictorial posture and epic description: "The posture of a poetic figure is . . . the description of [the] heroes in the performance of such or such an action. . . . " To illustrate this Dryden turns to Vergil, to the scene in the tenth book of the *Aeneid* in which Aeneas slays Lausus, who is defending his father, the Etruscan king Mezentius. Of this scene Dryden says:

> [Aeneas] considers Lausus rescuing his father at the hazard of his own life, as an image of himself, when he took Anchises on his shoulder, and bore him safe through the rage of the fire, and the opposition of his enemies; and therefore, *in the posture of a retiring man, who avoids the combat, he stretches out his arm in sign of peace, with his right foot drawn a little back, and his breast bending inward, more like an orator than a soldier.*[31]

The amazing fact about the portion of Dryden's comment that I have italicized is that Aeneas' elaborately described posture existed only in the mind of Dryden the critic: it is present neither in Vergil's original nor Dryden's own translation. The only gesture that could have suggested it is Aeneas' stretching forth his hand in pity to the youthful warrior after the death blow had been delivered. Dryden has responded to Vergil's hint by imaginatively carving the hero into a statue in the antique manner. Nothing could be more characteristic of the motion of the neoclassical mind than that. It is constantly freezing the motions of nature and of antecedent literary art into the picturesque.

Dryden himself did exactly that in his own verse-adaptations. In his version of the "Knight's Tale," which he entitled "Palamon and Arcite," he has elaborated upon Chaucer's description of the painting of Diana that hangs on the walls of her temple. Chaucer gave her only her silver bow and quiver and had her tread upon the crescent moon, her peculiar emblem. These details Dryden retains but dilates them into a fully developed iconic pose that resembles Correggio's and Rubens' famous Dianas, adding the details italicized in the following passage.

> The graceful goddess was array'd in green;
> About her feet were little beagles seen,

[31] *Works*, XVII, 318–19.

That watch'd with upward eyes the motions of their queen.
Her legs were buskin'd, and the left before
In act to shoot; a silver bow she bore,
And at her back a *painted* quiver wore.
She trod a wexing moon, that soon would wane,
And, drinking borrow'd light, be fill'd again.

[Book II, ll. 643–50]

What has happened to Chaucer is extremely revealing. Dryden has introduced metaphysical conceit and intellectual paraphrase. He has also added visual detail, stylized in a pictorial manner. The legs are buskined, and one of them, as in the imagined posture of Aeneas, is thrust forward in frozen action. The dogs look up to their queen and have something of the "air" of Guido's heads[32] (see Plate VIII, A, B). When we observe that exactly the same kind of ornamentation is added to Vergil and Chaucer by Pope and to Milton by Thomson and Collins, we must conclude that we here confront one of the dominant characteristics of neoclassical poetic expression.

It is not surprising, then, that it should be so prominent in Dryden's greatest play, the classically conceived *All for Love*. Some of its pictorial elements Dryden borrowed from his sources. The description of Cleopatra lying in her barge like "another sea-born Venus," surrounded by nymphs and fanned by boys who resemble cupids while the winds play about her face and lodge in the sails, is elaborately pictorial, but perhaps no more so than the magnificent passage in Shakespeare. In the final scenes, however, Dryden has intensified the pictorialism of his predecessors. In Plutarch, who liked pictorial effects even in prose history, the dead Cleopatra lies stretched out on a golden bed; Iras lies dead at her feet; Charmion, half-dead and about to fall, stands adjusting the queen's diadem. Samuel Daniel's setting is the same, and one of the details is worked into the lovely line: "And dying Charmion trimming of her head." In Shakespeare Charmion adjusts the crown which is awry; and when the first guard asks "Where is the queen?" Charmion replies: "Speak softly, wake her not," words reminiscent of Michelangelo's famous lines on his statue Night.[33] But Dryden's arrange-

---

[32] Of these lines Joseph Warton said perceptively: "The figure of the . . . goddess is a design fit for Guido to execute" (*An Essay on the Genius and Writings of Pope* [London, 1782], II, 15).

[33] See above, pp. 74–75.

ment, though obviously indebted to his literary predecessors, is even more pictorial. Antony, dead on one throne, is placed next to Cleopatra, who, though dead, sits erect on another. Charmion stands behind her dressing her hair, and Iras, already dead, is stretched out on the ground at her feet.[34]

"ALL FOR LOVE" AND THE "CHOICE OF HERCULES"

In placing *All for Love* alongside one of the most typical and famous paintings of the seventeenth century I do not wish to argue a conscious influence from canvas to play. Such influence is not at all unlikely or uncommon; it can be widely illustrated in the period we are studying. There is, however, no evidence for it in this instance; had it existed, it seems probable that Dryden would have said something about it in the Preface he wrote for the drama. But I do wish, in bringing *All for Love* and the "Choice of Hercules" together, to support what I have been arguing, that the play is an example of the neoclassical picturesque not only in certain of its details but in its total impression.

What was sometimes called the "Choice of Hercules" and at other times "Hercules at the Crossroads"[35] was a popular and influential representation of a story now almost forgotten. During the seventeenth and eighteenth centuries, however, this story was a kind of archetypal icon. It originated in antiquity, when Socrates allegedly used it to illustrate Hesiod's comment that the way of wickedness is easy and degrading and the way of virtue hard and ennobling.[36] While passing from boyhood to manhood, Hercules sat pondering in a quiet place in the forest where two ways met. He was approached by two women of great stature. The first was fair and tall, with modest eyes and a figure soberly clad in white. The second was soft and plump from high feeding, her face painted in an attempt to heighten its pink and white, and her dress

[34] These passages have been assembled by Bonamy Dobrée, *Restoration Tragedy* (Oxford, 1929), pp. 80–81.

[35] The fortunes of this theme during the Renaissance have been traced in two important studies: Erwin Panofsky, *Hercules am Scheidewege und andere antike Bildstoffe in der neueren Kunst* (Leipzig-Berlin, 1930); Theodor E. Mommsen, "Petrarch and the Story of the Choice of Hercules," *Journal of the Warburg and Courtauld Institutes*, XVI (July–December, 1953), 178–92.

[36] Xenophon *Memorabilia* ii. 1. 21–33.

disclosing most of her charms. She habitually looked to see whether anyone noticed her and stole glances at her own shadow. She told Hercules that she was called Happiness by her friends and Vice by her enemies, and she promised him all the joys of the flesh. The first woman, Virtue, summoned him to a high and noble road, but one that would cost him toil and effort. Choosing it, he would win renown as a hero and civilizer. There is no indication of which choice Hercules made, but his subsequent achievements witness that he chose the hard life of Virtue.

Of the long and varied fortunes of this legend we can here say little. Although told by Cicero and therefore known to the Middle Ages, it lay dormant through all the Christian centuries until Petrarch revived it, when it became one of the most popular themes of Renaissance Italy and Germany, giving to each of these countries a proverbial phrase—"Ercole al Bivio," "Hercules am Scheidewege." The legend underwent changes in emphasis and served various purposes at various historical moments. We shall discuss only a few of the leading seventeenth- and eighteenth-century uses of this subject in order to indicate how deeply it had penetrated into the baroque culture that Dryden drew upon and into the neoclassical culture that he helped to create.

Annibale Carracci was one of the most influential painters of the *Seicento*, partly because he was sponsored by Bellori as reviver of the noble art and as an idealistic counterinfluence to the vulgar naturalism of Caravaggio and partly because he understood a culture that wished to retain the splendors of the Renaissance but also to interpret them afresh. Besides that, Annibale was a painter of considerable power whom literary people found attractive. His version of the Hercules was one of the most famous paintings of the epoch; knowledge of it was widely diffused, not only through copying and engraving, but through the long and eloquent description and analysis of it given by Bellori in his biography of Annibale.[37]

[37] Bellori's reading of this painting is highly literary, dramatic, and psychological. He actually puts words in the mouth of Virtue (*Vite* [Pisa, 1821], 36–39). In our own day Carracci's painting has been called by Mahon "a veritable masterpiece" and by Venturi an *opera mancata* (Denis Mahon, "Eclecticism and the Carracci," *Journal of the Warburg and Courtauld Institutes*, XVI [July–December, 1953], 340). Luigi Lanzi wrote at the end of the eighteenth century: "To write the history of the Carracci is equivalent to writing the history of painting of the last two centuries" (cited by R. Wittkower, *The Drawings of the Carracci* [London, 1952], p. 9). Almost all the Eng-

On Carracci's canvas (Plate VII A), which in the seventeenth and eighteenth centuries was hung in the Farnese Palace in Rome, where it could be admired along with the same artist's famous ceiling and his other moral allegories, Hercules appears as a young giant, nude, beardless, a frown of indecision on his face. He stands in the center, almost equidistant from the two figures but slightly closer to Virtue, to whom he seems, though not decisively, to be inclining. Virtue faces the spectator, but her head is slightly turned toward Hercules. A modest creature, dressed in the robe and bearing the aegis of Athena, she points upward to a hill. By her side sits a bearded man, whose crown of laurel and open book reveal him to be an author who will celebrate Hercules' exploits if he chooses the proper path. To the right, her back to the spectator, stands the figure of sensuality, Voluptas, as she was usually called, clothed only in delicate and transparent stuff. She too looks at Hercules; her right arm, unlike that of Virtue, points downward. Two theatrical masks, an open songbook, and a musical instrument lie on the ground as the emblems of her blandishments.

Rubens also painted the theme (see Plate VII B and cf. Plate VI). On his canvas, which is now at the Uffizi Gallery in Florence, the three characters are bound closely together by strong and restless rhythms of line and light. Voluptas, a Rubensian Venus if there ever was one, is almost nude. Two winged *amori* and two maidens, one of whom has flowers in her hair, support her pleas. Virtue is Amazonian. Wearing a helmet and a breastplate, she is in every way soldierly and strong. Instead of the poet of Annibale's scene, Rubens has drawn Time as a winged being in descent; his presence symbolizes the future renown that will follow the choice of Virtue. The military nature of Virtue's cause is emphasized by a youth who holds a bridled horse ready to bear Hercules away to his arduous exploits. In this painting Hercules seems inclined to Voluptas: not only is he facing her but the look on his face is one of yielding languor. Rubens' is a clear presentation of the conflict between hard military honor and soft sensuality.

These are the graphic representations most relevant to Dryden's

lish travelers were impressed by the works of the Carracci; of them, Annibale's works at the Farnese, including "Hercules at the Crossroads," impressed them the most. See Adolfo Venturi, *I Carracci e la loro scuola* (Milan, 1895) and Paolo Della Pergola, *I Carracci* (Rome, 1932).

play. Later uses of the theme we can only mention: the painting by Pompeo Battoni, which obviously influenced that of Paolo Matthaeis, whose somewhat simpler eighteenth-century version has most of the neoclassical features that the Earl of Shaftesbury instructed him to include; the parodies of the theme by Hogarth in the "March to Finchley" and by Reynolds in his spirited "Garrick between Comedy and Tragedy"; and its several appearances in literature from the Renaissance to the Romantic movement in the verses of Ariosto, Ben Jonson, Metastasio, Shenstone, Lowth, and Akenside, in the libretto of Handel's opera on the theme, and in Coleridge. Such manifestations of the theme should perhaps be intensively studied. They would reveal how deeply the story had penetrated into neoclassical culture. It had become a universally accepted icon for difficult moral choice. Coleridge has his Laska in *Zapolya* say:

> Well then! Here I stand,
> Like Hercules, on either side a goddess.
> Call this (*looking at the purse*)
> Preferment; this (*holding up the key*) Fidelity!
> And first my golden goddess: what bids she?[38]

A soldier hesitating between wife and mistress, an actor wavering between the choice of tragedy or comedy, and a dramatic character unable to decide between preferment and fidelity to his trust have all, as these examples show, suggested the "Choice of Hercules" as symbol and emblem. There would have been much greater reason for making that story the emblem of Antony hesitating between Roman military virtue and Egyptian love, for Antony had been prominently associated with Hercules in Dryden's leading sources. In Plutarch he is presented as a descendant of Hercules, whom

[38] Act III, Sc. 1. Shaftesbury, "A Notion of the Historical Draught or Tablature of the Judgment of Hercules," *Second Characters*, ed. Benjamin Rand (Cambridge, Mass., 1914), pp. 360–61; Edgar Wind, "Borrowed Attitudes in Reynolds and Hogarth," *Journal of the Warburg and Courtauld Institutes*, II (1938–39), 182–85; Waterhouse, *op. cit.* (n. 19), p. 168; *Orlando Furioso* vi. 55 ff.; Metastasio, *Alcide al bivio*; Handel's interlude, "The Choice of Hercules" (1750); Alfred Owen Aldridge, "The Eclecticism of Mark Akenside's 'The Pleasures of the Imagination,'" *Journal of the History of Ideas*, V (June, 1944), 312–13; "Pleasure reconcil'd to Vertue," *Ben Jonson*, ed. C. H. Herford, Percy Simpson, and Evelyn Simpson, VII (Oxford, 1941), 483 ff. One of the latest uses of the theme in painting is the central compartment of the "new" ceiling, done earlier this century, by Lodovico Poliaghi for the Olympic Theater in Vicenza. For an earlier variant of the theme see Plate VI.

he resembled, a resemblance he sought "to confirme in all doings"—
in dress, gait, bearing, and speech.[39] The relationship with Hercules
is even more strongly suggested in Shakespeare. Cleopatra calls
him "this Herculean Roman" (Act I, Sc. 3), and Antony cries out

> The shirt of Nessus is upon me, teach me,
> Alcides, thou mine ancestor, thy rage [Act IV, Sc. 12].

When the second soldier, upon hearing the furtive and mysterious
music, says,

> 'Tis the god Hercules, whom Antony lov'd,
> Now leaves him [Act IV, Sc. 3],

Shakespeare has substituted Hercules for Bacchus, who in Plutarch's
account is believed to forsake Antony.

That association of Antony and Hercules Dryden maintained.
On three separate occasions[40] Antony addresses prayers and ejacula-
tions to his ancestor, and he is everywhere presented as a man of
heroic and godlike proportions, even in his sufferings.

These associations, however, do not in themselves make the
parallel with the painting valid. Such correspondence could not
be legitimately applied to Shakespeare's *Antony and Cleopatra*. It
is the total construction of *All for Love*, the arrangement of its
characters, and the nature of their alternatives that are pictorial.
In the enormous reduction of scenes and characters and in the
severe condensation of time Dryden has approached the neoclassical
picturesque—what he considered in his criticism the desirable economy of painting. Dryden's Antony—and this is not at all true of
Shakespeare's—is, like Hercules, unmistakably at the center of
the scene; Cleopatra, now somewhat reduced in scale and importance,
is more or less on the level of Ventidius, who has been elevated in
character and position until he can rival the queen herself; and both
queen and soldier stand on either side of the hero, as it were, each
urging the powerful and conflicting claims that lie at the center of
Antony's choice. The entire machinery of the play operates to
confront Antony with these two figures and the alternatives they
represent. The first act is devoted to Antony and Ventidius and

---

[39] Shakespeare, *Antony and Cleopatra*, ed. M. R. Ridley ("Arden" ed. [London,
1954]), pp. 160, 258, 262, 280 (where the relevant passages from Plutarch are re-
printed).

[40] Act II, Sc. 1 (twice); Act III, Sc. 1.

to the temporary triumph of Roman virtue. The second act is Cleopatra's triumph, as the first had been Ventidius'. And this type of alternating movement, though modified and complicated, continues through the drama. In its basic elements the choice of Antony is, then, the choice of Hercules: the dilemma of choosing between Ventidius, who represents military virtue, honor, friendship, and practical wisdom, and Cleopatra, who continues to represent, even in defeat and decline, the blandishments of love and the alluring pleasures of sense.[41]

In seeing this parallel we can also see how the author has transcended and enriched it. Dryden's Antony, an older man, cannot now be made to encounter the clean-cut alternatives of a Hercules just entering manhood. In fact, Antony, a great soldier and a great lover, has chosen to travel both paths and has already achieved some of the glory of the one and some of the delight of the other. Though he does lose the world in death, it is "the world well lost."

Nor is Dryden's Cleopatra an exact equivalent of the Venus or the Voluptas of the painted legend. One should not deny her, as some have, all sensual allurement and make her another Octavia. But it is certainly true that Dryden's queen is something vastly different from and inferior to Shakespeare's. Capable of sorrow and sweetness, she has few feminine wiles. By no means the serpent of old Nile, she cannot act the role of duplicity that Alexas urges on her. The greatest mistress of all history wants nothing more than to be a wife:

> Nature meant me
> A wife; a silly, harmless, household dove,
> Fond without art, and kind without deceit [Act IV, Sc. 1].

Cleopatra's combination of sensual allure and the desire for uxorial virtue is foreign to the modern mind, and it has been judged very

---

[41] Dryden continually makes us aware of the position of Ventidius and Cleopatra and of the nature of the conflict between them. When Ventidius first enters, Serapion says of him,

> "But, who's that stranger? By his warlike port,
> His fierce demeanour, and erected look,
> He's of no vulgar note" [Act I, Sc. 1].

Cleopatra's first words emphasize her conflict with Ventidius:

> "What shall I do, or whither shall I turn?
> Ventidius has o'ercome, and he will go" [Act II, Sc. 1].

harshly. Churton Collins called her "wretched." Such judgment as this may spring in part from our complete insensitiveness to a type of womanhood greatly admired in the seventeenth century and often represented in baroque art. In such women, whether saint or sinner, there was a combination of sexual and religious ecstasy, of Ovidian voluptuousness and Christian sweetness. Precisely those qualities appear in Guido Reni's Cleopatra (Plate VIII B), who, about to apply the asps to her breast, looks heavenward, in an ecstatic gaze typical of Guido's saints, her mouth slightly open, her hair chastely tied up. She is a kind of Mary Magdalen, whom, in Guido's mind, she closely resembled[42] (see Plate VIII A).

In closing the discussion of Dryden's play, I wish to repeat that I have not argued what is essentially unprovable, that Dryden borrowed directly from Annibale Carracci's canvas or one similar to it. It is true that in 1695 he knew the painting and Bellori's comment on it, for he described Annibale's "Farnesian gallery" as being morally instructive, "particularly the *Herculis Bivium*, which is a perfect triumph of virtue over vice; as it is wonderfully well described by the ingenious Bellori."[43] But strong though the likelihood is that this knowledge was his when he was writing *All for Love*, it cannot at present be proved. What I have intended by the juxtaposition is to make clearer the fundamentally pictorial nature of the tragedy. Whether that quality came to Dryden's imagination directly from the canvases and frescoes of baroque and Bolognese art, from the dramatic pictorialism of the French classical theater, from the masque, or from the pictorialist tradition of the ancient poetry that he admired and translated is not important. *All for Love* is a manifestation of *ut pictura poesis*, a realization of Simonides' dictum that poetry should be a speaking picture. It is not a closely concatenated action that unfolds moral justice. It is a gallery of related heroic poses intended to arouse our sympathy (because the characters remain human beings and share our common nature) and our admiration (because they are larger than life, ideal

---

[42] Collins' comment is quoted in Frederick Tupper and James W. Tupper, *Representative English Dramas* (New York, 1914), p. 42. J. Max Patrick, in a paper delivered at the Modern Language Association in 1955, said that the Cleopatra of Giraldi's *Cleopatra Tragedia* (1543) was the lamenting type, introduced in the sixteenth century as a neo-Senecan motif.

[43] *Works*, XVII, 305.

forms in heroic postures). This play is substantive evidence of what Dryden meant when he said that the general parallel between poetry and painting is "more complete in tragedy" than in any other literary genre.

THE "BAROQUE" ODES

In commenting on Dryden's general use of the analogy between the arts and in analyzing the "Annus mirabilis" and his satires we observed that his theoretical desire to achieve classical pictorialism was often frustrated in practice by his use of imagery in a metaphysical or baroque manner. This ambivalence is not characteristic of *All for Love*. In spite of its relation to paintings of the seventeenth-century eclectic and baroque masters, it is essentially a triumph of classical idealization, the kind that we have discussed in connection with statuary and pictorial allegory. *All for Love* may be viewed as a culmination of the classically pictorial in Dryden. The great odes should, on the other hand, be considered the culmination of those elements of the religious baroque already encountered in his verse.

In the introduction to this book I deplored the indiscriminate application of terms used in the visual arts to poetry, and it may seem that in the ensuing pages I have not heeded my own warnings. But in discussing the odes I shall concentrate on visual imagery; and it has seemed to me undeniable that in them Dryden has brought to English verse many of the visual themes, some of the splendors, and some of the excesses of the Continental art of the seventeenth century. For that reason I have ventured to call these odes "baroque."[44]

The great ode was, during the Restoration and the entire course of English neoclassicism, always considered the vehicle for freedoms not encouraged in other genres, where the rule of decorum was more austerely regulative. Usually the noble rage of this poetic form has been thought to reside principally in its irregular numbers, its declamatory fervor, its exalted religiosity. But the visual imagery of the ode is at the very least of co-ordinate importance with these

[44] "To appreciate [the cultivation of splendor in Dryden's epoch] we must keep in mind certain continental developments which are not fully paralleled in England, but which had their influence on the English sensibility: the glorification of despotism and the brilliance of Baroque art" (D. W. Jefferson, "Aspects of Dryden's Imagery," *Essays in Criticism*, IV [January, 1954], 33).

other elements. In fact, if we consider the nature of Restoration and eighteenth-century aesthetic psychology, we might be inclined to make the visual the most important single means of conveying the *furor poeticus*. Dryden once said that "imagining is, in itself, the very height and life of poetry," and to English critics since Hobbes "imagining" meant "seeing" and bringing to verbal form the content of physical vision. In defending Cowley's odes against their detractors, Dryden wrote:

> What fustian, as they call it, have I heard these Gentlemen find out in Mr. Cowley's *Odes!* I acknowledge myself unworthy to defend so excellent an author . . . ; only in general will I say, that nothing can appear more beautiful to me than the strength of those *images* which they condemn.[45]

Dryden seems to have felt that the *élan* of the sublime ode lay largely in its "images," its "pictures."

Dryden published his poem to the memory of King Charles II about a month after that monarch's death on February 6, 1685, and entitled it "Threnodia Augustalis: A Funeral-Pindaric Poem." The first of its notable pictorial elements appears in the second stanza in presenting the grief of the dead king's brother James, who will soon ascend the throne.

> Who can describe th' amazement in his face!
> Horror in all his pomp was there,
> Mute and magnificent without a tear.
> And then the hero first was seen to fear.
> Half unarray'd he ran to his relief,
> So hasty and so artless was his grief:
> Approaching greatness met him with her charms
> > Of pow'r and future state;
> > But look'd so ghastly in a brother's fate,
> > He shook her from his arms.

The bold personification of approaching greatness as a female figure embracing James is not unlike the figures in historical and mythological pieces whose faces were sometimes distorted into grimaces of fear, anger, wonder, and what not. One of the most famous expressions of this tendency (the subject, incidentally, of one of Marino's poems in the *Galeria*) was Caravaggio's "Head of

---

[45] "Defence of the Epilogue," *Essays of Dryden*, ed. W. P. Ker (Oxford, 1900), I, 186.

the Medusa" in the Uffizi, painted on a roundel of wood: the eyes bulge, the whites are prominent, the mouth is open in a scream (Plate X). In Guido Reni's "Massacre of the Innocents" the grieving and terrified women strike similar attitudes of open-mouthed horror (Plate XI). And Charles le Brun prepared a series of sketches of the human face expressing strong emotion, notably terror and amazement.[46] Such modes of expression were not, of course, confined to the seventeenth century—they are to be seen in the faces of the Laocoön group—but they were peculiarly characteristic of the baroque. Dryden does not delineate James's horror, except to say that it was in his face and that it was mute and tearless. But what was unquestionably in his mind—and what he undoubtedly felt was appropriate to a "Funeral-Pindaric"—was just the kind of baroque expression we have been referring to.

This impression would not arise from one element alone. But combined with others, like the one we are now to consider, the sense of baroque imagery in these odes becomes overwhelming. Most paintings of the period represent brisk movement between heaven and earth. Angels and saints in religious scenes and *putti* and pagan deities in classical ones ascend and descend like the angels in Jacob's dream.[47] Representations of such celestial commerce appear in almost every one of Dryden's great odes. In the present poem it appears in the third stanza, where the prayers for the life of Charles are personified and set in motion.

> With him th' innumerable crowd
> Of armed prayers
> Knock'd at the gates of heav'n, and knock'd aloud;
> The first, well-meaning, rude petitioners,
> All for his life assail'd the throne,
> All would have brib'd the skies by off'ring up their own.
> So great a throng not heav'n itself could bar;
> 'T was almost borne by force, as in the giants' war.

[46] Le Brun, Louis XIV's official painter, illustrated his essay "Expression des Passions" with faces expressing theatrical emotion. This work was widely known in England. Jonathan Richardson and Hogarth (who called it "the common drawing book of Le Brun") borrowed from it. See Brewster Rogerson, "The Art of Painting the Passions," *Journal of the History of Ideas*, XIV (January, 1953), 75, n. 8.

[47] Jacob's dream was actually painted in this period. Cf. Lodovico Carracci's painting (now at the Pinacoteca, Bologna), reproduced as Fig. II in Wittkower, *op. cit.* (n. 37).

In virtually all these poems Dryden draws some sort of analogy with painting, as if to alert the reader to the pictorial effects. In the "Threnodia" (stanza 8) it is drawn directly. Dryden, very much in the manner of Bellori, looks upon both pen and pencil as involved in the iconic representations he verbally renders.

> Thus far my Muse, tho' rudely, has designed
> Some faint resemblance of his godlike mind;
> But neither pen nor pencil can express
> The parting brothers' *tenderness*. . . .
> But what they did, and what they said,
> The monarch who triumphant went,
> The militant who stay'd,
> Like painters, when their height'ning arts are spent,
> I cast into a shade.

The fifteenth stanza is a kind of iconic poem, closely resembling the passage in *All for Love* in which Ventidius describes the "making" of the hero Antony. Its reference to the Cyclops' shield invokes the example of the earliest of all iconic poems, the description of Achilles' shield in the *Iliad*. The excellence of these lines attests the congeniality of high baroque expression to Dryden's imagination.

> Heroes in Heaven's peculiar mold are cast,
> They and their poets are not form'd in haste;
> Man was the first in God's design, and man was made the last.
> False heroes, made by flattery so,
> Heav'n can strike out, like sparkles, at a blow;
> But ere a prince is to perfection brought,
> He costs Omnipotence a second thought.
> With toil and sweat,
> With hard'ning cold, and forming heat,
> The Cyclops did their strokes repeat,
> Before th' impenetrable shield was wrought.
> It looks as if the Maker would not own
> The noble work for his,
> Before 't was tried and found a masterpiece.

In the final image of the poem old Neptune raises his head and brings the tribute of the sea to the realm of Charles and James. In closing this poem of patriotic and public exaltation, Dryden has once more introduced baroque decoration.

While starting from his oozy bed,
Th' asserted ocean rears his reverend head,
To view and recognize his ancient lord again;
And, with a willing hand, restores
The *fasces* of the main.

How often in the age of the baroque the public scene was adorned by the personification, in tapestry, sculpture, or painting, of river, land, sea, continent, and nation!

The pictorial elements of the first of these odes recur in most of the others. The personification of high emotion theatrically conceived, the use of clearly visualized celestial beings in large spatial motion, the invocation of the analogy with painting or another art, the adaptation of the iconic tradition to the mood and theme of the ode, the use of symbols (natural and national) that remind us of Ripa—these are the essential ingredients of the pictorialism of Dryden's odes. They are all reminiscent of baroque expression.

The first stanza of the ode to Mrs. Anne Killigrew, published late in 1685, is a forceful expression of celestial themes in the baroque plastic manner. The deceased young lady, addressed as the "youngest virgin-daughter of the skies," is imagined as bearing a palm in paradise, "rich with immortal green"; or as rolling above in "procession fix'd and regular," like a star; or as treading "with seraphims the vast abyss." Nowhere has Dryden so grandly achieved the massive interstellar movement and the bold conquest of space it was the genius of baroque art to accomplish. Such a detail as the palm of immortal green is highly characteristic of contemporary religious art. Sometimes borne by an angel to a dying martyr, sometimes held in the hand of the saint, it was a sign of the heavenly intercourse that almost every significant human relationship was thought to imply.

Dryden is here more deeply concerned than elsewhere with the relations of painting and poetry because, as the title says, the lady was "excellent in the two sister-arts of Poesy and Painting." Therefore the entire sixth and seventh stanzas are devoted to the young lady's accomplishments as a painter. There is nothing that need detain us here in this adaptation of the iconic tradition, an adaptation that suggests Marino's *Galeria* in highly abbreviated form. Each picture in Dryden's gallery is painted in a brief stroke of two lines or so. The flat, one-dimensional itemization introduces no perspective, foreground, background, middleground, or fore-shortening. The passage is notable chiefly because it constitutes an excellent summary of seventeenth-century taste in landscape; we are referred to sylvan scenes of herds and flocks; rich plains and barren rocks; brooks and floods; lofty trees and shades; landscapes, like innumerable ones by Nicolas Poussin, in which bright nymphs and shaggy satyrs appear; and ruin pieces in which the broken stones of Greece or Rome are still, "tho' defaced, the wonder of the eye."[48]

"Britannia rediviva," written in 1688 to celebrate the birth of a son to James II, has so many lines of dull compliment and exaggerated conceit that it is easy to miss its occasional moments of poetic intensity. Written in couplets, it does not formally belong to the genre we have been considering, but its manner of imagery is precisely that of baroque art. It contemplates the royal babe in the manner of the older iconic tradition, not, however, without the addition of baroque theatricality.

> When humbly on the royal babe we gaze,
> The manly lines of a majestic face
> Give awful joy.

Angels' voices are accompanied by harps; an avenging angel appears in mid-air; there is strife in heaven; Mercy, an emblem of Christ,

> . . . stretches out her hand, and saves
> Desponding Peter sinking in the waves.

On the day of the boy's birth, shortly before the summer solstice, when the sun

> Did farthest in his northern progress run,
> He bended forward, and ev'n stretch'd the sphere
> Beyond the limits of the lengthen'd year,
> To view a brighter sun in Britain born.

[48] "The popularity of ruin pieces was clearly great. Probably no other kind of landscape except the prospect was more admired during the second half of the century" (Henry V. S. Ogden and Margaret S. Ogden, *English Taste in Landscape in the Seventeenth Century* [Ann Arbor, Mich., 1955], p. 139). The only surviving paintings by Anne Killigrew are reproduced in the *Burlington Magazine*, XXVIII (December, 1915), 113–16. One is a portrait in oil of James II and may be compared with Dryden's lines, in the ode, on the lady's royal portraits. The other is entitled "Venus Attired by the Graces," which is not close to any of the types briefly delineated in Dryden's lines. The Italianate background, the light, and the trees suggest Dughet. If the subject is allegorical, it suggests the stylization of natural beauty implied in the painting by Rubens (see Plate IV).

These conceits and images are not unlike the exaggerated technical flourishes of seventeenth-century Continental art. But the following passages even more unmistakably establish the mood of the religious baroque—its Jesuitical zeal, its loyalty to the feasts and fasts of the church, its sensuous presentation of the divine, its association of the political and the religious that to a later day seems almost sacrilegious, its tendency to see natural events as supernatural epiphanies. The Sunday before the boy's birth was Whitsunday:

> Last solemn Sabbath saw the Church attend;
> The Paraclete in fiery pomp descend.

The day of his birth was Trinity Sunday.

> Or did the mighty Trinity conspire,
> As once, in council to create our sire?
> It seems as if they sent the newborn guest
> To wait on the procession of their feast;
> And on their sacred anniverse decreed
> To stamp their image on the promis'd seed.
> Three realms united, and on one bestow'd,
> An emblem of their mystic union show'd:
> The Mighty Trine the triple empire shar'd,
> As every person would have one to guard.

These last lines are as bold a stroke of baroque imagination as we find anywhere in Dryden. It is as though Rubens had added to his painting of the crowning of the infant Charles I in the Banqueting Hall at Whitehall (Plate XIV) the emblematic representation of the Trinity which appears on a separate canvas now in the academy at Mantua.[49]

The first of Dryden's famous odes for St. Cecilia's Day, "A Song for St. Cecilia's Day, 1687," is, in its first and last stanzas, a poem of musical power. Its relevance to the kind of pictorialism we are

[49] For a reproduction see Rudolf Oldenbourg, *P. P. Rubens* (Berlin-Leipzig, n.d.), p. 13. The spiritual affinities of Dryden to a painter like Rubens might be explored further. Rubens' combination of the secular and religious, his personal involvement in politics and diplomacy, his skill in various genres (landscape, portrait, history) all could be matched in Dryden's career. One of the most striking parallels exists between politico-religious odes like the "Threnodia" or "Britannia" and the ornamental celebration of good government and the apotheosis of James I that Rubens placed on the ceiling of the Banqueting Hall at Whitehall (see below, pp. 206–9 and n. 55).

now considering appears only at the end, when Dryden binds heaven and earth together in the manner of the baroque:

> But bright Cecilia rais'd the wonder high'r:
> When to her Organ vocal breath was giv'n,
> An angel heard, and straight appear'd,
> Mistaking earth for heav'n.

In the second musical ode, "Alexander's Feast" (1697), which was also written for the celebration of St. Cecilia's Day, the lines devoted to the saint come in the last stanza:

> At last, divine Cecilia came,
> Inventress of the vocal frame;
>
> . . . .
> Let old Timotheus yield the prize,
> Or both divide the crown;
> He rais'd a mortal to the skies;
> She drew an angel down.

St. Cecilia was one of the most popular subjects of baroque religious art, chiefly because the life and death of so attractive a martyr served the whole purpose, religious and aesthetic, of Counter-Reformation culture.[50] Raphael had earlier painted her in an influential picture (Plate XII) that portrayed the saint holding an organ in her hand and gazing upward to the singing angels that hang suspended in mid-air. Heaven and earth are divided by a horizontal line; the two spheres are not bridged literally but only symbolically by the saint's upward gaze. But in the seventeenth century matters are different. Angels appear on their way to the earth or already arrived on earth. And so it is in Dryden. An angel "straight appears"; "she drew an angel down."

Dryden's lines could have served as the motto for innumerable contemporary and earlier paintings of St. Cecilia. In Orazio Gentileschi's fine painting at the Brera in Milan, "I Martiri Valeriano, Tiburzio, e Cecilia" (Plate XIII), the subject is martyrdom; and the descending angel, a noble creature in magnificent motion and already in the room itself, bears the green palm leaf of paradise in one hand and the martyr's crown of roses and lilies in the other. The kneeling saint stretches forth one hand to the approaching angel *as though to draw him down.* In a painting at Montepellier attributed

[50] Émile Mâle, *L'art religieux après le Concile de Trente* (Paris, 1932), pp. 187 ff.

to Nicolas Poussin, an angel descends to the dying saint. In Bernardo Cavallino's excellent picture in the National Museum of Naples, the angel has touched the earth, his wings are at rest, and he is about to crown the saint. In Domenichino's scene an angel descends, and in Rubens' an angel appears with a martyr's crown.[51]

In most of the paintings of the subject the angel descends with a martyr's crown to the dying saint. Dryden, however, conceives of the saint's music as drawing the angel down. The association of organ and angel is prominently made in several of the paintings. Gentileschi places organ pipes in the room. In Domenichino's painting at the Louvre a small angel holds a musical score up to the saint, who plays a violincello, her eyes directed heavenward to suggest the celestial inspiration of her notes. Almost all the graphic representations suggest music, celestial ravishment, and the descent of an angel (see Plate IX). Dryden's originality lies in catching in memorably brief and epigrammatic lines the very motifs and associations of one of the most typical of baroque themes.[52]

Apart from the Christian conclusion, "Alexander's Feast" is not a religious poem but a celebration of art, of which Christian music is but a single, although climactic, manifestation. It consists of a series of vivid tableaux from pagan mythology and is an example of the pagan baroque, which, without direct religious relevance, nevertheless often attained the same kind of energy that in religious paintings moved angels across large surfaces of earth and sky.

[51] For Domenichino's painting, now at S. Luigi dei Francesi, Rome, see the reproduction in John Pope-Hennessy, *The Drawings of Domenichino in the Collection of His Majesty at Windsor Castle* (New York, 1948), Fig. 41. Rubens' St. Cecilia hangs in the Academy, Vienna. See Oldenbourg, *op. cit.* (n. 49), p. 207.

[52] Dryden's lines are fully serious. But their epigrammatic quality reminds us that in the eighteenth century the serious baroque was often parodied. So fixed was the tradition of associating angels in some kind of motion with the representations of the saint that when Reynolds' fashionable sitters were presented as St. Cecilia, angels, looking now more like *amorini*, are always present. In "Mrs. Billington as St. Cecilia," a tiny angel descends with a flowery garland; in "Mrs. Sheridan as St. Cecilia," the cherub, who has just descended and now rests on a pillowy cloud, inclines his ear to the harp that the society saint plays (see Ellis K. Waterhouse, *Reynolds* [London, 1941], Plates CLXV, CCC). Dryden was deeply interested in the subject of angels. In the "Discourse concerning Satire" (1692) he urged that Christian poets adopt angels as their machines in heroic poetry. He referred not to individual guardian angels but to the tutelary angels of nation and empire, present in the prophetic books of the Old Testament.

The pictorialism of this poem appears with great obviousness if we compare it to the first St. Cecilia's Day ode, which is to a very large extent intellectually abstract and musical. But here all is visualized, and the form follows what we have earlier called the picture-gallery manner of proceeding.[53] Tableau succeeds tableau. The whole arrangement is basically static, and what motion there is must be viewed against that stasis. Alexander *sits* aloft in "awful state" on his "imperial throne." His peers are "*plac'd* around," wearing roses and myrtles on their brows. By the emperor's side *sits* the blooming Thais. Timotheus is "*plac'd* on high." Such is the frame. On it are hung the mythological paintings. In one Jupiter rides "sublime on radiant spires." In another Bacchus comes in triumph. In still another—and this Sir Joshua actually made the subject of a painting[54]—the king with a flambeau in his hand and his peers with torches in theirs rush out to "fire another Troy."

The subject, ostensibly the power of music, is extended to all art. The artist, whatever his medium, is the real hero. That extension of meaning is partly accomplished by the very form of the poem. Music, the most abstract of all the arts, produces scenes that are as vividly visual as words can make them. This is an art poem, an iconic poem— or, more accurately, a subtle modification of the iconic genre (in which the subject is usually a work of plastic art). Here the subject is music, but music celebrated in plastic scenes verbally described. Dryden in a single poem has dissolved the boundaries between all the arts.

Once more we see the poet's relationship to the spiritual and artistic tendencies of baroque Europe. To no other period except the early eighteenth century were the boundaries of the arts less important. St. Luke, who was believed to be both writer and painter, became an important symbol. He was often represented with the scroll of his gospel and the portrait of the Virgin which is supposed to have come from his hand. In many of Rubens' paintings the Virgin is not directly represented; she appears instead in a framed painting carried through the air by a bevy of angels, the frame itself sometimes framed first by a garland of flowers and then by a ring of tiny angels. In Rubensian political allegory there is often art within art: statuary,

[53] See above, pp. 33, 105–6, 114, 180–81.

[54] "Miss Emily Pott (or Bertie) as Thais," in Waterhouse (n. 52), Plate CCXXIII.

architecture, other paintings are richly represented. Art in baroque Europe liked to contemplate itself, and that tendency was somehow communicated to Dryden.[55]

Perhaps we should be content merely to describe the relationship of Dryden to contemporary Continental painting, but it is tempting to ask how and why such baroque motifs as these reached the greatest poet of the Restoration. The seeds of Dryden's baroque flowering were in him from the very beginning. From Milton he inherited that kind of intellectual and religious imagery that went quickly from outer to inner reality. From Cowley, the master of his youth, and from other metaphysical poets he inherited the extravagant emblematic manner of his juvenilia. The amateurishness of these early conceits he fortunately soon outgrew, but the admiration for Cowley, especially for the power of his images, lasted throughout a long life. The restlessly imaginative side of Dryden was kept alive in creating heroic plays, in which, as Johnson saw, the poet achieved a kind of romantic sublimity, at times verging on the abyss of nonsense and chaos. Never dissipated by the urbane French classicism to which he had exposed himself or by the powerful Vergilian and Ovidian influences he helped bring to England in his translations and prefaces, these tendencies were quickened into high baroque expression by his conversion to Roman Catholicism in 1685 and the alterations in taste and thought that must have preceded and accompanied that commitment. Of his baroque sensibility the sublime odes of the later years are the chief vehicle.

Shortly after Dryden's conversion and the coronation of the Roman Catholic monarch James II, whom he served, Roger, the Earl of

[55] See St. Luke as represented in the fresco of Domenichino in Sant'Andrea della Valle, Rome, reproduced by Mâle, *op. cit.* (n. 50), p. 28, Fig. 9. See also the following paintings by Rubens: "St. Gregory and Other Saints" (Grenoble) and the "Madonna in a Garland of Flowers" (Munich), in Max Rooses, *Rubens*, trans. Harold Child (London, 1904), I, 88, 280; and the "Virgin Surrounded by Angels" (S. Maria in Vallicella, Rome) in Oldenbourg, *op. cit.* (n. 49), p. 24. The immediate historical reasons for these paintings lay in the Protestant attack on sacred images and paintings. But even apart from the iconoclastic controversy, the painting of the seventeenth century, like that of the eighteenth, tended to make other arts and the exaltation of art in general an important theme (see, for example, "L'inspiration du poet" [Louvre], reproduced in Walter Friedländer, *Nicolas Poussin* [Munich, 1914], p. 64). It is this tendency of seventeenth-century art that Dryden exemplifies in his musical odes. I discover I have been anticipated in the comparison of Dryden and Rubens by Samuel Holt Monk ("Dryden the Craftsman," *Sewanee Review*, LIV [Autumn, 1946], 720–27).

Castlemaine, was sent through France to Rome, accompanied by a retinue of gentlemen and one of the most magnificent trains of attendants ever to leave England for foreign soil. After a triumphal tour of France, the party came to Rome. For months and months— the celebrations were somewhat prolonged by the Pope's illness— there were state entertainments of unprecedented lavishness.

The story of Castlemaine's embassy was told in a handsome book, a translation of the account in Italian prepared by Michael Wright, chief steward of Castlemaine's house at Rome.[56] The book was adorned by the elaborate baroque engravings of Giovanni Battista Lenardi, which, accompanied by verbal descriptions of the expensive entertainments, brought to the English reader a sense of the power and magnificence of seventeenth-century Rome. The frontispiece (Plate XV), itself obviously influenced by the monumental public art of Rubens,[57] represents Innocent XI seated on his elevated throne, blessing the kneeling figure of the king's representative, who lays the secular crown at the feet of His Holiness. A female figure, perhaps representing Truth, points, in the manner of Virtue in the Hercules story, to the dome of St. Peter's and to Bernini's colonnades. *Putti* descend with a huge medallion on which is engraved the portrait of James II.

To the religious, political, and aesthetic tendencies represented by this engraving Dryden's great odes are very intimately related. In the visual images and references of his poems he alternates between baroque and classical: Pagan *amori* one day; celestial angels the next. The austerely classical lines to Oldham, with no hint of Christian immortality or resurrection one year; another year, the religiously decorated verses to Anne Killigrew, in which the sacred poets "foremost from the tomb shall bound."

> And straight, with inborn vigor, on the wing,
> Like mounting larks, to the new morning sing.

But even here Dryden was close to his age. His alternations are paralleled in the greatest architectural achievement of Restoration

---

[56] *An Account of his Excellence Roger Earl of Castlemaine's Embassy, from his Sacred Majesty James the IIe* . . . (London, 1688).

[57] Cf. Rubens' sketch, "The Union of England and Scotland," a model for the first of the large canvases in the ceiling decoration of the Banqueting Hall, Whitehall, reproduced as Plate LXX in Leo Van Puyvelde, *The Sketches of Rubens* (New York, 1951).

and Augustan England, St. Paul's Cathedral, the first stone of which was laid in 1675. The building blends classic and baroque, the motifs of seventeenth-century Jesuitical Rome—the Rome of St. Peter's dome and the towers of St. Agnes in the Piazza Navona—and the motifs of *le grand siècle*—of Mansart's dome of the Invalides and of Perrault's rationally and mathematically devised Louvre façade.[58]

[58] See F. Saxl and R. Wittkower, *British Art and the Mediterranean* (London, 1948), p. 46.

CHAPTER VIII

Alexander Pope

Coming to Pope from Dryden and from the entire pictorialist background, we receive a strong sense of continuing but subtly modified tradition. The ingredients of Dryden's pictorialism are all present but in somewhat different proportions. Dryden's "baroque" has not disappeared but has been modulated into a subordinate theme. His angels ascend and descend in full baroque motion, but Pope's only "lean from Heav'n to hear."[1] Pictorialism in Pope is more decisively that of the ancients and of the Renaissance, although it has been enriched by the intervention of the seventeenth century. It is more intense in his poetry than in Dryden's; Pope brings to a culmination some of the most characteristic features of the ancient pictorialist tradition. The "Temple of Fame" contains one of the most elaborate literary icons in English, and the satire on women is more obviously and consistently pictorial in form than any other poems we have hitherto considered. Pope's famous "texture," on which nearly everyone remarks in our day and which Miss Sitwell regards as one of the richest in English poetry,[2] is, to an extent before unrealized, woven of pictorial images.

POPE AND THE KINDRED ARTS

Pope's life, his critical doctrine, and his poetical practice reveal an unmistakable affiliation with the pictorialist tradition. Like some of the Italian poets of the Renaissance, he was himself a painter. He spent a year and a half studying the art in the studio of his painter friend Charles Jervas. He wrote to Caryll on August 31, 1713, that he had thrown away "three Dr Swifts, two Dutchesses of Montague,

[1] See above, p. 199; "Ode for Musick on St. Cecilia's Day," l. 130. Pope's verse is quoted, whenever possible, from the Twickenham edition (London, 1939——). Reference will be made to title and in longer poems to line.

[2] Edith Sitwell, *Alexander Pope* (London, 1930), pp. 266, 270.

one Virgin Mary, the Queen of England, besides half a score earls and a Knight of the Garter."[3] So happy were these months of painting that the desire to be a painter may for a time have supplanted that of continuing to be a poet.

Like Dryden, Pope was a friend of the painter Godfrey Kneller, who lived on from the Restoration into the age of Anne and for whom Pope wrote an epitaph that turns on the time-honored theme of iconic verse, the contest of art and nature.[4] Pope also wrote a poem to Jervas, Kneller's pupil and his own teacher, that was published in 1716 and that goes beyond its model, Dryden's poem to Kneller, in stressing the association of the arts and of artists. The friendship between Pope and Jervas is viewed as expressing the tradition:

> Smit with the love of Sister-arts we came,
> And met congenial, mingling flame with flame [ll. 13–14].

Pope, as if to emphasize the continuity of a tradition, sent the poem to Jervas with a copy of Dryden's translation of Dufresnoy's poem on painting.

> Read these instructive leaves, in which conspire
> *Fresnoy*'s close art, and *Dryden*'s native fire:
> And reading wish, like theirs, our fate and fame,
> So mix'd our studies, and so join'd our name,
> Like them to shine thro' long succeeding age,
> So just thy skill, so regular my rage [ll. 7–12].

It is not recorded that Pope and Jervas ever thought of the kind of collaborative enterprise Goethe and Tischbein dreamed of later, but Pope did believe firmly in the kinship of the arts and deeply loved

[3] *The Correspondence of Alexander Pope*, ed. George Sherburn (Oxford, 1956), I, 189. See also Norman Ault, "Mr. Alexander Pope: Painter," in his *New Light on Pope* (London, 1949), p. 70. I am indebted to Ault's sensitive essay for many details, but I find his method somewhat limited. To concentrate on color alone does not by any means exhaust pictorial possibilities, and his method may be too rigidly applied even to color (see D. S. Bland, "Pope's Colour-Sense: A Comment," *Durham University Journal*, XLVII [June, 1955], 104–9; Robert J. Allen, "Pope and the Sister Arts," in *Pope and His Contemporaries*, ed. James L. Clifford and Louis A. Landa [Oxford, 1949], pp. 78–88). In a study of Pope, it should be made clear that his pictorialism, though unquestionably sharpened by his studio experience, is related to the tradition of literary pictorialism and to great Italian art. Pope's entire visual context was by no means provided by Kneller and Jervas, and his poetry would have been pictorial had he never handled a brush.

[4] "Epitaph on Sir Godfrey Kneller, in Westminster-Abby, 1723."

the art of painting. As Joseph Warton said, painting was "a subject of which Pope always speaks *con amore*. Of all poets whatever, Milton has spoken most feelingly of music, and Pope of painting."[5] Pope's love of gardening, which expressed itself both at Twickenham and on the printed page, may itself have been an outgrowth of his love of painting. Anticipating the picturesque garden of the later eighteenth century, he conceived of gardening as closely analogous to painting. The "Genius of the Place," he writes in one of the "Moral Essays"

> Calls in the Country, catches opening glades,
> Joins willing woods, and varies shades from shades,
> Now breaks, or now directs, th'intending Lines;
> Paints as you plant, and, as you work, designs
>> [Epistle IV, ll. 57, 61–64].

In Pope's criticism poetry is frequently compared to painting.

> Our sons their fathers' failing language see,
> And such as Chaucer is, shall Dryden be.
> So when the faithful pencil has designed
> Some bright Idea of the master's mind,
> Where a new world leaps out at his command,
> And ready Nature waits upon his hand;
> When the ripe colours soften and unite,
> And sweetly melt into just shade and light;
> When mellowing years their full perfection give,
> And each bold figure just begins to live,
> The treach'rous colours the fair art betray,
> And all the bright creation fades away!
>> ["Essay on Criticism," ll. 482–93].

Dryden had several times drawn the same analogy but never with such eloquence and emotion.

The analogy with painting has often been said to support the view that style is ornamental—that language is color and can be similarly imposed upon already created design or form. Pope does indeed seem to separate language and meaning. In actual critical practice, however, he seldom argues positively from the analogy. He uses it most often in order to censure. False eloquence he compares to gaudy colors. He writes as follows to Cromwell about the poetry of Crashaw:

[5] *An Essay on the Genius and Writings of Pope* (London, 1806), I, 149. "Our author is never happier than in his allusions to painting, an art he so much admired and understood" (*ibid.*, II, 182).

All that regards Design, Form, Fable, (which is the Soul of Poetry) all that concerns exactness, or consent of parts, (which is the Body) will probably be wanting; only pretty conceptions, fine metaphors, glitt'ring expressions, and something of a neat cast of Verse, (which are properly the dress, gems, or loose ornaments of Poetry) may be found in these verses. . . . And (to express my self like a Painter, their *Colouring* entertains the sight, but the *Lines* and *Life* of the picture are not to be inspected too narrowly.[6]

Style and meaning, form and color, Pope was capable of seeing as separable things. But this distinction he used not to encourage the laying on of superficial and splendid ornament but to blame those who did precisely that. Pope loved both color and poetic metaphor but believed them inferior to design and meaning. The distinction was therefore made in order to put things in their proper places. The analogy exists, but it does not sanction the doctrine of superficial ornamentalism—a doctrine that in Dryden and Pope does not occupy the central position usually assigned it.

Pope said on two occasions that images are reflected from art to art.[7] Such statements invite us to look for specific cross-artistic correspondences. As we shall shortly see, they do exist, and it is not impossible, in view of Pope's intimate association with painters and paintings, that such borrowings from the graphic arts are more abundant than I have detected. But Pope's pictorialism is, I believe, more pervasive than direct borrowings alone might indicate. It arose from a life-long acquaintance with the sister arts and with the entire tradition of literary pictures.

Pope's pantheon was that of his age.[8] His taste in graphic art embraced ancient marbles and Italian canvases. He was intellectually and spiritually a son of the Renaissance and its seventeenth-century afterglow, an affiliation revealed everywhere in his writings but notably in the "Essay on Criticism" and in those highly personal and obviously sincere lines of the "Epistle to Mr. Jervas" in which the poet imagines that he and his painter friend have gone together to Italy.

> Together o'er the *Alps* methinks we fly,
> Fir'd with ideas of fair *Italy*.

[6] Dec. 17, 1710, Sherburn, *op. cit.* (n. 3), I, 109–10.

[7] "To Mr. Addison Occasioned by His Dialogues on Medals," l. 52; "Epistle to Mr. Jervas," l. 20.

[8] See above, pp. 162–70.

> With thee, on *Raphael*'s Monument I mourn,
> Or wait inspiring dreams at *Maro*'s Urn: . . .
> Here thy well-study'd Marbles fix our eye;
> A fading Fresco here demands a sigh:
> Each heav'nly piece unweary'd we compare,
> Match *Raphael*'s grace, with thy lov'd *Guido*'s air,
> *Caracci*'s strength, *Correggio*'s softer line,
> *Paulo*'s free stroke, and *Titian*'s warmth divine
> > [ll. 25–28, 33–38].

Raphael of Rome is mentioned first, but then so are Veronese and Titian of Venice. Pope's Renaissance included the once warring masters of form and color. The seventeenth-century Bologna of Annibale Carracci and Guido Reni is prominent. "Strength" belongs to Annibale and not to Michelangelo. Grace everywhere dominates. Assigned by name to the Prince of Painters, it is also present, as anyone who knows the vocabulary of eighteenth-century taste cannot fail to notice, in the "air" of Guido and the "softer line" of Correggio. For Pope, as for his age, the pictorial tradition was characterized by grace, delicacy, and elegance.[9]

THE EARLY POEMS

Traditional pictorialism appears everywhere in Pope, even in the minor poems: in the adaptation of Waller's iconic verse; the translation of Castiglione's poem on a statue; the slight poetic responses to medals, gardens, coins, paintings; the imitation of the "bowl" of Theocritus; and the frequent association of epigram and art object.[10] A writer in the *Guardian* said in 1713 that he reflected with no little pleasure on the fact that "I have got over that childish part of Life, which delights in Points and Turns of wit; and that I can take a manly and rational Satisfaction in that, which is called Painting in Poetry."[11] "Windsor Forest," which the *Guardian* writer specifically mentions, was calculated to produce such "manly and rational Satisfaction" by properly rendering landscape and natural object. Comparing Windsor to Eden, Pope says:

[9] See above, pp. 169–70.

[10] See *Minor Poems*, ed. Norman Ault and John Butt (Twickenham ed.; London, 1954), pp. 9, 45, 66, 202, 211, 212, 290, 312, 313, 373, 382. See also "Spring: The First Pastoral," ll. 35 ff.

[11] No. 86 (June 19, 1713).

Here hills and vales, the woodland and the plain,
Here earth and water seem to strive again; . . .
Here waving groves a chequered scene display,
And part admit, and part exclude the day; . . .
There, interspersed in lawns and opening glades,
Thin trees arise that shun each other's shades.
Here in full light the russet plains extend:
There wrapt in clouds the blueish hills ascend.
Even the wild heath displays her purple dyes,
And 'midst the desert fruitful fields arise
[ll. 11–12, 17–18, 21–26].

I have quoted only a part of the passage, omitting those lines in which the scene is contrasted to primeval chaos and likened to "order in variety," in which the shade admitting the light is compared to a coy nymph who can neither quite indulge nor quite repress her wishes. Even the purely descriptive portion, however, is stylized. "Here" and "there" always emphasize a contrast: dark against light, plain against hill. The composition is not developed into the later "picturesque" of foreground, middleground, and background. But the seeds of such painterly sophistication are here, and Pope, more than Dryden ever did, has paid attention to the plastic values of the natural world. He is interested in the contrasts of light and shade, of far and near, of high and low, and in the soft blend of russet, blue, and "purple."[12] Nature comes to Pope's mind stylized along the lines of pictorial composition.

In Pope's still-life scenes the arrangement is even simpler, consisting of little more than enumerated detail. But the colors are more painterly than natural. The fish of the following lines from "Windsor Forest" are the painted fish of still life, their hues heightened by the palette:

Our plenteous streams a various race supply,
The bright-eyed perch with fins of Tyrian dye,
The silver eel, in shining volumes rolled,

[12] Elizabeth Wheeler Manwaring (*Italian Landscape in Eighteenth Century England* [New York, 1925], p. 97) finds this passage "close to Claude." It should be compared with the similarly colored and stylized landscape in Pope's "Spring: The First Pastoral," ll. 29–34; "here" are "bright" crocuses, "blue" violets, and "breathing roses"; "there" or "yon" are "slow oxen" and a lamb playing near a fountain. "Here," "there," and "yon" are pointers that reveal a picturesquely conceived scene.

> The yellow carp, in scales bedropped with gold,
> Swift trouts, diversified with crimson stains,
> And pikes, the tyrants of the watery plains
> [ll. 141–46].

The pheasant's colors are made intense to emphasize the pathos of his death. The gorgeous creature springs from the brake and while mounting in exultation is shot down.

> Ah! what avail his glossy, varying dyes,
> His purple crest, and scarlet-circled eyes,
> The vivid green his shining plumes unfold,
> His painted wings, and breast that flames with gold?
> [ll. 115–18].

But Pope does not luxuriate in these colors for their own sensuous sake. Though keeping his eye on the object, he has stylized the visual detail to make it intellectually and emotionally expressive.

In addition to reproducing natural detail in a manner that looks across the seventeenth century to the Renaissance, Pope reproduces pictorially conceived personifications that remind one of antiquity. Some are mythological: "Here blushing Flora paints th'enamelled ground" (l. 38); others, moral: "There purple Vengeance bathed in gore retires" (l. 417); still others, natural: "The blue, transparent Vandalis [the Wandle River] appears" (l. 345).

We have earlier discussed the requirement of eighteenth-century criticism that personifications be pictorial.[13] Barbarous discord, mad ambition, and cruel hate are not pictorial since they are not paintable. But the following, which bear their proper insignia in the manner of an icon of Ripa, are:

> There hateful Envy her own snakes shall feel,
> And Persecution mourn her broken wheel:
> There Faction roar, Rebellion bite her chain,
> And gasping Furies thirst for blood in vain [ll. 419–22].

Such pictorial personifications Pope liked to create. He apparently looked upon them as one of the great beauties of poetry, and his im-

---

[13] To the earlier discussion (above, pp. 147–49) I add only two examples. John Hughes calls personifications of morning, including the famous one in *Hamlet*, "poetical pictures" (*Poems on Several Occasions* [London, 1735], II, 334). Joseph Warton, who required the epithets of personifications to be "particular and picturesque," was reminded by Pope's successful ones of "the pencil of Rubens or Julio Romano" (*op. cit.* [n. 5], I, 27–28).

agination liked to elaborate them into full-scale allegorical paintings. Dryden had thus described the personified Thames in "Annus mirabilis":

> Old father Thames rais'd up his reverend head,
> But fear'd the fate of Simoeis would return:
> Deep in his *ooze* he sought his sedgy bed,
> And shrunk his waters back into his urn [ll. 925–28].

Pope's Thames appears as follows in "Windsor Forest":

> In that blest moment from his oozy bed
> Old father Thames advanced his rev'rend head.
> His tresses dropped with dews, and o'er the stream
> His shining horns diffused a golden gleam:
> Graved on his urn appeared the moon, that guides
> His swelling waters and alternate tides;
> The figured streams in waves of silver rolled,
> And on their banks Augusta rose in gold.
> Around his throne the sea-born brothers stood,
> Who swell with tributary urns his flood [ll. 329–38].

In Dryden the urn alone appears as the signum of the river. On Pope's urn a moon has been engraved. Dryden's Thames has little more than "a reverend head." Pope's Thames has that, too; but in addition his tresses drop dew and he wears shining horns that provide the central golden light of the scene. In Pope the rivers are silver, the city rises in gold; and there are several accompanying figures surrounding the central one, who stands, "High in the midst, upon his urn reclined" (l. 349). The tendency to sophisticate the simple and single image of Dryden into a conventional but splendid verbal tapestry is highly characteristic of Alexander Pope. In this manner he everywhere enriches the pictures of his predecessor.

Pope uses visual details that have a long literary history. The habit of personifying rivers, for example, is a venerable one present in Dryden, Milton, Jonson, Spenser, Chaucer, Vergil (who in the eighth book of the *Aeneid* introduces Father Tiber clothed in a thin garment of sea-green linen, wearing reeds in his hair), and Claudian (who introduces the god Eridanus above the floods, his golden horns shining on his head and under his arms the conventional urn).[14] But the long presence in poetry of such icons should not be allowed to rub off

---

[14] Pope, *Works*, ed. Whitwell Elwin and William J. Courthope (London, 1871), I, 360–61.

their pictorial gloss. For pictorial they surely are. Waller associates them primarily with painting:

> Those which inhabit the celestial bower,
> *Painters express* with emblems of their power;
> His club Alcides, Phoebus has his bow,
> Jove has his thunder, and your navy you.[15]

No poet living in the age of Pope, even though he may have been consciously borrowing from Claudian or Vergil, could fail to be influenced by the appearance of such figures in Ripa, Rubens, and dozens of other pictorial allegorists.[16] Pope's icon, especially if it is compared to the simpler ones of Dryden and the classical poets, has all the marks of pictorial arrangement: design, light, color, and the grouping of subordinate figures around a central one.

Pope returns to this kind of personification with heightened power in "Eloisa to Abelard," precisely the kind of poem for which he would have wanted to create visual imagery of the most effective type. As Dryden and others had said, human passion is best represented in "imaginings" (the visual creations of the fancy), and this is a poem of passionate love. The pictorial Ovid had established in his *Heroides* the tradition of creating sympathetic landscape as a kind of visual accompaniment to the emotions. Pope, using the Ovidian genre, does the same thing. The setting—"deep solitudes," "awful cells," "moss-grown domes with spiry turrets crowned," "some mould'ring tow'r" covered with "pale ivy," and "low-brow'd rocks [that] hang nodding o'er the deeps"—is appropriate to the expression of profound emotion.

It is not on effects like these (reminiscent of Salvator Rosa and the sublimity of terror) that we wish to dwell but on the presence of a pictorially conceived persona. In one of the most memorable moments in the entire poem, Pope describes the figure of Melancholy:

---

[15] "Instructions to a Painter," ll. 313–16, in *Poems of Edmund Waller*, ed. G. Thorn Drury (London, 1901), I, 5–9. Italics mine.

[16] In Ripa's *Iconologia* (see above, pp. 91, 99) the Po, represented as leaning on an urn, has the face of a bull with horns in order to suggest, as Ripa says, the fact that in its course the river makes the sound of an ox and in its turns and windings resembles the horns of a bull. Rubens, whom Joseph Warton mentions as creating allegorical personifications similar to those of Pope, painted an allegorical picture of the Tiber in which the personified river holds a trident in his right hand and rests his left arm on an urn, from which pours a flood of water (H. Knackfuss, *Rubens* [Leipzig, 1898], p. 16).

But o'er the twilight groves, and dusky caves,
Long-sounding aisles, and intermingled graves,
Black Melancholy sits, and round her throws
A death-like silence, and a dread repose:
Her gloomy presence saddens all the scene,
Shades ev'ry flow'r, and darkens ev'ry green,
Deepens the murmur of the falling floods,
And breathes a browner horror on the woods
[ll. 163–70].

The passage is effective because it brings to a focus almost all the visual details in the poem. For Pope, as for many painters of his own and earlier epochs, the physical scene alone will not do. A figure, real or personified, must appear to explain the distribution of light and shade, the relation of subordinate to central detail. It is thus that an eighteenth-century critic read Pope's passage and viewed Pope's image: "The Image of the Goddess Melancholy sitting over the convent, and, as it were, expanding her dreadful wings over its whole circuit, and diffusing her gloom all around it, is truly sublime, and strongly conceived."[17]

An essential quality of Pope's mature iconic visualization will appear if we compare his image with the famous engraving of Albrecht Dürer, "Melancholy I," which, for want of evidence, cannot be claimed as a direct influence but which Pope in all likelihood knew[18] (Plate XX; cf. Plate II). In the Renaissance masterpiece Melancholy appears as a female being with folded wings, an angel of night whose darkened face rests in her hand, her elbow in turn resting on her knee. She sits in an unfinished building and is surrounded by an hourglass, a pair of scales, a bell, a wooden ladder, and the tools of geometry, architecture, and carpentry. A gloomy and partially darkened *putto* sits near the goddess, and into the picture at the upper left flies a squeaking bat bearing a motto, the title of the picture.

Of these details in the engraving—and I have enumerated only a few and have interpreted none—Pope's figure embodies only two: Melancholy is feminine, and she is surrounded with gloom and darkness. Pope has appropriated one of the most powerful qualities of Dürer's masterpiece: the dark goddess shares her darkness not only

[17] Warton, *op. cit.* (n. 5), p. 315.

[18] On Dürer's engraving and its meaning and influence see the classic account by Erwin Panofsky, *Albrecht Dürer* (Princeton, 1943), I, 156–71.

with the indoor objects near her but also with the land and the sea outside. Pope has gone beyond Dürer in one respect. Eliminating from his icon all moral and philosophical meaning, he has made his goddess, as Dürer's is not, an agent. She is not acted upon; she acts. She does not merely share the surrounding gloom; she creates it— "Shades ev'ry flow'r, and darkens ev'ry green." In thus developing one effective quality and in omitting all extrinsic detail, Pope obeyed the injunctions of Shaftesbury, Spence, and other neoclassical critics and attempted to achieve the simplicity and directness of ancient allegory, which was often capable of creating its effect with a single iconic sign, a single attendant circumstance.[19] Most modern readers will doubtless prefer this radically simplified icon to the elaborately embroidered Father Thames. But there are no absolutes here. "Windsor Forest" is a poem of elegant description; "Eloisa," of intense passion. Each type of image is appropriate to its context. And in Pope's creative use of pictorial imagery in the next poem we shall examine we shall see that the elegant and elaborate icon can be fully as persuasive as the direct and simple.

The "Rape of the Lock" has often been called rococo. But if one wishes a pictorial analogue for the whole poem, none is more appropriate than the work of Correggio as it was understood by the eighteenth century[20] (see Plate III). In the description of the sylphs —"Some to the Sun their Insect-Wings unfold"—grace triumphs, and harsh, defining form tends, in this play of soft and blended color, to sink in clouds and dissolve in light.

> Transparent Forms, too fine for mortal Sight,
> Their fluid Bodies half dissolv'd in Light
>
> [Canto II, ll. 59, 61–62].

This rendition of delicate motion—of transient colors and waving wings—is surely the closest that any poet has ever come to the *sfumato* of Correggio.[21]

---

[19] Joseph Spence, *Polymetis* (London, 1747), p. 292, Dialogue XVIII; Shaftesbury, *Second Characters*, ed. Benjamin Rand (Cambridge, Mass., 1914), pp. 30–61; Muratori, *Della perfetta poesia italiana*, I, xiv (see above, pp. 160–61).

[20] See above, pp. 169–70.

[21] Pope was compared to Correggio in the eighteenth century by Daniel Webb, who says of the "Rape of the Lock": "The painting of Correggio alone verges on these poetic ideas. . . . One would imagine that Pope had been animated with the

The description of Belinda at her toilet, the concluding scene of the first canto, is richly pictorial.

> And now, unveil'd, the *Toilet* stands display'd,
> Each Silver Vase in mystic Order laid.

The words "unveil'd" and "display'd" are slight but unmistakable hints that the scene is to be treated as though it were a work of visual art.

> First, robed in White, the Nymph intent adores
> With Head uncover'd, the *Cosmetic* Pow'rs.
> A heav'nly Image in the Glass appears,
> To that she bends, to that her Eyes she rears;
> Th'inferior Priestess, at her Altar's side,
> Trembling, begins the sacred Rites of Pride.
> Unnumber'd Treasures ope at once, and here
> The various Off'rings of the World appear;
> From each she nicely culls with curious Toil,
> And decks the Goddess with the glitt'ring Spoil.
> This Casket *India*'s glowing Gems unlocks,
> And all *Arabia* breathes from yonder Box.
> The Tortoise here and Elephant unite,
> Transform'd to *Combs*, the speckled and the white.
> Here Files of Pins extend their shining Rows,
> Puffs, Powders, Patches, Bibles, Billet-doux.
> Now awful Beauty puts on all its Arms;
> The Fair each moment rises in her Charms,
> Repairs her Smiles, awakens ev'ry Grace,
> And calls forth all the Wonders of her Face
>
> [Canto I, ll. 121–42].

The scene can be annotated by references to painting: to the famous canvases of Titian ("Young Woman at Her Toilette" in the Louvre and "Venus with a Mirror" in Washington) and to Rubens' "Toilette of Venus" in Vienna (Plate XVI), in which the goddess looks into a mirror held by Cupid while an Ethiope (in an office similar to that of Belinda's Betty) stands at Venus' side.

In this brilliant scene the pictorial is the servant of a witty mean-

---

spirit of Correggio, that had taken possession of his pencil when he thus pictured the sylphs:

> *Some in the field of purest aether play,*
> *And bask and whiten in the blaze of day"*

(*An Inquiry into the Beauties of Painting* [London, 1760], pp. 129–30).

ing that does much more than parody the arming of the hero in epic poetry. These are "sacred Rites"—a mock mass offered on the altar of vanity. Each vase is laid in "*mystic* Order." Belinda, accompanied by an acolyte (the "inferior *Priestess*"), "rears" her eyes in the manner of one of Guido Reni's adoring saints (Plate VIII A; cf. Plates XII, XXI) to the "*heavenly* Image" in the glass. Pope's metaphor has been preserved in Reynolds' "Lady Sarah Bunbury Sacrificing to the Graces" (Plate XVII), in which the lady, caught in a posture of genuflection, pours incense on a smoking urn, while her "inferior Priestess" pours the water of libation into a vessel.[22]

Such scenes as these by no means exhaust the pictorial elements in the "Rape of the Lock." One has only to think of the allegorical portrait of Spleen with her handmaidens Ill Nature and Affectation by her side or of the outdoor scene in which the progress of Belinda on the river, surrounded by "fair Nymphs and well-drest Youths," suggests Cleopatra on the barge or a recumbent Venus. But these pictorially conceived scenes alone do not reveal the total pictorial form. For the manner of proceeding is essentially that which we considered in connection with the Greek romances, commented on in connection with Marino, Le Moyne, Marvell, and Dryden, and shall observe again in connection with Pope's satire on women.[23] We move from scene to scene, not in narrative progress (even though the mock epic is used as a central metaphor) but as though we were in a gallery. We first see Belinda's bedroom, then the aerial squadron, then the scene at the toilet. And so through the entire poem: we move visually from the inside to the out-of-doors and then back to the salon again until at the very end with the sylphs we "behold" the lock "kindling as it flies," drawing behind it "a radiant trail of hair." This is not like Homer's and Vergil's form, a narrative with occasional supporting pictures. It is a picture gallery with supporting comment and some narrative links.

THE "TEMPLE OF FAME"

Pope's adaptation of Chaucer's "House of Fame" constitutes a thorough realization of *ut pictura poesis*. The subject of the first and

[22] Reynolds has altered the scene. There is no mirror; a statue of the Graces has taken the place of Belinda's image in the glass. Sir Joshua has not dared to place his subject in a posture of bemused self-contemplation.

[23] See above, pp. 33, 105–6, 114, 117, 180, 181, 206, and below, pp. 238–39.

longer of the two sections of the poem is an enormous work of architecture and sculpture. In describing it the poet has largely limited himself to graphically representable detail. We shall analyze the first 275 lines in some detail, ignoring the remaining 249 lines, which are concerned in part with the pronouncement of Fame's judgment and in part with the Temple of Rumor, a structure which, because of the demands of the allegory, cannot be the stable edifice we are now about to view.

Pope has composed a "Train of Phantoms" into an "Intellectual Scene." That is, his temple is imaginatively created in imitation of no single work of art or scene but only in response to his own didactic and aesthetic requirements. It therefore enables us to observe Pope working with imaginative freedom in the iconic tradition, which all too often tied the poet to the creation of another artist.

The description begins with a landscape, observed from a position somewhere "betwixt Earth, Seas, and Skies." Excellently conceived and somewhat like Claude's paintings in detail, it shows no change from the composition by contrast and antithesis characteristic of "Windsor Forest." The words "here," "there," and "now" guide the eye to antithetically placed compositional masses: rocks and cities, wastes and forests, ships and temples, a clear sunny scene and one lost in clouds. The temple itself, which resembles Parian marble in its whiteness and which lies so high on a rock of ice that its summit is concealed in clouds, is introduced by one of Pope's most brilliant descriptions, a winter scene done in glittering white, for which there is no parallel in Chaucer's original.

> So *Zembla*'s Rocks (the beauteous Work of Frost)
> Rise white in Air, and glitter o'er the Coast;
> Pale Suns, unfelt, at distance roll away,
> And on th' impassive Ice the Lightnings play:
> Eternal Snows the growing Mass supply,
> Till the bright Mountains prop th' incumbent Sky:
> As *Atlas* fix'd, each hoary Pile appears,
> The gather'd Winter of a thousand Years.[24]

---

[24] Ll. 53–60. The pictorial qualities of this description were admired in the eighteenth century. "A real lover of painting will not be contented with a single view and examination of this beautiful winter-piece. ... The images are distinct, and the epithets lively and appropriate, especially the words, *pale, unfelt, impassive, incumbent, gathered*" (Warton, *op. cit.* [n. 5], I, 342).

The temple itself, with four brazen gates that "salute the diff'rent Quarters of the Sky," resembles Palladio's *La Rotonda*, a villa on a hill near Vicenza that was greatly admired in the eighteenth century.[25] Pope has modernized Chaucer's gothic. Gone are tower and hall, bower and gargoyle. But Pope's structure is Palladian only in its quadrangular shape. It otherwise bears no resemblance to the country seat of an eighteenth-century English gentleman. It is the construction of a mind intent upon representing in visual form the cultural and ethical achievements of mankind. Each side represents a different style. The western front is Grecian, supported by Doric pillars of white marble; the eastern is Assyrian-Persian, splendid in its elaborate and weird ornamentation; the southern is Egyptian; the northern, gothic. Each façade, except the gothic, is presented as a work of meaning and majesty. The Grecian is "sumptuous"; the eastern, "glorious"; the Egyptian, impressive; but the gothic is "o'er-wrought with Ornaments of barb'rous Pride," where Odin dies in a trance and the rude iron columns are smeared with blood.

Each of these "Frontispieces," as Pope calls them, is adorned with sculptures:

> Heroes in animated Marble frown,
> And Legislators seem to think in Stone [ll. 73–74].

These words, which recall similar phrases of Lovelace and Dryden, have a traditional iconic-epigrammatic quality. Some details are borrowed directly from particular statues:

> There great *Alcides*, stooping with his Toil,
> Rests on his Club, and holds th' *Hesperian* Spoil—

lines which Pope says he wrote "with an eye to the Position [i.e., posture] of the famous Statue of Farnese," a statue of Hercules greatly admired in the eighteenth century[26] (Plate XVIII A).

---

[25] In the same year (1715) that Pope's poem was first published there appeared the magnificently presented translation of Giacomo Leoni's *Architecture of A. Palladio*, to which were added several previously unpublished notes by Inigo Jones and which bore a Preface translated from the French of Du Bois. Among subscribers to these two volumes were Bridgewater, Marlborough, and Richard Steele. The publication did not create the Palladian vogue in England; it was symptomatic of it.

[26] Ll. 81–82 and Pope's note in the editions of 1715 and 1736. "The easiness, the strength, the beauty, and the muscles of the Hercules cannot be too much admired" (Berkeley, "Journal of a Tour in Italy 1717, 1718," in Alexander Campbell Fraser, *Life and Letters of George Berkeley* [Oxford, 1871], p. 517). Pope's friend Jervas made

Such details, borrowed directly from an ancient statue, would naturally tend to embody the stability of classical sculpture. But other sculptured details are in motion: trees move to Orpheus' music; Thebes rises to Amphion's lyre:

> The growing Tow'rs like Exhalations rise,
> And the huge Columns heave into the Skies.[27]

The description of the inside of the temple, where the roof is fretted with gold, the pillars wreathed in laurel, the walls made of transparent beryl, is similarly iconic. It is somewhat reminiscent of the setting of Raphael's "School of Athens," in which classically draped figures are placed in a temple of imposing proportions, and of the interior of the Pantheon in Rome as it was seen by eighteenth-century eyes. Historians, who will adjudicate the worth of heroic deeds, are dressed in white. Over their seats stands the figure of Time, his scythe reversed, his pinions bound—a pictorial personification not unlike those of "Windsor Forest."[28] Of similar nature are the heroes next presented. It may be true, as has been suggested,[29] that behind these descriptions lay knowledge and admiration of antique statues. But behind them also lay the tradition of iconic poetry. Pope contemplates the statue itself, introducing it by means

---

at least four drawings of the Farnese Hercules (*Rape of the Lock*, ed. Geoffrey Tillotson [Twickenham ed.; London, 1950], p. 231) and on one occasion painted the statues of Venus, Apollo, and Hercules for Pope. Unquestionably Pope was familiar with Jervas' collection of sketches and reproductions of the ancient marbles.

[27] Ll. 91–92. John Dennis (*Critical Works*, ed. Edward Niles Hooker [Baltimore, Md., 1943], II, 143) criticized the "pretence" that sculptured stone can imitate motion. Of these lines he said: "*Trees starting from their Roots*, a *Mountain rolling into a Wall*, and a *Town rising like an Exhalation* are Things that are not to be shown in Sculpture." But Dennis flies in the face of what both sculpture and painting, especially in the baroque mode, had attempted to do. The very scene Pope describes was not considered too difficult for painting: in Tiepolo's "The Power of Eloquence," a ceiling fresco in the Palazzo Sandi, Venice, the chief episode portrays Amphion standing on a rock and striking his lyre. Bricks and stones are, by the power of music, being "blown" into their places on the growing walls. See Antonio Morassi, "Some 'Modelli' . . . by Tiepolo," *Burlington Magazine*, XCVII (January, 1955), 4–12, for a reproduction and analysis. Milton (*Paradise Lost* i. 711) says that Pandemonium "Rose like an Exhalation."

[28] "Temple," ll. 146–48. The reversing of insignia indicates dishonor (Tillotson, *op. cit.* [n. 26], p. 254). Time has been challenged and defeated by human achievement.

[29] *Ibid.*, pp. 232–33.

of the identifying signum (Alexander's "horn'd Head," for example) and the characteristic posture ("Unconquer'd *Cato* shews the Wound he tore"). He then adds the brief, epitaph-like summary of the subject's leading characteristics:

> And wise Aurelius, in whose well-taught Mind
> With boundless Pow'r unbounded Virtue join'd,
> His own strict Judge, and Patron of Mankind
> [ll. 154, 176, 165–67].

Such a combination of graphic detail and succinct comment goes to the very heart of the iconic tradition. It reminds us of the seventeenth-century emblem, which unites design and mot; of the *Greek Anthology*, where epigrams tersely interpret works of art; and of the very ancient association of tomb and epitaph, urn and inscription, statue and motto.

At the very center of the scene, around the throne of Fame herself, stand the statues of the literary great. Here Pope's virtuosity is at its highest. Homer and Vergil, Pindar and Horace, Aristotle and Cicero are presented in antithetical and balanced scenes. Antithesis is itself one of the hallmarks of Pope's wit and verbal structure, but here, as in the landscapes, it is graphically expressed. The cultural past is given intellectually stylized visual form. Cultural history and literary value are presented pictorially. The qualities of each writer are distinguished by means peculiar to the spatial arts. The posture of Cicero,

> Gath'ring his flowing Robe, he seem'd to stand,
> In Act to speak, and graceful, stretch'd his Hand [ll. 240–41],

is that of an antique statue. It could, in fact, be a description of the statue of Augustus now in the Vatican (Plate XVIII B).

Pindar, in contrast, is presented in a sculptured mythological progress.

> Four Swanns sustained a Carr of Silver bright,
> With Heads advanc'd, and Pinions stretch'd for Flight:
> Here, like some furious Prophet, *Pindar* rode,
> And seem'd to labour with th' inspiring God.
> A-cross the Harp a careless Hand he flings,
> And boldly sinks into the sounding Strings.
> The figur'd Games of *Greece* the Column grace,

Neptune and *Jove* survey the rapid Race:
The Youths hand o'er their Chariots as they run;
The fiery Steeds seem starting from the Stone;
The Champions in distorted Postures threat,
And all appear'd Irregularly great [ll. 210–21].

Pope has carved this statue in the high baroque of Bernini, in which stone is rhythmically expressive of dramatic movement and emotional excitement. The heads of the swans are thrust forward, their wings stretched for flight. The poet is caught in a moment of rapture, and the stone is made to do the visually impossible, for Pindar "boldly sinks into the sounding Strings." In the race on the adjoining column young men hang over their chariots and, "The fiery Steeds seem starting from the Stone."

Such is the virtuosity of Pope and such the range of his artistic enthusiasms that he can in one paragraph present the monumental fixity of Roman art and in the next the flowing lines and agitated movement of Bernini. All this is appropriate, of course, to Pope's meaning, of which the visual details are the sole instruments. Pope's is not a Bower of Bliss or a Palace of Art. It is a brilliant but essentially sober attempt to tell, in visual icons, the truth about history. Pope has, with that feeling for decorum that never deserted him, suited scene to sense.

In some respects Pope has surpassed his original, not in narrative motion or in the fresh, naïve charm that will always remain one of the permanent endearments of Chaucer, but in magnificence of scene and descriptive power. There is nothing in the "House of Fame" to equal the jewel-studded brocade of the "Temple," ablaze with color and light. Chaucer is not insensitive to the beauty that surrounds him, but his usual response is that of stupefied silence. He finds

> That al the men that ben on lyve
> Ne han the kunnynge to descrive
> The beaute of that ylke place,

and

> That hit astonyeth yit my thought,
> And maketh al my wyt to swynke
> [Book III, ll. 1167–69, 1174–75].

Chaucer describes the goddess' throne as follows:

> But al on hye, above a dees,
> Sitte in a see imperiall
> That mad was of a rubee all,
> Which that a carbuncle ys ycalled,
> Y saugh, perpetually ystalled,
> A femynyne creature,
> That never formed by nature
> Nas such another thing yseye
> [Book II, ll. 1360–67].

But Chaucer's extremity is Pope's opportunity.

> Full in the midst, proud *Fame*'s Imperial Seat
> With Jewels blaz'd, magnificently great;
> The vivid Em'ralds there revive the Eye;
> The flaming Rubies shew their sanguine Dye;
> Bright azure Rays from lively Saphirs stream,
> And lucid Amber casts a Golden Gleam.
> With various-colour'd Light the Pavement shone,
> And all on fire appear'd the glowing Throne;
> The Dome's high Arch reflects the mingled Blaze,
> And forms a Rainbow of alternate Rays [ll. 248–57].

The "Temple of Fame" does not deserve the neglect into which it has fallen in our time.[30] It is admittedly not Pope at his best and often shows the strain of its own virtuosity. But it cannot be neglected by anyone who wishes to understand Pope's visual imagination, since it experimentally embodies the leading elements of Pope's pictorialism. It is also of historical importance as an expression of the iconic tradition and as an illustration of Pope's relation to baroque as well as classical art. But above all it demonstrates the poet's incredible visual-verbal virtuosity—his ability to absorb styles of the greatest diversity and to manipulate visual details to express complex meanings. The "Temple of Fame" allows us to see Pope's pictorial imagination in full and uninhibited play and alerts us to qualities that in better poems may lie below the surface. A similar opportunity is presented by the translation of the *Iliad*.

[30] An exception is G. Wilson Knight, "Symbolic Eternities: An Introduction to *The Temple of Fame*," *Laureate of Peace* (London, 1954), pp. 79–110.

Petrarch, following the example of Cicero and other ancients, introduced into Western culture the habit of calling Homer a painter. Pope indulges the same habit. Among the many examples of Homer's inventive genius—and Homer's invention is specifically the subject of Pope's Preface to the *Iliad*—is his ability to "draw his characters with so visible and surprising a variety" that "no painter could have distinguished them more by their features." He was also a creator of landscape: "He not only gives us the full prospects of things, but several unexpected peculiarities and side-views, unobserved by any painter but Homer." Homer's epithets Pope regards as pictorial, as providing "a sort of supernumerary picture of the persons or things to which they are joined." Pope's explanatory notes, intended to comment on Homer as poet, also express the view that to be a poet was to be a painter. Pope obviously regards the *Iliad* as a pictorial poem. Certain of its passages remind him of Raphael and Giulio Romano, of Guido Reni and Rubens. He admires the description of the duel in Book II as an "exact Piece of Painting where we see every Attitude, Motion, and Action of the Combatants particularly and distinctly." He finds as the distinguishing beauty of Book X—and here Pope invokes the ancient principle of *enargeia*—"the Liveliness of its Paintings": "the chief Beauty of it is in the Prospect, a finer than which was never drawn by any Pencil." Here is "the most natural Night-Scene in the World"; "we see the very Colour of the Sky," the "marshy spot" where Dolon is killed, "the aquatic plants on which they hang his spoils, the heaped reeds"—details "the most Picturesque imaginable."[31] It is manifestly wrong to say that only in Thomson and the poets of the later eighteenth century was there appreciation of literary landscape. It exists full-blown in the literary taste of Pope.

But if he found his original to be highly pictorial, he has made it even more so in translation.[32] This heightening of the visual manifests itself in many ways. Often when Homer's scene is in black and white, Pope's is in color. Homer repeats the same color from

[31] I quote from the notes to the first edition of Pope's translation of the *Iliad* (London, 1715–20), I, 3; III, 140. See also Austin Warren, *Alexander Pope as Critic and Humanist* (Princeton, N.J., 1929), p. 111.

[32] See Thomas Twining, "On Poetry Considered As an Imitative Art," *Aristotle's Treatise on Poetry* (2d ed.; London, 1812), I, 46 ff.

epithet to epithet; Pope changes it, or at least varies the hue. Homer's color is usually single and conventional; Pope's colors provide vivid contrast or blend into chordlike harmonies in which scene is related to scene, figure to figure, and sometimes person to landscape.[33]

Pope's translation elaborates the pictorial images of the original by altering line and design, by rearranging the position of objects, and by using English verbs that carry visual images not present in the Greek. These changes may be illustrated in the following passage, in which the visual words and phrases not present in Homer are italicized:

> Now *circling round* the walls their course maintain,
> Where the *high* watch-tower *overlooks* the *plain;*
> Now where the fig-trees spread their *umbrage broad*
> (A wider compass), *smoke* along the road.
> Next by Scamander's double source they bound,
> Where two famed fountains burst the parted ground:
> This hot thro' scorching clefts is seen to rise,
> With exhalations steaming to the skies;
> That the *green* banks in summer's heat o'erflows,
> Like *crystal clear*, and cold as winter snows.
> Each gushing fount a *marble* cistern fills,
> Whose polish'd bed receives the falling rills

[Book XXII, ll. 191–202].

Pope's tendency to pictorialize is also found in the indexes that follow the translation. One of these, called a "Poetical Index," is a guide to the various beauties of Homer. One of its headings is "Descriptions or Images," and among its many subheadings (places, persons, things, times, and seasons) there is one that deserves mention: *"Descriptions of the* Internal Passions, or of *their visible effects."* Pope's phrasing reminds us of the theory of expression used in the seventeenth century to explain the art of portrait painting. The skill of the portraitist lies precisely in his ability to render "internal passions" by their "visible effects." That painterly skill Pope finds eminently illustrated in Homer—in the description of Agamemnon, for example, who suffers and sighs while he sleeps, his limbs trembling; of Achilles reclining on his arm and wearing a brow of gloom. Here the admiration of the sculpturesque pose is consciously expressed; it is justified on the grounds that aesthetic

[33] In this paragraph I am indebted to Ault, *op. cit.* (n. 3).

beauty resides in the ability to show emotion and meaning through arrested physical motion and visual detail.

In another index appended to the translation, the "Index of Arts and Sciences," there is the heading, "Painting, Sculpture, &c." The reader is referred to passages that Pope evidently considered picturesque or statuesque. Under "Beauty" Pope refers to the "alluring" beauty of Venus, the "majestic" beauty of Juno, the womanly beauty of Helen, and the youthful male beauty of Paris. "Majesty" is also variously classified and illustrated by Jupiter, Mars, Agamemnon; by wise old men like Nestor; and by a young hero like Achilles. Again one feels the presence in Pope's imagination of the recollection of sculptured stone. He sees, as Reynolds was to see later, the generic forms of general nature in terms of the classical marbles. But this habit of mind should not be exaggerated. For Pope also had a sense of the grotesque, which he associated with the pictorial. Under "Painting, Sculpture, &c." he includes the category "deformity" and illustrates it by the description of Thersites. This qualification is important. Pictorial beauty is not exclusively ideal beauty for Pope. We are justified in viewing the visual grotesquerie of the "Dunciad" as a part of Pope's pictorialism.

Under the same heading, "Painting, Sculpture, &c.," Pope refers to the famous description of Achilles' shield as an "image of the whole world" (*clypeus vasti coelatus imagine mundi*, as Ovid said).[34] Having discussed the Homeric passage earlier, we shall now examine it only in the workshop of Pope. This passage in the eighteenth book of the *Iliad* showed, he believed, Homer's "Genius for description" in its "full Lustre": and Pope regarded as the most fundamental task of the critic that of appreciating

the Piece as a complete *Idea* of *Painting*, and a Sketch for what one may call an *universal Picture*. This is certainly the Light in which it is chiefly to be admired, and in which alone the Criticks have neglected to place it.[35]

Because this is Pope's view of the shield—and how unlike Lessing's that view is!—it is not surprising that he should have published Boivin's attempt to reduce Homer's verse to design and given sanction to the pictorialist criticism that regarded Homer's verse as blameless from the graphic artist's point of view, possessing

---

[34] Cited by Pope, *op. cit.* (n. 31), V, 129.   [35] *Ibid.*, p. 138.

design, disposition, and aerial perspective.[36] Nor is it surprising that in translating this passage Pope should strengthen the pictorial and iconic elements by heightening the colors, sharpening the design, elaborating the detail, and stressing the purely aesthetic qualities of the object.

Pope compared to Homer reveals the same qualities as Pope compared to Chaucer. The pictorialist theory of his age, to which he fully subscribed, the force of the iconic tradition, and the natural bent of his mind led him to diminish and simplify narrative and to heighten and elaborate scene. From this there is aesthetic loss and aesthetic gain. The movement is slower; the texture correspondingly richer. Most modern readers would unquestionably feel that the loss has outweighed the gain, that splendor of scene cannot compensate for the diminution of narrative energy, that what Johnson called "Ovidian beauties" are not adequate substitutes for Homer's narrative verve.

But even while conceding that the textures of the "Temple of Fame" and the *Iliad* are excessively embroidered and that the resemblance to plastic art is sometimes pushed too far, we must say that Pope's poetry in its totality would have suffered without such works as these and that his best poetry would have been something vastly different from what it is had he not given his mind so unstintingly to pictorial effects. We are beginning to realize, more fully than the nineteenth century ever did, that Pope was a poet of sensuous richness. Some of that richness is owing to the splendor and sophistication of his pictures. In "Eloisa," the "Rape of the Lock," and some of the satires, pictorial forms are used with creative relevance. And to that poetic achievement the more experimentally pictorial poems made their contribution.

The "Temple of Fame" and the *Iliad* are also of historical importance. They not only embodied the pictorialist tradition; they helped perpetuate it. Steele said the Temple has "a thousand beauties," and Johnson observed of it that "every part is splendid; there is great luxuriance of ornaments."[37] Goldsmith said of the

---

[36] *Ibid.*, pp. 129–30; 135 ff.; 151. See also William Whitehead, "Observations on the Shield of *Aeneas*," in *Works of Vergil*, trans. Joseph Warton and Christopher Pitt (London, 1753), III, 457–92.

[37] *Works of Samuel Johnson* (Oxford, 1825), VIII, 326, where Steele's comment is quoted. It should be added that Johnson qualified his praise by remarking on this allegory's remoteness from life.

translation of Homer: "The Grecian bard says simply, the sun rose; and his translator gives us a beautiful picture of the sun rising. . . . If this be a deviation, it is at the same time an improvement."[38] And it may not be fanciful to see in Pope's view of the pictorial and statuesque beauty of Homer an anticipation of Count Caylus, who some forty-two years later published his *Tableaux tirés de l'Iliade, de l'Odyssée . . .*, an anthology of pictorial passages in the epics recommended as subjects to painters, and of Winckelmann, who, like Pope, classified Greek beauty into Phidian majesty and Lysippian and Appelean grace.[39]

SATIRICAL PICTURES

Much has been made of those lines in Pope's satires in which he says that he turned from "Fancy's maze" (where "pure Description held the place of Sense"), "stooped to Truth, and moralized his Song"; that, led by the philosopher Bolingbroke, he

> . . . turn'd the tuneful art
> From sounds to things, from fancy to the heart;
> For Wit's false mirror held up Nature's light.[40]

These statements, often interpreted as a confession of change in literary program, need not be taken so seriously. Pope never really abandoned wit or fancy; he never turned *from* sounds, and he had never really had to turn *to* things, sense, or Nature's light, all of which had held his allegiance from the beginning. It is true that he did write didactic and satiric verse almost exclusively in his later years. Because the satiric muse was considered the meanest of the nine and because didactic verse was considered less imaginative than other poetry, Pope may have been unconsciously piqued

[38] Cited by C. V. Deane, *Aspects of Eighteenth Century Nature Poetry* (Oxford, 1935), p. 53.

[39] The date of the *Tableaux* is 1757–58. See Winckelmann, *History of Ancient Art*, trans. G. Henry Lodge (1881), II, 132 ff. For additional comments by Pope that illustrate this tendency of his criticism see *op. cit.* (n. 31), Vol. VI, "Index of Arts and Sciences" under "painting," "sculpture," "beauty," and "majesty." In view of the fact that Winckelmann had read Spence, it is not entirely unlikely that there was a relationship between the classicism of Pope and his circle and that of the sculpture and design of the late eighteenth century and the Napoleonic era.

[40] "Epistle to Dr. Arbuthnot," ll. 148, 340–41; "Essay on Man," Epistle IV, ll. 391–93.

into a justification of his choice in terms somewhat more honorific than they need be.

At any rate, most of the changes in Pope's verse can be explained by generic requirements, to which he always paid close attention. They do not involve a change of aesthetic or philosophical principle or a serious alteration in his taste. The "Dunciad"—with its controlling metaphors of Chaos and Old Night, its vivid embodiments of crawling, damp, embryonic inchoateness, its mock-heroic scenes and stances, its verse forms and textures that reveal the pressure of the subject—is as much a work of mimetic, imaginative art as the "Rape of the Lock." Even the "Essay on Man" is more than versified argument and may properly be viewed as a dramatic-rhetorical monologue addressed to a person who is characterized as morally proud and ethically complacent, to whom the somewhat urgent and agitated imperatives, "ask," "go," "mark," "see," and "know," are addressed, and before whom is unrolled the entire panorama of man, nature, and society.

It is surely wrong to assume that the pictorial artist died when Pope turned to moral and satirical poetry. Color words do, upon actual count, become fewer; the set scene, inserted and enjoyed for its own sake, less prominent (but actually that had never been very prominent in Pope); and painterly epithets less frequent.[41] But again these changes can be mostly explained by the requirements of the genre to which Pope turned. There is an adaptation to a different verse form but not an abandonment of the pictorialism of his earliest period.

We have already observed the association between satire and painting present in the works of Marino, Marvell, and Dryden. That association Pope maintained and extended. He maintained, for one thing, the comparison of the satirical character to a portrait. He said that his satire "against the misapplication of [human reason and science]" is to be exemplified by "pictures, characters, and examples."[42] In the Advertisement of the "Epistle to Dr. Arbuthnot," he said: "Many will know their own pictures in it." Such offhand phrases should not be pushed too far. They may, like the verbs "draw" and "paint" when used for "describe" or "write," have lost most of their metaphoric force. But the fact that

[41] See Ault, *op. cit.* (n. 3), p. 100.

[42] Elwin and Courthope, *op. cit.* (n. 14), VII, 341.

Pope does make creative use of the metaphor in his satires gives some importance even to its casual manifestations in his commentary.

Pope continued to the very end of his career to introduce, when relevant, the paintable allegorical personification. Prudence appears with her glass; Justice with her scales; and in one place the Pythagorean Y stands for the choice of life (elsewhere elaborated into the Choice of Hercules).[43]

Pope learned from Dryden that a satirical character was not delineated chiefly by pictorial and visual detail and that all the abstract, intellectual, and non-imagistic powers of language should be levied for their contribution. Pope's "portraits," like Dryden's, are essentially rhetorical analyses—brilliant, concise summaries of the intellectual and moral qualities of the victim. The same is true of the panegyrical characters that appear in the "Essay on Criticism" and "To Augustus."

Pope's characters, however, are less declamatory than Dryden's and more elaborately aesthetic.[44] This quality arises partly from a more subtle and skilful use of all the devices that we have come to recognize as indispensable to Pope's poetic art: the antithesis, the pun, the zeugma, the rhyme itself, the onomatopeia, occasional chiasmus, bathos, and all the varieties of comparison from the witty to the sublime. But greater aesthetic richness in Pope also arises from greater pictorial richness in the imagery. Full-blown Bufo sitting on his forked hill is a *picture* of fatness and flatulence, to which almost every detail—the auditory, the kinesthetic, the purely intellectual—contributes its bit. Timon and his villa are visualized in a pattern, and on that patterned visualization is built the entire passage. Almost all the details are designed to irritate what Pope calls in one of the lines "the suffering eye." The successful portrait, of course, rises above merely pleasing or irritating the eye. Visual detail contributes to moral vision. In the lines on Timon we see monstrous grandeur as an ironic revelation of moral and

[43] "Dunciad" (A), Book I, ll. 50–52; "Dunciad" (B), Book IV, ll. 151–52 and Pope's note on the last. See above, pp. 190–93.

[44] See Maynard Mack, " 'Wit and Poetry and Pope': Some Observations on His Imagery," in Clifford and Landa, *op. cit.* (n. 3), pp. 20–40. Robert W. Rogers has clearly perceived the importance of the analogy between painting and the characters in Pope's satirical poetry (*The Major Satires of Alexander Pope* [Urbana, Ill., 1955], pp. 60–61).

emotional smallness. To that vision of poverty amidst profuseness all the details—from the gladiators that fight and die in flowers to the rich buffet adorned with "well-colour'd Serpents"—contribute form and meaning. "Lo, what huge heaps of littleness around!"[45]

Dryden was the master of the brief visual image that brightens a rhetorical passage. Pope was capable of that effect too.

> *Eve*'s tempter thus the Rabbins have exprest
> A Cherub's face, a reptile all the rest.[46]

But it is a part of Pope's aesthetic enrichment of Dryden that he has brought to so didactic and witty an art as that of satire the ability to make visual metaphor serve as a guiding and governing image.

The sustaining of pictorial metaphor in satire is nowhere better illustrated than in "Of the Characters of Women," Epistle II of the "Moral Essays." The image that unifies and controls the entire satire is drawn from the art of painting. The satire is a consummate variant of the genre of satiric iconic poetry. And in its manner of proceeding it clearly reveals total pictorial form.

In the opening lines Pope introduces the theme—*la donna é mobile.* Even here, before the ruling metaphor has been presented, he delicately anticipates it by referring to the characters of women as "matter" too "soft" to bear a lasting mark and to our habit of distinguishing women by their coloration.

> Nothing so true as what you once let fall,
> 'Most Women have no Characters at all.'
> Matter too soft a lasting mark to bear,
> And best distinguish'd by black, brown, or fair.

In the next paragraph Pope introduces the comparison with painting. Its immediate function is to illustrate the variability of the sex, apparent in its desire to be painted in different historical and mythological roles—roles, incidentally, that express with brilliant irony profound inconsistencies of moral character and social position.

> How many Pictures of one Nymph we view,
> All how unlike each other, all how true!
> Arcadia's Countess, here, in ermin'd pride,

[45] See "Arbuthnot," ll. 231–50; "Moral Essays," Epistle IV, ll. 99–168.

[46] "Arbuthnot," ll. 330–31. For Dryden, see above, pp. 181–84.

Is there, Pastora by a fountain side.
Here Fannia, leering on her own good man,
And there, a naked Leda with a Swan.
Let then the Fair one beautifully cry,
In Magdalen's loose hair and lifted eye,
Or drest in smiles of sweet Cecilia shine,
With simp'ring Angels, Palms, and Harps divine.

These literary portraits embody some of the motifs of high Renaissance and baroque painting that, in the fashionable studios of the eighteenth century, were to appear again as witty, delicate, and sometimes merely outrageous society allegories. The first picture of the countess reflects not only the fashionable Arcadianism of the period but the love of painting rich stuffs and materials characteristic of two centuries of portraiture, from Raphael d'Urbino to Raphael Mengs.[47] The portrait of the same lady as Pastora may actually "quote" a contemporary painting of Margaret Sawyer, the Countess of Pembroke, by John Van der Vaart, in which the lady fondles a fleecy lamb.[48] Fannia, "leering on her own good man," is a husband-wife portrait, of which the self-portrait of Rubens with his first wife is one of the most famous examples. The uses of Leda and the Swan are too numerous to mention. Mary Magdalen with "loose hair and lifted eye" is an excellent one-line description of Titian's famous canvas in the Pitti [Plate XXI] and is not unlike some of Guido's heads (Plate VIII). St. Cecilia with angel, palm, and harp was, as we have seen, one of the favorite themes of serious baroque art and was later to be parodied wittily and elegantly by Reynolds (see Plates IX, XII, XIII).

In the next lines Pope draws the metaphoric noose still tighter. The ladies have been painted before; they shall be painted again in this poem. Pope the poet poses as Pope the painter.

Whether the Charmer sinner it, or saint it,
If Folly grows romantic, I must paint it.
Come then, the colours and the ground prepare!

[47] See, for example, the magnificent gold- and fur-trimmed garments in Mengs's (1728–79) "Ritratto del Cantante Domenico Annibale" in the Brera, Milan, or in the portrait of the Marquess of Monthermer now in the collection of the Duke of Buccleuch (printed in color opposite page 3 in the *Connoisseur*, February, 1955).

[48] Reproduced in Pope, *Epistles to Several Persons*, ed. F. W. Bateson (Twickenham ed.; London, 1951), opposite p. 48.

Dip in the Rainbow, trick her off in Air,
Chuse a firm Cloud, before it fall, and in it
Catch, ere she change, the Cynthia of this minute.

Again, these lines serve an immediate purpose. "Air," "rainbow," and "the Cynthia of *this minute*" enforce the theme, the infinite variableness of women. But they also point to the satiric-iconic tradition we have discussed in earlier chapters. Both in literature and life, poets, as we have learned, had been accustomed to instruct painters. In writing political satires Marvell had pretended to be giving instructions to a painter; Ben Jonson had done the same in writing social panegyric.[49] Marino, in preparing his literary *Galeria*, commissioned many painters to do his bidding, and Shaftesbury on one occasion gave specifications to Paolo Matthaeis for a "Judgment of Hercules" and on another occasion tried to get the Roman sculptor Guidi to collaborate in executing statues to represent the different virtues.[50] There was ample precedent in both art and history for the imperatives "the ground prepare," "dip in the Rainbow," and "trick her off in Air."

The remarks now to be made concerning total form will be fully persuasive only if they are related to our earlier discussions of Marino and Marvell, both of whom used the word "gallery" in their titles, and of Pierre le Moyne, who used throughout his entire *Peintures morales* the analogy of a gallery[51] [see Plate I]. There were other galleries, closer at hand, that Pope may also have known.[52] The most important consideration, however, does

[49] See above, p. 121. Jonson's is a variant of the usual type of instruction. The poet admits that the painter had drawn Lady Venetia's body with skill. He is therefore summoned to paint her mind as well, but is soon scornfully dismissed by the poet, who says: "This work I can performe alone" ("Eupheme; or, the Faire Fame . . . of . . . the Lady Venetia Digby," secs. 3, 4, in *Under-Wood* [London, 1640]). See Bernard H. Newdigate (ed.), *The Poems of Ben Jonson* (Oxford, 1936), pp. 205–8.

[50] See above, p. 102, and E[dgar] W[ind], "Shaftesbury as a Patron of Art," *Journal of the Warburg Institute*, II (1938–39), 186–88.

[51] See above, pp. 105–6. On one occasion Pope compared the several descriptions of Achilles to "a gallery full of pictures" (*op. cit.* [n. 31], XIX, 197 n.).

[52] In the *Beaux' Stratagem*, Act IV, Aimwell, Dorinda, Mrs. Sullen, and Archer go through the country house looking at paintings, which are briefly described and then used by the clever Archer to further his own gallantries. In *Spectator*, No. 83— itself influenced, I believe, by Marvell's if not Marino's poem—Addison sees in a

not concern the specific source but the embodiment in this poem of the picture-gallery manner of proceeding. Here there is a deliberate and unmistakable use of a form which governs the construction of much neoclassical poetry. We move in this poem from portrait to portrait, just as in other poems we move from scene to scene, tableau to tableau, pageant to pageant.

The analogy with painting not only provided Pope with his form but with his message as well. The metaphor touches Pope's meaning at three points. The first we have already discussed: the same woman adopts a new and contradictory role for each portrait in which she appears—a fact that becomes symbolic of the moral paradox Pope finds in each character he delineates. The second contact is revealed in the following passage:

> . . . Artists! who can paint or write,
> To draw the Naked is your true delight.
> That Robe of Quality so struts and swells,
> None see what Parts of Nature it conceals.
> Th'exactest traits of Body or of Mind,
> We owe to models of an humble kind.
> If Queensberry to strip there's no compelling,
> 'Tis from a Handmaid we must take a Helen,
> From Peer or Bishop 'tis no easy thing
> To draw the man who loves his God, or King:
> Alas! I copy (or my draught would fail)
> From honest Mah'met or plain Parson Hale
> [ll. 187–98].

Pope uses the metaphor, in a Swiftian manner reminiscent of the clothes philosophy of *A Tale of a Tub*, to deny the possibility of achieving worth in society portraits, where neither naked truth, naked beauty, nor naked virtue can possibly appear. In Titian's "Sacred and Profane Love" in the Borghese Gallery, sacred love is nude and profane love clothed.[53] In the world Pope satirizes there is no sacred love; all is profane, all is clothed and covered. For

dream a gallery of living and dead painters. Galleries devoted exclusively to portraits of women were not unknown in the eighteenth century. One room in the Palace of Peterhof, near Petrograd, contained a series of 863 portraits painted by Count Rotari (1707–62), a pupil of Solimena, on the order of Catherine II (Sacheverell Sitwell, *Southern Baroque Art* [London, 1924]).

[53] Erwin Panofsky, *Studies in Iconology* (New York, 1939), pp. 151 ff.

true beauty one must turn to the handmaid; for honest virtue, to the Turkish servant or the humble parson.

The third point at which the comparison serves Pope's deepest satirical meaning concerns color.

> Some wand'ring touches, some reflected light,
> Some flying stroke alone can hit 'em right:
> For how should equal Colours do the knack?
> Chameleons who can paint in white and black?
>
> [ll. 153–56].

If equal (that is, simple, unmixed) colors and black and white will not do for such "variegated Tulips" as women, one must of course dip the brush in the rainbow. Rainbows are beautiful—and Pope, as we have seen, was a lover of color who mixed the hues and tints delicately on his poetic palette. But these facts should not blind us to Pope's meaning in this poem, the theme of which is *varium et mutabile est semper femina*. Women must be painted in blended colors, not primarily because they are beautiful—although they are surely that—but because they are evanescent, superficial, ephemeral.

Such a Swiftian view of color had, paradoxically, been present in Pope from the very beginning. It had also been present in Western thought at least as early as the protest of the patristic authors against pagan sensuousness. In the "Essay on Criticism" the lines of a drawing were used to represent good sense; the colors, false learning (ll. 22–25). In another passage the "treacherous colours" fade and betray the whole design (ll. 483–94). In the first of the "Moral Essays" the phrase "Opinion's colours" is followed by these lines:

> All Manners take a tincture from our own,
> Or come discolour'd thro' our Passions shown.
> Or Fancy's beam enlarges, multiplies,
> Contracts, inverts, and gives ten thousand dyes.[54]

These are the pejorative associations of the term "color"— falseness, fancifulness, transience. They affect the meaning of Pope's

[54] Ll. 22, 25–28. Maynard Mack points out that the analogy with painting was frequently used in psychological and ethical discussions. He cites several examples from Senault, La Bruyère, and Edward Young (*Essay on Man*, Epistle II, ll. 119–22 and n. [Twickenham ed.; London, 1950], p. 69).

satire on women and explain why the painter-poet prepared the colors, dipped his pencil in the rainbow, and compared the fair to "variegated Tulips."

Could any analogy be more essential to a poem than Pope's is to this satirical epistle? It provides him with his general form and pose; and three specific practices of contemporary and earlier portraitists—the use of allegorical and mythological fables, the habit of painting the subjects fully and elaborately clothed, and the use of variegated colors—are keys that open the moral meaning. And that meaning unfolds with relevant and persuasive force because all these analogical elements—garments and postures, canvases and colors—point to the glittering but unstable surfaces of fashionable life. Never have the analogy with painting and the iconic tradition been put to subtler and more effective satiric use.

We began this chapter by comparing Pope to Dryden, and it may serve to summarize the peculiar contribution of each to literary pictorialism if we now conclude that comparison. Both, with revealing frequency, drew the analogy between poetry and painting and demonstrated through many signs that they were inheritors of the entire pictorialist tradition. Both knew intimately the leading painters of their own day, but Pope, himself a painter, was perhaps in closer touch with the aesthetic tendencies of Augustan England than Dryden was with those of the Restoration. Both poets adapted the icons of Ripa and of the classical tradition, but Pope's icons are more elaborate, denser in detail, richer in texture.

Both poets possess qualities that must be called baroque. It is important that we notice this fact in Pope, for any analysis that concentrates exclusively on his dominant classical qualities misses an element of richness and complexity. Pope is of course further from Guercino and Domenichino, Rubens and Bernini, than was Dryden; but baroque impulses had not yet spent themselves, and they are present in Pope as an important if secondary strain. One thinks of the dark and sinister visual movements of the "Dunciad" and its brilliant adaptation of Miltonic imagery, coming to a baroque climax when Chaos, the dread anarch, like a dark and evil angel in the upper right-hand corner of a seventeenth-century eschatological canvas, "Lets the curtain fall; / And Universal Darkness buries All." Or one thinks of Eloisa, now a nun, imagining her own death in the presence of Abelard, who holds the cross before her lifted eyes:

> See my lips tremble, and my eye-balls roll,
> Suck my last breath, and catch my flying soul!
> Ah no—in sacred vestments may'st thou stand,
> The hallow'd taper trembling in thy hand,
> Present the Cross before my lifted eye,
> Teach me at once, and learn of me to die [ll. 323–28].

Or, again, one thinks of Eloisa's imagining the death of Abelard:

> In trance extatic may thy pangs be drown'd,
> Bright clouds descend, and Angels watch thee round,
> From opening skies may streaming glories shine,
> And Saints embrace thee with a love like mine [ll. 339–42].

These are echoes of the Counter Reformation, reminiscent of Domenichino's "Communion of St. Jerome"[55] (Plate XXII). The dying saint, now an old man, receives his viaticum in a church. Much as Abelard holds cross and taper before the dying Eloisa, so an old priest extends the wafer on a paten while a younger priest holds up the chalice. The saint, already in "trance extatic," lifts his eyes, like those of the dying Eloisa, to the host held before them and beyond it to the opening heavens, where a bevy of angels hover.

Yet baroque moments like these come less frequently in Pope than in Dryden. The word "baroque" can justly be applied to Dryden's odes as a whole but not to an entire poem of Pope, to say nothing of a whole genre. One entire side of Dryden's imagination can be illuminated by a comparison with Rubens, who is not consistently congenial to the genius of Pope. Rubens is of course occasionally relevant, but Pope's scene is so endlessly varied that no single painter and no single school within the large tradition can claim dominant rights. The "Rape of the Lock" suggests the grace of Correggio; "Windsor Forest" has Claude-like moments; "Eloisa" recalls Salvator Rosa. The "Temple of Fame" alternately reminds us of classical marbles, Bernini, Raphael, and perhaps also of the Farnese ceiling of Annibale Carracci.

---

[55] This parallel was suggested by Joseph Warton, *op. cit.* (n. 5), I, 325–26. Domenichino's was one of the most admired paintings of the period. Thomson's line (". . . and, as angels look / On dying saints, his eyes compassion shed" ["Summer," ll. 1202–3]) seems to be an echo (*Complete Poetical Works*, ed. J. Logie Robertson [Oxford, 1908]).

CHAPTER IX

James Thomson

The pictorialism of James Thomson has usually been viewed as a cause and not an effect. Joseph Warton said in 1756 that "the Seasons of Thomson have been very influential in diffusing a taste for the beauties of nature and landscape";[1] and ever since, Thomson's visual scene has been associated with landscape and conceived of as an influence upon romantic naturalism in garden, painting, and poem. Even studies of background and source have been chiefly concerned with Thomson as the first in a line of Claudian landscapists, important because of his anticipation of the "picturesque" of later poets and gardeners.[2]

This view of Thomson's influence on later culture cannot here be assessed, since this is a history of neoclassical and not romantic pictorialism. But the traditional point of view has had unfortunate consequences for the understanding of Thomson's verse both as a thing in itself and in its pictorial relations. By detaching Thomson from Pope and his contemporaries, it has discouraged us from seeing Thomson's imagery in its proper setting and proper historical relationships. By influencing us to look forward instead of back, it has diverted us from the true visual context of Thomson's work, which includes more than the art of Claude and Salvator Rosa. The traditional interpretation has also, by confining the picturesque

---

[1] *An Essay on the Genius and Writings of Pope* (London, 1806), II, 180.

[2] I refer chiefly to two influential studies with views that go back to Thomas Twining, Richard Graves, the Wartons, Percival Stockdale, and others in the eighteenth century: Elizabeth Wheeler Manwaring, *Italian Landscape in Eighteenth Century England* (New York, 1925), esp. pp. iii, 96, 101-8; and Christopher Hussey, *The Picturesque* (London, 1927), pp. 30-35. Unfortunately, the expert attention of Alan Dugald McKillop (*Background of Thomson's Seasons* [Minneapolis, Minn., 1942]) was not occupied with Thomson's pictorialism in the *Seasons;* but he has done pioneer research on pictorial theory in the *Background of Thomson's Liberty* (Rice Institute Pamphlet No. 38 [July, 1951], pp. 71-73).

almost exclusively to Salvatorian and Claudian prospects, obscured
Thomson's relations to iconic poetry, to ancient sculpture, and
to the central tradition of Renaissance and seventeenth-century
art. But perhaps the most serious charge that can be made against
it is that it has inadequately described even what it set out to
describe, Thomson's own landscape art.

THOMSON AND POPE: ICONIC IDEALIZATION

Our first task is to reverse the tendency of such scholarship
and criticism and, in the interest of proper historical perspective,
to separate Thomson from the forerunners of romanticism and
place him firmly among his neoclassical contemporaries. Without
denying that he was important in the rise and development of
romantic naturalism and without denying that there are substantial
differences in subject and manner between Pope and Thomson,
we must now view the two poets as intellectual and aesthetic contemporaries. In creating their visual scenes they responded to the
same traditions of pictorialism. Both, with relatively minor differences of emphasis, accepted the same pantheon of ancient and
modern graphic artists. Both looked to antiquity for inspiration;
both accepted as axiomatic the excellence of the art of the high
Renaissance and the seventeenth-century eclecticism. Like Pope
and Dryden, Thomson read and absorbed French art criticism—the
treatises of De Piles, Félibien, Dufresnoy, Du Bos, and Le Brun;
and he owned such standard English words on graphic art as Turnbull's history of painting and Spence's *Polymetis*. Like Pope and
Pope's circle of noble friends, Thomson admired Palladio and supported Palladianism. He also spoke on the subject of gardening to
none other than Shenstone, to whom he made specific recommenda-
tions for improving the Leasowes. Pope, as we have seen, was devoted
to paintings of ancient statues. So was Thomson, for among the
eighty-three engravings of paintings that he possessed there were
several drawings by Castelli of the most admired of the ancient
statues. The painters most frequently represented in Thomson's
personal collection of copies and prints were, in order of the number
of works by each that he owned, Carlo Maratti, Nicolas Poussin,
Raphael, Annibale Carracci, and Domenichino.[3] These are precisely

[3] My information about the engravings, copies of paintings, and art treatises
owned by Thomson comes from *A Catalogue of All the Genuine Houshold* [*sic*] *Furni-*

the painters most congenial to neoclassical taste, the painters French criticism had taught English gentlemen to appreciate. In matters related to traditional pictorialism there is little basic difference between Pope and Thomson.

Even in his personal contacts Thomson resembled his fellow poets. One is tempted to say that life as well as poetry imitates the conventions of the pictorialist tradition. Dryden was the friend of Kneller, and Pope the friend of Kneller, Jervas, landscape gardeners, architects, and noble patrons of these arts; Thomson, similarly, was on intimate terms with the painter Aikman, to whom, in the conventional manner, he addressed a poem of which the first stanza is a celebration of art and artist in terms sanctified by long and universal practice. He was also a friend of the painter-poet Dyer; of the gentlemen of the Prince of Wales's circle, largely men of taste and the collector's instincts; and of the Countess of Hertford, his patroness, who was a collector of paintings and prints and was herself something of a painter.[4]

In his travels it was apparently the landscape of Italy, so dear to Claude, Salvator Rosa, and their English followers, that impressed Thomson the least, even though one of his aims in going abroad had been to store his imagination with "ideas of all-beautiful, all-great, and all-perfect Nature"—the "pure *Materia Poetica*." In fact, he was greatly disappointed in the countryside through which he passed. What, then, did impress him? The "antique statues (where several of the fair ideas of Greece are fixed forever in marble)" and "the paintings of the first Masters." These were "indeed the most enchanting objects" that he saw. The paintings of Italy themselves were "vastly Superiour to the painting of all other Nations" not chiefly because the painters lived amid Claudian and Salvatorian natural scenery but because they were constantly exposed to the remains of Greece and Rome.[5] Thomson the traveler more often

ture: Plate, China, Prints and Drawings &c. of Mr. James Thomson (1749), a photostatic copy of which was lent me by Professor McKillop. For Thomson and Shenstone see Isabel Wakelin Urban Chase, *Horace Walpole: Gardenist* (Princeton, 1943), pp. 112–13.

[4] Manwaring, *op. cit.* (n. 2), p. 102; G. C. Macaulay, *James Thomson* (London, 1908), pp. 23–24, 35, n. 1, 45, 50–52, 153, 166.

[5] Douglas Grant, *James Thomson: Poet of "The Seasons"* (London, 1951), pp. 117, 127, 131.

reminds us of the neoclassical Joseph Addison than he does of William Beckford.

When we consider the visual passages of Thomson's poetry, we find that he is far from being exclusively a describer of external nature. The theme that attracts his eye is art *and* nature more often than nature alone, and from one point of view even his nature is art, "the finished university of things,"[6] in which design and not chance have determined form and established meaning. In Thomson's later poems, it is the art and industry of man that are celebrated as civilizing forces, that make nature available to man. In the "Castle of Indolence" the "Knight of Arts and Industry" is the hero who rescues victims of both natural and supernatural magic. In *Liberty* Thomson constructs a "palace of the laws"[7] and reads in the artistic memorials of mankind the civilizing deeds of heroes and legislators:

> If not by them, on monumental brass,
> On sculptured marble, on the deathless page
> Impressed, renown had left no trace behind:
> In vain, to future times, the sage had thought,
> The legislator planned, the hero found
> A beauteous death, the patriot toiled in vain.
> The awarders they of fame's immortal wreath!
> They rouse ambition, they the mind exalt,
> Give great ideas, lovely forms infuse,
> Delight the general eye, and dressed by them,
> The moral Venus glows with double charms
>
> [Part V, ll. 389–99].

This passage, which provides the point from which we must view Thomson's iconic scene, suggests that the descriptive portions of *Liberty* correspond in many ways to Pope's "Temple of Fame." The earlier poem describes an artificial, visual embodiment of cultural tradition and value. Thomson's story of Liberty's progress from nation to nation and culture to culture, ending finally in con-

---

[6] "To the Memory of Sir Isaac Newton," l. 140. Thomson's poetry is quoted from the *Complete Poetical Works*, ed. J. Logie Robertson (Oxford, 1908). When an early or variant draft of the *Seasons* is used, that fact is noted. Reference is made to title and line only.

[7] Part IV, l. 1180. The goddess Liberty uses the phrase to describe her "fabric" that "swells immense o'er many-peopled earth."

temporary England, is less statically conceived, but it too is a monument to the tradition of culture. Thomson's, however, is a more publicly and politically conceived tradition than is Pope's, a tradition not chiefly concerned with individual artists and isolated works of art, with an esteemed friend's painterly prowess, or with art as art or artist purely as artist, achieving the miracle of meaning and form in spite of intractable materials and insuperable obstacles. Thomson's poetical statues stand in a "palace of the laws," a kind of national museum where civic virtue is more important than purely artistic achievement.

So extensive a preoccupation with art did, of course, inevitably include many considerations of purely aesthetic concern. Some of Thomson's lines discuss the arts as a whole and attempt to develop a philosophy of their history and relationships. Sculpture was the eldest, teaching the fundamental laws of correct design—a primacy that we should not allow to go unnoticed in view of the basic importance of scultpure to eighteenth-century aesthetic idealism. From sculpture painting learned how to achieve her greatest grace, linear form. Other powers followed: the ability to express the motions of the soul, to achieve just and unified composition, to employ the morally significant fable, and to render the rural scene—all of them abilities shared equally by poetry. Everywhere—and here his resemblance to Pope's orientation to ancient and Renaissance aesthetic values is striking—Thomson celebrates the virtue of verisimilitude (of *enargeia*), demonstrated in the ability of the pencil to "shed mimic life" and of the chisel to become "the boast of well pleased nature."[8]

Many passages thus celebrate Grecian sculpture in general. But there are also detailed descriptions of individual masterpieces. In a noteworthy passage Thomson calls the roll, one by one, of the

[8] *Liberty*, Part II, ll. 314, 293. Cf. the lines on Grecian sculpture in general:
> ". . . Each dimple sunk,
> And every muscle swelled, as nature taught.
> In tresses, braided gay, the marble waved;
> Flowed in loose robes, or thin transparent veils;
> Sprung into motion; softened into flesh;
> Was fired to passion, or refined to soul"
> [Part II, ll. 307–12].

Such lines obviously stand in the iconic tradition.

most admired ancient marbles. They are all here, those statues which
Pope admired and by which he was inspired in his "Temple of Fame"
—statues that did not lose their hold upon English poets until well
after the discovery of the Elgin marbles. Hercules appears first:

> In leaning site, respiring from his toils,
> The well known hero who delivered Greece,
> His ample chest all tempested with force,
> Unconquerable reared. She saw the head,
> Breathing the hero, small, of Grecian size,
> Scarce more extensive than the sinewy neck;
> The spreading shoulders, muscular and broad;
> The whole a mass of swelling sinews, touched
> Into harmonious shape [see Plate XVIII A]

and following him Meleager, with "his beauteous front"; the "raging
aspect" of the Fighting Gladiator; the Dying Gladiator, "supported
on his shortened arm"; Apollo Belvedere in "graceful act," "His
arm extended with the slackened bow" (Plate XIX A); the Medicean
Venus, sentimentally viewed as a combination of modest shame
and "slippery looks of love" but so lifelike, "That the deluded eye
the marble doubts" (Plate XIX B); and finally as the "utmost masterpiece" the Laocoön group, of which the "miserable sire, / Wrapt
with his sons in fate's severest grasp," fired Vergil to one of his greatest poetic achievements.

> . . . Such passion here,
> Such agonies, such bitterness of pain
> Seem so to tremble through the tortured stone
> That the touched heart engrosses all the view.[9]

No one has ever argued that Thomson's *Liberty* is a great poem
or that the public neglect, which it encountered almost at once,
has been undeserved. It has of course been surpassed by the more
passionate and energetic verses of Byron, who in describing the
same works of art, though from an entirely different point of view,
has made it unlikely that anyone will ever turn to Thomson. But
the descriptive portions, even though occasional lines betray their
origins in the treatises of Félibien and De Piles, are more than

[9] *Ibid.*, Part IV, ll. 140–206. See Stephen A. Larrabee, *English Bards and Grecian
Marbles* (New York, 1943), pp. 77–82.

poetical waxworks. They respond to and dignify an ancient tradition, and there is something in what the eighteenth century would call their "noble simplicity" that is not entirely unpleasing. Thomson writes from firsthand observation and in genuine appreciation. The verses occupy an important historical place in the venerable tradition of iconic poetry and are invaluable as a historic index of Augustan artistic taste.

Thomson saw most of these statues on his trip to Italy, but he must have known them before, in engraving and pictorial copy, since he seems to have made poetic use of certain of them in his earlier versions of the *Seasons*. Like many an Italian landscapist of the seventeenth century, Thomson placed statuary in his gardens and marble figures in his forests. Like many a French classical dramatist and like many an English neoclassical poet, he conceived of his idealized human figures as classical marbles. In one passage of "Summer" Thomson remembers the story of Niobe and the conceit of men turning to stone under the influence of great passion. Young Celadon undergoes the melodramatic experience of having his beloved Amelia struck dead by lightning while he holds her in his arms.

> But who can paint the lover as he stood
> Pierced by severe amazement, hating life,
> Speechless, and fixed in all the death of woe?
> So, faint resemblance! on the marble tomb
> The well-dissembled mourner stopping stands,
> For ever silent and for ever sad [ll. 1217–22].

Another passage from the same poem, unfortunately unredeemed by a beautifully Keatsian line like the last one, is interesting because it demonstrates that Thomson had early adopted the habit of viewing an actor in a human scene in the form of a well-known sculpture. Musidora, when she learns that Damon her lover has observed her bathing, becomes, in spite of his fully sincere vows of eternal protection, void of sense. By an old law of poetic conceit she turns to stone, out of which Thomson carves a copy of the Venus de' Medici.

> . . . With wild surprise,
> As if to marble struck, devoid of sense,
> A stupid moment motionless she stood:

So stands the statue that enchants the world;
So, bending, tries to veil the matchless boast,
The mingled beauties of exulting Greece[10]
[see Plate XIX B].

Thomson must take his place in the long list of neoclassical poets for whom poetic idealization was associated with classically sculptured stone.

THE NATURAL SCENE

The traditional view of Thomson's pictorialism has taken no notice of what we have just considered. But even in commenting on his natural scene, which has always and properly been recognized as Thomson's chief claim to poetical distinction, students of his imagery have not sufficiently dwelt on its true characteristics and its most important relationships.

Thomson's contribution lay in bringing to verse what was an already firmly rooted tradition in the visual arts. In writing of the seasons of the year he used a theme with roots deep in ancient and modern culture. There has survived from the third century A.D. a Roman sarcophagus known as the "Season" sarcophagus, on which Dionysus holds court surrounded by figures of the seasons. This work of ancient art, acquired in the eighteenth century by the third Duke of Beaufort on the Grand Tour and brought to England, stood on a base and was surrounded by a special decor designed by Thomson's illustrator, the artist William Kent.[11] In the Uffizi Gallery there are four sixteenth-century tapestries, woven after a design by Francesco Bachiacca, entitled "I mesi dell'anno." The first four numbers of Antonio Vivaldi's "Opus VIII" are devoted to the four seasons. In the fifteenth and sixteenth centuries pictures of the months in books of hours "almost reached the status of pure landscape," and in seventeenth-century art the season piece was

---

[10] Ll. 1344–49. The lines drawing a comparison with the Medicean Venus read as follows in the original version:

"So stands the statue that enchants the world,
Her full proportions such, and bashful so
Bends ineffectual from the roving eye."

See Robertson, *op. cit.* (n. 6), p. 102 n.

[11] *New York Times*, Oct. 16, 1955.

a popular genre, painted by artists of such stature as Bassano, Brill, Nicolas Poussin, and Rubens, and by many lesser men as well.[12] The theme came to Thomson accompanied not only by the conventions of a literary tradition that includes Vergil and Spenser but also by firm and ancient associations with other arts, notably the arts of visual design.

But Thomson's contribution and the nature of his relationship to preceding example can better be understood if we broaden our consideration beyond season antecedents alone to include seventeenth-century landscape as a whole. In England during the seventeenth century, as we now know, taste for landscape had already been established. That taste appreciated scenes of forests, harbors, rivers, estates, ruins, farms with cattle, moonlit vistas, sunrises, mountains, waterfalls, prospects with diffused light, and distances. By some of these canvases "delightful horror" was created; by others, nostalgic sadness at the decay of civilization; by still others, a sense of Christian optimism, well-being, and prospering activity that gloried in the God-given beauties of the physical world.[13]

Thus, long before the literary doctrine of Longinian sublimity took hold in England and long before Shaftesburian benevolism had been expressed, there had already been created a vigorous artistic taste that included elements usually associated only with the eighteenth century in general and Thomson in particular. The creation of the pantheon that we described earlier had established a taste for natural scenery in England very much like the one present in the *Seasons*. In fact, it may be said that the originality

---

[12] Henry V. S. Ogden and Margaret S. Ogden, *English Taste in Landscape in the Seventeenth Century* (Ann Arbor, Mich., 1955), pp. 48–49. I am deeply indebted to this pioneer study. These authors do not discuss Thomson, but they delineate the general visual background for Thomson's scene. One of the most striking parallels to Thomson in the visual arts is to be found in Nicolas Poussin's paintings of the "Four Seasons," now in the Louvre, reproduced in Ulrich Christoffel, *Poussin und Claude Lorrain* (Munich, 1924), pp. 120, 121, 124, 126. In these paintings the seasons are idealized by association with biblical story. "Spring" is subtitled "Adam and Eve"; "Summer," "Boas and Ruth" (here the anticipation of Thomson is striking, since he tells the story of Ruth gleaning in the fields in the idyl of Palemon and Lavinia that appears in "Autumn"); "Autumn" represents two Israelites carrying a bunch of huge grapes on their return from spying out the land of Canaan; and "Winter" bears the subtitle "The Deluge," a pictorial representation of what was a favorite Thomsonian theme.

[13] Ogden and Ogden, *op. cit.* (n. 12), pp. 134 ff.; see also pp. 49–50.

of Thomson's visual scene lay in bringing to poetry the very themes most prominent in seventeenth-century landscape. If this is true, it radically alters our view of Thomson's position in the cultural history of England.

Neoclassical aesthetics bade the poet follow nature. While "nature" was broader than the physical world, it did include the physical world—earth, sea, and sky, and it was Thomson's happy destiny as a poet to remember that it did. Hence, in responding to Pope's imperative, "First follow nature,"[14] by exploring the natural scene, Thomson was doing no more than his age required.

Thomson said in his Preface to the second edition of "Winter" that he knew of "no subject more elevating, more amusing; more ready to awake the poetical enthusiasm, the philosophical reflection, and the moral sentiment, than the works of Nature." The Preface is too brief and summary to provide much help in analyzing Thomson's rendition of the "fair, useful, and magnificent"[15] in nature—a phrase that reminds us of Addison's classification of the "pleasures of the imagination" in the *Spectator*.[16] But his practice reveals that his achievement in visual description has been fourfold: (1) He has responded to the *light* (and the lights) of the natural world, giving us what may be the best poetic light-imagery in English outside Milton and what is perhaps the richest imagery of natural light ever written. (2) He has rendered the *color* of the natural world with greater eloquence and fidelity than any other writer on so large a scale. (3) He has achieved on his verbal canvas the grace of *natural motion* that was greatly admired in seventeenth- and eighteenth-century aesthetic thought. (4) He has attempted to solve the problem of *landscape form* in verbal description by humanizing and mythologizing the world in the manner of baroque and Renaissance landscape. These contributions are worth examining one by one.

1. As one of the leading and most sensitive of the eighteenth-century Miltonists, Thomson could scarcely have failed to profit by his exemplar's great achievement in writing the poetry of light. Milton's light, however, is not the light of nature any more than is the light of the seventeenth-century religious paintings—the paintings of Rembrandt, Guercino, Caravaggio, Domenichino. But

---

[14] "Essay on Criticism," l. 68.

[15] Robertson, *op. cit.* (n. 6), pp. 240–41.

[16] See above, p. 136.

Thomson's is, and as such differs greatly from the "holy light" or the "dimm religious light" of seventeenth-century art. It also differs from the light of Pope's *vers de societé* and of fashionable rococo painting in that it is directly antithetical to the brilliant and glittering light of society. Thomson's natural light, as he felt, caused the "little glittering prettinesses" to fade into drawing-room insignificance.

Although Thomson was directly inspired by Milton, he is careful not to attempt Milton's greatest theme.

> How shall I then attempt to sing of Him
> Who, Light Himself, in uncreated light
> Invested deep, dwells awfully retired
> From mortal eye or angel's purer ken?
>
> ["Summer," ll. 175–78].

He turns rather to the light of the physical world, which, though it derives from and points to the uncreated light, is material and natural.

> Prime cheerer, Light!
> Of all material beings first and best!
> Efflux divine! Nature's resplendent robe,
> Without whose vesting beauty all were wrapt
> In unessential gloom; and thou, O Sun!
> Soul of surrounding worlds! in whom best seen
> Shines out thy Maker! May I sing of thee?
>
> [*ibid.*, ll. 90–96].

2. Thomsonian color derives from nature itself and, in "To the Memory of Sir Isaac Newton," nature's interpreter, Newton.

> Even Light itself, which every thing displays,
> Shone undiscovered, till his [Newton's] brighter mind
> Untwisted all the shining robe of day;
> And, from the whitening undistinguished blaze,
> Collecting every ray into his kind,
> To the charmed eye educed the gorgeous train
> Of parent colours. First the flaming red
> Sprung vivid forth; the tawny orange next;
> And next delicious yellow; by whose side
> Fell the kind beams of all-refreshing green.

> Then the pure blue, that swells autumnal skies,
> Ethereal played; and then, of sadder hue,
> Emerged the deepened indigo, as when
> The heavy-skirted evening droops with frost;
> While the last gleamings of refracted light
> Died in the fainting violets away [ll. 96–111].

Thomson finds the "refractive law" both "just" and "beauteous" and, of course, considers virtually divine that genius who "untwisted all the shining robe of day" into parent colors. But it is the colors in nature, not colors abstractly and scientifically considered, that awaken his fullest response.

> These [the colors], when the clouds distil the rosy shower,
> Shine out distinct adown the watery bow;
> While o'er our heads the dewy vision bends
> Delightful, melting on the field beneath.
> Myriads of mingling dyes from these result,
> And myriads still remain—infinite source
> Of beauty, ever flushing, ever new.
> Did ever poet image aught so fair,
> Dreaming in whispering groves by the hoarse brook?
> [ll. 112–20].

Thomson's literary use of color in response to Newtonian physics is effective. But it has its precedents. It belongs generally to the eighteenth-century version of *enargeia*, which, as we saw in connection with Addison's aesthetics, owed much to the new psychology of Locke. It is also reminiscent of Leonardo's co-operation with the new scientific impulses that led men to explore the physical world; Thomson's color is related to Leonardo's because both were inspired by a scientific view of reality and scientific achievement. But, as Thomson implies, these origins do not adulterate the beauty: he asks if poets have ever imagined anything so poetical as the natural colors themselves. To render these newly understood and scientifically analyzed colors in their natural setting, Thomson uses all his poetical skill. He describes "the red fiery Streaks" of a "louring Sky" or the "darkly red" eastern sky that "breathes forth / An Icy Gale." He notices the blackening of a field of ripened wheat alternately swept by sun and shadow. Although he denies that literary expression can paint "with hues on hues" the "breath of Nature and her endless bloom," he attempts precisely that:

> Fair-handed Spring unbosoms every grace—
> Throws out the snow-drop and the crocus first,
> The daisy, primrose, violet darkly blue,
> And polyanthus of unnumbered dyes;
> The yellow wall-flower, stained with iron brown,
> And lavish stock, that scents the garden round:
> From the soft wing of vernal breezes shed,
> Anemones; auriculas, enriched
> With shining meal o'er all their velvet leaves;
> And full ranunculus of glowing red.[17]

3. During both the seventeenth and eighteenth centuries men found the motion of nature one of its most attractive qualities. As early as Lomazzo's *Treatise of the Art of Painting* of 1584 motion had been considered a natural quality that the painter should strive to represent, and Lomazzo, who entitled one of his chapters "Of the Motions of Trees and All Other Things That Are Moved," described in detail the motion of plants, waves, waterfalls, clouds, and fire. The authority on ancient painting, Franciscus Junius, stated the same principle in advising connoisseurs what to learn from nature: "They doe marke ... how the great Lampe of light up rearing his flaming head above the earth, causeth the dawning day to spread a faint and trembling light upon the flickering gilded waves."

John Evelyn was sensitive to natural movement; he described a valley where he saw the "trembling serpenting of some Chrystal rivolet, fringed with the curtous [*sic*] diaper of the softer meadows, the umbrage & harmonious warblings of the cooler groves, the frisking and lowing of the wandering cattle."[18] When Addison saw a scene on the wall of a camera obscura, he called it the "prettiest Landskip I ever saw," superior to most artificial scenes chiefly because of "the Motion of the Things it represents"—the motion

---

[17] "Spring," ll. 529–38. The immediately preceding citations come from *ibid.*, ll. 554–55; "Winter" (1726 ed.), ll. 155, 307–8; "Autumn," ll. 37–42. Cf. the gorgeous passage in "Spring," ll. 186 ff.

[18] The quotations from Lomazzo, Junius, and Evelyn appear in Ogden and Ogden, *op. cit.* (n. 12), pp. 37–38.

of a ship entering the scene and sailing slowly through it, the waving of green shadows, the leaping of herds of deer.[19]

There was ample precedent, then, for James Thomson's appreciation of the motion and animation of nature. He attempted to achieve in poetic landscape what pictorial landscapists had been bidden to imitate for nearly two centuries.

Of the lover of nature, whom we see out-of-doors in "Spring," Thomson says that he can "catch" the landscape "gliding swift / Athwart imagination's vivid eye" (ll. 458–59). He himself, in his notes to "Spring," refers to one section of the poem as a "landskip of the shepherd tending his flocks with the lambs frisking around him." His "stately swan / Gives out his snowy plumage to the gale" (*ibid.*, ll. 778–79). And if natural details do not move, dancing girls imbue the static scene with grace,

> . . . with smooth step,
> Disclosing motion in its every charm,
> To swim along, and swell the mazy dance
> [*Autumn*, ll. 594–96].

4. Thomson's total form had to take account of what Dr. Johnson called "appearances subsisting all at once,"[20] and the only manner of proceeding he could use to express such appearances was the picture-gallery method of "see and respond." This, as we have seen, was a form common in neoclassical England; Thomson in the *Seasons* has given this form of alternating description and reflection one of its most notable uses. Of the total form little more need be said than this, since the process need only be identified to be understood. But for Thomson's form in the individual scene, in the short passage of description, closer analysis is required. Basically, the method is not new to us. We have seen something of it in "Windsor Forest" and in more rudimentary form in "Annus mirabilis"; and back of these poems lie the examples of Milton, the Jonsonian masque, Ovid, and the whole tradition of classical pictorialism. The technique consists simply of making pictorialized

---

[19] *Spectator*, No. 414.

[20] "The great defect of the Seasons is want of method; but for this I know not that there was any remedy. Of many appearances subsisting all at once, no rule can be given why one should be mentioned before another; yet the memory wants the help of order, and the curiosity is not excited by suspense or expectation" ("Life of Thomson," *Works of Samuel Johnson* [Oxford, 1825], VIII, 378).

natural personification the central formal element in rendering landscape. If we refer back to the last passage quoted in the section on color, we see that both unity and movement result from the presence of the personified spring—"Fair-handed Spring," who "unbosoms every grace" and discloses the charms of her own body by "throwing out" flower after flower. Even in the passage on Newton's colors, each one is personified and given a pictorial epithet and an appropriate action.

Before we examine the details of Thomson's scenic form, we must narrow and bring to sharper focus his relationship to the landscape painting that preceded him. But we cannot narrow it, as some have, to the natural landscapes of Salvator Rosa and Claude Lorrain alone, since such limitation would obscure the true nature of Thomson's image.[21] Thomson's landscape art is related to the kind of pictorial landscape variously described as idealized, generalized, and heroic—the landscape of the high Renaissance and the seventeenth-century baroque. That type of art included certain works of Claude, Salvator Rosa, and Gaspard Dughet, but not chiefly the works of naturalistic art usually associated with Thomson. It also included Guido Reni, of whom we shall presently speak at some length, Guercino, Rubens,[22] Nicolas Poussin,[23] Spa-

---

[21] Manwaring, *op. cit.* (n. 2), p. v and *passim*. Whatever may be true for the later eighteenth century, Miss Manwaring's emphasis on Gaspard, Claude, and Salvator Rosa is, for Thomson, mistaken. I find the following fact corroborative of my position—though I do not think it depends on this kind of evidence: in the sale catalogue of Thomson's effects (*op. cit.* [n. 3]), among eighty-three separate engravings, there is not a single one of the paintings by Miss Manwaring's trio, though there are many examples of the works of other painters. The catalogue enforces the view that Thomson's taste ran to heroic landscape. I am not the first who has found it necessary to qualify Miss Manwaring's work. McKillop, in his work on *Liberty, op. cit.* (n. 2), says, "Miss Manwaring's claims for Claudian and Salvatorian influences in Thomson's early work must be considerably toned down" (p. 71). See also C. V. Deane, *Aspects of Eighteenth Century Nature Poetry* (Oxford, 1935), pp. 71–75, and B. Sprague Allen, *Tides in English Taste* (Cambridge, Mass., 1937), II, 147–48.

[22] Horace Walpole regarded Rubens as a greater landscapist than Claude, because he possessed greater variety. "Seldom as he practiced it, Rubens was never greater than in landscape; the tumble of his rocks and trees, the deep shadows in his glades and glooms, the watery sunshine, and dewy verdure, show a variety of genius, which are [*sic*] not to be found in the inimitable but uniform glow of Claud Lorrain" (*Anecdotes of Painting* [2d ed.; Strawberry Hill, 1765], II, 89).

[23] See Anthony Blunt, "The Heroic and the Ideal Landscape in the Work of Nicolas Poussin," *Journal of the Warburg and Courtauld Institutes*, VII (1944), 154–68.

gnoletto,[24] and Annibale Carracci[25] of the seventeenth century, and Leonardo, Giorgone, and Titian[26] of the sixteenth.

One basic characteristic of this landscape art—and there were of course many divergencies within the tradition—was that it was not usually solely or exclusively concerned with nature in its purely natural forms but with nature as a manifestation of heroic, pastoral, or religious ideals. These ideals were sometimes conveyed by portraying a human or mythic action and making the natural environment a sympathetically interpretative stage setting. Titian's "St. Jerome" at the Louvre; some of his mythological stories, like the "Death of Actaeon" (Lord Lascelles, London); Annibale's "Repose on the Flight to Egypt" (the Doria, Rome); many of Gaspard's biblical scenes and many of the mythological and "historical" Claudes now in England—these and similar paintings provide us with Thomson's most immediately relevant visual context.[27] His view of the Spanish armada reflecting the gleams of the setting sun is a heroic, historical scene set in nature.[28] The "monarch-swain" of the pastoral tradition sleeping on downy moss "his careless arm / Thrown round his head"; the scene in which a youth stands, like Narcissus, on the edge of a crystalline flood, "Gazing the inverted

[24] Used by Joseph Warton to illustrate the quality of "incomparable wildness" of vision. See *op. cit.* (n. 1), II, 17.

[25] The high regard for Annibale as a landscapist appears in a comment like this of the Abbé du Bos: "the finest landskip, were it even Titian's or Carraccio's" (*Critical Reflexions on Poetry, Painting and Music*, trans. Thomas Nugent [London, 1748], II, 44).

[26] In defending landscape as a genre, claiming for it the very next rank to history-painting, Joseph Warton says: "Titian thought it no diminution of his genius, to spend much of his time in works of [this] species" (*op. cit.* [n. 1], I, 49).

[27] The following paintings also belong to the type Thomson admired. Titian: "The Three Ages of Man" in the Bridgewater House, London; the Prado "Venus," Madrid; "A Landscape with a Flock of Sheep," Buckingham Palace, London. Gaspard Dughet: "Landscape: Abraham and Isaac Approach the Place of Sacrifice"; "Storm: the Union of Dido and Aeneas"; "Storm with Biblical Figures." Claude: "Landscape: The Reconciliation of Cephalus and Procris"; "Landscape: David at the Cave of Abdullam"; "Landscape: The Marriage of Isaac and Rebekah"; "Landscape: Hagar and the Angels." These paintings by Claude and Gaspard are reproduced in *French School* ("National Gallery Catalogues," London, 1950), Plates XV, XVII, XVIII, XXIII, XL, XLIII, XLVI. See also Salvator Rosa's "Grove of the Philosophers" in the Pitti, in Aldo de Rinaldis, *Neapolitan Painting of the Seicento* (Florence, 1929), Plate LXXI.

[28] "Britannia," ll. 63–71.

landscape"[29]—these and many others like them remind us of the painters mentioned and could in many instances be illustrated by specific paintings on the same or similar themes.

Thomson borrowed many specific devices of visual presentation from heroic landscape. One is simple and requires no discussion. He often places a human figure in a natural setting. Another is equally simple: he often renders the scene classical by placing architecture and sculpture in it and thus makes of wild nature a garden. Still another we have noticed earlier; Thomson presents human figures in sculptured poses. But the technique of heroic landscape most peculiarly amenable to verbal art is natural personification, and by means of it Thomson achieves his characteristic form.

This form may be observed if we compare the original and the revised passage on the advent of summer. The original passage, from the first edition of 1727, personifies the season and begins as follows:

> Parent of Seasons! from whose rich-stained rays,
> Reflected various, various colours rise: . . .
> The branching grove the lusty product stands,
> To quench the fury of thy noon-career;
> And crowd a shade for the retreating swain,
> When on his russet fields you look direct.[30]

The personification is carried in this manner through several stanzas and the "Parent," directly addressed, is made the active cause of beauty and fruitfulness. But the persona is not clearly visualized or pictorially conceived. The only suggestion of organizing motion is conveyed by the single word "noon-career," and its implications are not pursued.

In the final version of this passage, however, written for the edition of 1744 after Thomson's trip to Italy and perhaps in part as a result of his greatly widened knowledge of painting, the personification is pictorialized and made more elaborate, is surrounded with other allegorical figures, and is organized into a tightly knit

[29] "Summer," ll. 493–94, 1244–56. "Inverted landscapes" were very common. See Claude's "Landscape: Narcissus" (in *French School* [n. 27], Plate 20) and Richard Wilson's later "Landscape" in the Louvre (Tancred Borenius, *English Painting in the XVIIIth Century* [London, 1938], Plate 24), where ruined tower and the land promontory are reflected in the water.

[30] Printed in Robertson, *op. cit.* (n. 6), p. 121.

visual scene, spatially bounded but full of relevant and graceful motion. The revised passage contains an excellent example of the neoclassical picturesque:

> Parent of Seasons! who the pomp precede
> That waits thy throne, as through thy vast domain,
> Annual, along the bright ecliptic road
> In world-rejoicing state it moves sublime.
> Meantime the expecting nations, circled gay
> With all the various tribes of foodful earth,
> Implore thy bounty, or send grateful up
> A common hymn: while, round thy beaming car,
> High-seen, the Seasons lead, in sprightly dance
> Harmonious knit, the rosy-fingered hours,
> The zephyrs floating loose, the timely rains,
> Of bloom ethereal the light-footed dews,
> And, softened into joy, the surly storms.
> These, in successive turn, with lavish hand
> Shower every beauty, every fragrance shower,
> Herbs, flowers, and fruits; till kindling at thy touch,
> From land to land is flushed the vernal year [ll. 113–29].

That revision was made, I suggest, under the guidance of Guido Reni's famous fresco, "Aurora" [Plate XXIV], of which Thomson himself owned an engraving.[31] Guido's pictorial allegory is presented in brilliant colors and rhythmic, graceful motion. Apollo, bathed in golden light, sits on a classical car drawn by spirited horses. Aurora flies on ahead of the horses; she is surrounded with soft rosy light that tints the clouds and begins to illumine the expanse of sea and land below. Dressed in swirling robes, she not only brings light but is about to scatter roses from both her hands.[32] Around the

---

[31] Thomson owned three Guidos, all engraved by Frey: "Bacchus and Ariadne," "Song of Our Blessed Virgin," and "Aurora" (see the sale catalogue [n. 3]). The fresco "Aurora" was greatly admired by Englishmen. The correspondence of the artist William Kent, who illustrated Thomson, reveals that his patrons expected him to make copies of this painting (see Edward Croft-Murray, "William Kent in Rome," in *English Miscellany*, ed. Mario Praz, I [Rome, 1950], 221–29). For an excellent discussion of the Aurora theme in paintings by Agostino Carracci, Domenichino, and Guercino see Irving Lavin, "Cephalus and Procris," *Journal of the Warburg and Courtauld Institutes*, XVII (July–December, 1954), 284 ff.

[32] Cf. Thomson's lines from "Summer":

> "And every beauty softening, every grace
> Flushing anew, a mellow lustre shed—
> As shines the lily through the crystal mild,

sun god, who is intent upon guiding his horses, seven beautiful maidens dance in circular motion. These are the personified hours, who hand in hand weave an accompanying pattern about the forward progress of the flying Aurora and of Apollo in his horse-drawn chariot. These are the lines of pictorial representation and composition that Thomson followed in revising his scene. The parent season—and it is only a detail that Guido's dawning day has become Thomson's dawning season—is "high seen" in a "beaming car." The other seasons lead a harmoniously knit and sprightly dance around the car, and among the dancers are the "rosy-fingered hours" of Guido's canvas. From them and from other dancers are strewn all the blessings of summer, until the land beneath is kindled by the agency of this mythologically conceived progress. Guido's basically literary treatment is easily transferable to poetry. Thomson's revised scene is admittedly more artificial than his first; but it has a grace and motion as well as an imagistic unity that his first draft was far from achieving. The passage, however, is important not only for its own sake but because it so clearly exposes what must have taken place constantly in the creation of neoclassical poetry.[33]

PERSONIFIED NATURE

Thomson's personifications range from implicit, unvisualized figures, lurking suggestively behind his natural details, to those in the fully developed pictorial "action" we have just noticed. But there are subtleties beyond those of mere variety, and these we must also attempt to understand.

Each of the four poems in the *Seasons* begins with the coming of the personified season, iconically invested with appropriate signa and invited, in noble invocation, to come to earth and possess

---

Or as the rose amid the morning dew,
Fresh from Aurora's hand, more sweetly glows"
[ll. 1323–27].

[33] Cf. Pope's conclusion of the "Dunciad," where the coming of Night is perceived as the coming of an anti-Aurora:

"She comes! she comes! the sable Throne behold
Of *Night* Primæval, and of *Chaos* old!
Before her, *Fancy*'s gilded clouds decay,
And all its varying Rain-bows die away"
["Dunciad" (B), Book IV, ll. 629–32].

nature. These invocations would have been impossible had not each season been conceived of as a persona, exalted and semidivine.

Come, gentle Spring, ethereal mildness, come ["Spring," l. 1].

. . . .

From brightening fields of ether fair-disclosed,
Child of the sun, refulgent Summer comes
In pride of youth, and felt through nature's depth;
He *comes*, attended by the sultry hours
And ever-fanning breezes on his way;
While from his ardent look the turning Spring
Averts her blushful face, and earth and skies
All-smiling to his hot dominion leaves ["Summer," ll. 1–8].

. . . .

Crowned with the sickle and the wheaten sheaf
While Autumn nodding o'er the yellow plain
Comes jovial on . . . ["Autumn," ll. 1–3].

. . . .

See, Winter *comes* to rule the varied year,
Sullen and sad, with all his rising train—
Vapours, and clouds, and storms ["Winter," ll. 1–3].

In this manner each of the poems begins; the season, personified as an allegorical being of dignity and power, *comes* to the earth as a celestial visitation. This is the pivotal conception of the whole poem. But it is not only these large introductory scenes that are so presented. In one of Thomson's most celebrated and beautiful passages he describes the rising of the sun as a royal progress.

But yonder comes the powerful king of day
Rejoicing in the east. The lessening cloud,
The kindling azure, and the mountain's brow
Illumed with fluid gold, his near approach
Betoken glad. Lo! now, apparent all,
Aslant the dew-bright earth and coloured air,
He looks in boundless majesty abroad,
And sheds the shining day, that burnished plays
On rocks, and hills, and towers, and wandering streams
High-gleaming from afar ["Summer," ll. 81–90].

This has been considered a Claudian sunrise.[34] But because its

[34] By Miss Manwaring, (*op. cit.* [n. 2], p. 102), who fails to notice the beauty and organizing centrality of the personification—a fact that would significantly alter the pictorial analogues to this passage.

most striking feature is the personification of day as a powerful king, coming in golden pomp to the earth, it is closer to Guido's "Aurora." Thomson's imagination seems to have kindled at this fresco, in which the sky streams not only with vague unembodied glories but with glories attached to large and lovely human figures in general progress and also in graceful motion within that forward progress. The passages already cited from Thomson suggest the mythological and allegorical triumph dear to the seventeenth-century painter: Annibale Carracci's "Triumph of Bacchus" in the Farnese, Rome; his "Triumph of Pan" in the Louvre; Nicolas Poussin's "Triumph of Flora" in the Louvre; and the same artist's "Kingdom of Flora" in Dresden, in which Flora, a smiling, delicate creature, strews petals in the garden while above in the sky, fully visible but not sharply delineated, Apollo drives the horses of the sun [Plate XXVI A].

The parallel we have attempted to establish receives support from the design that William Kent drew for the 1730 edition of the *Seasons* [Plate XXIII]. That design is no triumph of form—its lines are somewhat awkward and the celestial beings do not have the graceful motion necessary for such bold and unnatural levitation. Nonetheless, it is an excellent commentary on Thomson's landscape art. Kent has drawn a natural scene—mountain, hill, lake, tree, and generously represented sky—but one that is also idealized in the manner we have been describing. A structure, stylized in the manner of Palladio or the Greeks, stands to the right. The pastoral tradition is alluded to by the introduction of a shepherd and his sheep and of two pairs of rural lovers, in one of which the swain plays on his oaten pipe. A rainbow, suggestive of Thomson's relations to both nature and Newton, spans the sky. But the justest, though artistically by no means the most successful, touch of all is the opening of the sky to permit the descent of a goddess bearing a garland of flowers, strewing petals on the earth beneath, surrounded with a bevy of winged *putti* and accompanied by a winged creature that recalls the Aurora of Guido's allegory.

Thomson's personifications are not always sharply visualized or relevantly active. But enough of them are to endow his scene with neoclassical picturesqueness of a high order of competency. Though his moral personifications tend to be lifeless, his natural personifications are usually bright, individual, and moving. It is here that his characteristic excellence resides. This excellence appears if we introduce a passage from Pope, his translation of the concluding scene in the eighth book of the *Iliad*, in which many of the details and the general scenic arrangement belong to the translator and not to Homer.

> The troops exulting sat in order round,
> And beaming fires illumin'd all the ground.
> As when the moon, refulgent lamp of night,
> O'er Heav'n's clear azure spreads her sacred light,
> When not a breath disturbs the deep serene,
> And not a cloud o'ercasts the solemn scene;
> Around her throne the vivid planets roll,
> And stars unnumber'd gild the glowing pole,
> O'er the dark trees a yellower verdure shed,
> And tip with silver ev'ry mountain's head;
> Then shine the vales, the rocks in prospect rise,
> A flood of glory bursts from all the skies.
> The conscious swains, rejoicing in the sight,
> Eye the blue vault and bless the useful light.

Although it is asserted that the planets roll and the flood of glory "bursts from all the skies," how static the scene remains! Apart from its inaccuracies of observation, it would probably deserve the censure of a Lessing as an artificial and imperfectly fused itemization of quasi-visual details.[35]

Compare Thomson's description of moonlight in a scene alive with motion, motion conveyed in the flexible rhythms Thomson uses to portray the scene but arising from the Guido-like and Poussin-like viewing of the scene in organic relation to the central persona.

> ... Meanwhile the moon,
> Full-orbed and breaking through the scattered clouds,
> Shows her broad visage in the crimsoned east.
> Turned to the sun direct, her spotted disk ...
> A smaller earth, gives all his blaze again,
> Void of its flame, and sheds a softer day.
> Now through the passing cloud she seems to stoop,
> Now up the pure cerulean rides sublime.
> Wide the pale deluge floats, and streaming mild
> O'er the skied mountain to the shadowy vale,

[35] For a discussion of this description that quotes both the rapturous approval of James Hervey and the scornful comments of Wordsworth and Southey see C. E. de Haas, *Nature and the Country in English Poetry* (Amsterdam, 1928), pp. 10–12.

> While rocks and floods reflect the quivering gleam,
> The whole air whitens with a boundless tide
> Of silver radiance trembling round the world
> > ["Autumn," ll. 1088–1102].

The moon is given a visage, is placed in a triumphal chariot that rides through the skies, and is directly responsible for the "silver radiance" that trembles round the world. The personification in motion permits the use of a temporal scheme so much more congenial to poetry than the static, spatial itemization of Pope. Thomson's scene moves from the rising of the moon in the east while the sky is still red with the light of the setting sun to her full nighttime splendor.

Thomson's own excitement in contemplating his figures is sometimes conveyed by his brief but urgent outbursts: "see," "behold," "lo," "yonder," "look." All these imperatives direct the eye. It is almost as though Thomson were present in his own scene, pointing a finger at the personification, much in the manner of a Renaissance painter who occasionally put himself or his patron in a lower corner of the canvas, his index finger pointing to the Virgin.

Another of Thomson's most frequently used imperatives is "come," the *veni* of religious invocation. Although not primarily religious, these moods are not factitious. They represent an appropriate response to a natural object or event that has been heightened into classical abstraction and animated into sentience.

Almost more than anything else in the poem these poetic supplications give to Thomson's natural scene a sense of personal intimacy and reverential responsiveness that cannot always vie with the effects of Cowper and Wordsworth but, in notable degree, anticipates them both. Thomson's addresses are varied. Sometimes he speaks to a season; sometimes to a color: "But chiefly thee, gay green! / Thou smiling Nature's universal robe"; or to trees:

> Welcome, ye shades! ye bowery thickets, hail!
> Ye lofty pines! ye venerable oaks!
> Ye ashes wild, resounding o'er the steep!
> Delicious is your shelter to the soul . . .

or to a nature goddess:

> Bear me, Pomona! to thy citron groves;
> To where the lemon and the piercing lime,
> With the deep orange glowing through the green,
> Their lighter glories blend;

and finally to Nature herself, in the paean that ends "Autumn":

> O Nature! all-sufficient! over all
> Enrich me with the knowledge of thy works;
> Snatch me to heaven; thy rolling wonders there,
> World beyond world, in infinite extent
> Profusely scattered o'er the blue immense,
> Show me....[36]

These last addresses are not essentially pictorial. They were selected to exemplify the prayerful "come!" But they would lose their impelling force, as well as their graceful comings and goings, were they not associated with the "see!"—with the highly pictorial persona that walks across the pages of the *Seasons*.

Thomson's images come in part from the landscape of his childhood, the Cheviot massif and the valley of the Jedwater and Teviotdale, a scene which, according to one observer, had already been arranged into foreground, middle distance, and background.[37] But natural nature is for Thomson only a beginning, an unadorned frame. His finally and fully contrived literary landscape has been subjected to a pictorial transformation that came from a conscious and unconscious absorption of the heroic landscapists of the previous century. Like Guido Reni, Annibale Carracci, Nicolas Poussin, and, to a lesser extent, Titian and Giorgione, Thomson has raised natural form to the ideal form required by eighteenth-century philosophical thought, by the classical tradition, and by the requirements of his medium.

His chief instrument in creating the pictorial image is the personification. His personae must be *seen* if we are ever again to recover the pleasures of reading Thomson. They were seen in the eighteenth and early nineteenth centuries—a fact that partly explains the enormous fame of Thomson that impressed Coleridge and upon which he remarked when he encountered in an inn a dog-eared copy of the *Seasons*. During the eighteenth century a writer in the *British Magazine* quoted the following lines from "Summer":

> O vale or bliss! O softly-swelling hills!
> On which the power of cultivation lies,
> And joys to see the wonders of his toil [ll. 1435–37].

[36] "Spring," ll. 83–84; "Summer," ll. 469–72, 663–66; "Autumn," ll. 1352–57.
[37] See Grant, *op. cit.* (n. 5), p. 10; Deane, *op. cit.* (n. 21), pp. 72, 105.

At first reading these lines seem to us unvisual, without prominent or particularized personification. But not to an eighteenth-century reader. For the writer who quoted them went on to comment as follows:

> We cannot conceive a more beautiful image than that of the Genius of Agriculture distinguished by the implements of his art, embrowned with labor, glowing with health, crowned with a garland of foliage, flowers, and fruit, lying stretched at ease on the brow of a gentle swelling hill, and contemplating with pleasure the happy effects of his own industry.[38]

Pictorialist poets breed pictorialist readers. The comment reveals unmistakably that a reader trained to see pictures in poetry would see one even when the poet gave him only the slightest visual hint. This particular eighteenth-century reader may have seen too much, but he saw appropriately. For to see an allegorical figure clearly delineated and placed in a natural scene was to see with the eyes of Thomson himself.

[38] Quoted by Donald Davie, *Purity of Diction in English Verse* (London, 1952), p. 40, n. 1.

CHAPTER X

William Collins

ODES DESCRIPTIVE AND ALLEGORIC

In December of 1746—the date 1747 appears, however, on the title page—there issued from the press a volume bearing the suggestive title *Odes on Several Descriptive and Allegoric Subjects.* In combining the "allegoric" and "descriptive" the author reflected the aesthetic position of the 1740's, specifically that of the Warton circle, which made as one of its central requirements of poetry the imaginative creation of pictorial personification.[1] These personifications contribute greatly to the peculiarly effective and insistent unity of the poems—a quality that in its final effect is unmistakably Collins' and represents a minor triumph of architectonic skill.

Collins' form at its purest may be seen in the "Ode to Pity," the first poem in the volume of 1746. It consists of five closely related sections presented in the following order: (1) the invocation to the personified quality, beginning here and elsewhere "O Thou"; (2) the description of the personification and its attendant train (a section that resembles the assigning of descriptive attributes to the Deity in prayer); (3) the manifestations—or the incarnations —of the quality in past literary and cultural history; (4) the present need in England and in the poet himself, a need that is, however, not presented satirically or rhetorically but in penitent humility of spirit as though the presentation were a prayer of humble access; and finally (5) the supplication of the personified quality to dwell once again among men and the pledge that the heart of the suppliant will be prepared to receive the indwelling.[2]

---

[1] For Joseph Warton's views on personification see above, p. 147, and below, n. 9. For a discussion of Collins' intimate association with the Wartons see J. S. Cunningham, "Thomas Warton and William Collins," *Durham University Journal,* XLVI (December, 1953), 22–24.

[2] Cf. the analysis of the allegorical ode by Norman Maclean, "From Action to Image," in *Critics and Criticism,* ed. R. S. Crane (Chicago, 1952), pp. 441–42.

Although Collins' subjects are usually literary and aesthetic, occasionally political and patriotic, but never directly religious, the mood created is that of religious devotion. The entire ode is usually presented as a prayer, which becomes the unifying metaphor of the poem.

There are variants in other odes of the formula of the "Ode to Pity." The "Ode to the Passions," for example, is radically different in basic scheme; the "Ode to the Poetical Character" lacks the invocation and is presented not as a prayer but as a mythic and cosmological event; and the "Ode to Evening" lacks the concluding supplication and ends in an allegorical *conversazione*. But even in these three poems basic elements remain that relate them closely to most of the other odes, in which the formal progress we have described remains intact.

The form is Collins' creation, but he is indebted for specific features of it to Thomson and Milton. We have observed that Thomson used not only such imperatives as "see" and "behold" (invitations to the reader to contemplate a natural scene) but also such imperatives as "come," "be present" (indications of a posture of prayer before the personified natural object or phenomenon). There are passages in the *Seasons* that combine description and prayer in a way that unmistakably anticipates Collins. Moreover, the almost endlessly described progress of the goddess Liberty from Greece to Rome and finally to England is an earlier and by comparison titanic version of Collins' brief lyric surveys of the progress of poetic qualities over substantially the same cultural terrain.

But greatly though Collins is indebted to Thomson—and he seems to acknowledge that debt in general, although he does not accurately describe it[3]—he is even more indebted to Milton. The closest antecedent parallels to the allegorical and descriptive odes of 1746 are found in "L'Allegro" and "Il Penseroso." The formula that governs these poems bears close resemblance to that governing Collins' odes: the banishment of the opposite quality in invoking the desired quality; the naming and description of the personified quality; the description of its train and associations; the manifestations of the quality in symbolic landscape; its manifestation in sympathetic forms of art and thought; and the conditional dedication to the subject quality provided it can indeed supply the pleasures

[3] "Ode Occasion'd by the Death of Mr. Thomson" (1749).

poetically contemplated. This Collins inherited. But he sufficiently altered its several parts in final combination so that he must be credited with considerable originality. He has endowed the Miltonic form with a new soul: less objective than Milton's poems, Collins' odes are prayers that breathe a kind of religious-lyrical awe present only occasionally and only for a limited purpose in the more brilliant but more external moods and scenes of Milton's poetic twins.

Our subject, however, is neither Collins' poetry as a whole nor the extent of its indebtedness, but rather its pictorial elements. Where, in this form, is the pictorial most prominently and effectively present? Obviously in the description of the personification and its attendants. In these sections Collins has fully absorbed the basic tenet of the Warton circle that poetry ought to be imaginative, that to be imaginative is to be pictorial, and that the pictorial is principally expressed in allegorical personae "picturesquely" rendered. But Collins' pictorialism was by no means confined to these sections, even though it is most prominent there. Some of the most successful pictorial images appear elsewhere: in the invocation, the supplication, and in fact at any and all points indifferently.

Such pervasiveness as this suggests that Collins' pictorial qualities are related to a basic aesthetic conception; and there is none more basic than his conception of the imagination,[4] a power to which he was almost religiously dedicated and from which, it may be assumed, all the elements of his poems, but particularly the pictorial, were in some way derived.

To Dr. Johnson, Collins was a poet "eminently delighted with those flights of imagination which pass the bounds of nature." Such preoccupation resulted in occasional "sublimity and splendour" and also in "allegorical imagery."[5] Johnson's language reveals that for him there was an intimate association between the imagination and literary description, an association that goes back to the etymological view that the imagination is basically the maker of pictures.

In making this association Johnson reflected the opinion of his age and the immediately preceding one. All critics and poets of whatever school accepted the association conveyed in the common

[4] See A. S. P. Woodhouse, "Collins and the Creative Imagination," in *Studies in English by Members of the University College* (Toronto, 1931).

[5] "Life of Collins," *Works of Samuel Johnson* (Oxford, 1825), VIII, 401-2.

phrase "Fancy's pictures." Neoclassic poets like Pope, Gay, Swift, and Prior consistently associated fancy and painting.[6] In Matthew Green's lively poem "The Spleen," for example, Fancy is given "limning skill" and "sketching power," the power to "draw and colour at her will."[7] In Fanny Burney's *Evelina* the Reverend Mr. Villars chides his lovely ward for her as yet unacknowledged preference for Lord Orville:

> *Imagination* took the reins . . . ; her glowing pencil, dipt in the vivid colours of her creative ideas, painted to you, at the moment of your first acquaintance, all the excellencies, all the good and rare qualities, which a great length of time, and intimacy, could alone have really discovered.[8]

Of "imagination" in a pejorative sense—as in Johnson's memorable "dangerous prevalence of imagination" in *Rasselas*—we shall do no more than note that painting and its colors were associated with the term even under these conditions. Among the Wartons and their associates imagination and color remain linked, but the pejorative connotation has disappeared. These poets—and Collins must be numbered along them—avowedly wished to counteract the didactic poetry that appealed to the mind by writing the more sensuous poetry that appealed to the fancy.[9] When they won support, it was by these canons that they were judged. In 1764 the *Monthly Review* praised Collins for "luxuriance of *imagination*, a wild sublimity of *fancy*" and said that the "Ode to Fear" was "so nervous, so expressive, and so *picturesque* throughout, that we have seen no lyric performance superior to it in the English language."[10]

Comment could be multiplied to show that it was a common thing for critics and poets of the school of the forties to associate the imaginative and pictorial. Exactly what was the imaginative-pictorial? It was clearly not the naturalistic picturesque of the later century that derived from Claudian and Salvatorian landscape. It was, rather, a quality associated chiefly with allegorical personification and heroic landscape. Although fundamentally related,

---

[6] See above, pp. 240–41, for Pope's use of color in a satirical context.

[7] Ll. 450–51, 497.

[8] Letter LXVII, September 28 ("Everyman's Library" [London, 1909], p. 285).

[9] Warton, "Advertisement," *Odes on Various Subjects* (London, 1746), p. [3].

[10] XXX (January, 1764), 21, 22. Italics mine.

there is this difference between Thomson's and Collins' imagery. Thomson's at its best arises from the vivid personification of *natural* detail and the organization of the scene around that personification, but Collins at his most typical personifies the *moral* and *psychological* abstraction and makes that personification central to the entire poem.

Although inevitably more shadowy than personified natural detail, these allegorical moral beings were nonetheless conceived pictorially. The *Monthly Review* calls the following lines of allegorical personification from the "Ode to Fear" a "picture":

> *Danger*, whose Limbs of Giant Mold
> What mortal Eye can fix'd behold?
> Who stalks his Round, an hideous Form,
> Howling amidst the Midnight Storm,
> Or throws him on the ridgy Steep
> Of some loose hanging Rock to sleep.

The same reviewer said that the following lines from the "Ode to Mercy" affords the finest subject for a picture that imagination can form":

> O Thou, who sit'st a smiling Bride
> By *Valour*'s arm'd and awful Side,
> Gentlest of Sky-born Forms, and best ador'd:
> Who oft with Songs, divine to hear,
> Win'st from his fatal Grasp the Spear,
> And hid'st in Wreaths of Flow'rs his bloodless Sword!

These lines are indeed pictorial, reminiscent of high Renaissance paintings of Mars disarmed by Venus. The *Monthly Review* also said of the lines just quoted that "Horace's rule of *ut Pictura Poesis* was never better observed."[11]

The contemporary critic was essentially sound but insufficiently specific. To whom and what in the long and diverse pictorialist tradition is Collins peculiarly related? Milton has already been introduced in discussing the total form of the odes. But the pictorial

---

[11] *Ibid.*, pp. 22, 24, 25. Collins would doubtless have approved of this criticism. He once praised his friend Cooper for his *"picturesque* and forcible allegory" (cited by Woodhouse, *op. cit.* [n. 4], p. 100, n. 20). For an interesting example of a "picturesque" allegory in prose see the sketch for a future poem written by Joseph Warton at the age of eighteen. It is full of pictorial personifications (*Biographical Memoirs of the late Revd Joseph Warton, D.D.* [London, 1806], pp. 10–13).

elements do not derive primarily from "L'Allegro" and "Il Penseroso." It is, rather, *Comus* that anticipates Collins' pictorialism in such personified abstractions as "gray-hooded Eev'n," "pure-ey'd Faith," "white-handed Hope," "bold Incontinence," and winged Wisdom that seeks "sweet retired Solitude" and her nurse Contemplation.[12] To the creation of imaginatively effective personifications Milton in this poem devoted his highest powers; in the following passage the animation of the natural scene by a personification is a brilliant poetic achievement. Comus says of Echo's song—those "raptures" that moved "the vocal air":

> How sweetly did they float upon the wings
> Of silence, through the empty-vaulted night
> At every fall smoothing the Raven doune
> Of darkness till it smil'd [ll. 248–51].

How gently but miraculously the forbidding darkness is transformed by music into an attractive human sentience that smiles at the loveliness of sound!

This passage is not particularly visual and not at all pictorial. But there are other passages in *Comus* from which Collins may have learned how to create the allegorical pictures so eminently characteristic of his poetry. In response to the attendant spirit's invocation Sabrina rises, attended by water nymphs, and sings the following song—itself a veritable allegory by Guido Reni or Nicolas Poussin:

> By the rushy-fringed bank,
> Where grows the Willow and the Osier dank
> My sliding Chariot stayes,
> Thick set with Agat, and the azurn sheen
> Of Turkis blew, and Emrauld green
> That in the channell strayes,
> Whilst from off the waters fleet
> Thus I set my printless feet
> O're the Cowslips Velvet head
> That bends not as I tread,
> Gentle swain at thy request
> I am here [ll. 889–900].

[12] Ll. 187, 212, 396, 374–75. I do not wish to make too sharp a distinction between the influence of *Comus* and of "L'Allegro" and "Il Penseroso." Nor should it be forgotten that Collins frequently echoed "Lycidas." For a convincing analysis see F. R. Leavis, *Revaluation* (London, 1949), pp. 131–33.

Comus as a masque obviously belonged to the pictorialist tradition. Although a direct influence of the masque upon Collins cannot be proved, it is not unlikely that impulses from this form were mediated to him through Milton; or perhaps his absorption of the very iconological forms that entered into the masque may have predisposed his imagination to masquelike effects. Jonson's *Masque of Beautie*, for example, anticipates Collins. In it such allegorical abstractions as *Splendor*, *Serenitas*, *Laetitia*, and *Dignitas*, all elements of the general quality "beauty," are represented as sculptured figures, standing on a cornice between pilasters, in front of which fly little cupids waving wreaths.

SERENITAS

In a garment of bright-*skie*-colour, a long tresse, and waued with a vaile of diuers colours, such as the golden skie sometimes shews: vpon her head a cleare, and faire *Sunne* shining, with rayes of gold striking downe to the feet of the figure. In her hand a *Christall*, cut with seuerall angles, and shadow'd with diuers colours, as caused by refraction.[13]

Who reading this can fail to think of Collins' Mercy, "gentlest of Sky-born Forms," or of Pity with

> Thy sky-worn Robes of tend'rest Blue,
> Thy Eyes of dewy Light?

Perhaps this comparison will not seem far-fetched if we remember that Spenser, whose poetry cannot escape some kind of association with the masque,[14] was an especial favorite of the Warton circle and that neoclassical criticism interpreted Spenser in particular and allegorical poetry in general as peculiarly pictorial. Of Spenser, John Hughes commented that his fable, "tho' often wild, is . . . always emblematical," and of allegorical poetry as a whole that "the Resemblance which has been so often observ'd in general between Poetry and Painting, is yet more particular in Allegory; which . . . is a kind of Picture in Poetry."[15]

THE ALLEGORICAL PERSONIFICATIONS

In his *Persian Eclogues*, which he himself had intended as an expression of "Elegancy and Wildness of Thought" in a style

[13] *Ben Jonson*, ed. C. H. Herford, Percy Simpson, and Evelyn Simpson, VII (Oxford, 1941), 187. See above, pp. 88–92.

[14] Enid Welsford, *The Court Masque* (Cambridge, 1927), pp. 302–7.

[15] *Works of Spenser*, ed. John Hughes (London, 1715), I, lxii, xxx.

"rich and figurative,"[16] Collins had undoubtedly hoped to make his figures pictorially lively. He was not successful. In his first eclogue Wisdom weds the "fair-ey'd Truth" and fathers Peace and Plenty. But not much more than a capital letter distinguishes these highly generalized and conventional beings. Modesty blushes; Pity is friendly; Chastity's heart is cold; Meekness has "low-cast eyes"—a faint suggestion of Guido Reni (see Plate VIII).

In the odes of 1746, for which Collins created the form described at the outset, there are fewer personified stereotypes. To his contemporaries Collins seemed to be most effective in the originality, particularity, and beauty of the personae of these poems. One reason for the improvement is the increase in animation. In the *Eclogues* it was sufficient that Pity was friendly; in the "Ode to Pity" the goddess, still a "friend of Man," binds up his wounds. In addition to being more animated, the personification is pictorially more vivid and iconically richer. In the same ode Pity, who is an anchorite, bears, like a figure from Ripa, her peculiar and appropriate signa (the wren, the turtles, and the sacred myrtle). She wears "a sky-worn Robe of tend'rest Blue," and her eyes are wet with dewy light—a faintly synesthetic image that anticipates Shelley.

Increased animation and heightened pictorialism characterize the figures in all the odes of 1746. Fear—"frantic *Fear*," with "hurried Step" and "haggard Eye"—is felt as an immediate presence: "I see, I see Thee near." She, too, is a nymph but, unlike Pity, a mad nymph, creating disturbance in human life and even in nature. Since she can be tamed only by the artistic imagination, the poem itself becomes a prayer to a Fury, a kind of literary charm. But its force is felt only if the sense of danger is keenly felt, and that is possible only if the personifications create a feeling of immediacy. In the "Ode to Fear" we can see clearly why the persona must be more than a capitalized noun. To justify the attitude of prayer the central and the attendant figures must seem iconically real enough to produce at least a genuflection.

In those odes of the 1746 volume that can be called slightly irregular if the form of the "Ode to Pity" is considered normative, there is substantially the same kind of pictorialism. Collins never clogs

---

[16] Preface to the *Persian Eclogues* (London, 1742). This and all other citations from Collins come from *Poems of Gray and Collins*, ed. Austin Lane Poole (4th ed.; Oxford, 1948). Reference will be made to only the titles of poems.

his visual passages with an excessive amount of sensuous and iconic detail. "How Sleep the Brave" is even less sensuous than the rest. An exquisitely chaste and disciplined poem—there is not a single indisputable metrical substitution in any of its iambic feet—its personifications appear as shadowy and wraithlike figures at the graves of the fallen soldiers. The visualization is extremely slight, but the action of each figure is delicately appropriate to it and to the total action.

The "Passions" is Collins' ode to Music. It lacks the metrical suppleness and the dramatic human scenes of Dryden's "Alexander's Feast," to which it is remotely related. Entirely allegorical, the action presents the personified passions thronging about the cell of Music, each in its turn snatching one of her instruments and revealing its own nature in what it plays and what it sings. The ode has been excessively admired. Langhorne in 1765 called it "the finest ode in the English language."[17] As a whole, however, it lacks inspiration, a fact revealed not only by its artificial series of unrelated theatrical appearances but also by its lines that are entirely filled with lists of words in unsubordinated relationship:

> Exulting, trembling, raging, fainting
> . . . .
> Warm, Energic, Chaste, Sublime!

In some of its scenes the rhetoric outruns the emotion, and the personae are abstract and ineffectual.

For these reasons the modern reader cannot appreciate the entire poem. But he can, by an effort of the historical imagination, understand what the sections devoted to Melancholy, Cheerfulness, and Joy must have meant to a contemporary reader. Their appeal lay in their evocation of splendid Renaissance and seventeenth-century pictorial allegories in which lovely mythological or allegorical personages were placed in appropriate landscapes.

> With Eyes up-raised, as one inspir'd [Plate VIII]
> Pale *Melancholy* sate retir'd,
> And from her wild sequester'd Seat,
> In Notes by Distance made more sweet,
> Pour'd thro' the mellow *Horn* her pensive Soul:

[17] *Poetical Works of Mr. William Collins*, ed. J. Langhorne (London, 1804), p. 143 (1st ed., 1765).

And dashing soft from Rocks around,
Bubbling Runnels join'd the Sound;
Thro' Glades and Glooms the mingled Measure stole,
Or o'er some haunted Stream with fond Delay,
Round an holy Calm diffusing,
Love of Peace, and lonely Musing,
In hollow Murmurs died away.

But O how alter'd was its sprightlier Tone!
When *Chearfulness*, a Nymph of healthiest Hue,
Her Bow a-cross her Shoulder flung,
Her Buskins gem'd with Morning Dew,
Blew an inspiring Air, that Dale and Thicket rung,
The Hunter's Call to *Faun* and *Dryad* known!
The Oak-crown'd *Sisters*, and their chast-eye'd *Queen*,
Satyrs and sylvan Boys were seen,
Peeping from forth their Alleys green:
Brown *Exercise* rejoic'd to hear,
And *Sport* leapt up, and seiz'd his Beechen Spear.

Last came *Joy*'s Ecstatic Trial,
He with viny Crown advancing,
First to the lively Pipe his Hand address'd,
But soon he saw the brisk awak'ning Viol,
Whose sweet entrancing Voice he lov'd the best.
They would have thought who heard the Strain,
They saw in *Tempe*'s Vale her native Maids,
Amidst the festal sounding Shades,
To some unwearied Minstrel dancing,
While as his flying Fingers kiss'd the Strings,
Love fram'd with *Mirth*, a gay fantastic Round,
Loose were Her Tresses seen, her Zone unbound,
And HE amidst his frolic Play
As if he would the charming Air repay,
Shook thousand Odours from his dewy Wings.

This is a pattern of rich and subtle sound, but it is the pictorial effects that are the loveliest: Cheerfulness is a Diana-like figure ("Her buskins gem'd with Morning Dew"); the satyrs and other sylvan creatures are seen emerging from the woods ("Peeping from forth their Alleys green"); the "gay fantastic Round" in which Mirth dances with streaming hair and flowing robe is a pictorial bacchanal.

Collins' "Ode to Evening" will remain for the modern reader the most beautiful of his poems. Since it is an exquisite adaptation to a natural scene of the formula used in purely literary and aesthetic allegory, the personified figure is necessarily of central importance. Evening is addressed as "pensive Eve,"[18] "*Nymph* reserv'd," "*Maid* compos'd," "calm *Vot'ress*,"[19] and "meekest *Eve*" at regular intervals throughout the poem. To this goddess the poet kneels in supplication. The characterization of the approaching goddess sustains and amplifies the evensong mood of invocation.

This poem, long praised for its delicate and appropriate music and the evocative beauty of its aural imagery, is also pictorial —in the manner of Guido Reni, not of Claude. Evening "returns" on a "shadowy Car," which has been prepared by the "*Hours*" and "*Elves*" and "many a *Nymph* who wreaths her Brows with Sedge." The conception is similar to Thomson's coming of the dawn, which, as we have argued, can be viewed as a literary transcription of Guido's famous fresco "Aurora" (Plate XXIV). Collins describes not the coming Aurora but the coming Vesper, and the chromatic values must necessarily be different. But there is no mistaking the fact that Collins' lines, like Thomson's, find their closest pictorial analogues in Guido's fresco or in the closely similar natural allegories of Italian art.

There are also other important pictorial qualities in the ode. The action of Evening—

> Thy Dewy Fingers draw
> The gradual dusky Veil[20]

—is reminiscent of the baroque angel who stands in an upper corner of the canvas, about to let the draped curtain fall upon the represented scene. And the coming of Evening is viewed near a ruin or

---

[18] Cf. Milton's "Com pensive Nun" ("Il Penseroso," l. 31) and the description of "still Evening" in *Paradise Lost* iv. 598, a passage to which Collins' ode should carefully be compared.

[19] This particular apostrophe was added later and appears in the text of Dodsley's *Collection* of 1748. I find the later superior to the original lines of the 1746 volume because they keep the central personification before our eyes and enforce a consistent mood of prayerful supplication (see Poole, *op. cit.* [n. 16], p. 314).

[20] Compare the action of Milton's personified Moon ("And o're the dark her Silver Mantle threw") in *Paradise Lost* iv. 609 and also Ariosto's "Stendon le nubi un tenebroso velo" in *Orlando Furioso* xviii. 142.

else from a hut placed in a scene at once Salvatorian and Claudian—
one of the very few occasions on which Collins invokes scenes characteristic of these painters:

> Then let me rove some wild and heathy Scene,
> Or find some Ruin 'midst its dreary Dells,
>   Whose Walls more awful nod
>   By thy religious Gleams.
> Or if chill blustering Winds, or driving Rain,
> Prevent my willing Feet, be mine the Hut,
>   That from the Mountain's Side,
>   Views Wilds, and swelling Floods,
> And Hamlets brown, and dim-discover'd Spires.

COLLINS AND THE PLASTIC ARTS

If it is true that Salvator Rosa and Claude are subordinate to
Guido Reni in Collins' poetry, then many of the suggestions of
modern criticism about his pictorial antecedents and analogues
are either mistaken or irrelevant. Equivalences have been drawn
between the odes of Collins and the paintings of Gainsborough,
Claude, Girtin, J. R. Cozens, Nicolas Poussin, and Corot.[21] Most
of these parallels are intended to isolate a particular quality in the
poetry: the mistiness of the scene, the serenity of the landscape,
the gentleness of the colors. But such commentary has missed
the main point. Collins is not essentially a landscapist; and, lovely
and suggestive though his occasional use of color assuredly is, his
colors are seldom natural but usually allegorical and moral.

Another kind of criticism that also falls wide of the mark finds
Collins an aural and not a visual poet and implies that because

---

[21] Herbert Read, *In Defence of Shelley* (London, 1936), p. 243; Edmund Blunden
(ed.), *Poems of William Collins* (London, 1929), p. 38; Nathan Drake, *Literary Hours*
(Sudbury, England, 1798), p. 391; C. V. Deane, *Aspects of Eighteenth Century Nature Poetry* (Oxford, 1935), p. 78. Professor Wylie Sypher has suggested that Collins'
"order-disorder" ambiguity is paralleled in the *genre pittoresque*, one of those fantastic and asymmetrical *morceaux de caprice* that developed within the French rococo ("The *Morceau de fantasie* in Verse: A New Approach to Collins," *University of
Toronto Quarterly*, XV [October, 1945], 65–69). The suggestion I do not find sound.
Collins does not seem to me to be French-oriented or rococo in any way. This parallel
diverts attention from Collins' true pictorial affiliations. Moreover, I cannot accept
Professor Sypher's assumption that there is asymmetry in Collins beyond some
grammatical and syntactical confusion, which surely does not need a visual analogue
to explain it. I find his total form firmly and steadily controlled, almost classical in
its symmetry.

there are very few Claudian landscapes in his verse, he was not pictorial at all.[22] This error arises from confining the picturesque to Claudian and Salvatorian effects and from denying that anything except landscape is pictorial.

Another reason that some have failed to find the pictorial in Collins is that his visualizations are slight and unextended. His effects are conveyed in brief compass, often by the suggestion of a single word. His method is to suggest rather than paint a picture. He does at times draw up rather detailed specifications for an allegory, placing and distinguishing his figures in the pictorial manner. But more frequently he merely hints at the pictorial effect and attempts to stimulate the reader's imagination to do the rest. That hint remains peculiarly pictorial, and the imagination is guided to the canvases of the great allegorists. When Langhorne in 1765 said that Collins had drawn "a moral picture," in which the truth or precept arises from the memory and the picture from the imagination, he is making the proper emphasis and approaching Collins from the right point of view. And when he further says that it is the personification that gives to the poetry its "chief powers and graces," the judgment may indeed be challenged, but he has defined the area in which critical debate should take place and in which the pictorial is located.[23] Similarly, James Montgomery in 1825 revealed that he found the pictorial to reside in allegorical personification and was willing to be stimulated even by the slightest hints of pictorialism. He says of "How Sleep the Brave" (a poem that a modern reader, taught to expect the extended prospect or the Salvatorian picturesque, would find highly aural and unvisualized): "The following stanzas are almost unrivalled in the combination of poetry with painting. . . ."[24]

All Collins' poetry supports what the comparison of Guido's "Aurora" and Collins' "Evening" suggests, that his pictorial af-

---

[22] Elizabeth Wheeler Manwaring, *Italian Landscape in Eighteenth Century England* (New York, 1925), p. 112. The recently discovered verse fragments seem to support the view that Collins was pictorial and iconic. In them he confesses to a deep love of painting, mentions by name Claude, Ruisdael, Salvator Rosa, Michelangelo, Leonardo, De Piles, and Thornhill, and seems to refer to Titian and Tintoretto (*William Collins: Drafts & Fragments of Verse*, ed. J. S. Cunningham [Oxford, 1956], pp. 11, 12, 14, 15, 19–20, 26, 32, 35).

[23] Langhorne, *op. cit.* (n. 17), pp. 124, 126.

[24] Cited in *Poems of Collins*, ed. Walter C. Bronson (Boston, 1898), p. 104.

filiations were basically those of all English poets from Dryden to Gray. His pantheon consisted of paintings of the high Renaissance and the seventeenth century and of the marbles of ancient Greece and Rome.

There are also the signs, which in a neoclassical poet we have come to expect, that the traditions of *ut pictura poesis* and of iconic poetry are operative. In his "Verses . . . to Sir Thomas Hanmer," in which he surveys the progress and historical manifestations of the arts, he seems fully to accept the Italian Renaissance as a reviver of all the arts. He has often been considered a "preromantic," in a line that connected Gray, Walpole, Beckford, Macpherson, and many others. But there is not a trace of literary gothicism or medievalism in the odes of 1746. In the "Verses to Hanmer" he considered even the Elizabethan age as a "beauteous Union" "Of *Tuscan* Fancy, and *Athenian* strength." He also expressed the notion that all the arts are sisters, notably painting and poetry. In the same poem he views poetry as in a special way the inspirer of painting:

> O might the Muse with equal Ease persuade
> Expressive Picture to adopt thine Aid!
> Some pow'rful *Raphael* shou'd again appear,
> And Arts consenting fix their Empire here.

Then, in the immediately ensuing passage, Collins has a prophetic vision in which he sees what was to be realized a generation later under Alderman Boydell: a gallery of native English paintings inspired by scenes from Shakespeare. The lines about to be quoted are also noteworthy because they are iconic in a special way. They do not describe pictures that have been painted; they describe pictures that it is hoped will be painted. Collins is, as it were, instructing a painter how to improve *Julius Caesar* and *Coriolanus* into fashionable pictorialism. Dramatic action has become frozen gesture and arrested motion.

> Methinks ev'n now I view some fair Design,
> Where breathing Nature lives in ev'ry line:[25]
> Chaste, and subdu'd, the modest Colours lie,
> In fair Proportion to th'approving Eye.—
> And see, where *Antony* lamenting stands

[25] Observe the conventional expression of *enargeia* in this line.

In fixt Distress, and spreads his pleading Hands![26]
O'er the pale Corse the Warrior seems to bend,
Deep sunk in Grief, and mourns his murther'd Friend!
Still as they press, he calls on all around,
Lifts the torn Robe, and points the bleeding Wound.
　　But who is he, whose Brows exalted bear
A Rage impatient, and a fiercer Air?
Ev'n now, his Thoughts with eager Vengeance doom
The last sad Ruin of ungrateful *Rome*.
Till, slow-advancing o'er the tented Plain,
In sable Weeds, appear the Kindred-train:
The frantic Mother leads their wild Despair,
Beats her swoln Breast, and rends her silver Hair.
And see he yields! . . . the Tears unbidden start,
And conscious Nature claims th'unwilling Heart!
O'er all the Man conflicting Passions rise,
Rage grasps the Sword, while *Pity* melts the Eyes.

These are the only lines in which Collins is avowedly iconic—in which, that is, his presentation of details is obviously guided by an imagined painting. If, however, we use these unmistakably iconic verses as a touchstone to detect the pictorialism of Collins' other poetry, we shall find how genuinely and pervasively pictorial he is. Nearly every one of the odes gives the impression that it was written with real or imaginary allegorical pictures in the back of the poet's mind.[27]

Rubens and Raphael have been suggested as particularly analogous to Collins by the only modern scholar who has correctly understood Collins' general pictorial affiliations.[28] There are indeed Rubensian moments in Collins' verse; but on the whole Rubens' colors are too bright and rich, his canvases too crowded, and his allegorical figures too fleshly and substantial to provide useful analogues. There are certainly Raphaelesque moments: "chaste

[26] Observe how sculpturesque this pose is. This is neoclassical idealization of the type described earlier (above, pp. 144–46).

[27] I do not wish to suggest that Collins' form derives from a steady contemplation of real or imaginary graphic art. That would negate what I said earlier about Collins' form. It is not totally pictorial in that manner. Collins gives, rather, the impression of glancing up at a picture that is not steadily contemplated but always ready to furnish pictorial and iconic details when called upon.

[28] Woodhouse, *op. cit.* (n. 4).

Eve," the hermit Freedom, the pilgrim Honor, the gentle skyborn Mercy, and Pity with blue robes and dewy eyes have about them the restrained classical delicacy and the Christian tenderness of Raphael's Madonnas. But Raphael seems somewhat remote and the parallels too faint to provide much illumination, and Raphael-esque qualities reappear in Guido Reni under circumstances that make him a more satisfactory analogue.

The much-admired "air" of Guido's heads—their grace, tender-ness, and sweet, resigned religiosity recently so much out of favor—easily became theatrical, and the figures in his more "sublime" and "terrible" history-pieces are often presented in attitudes of literally open-mouthed horror and in stagy postures of fear and anger[29] (Plate XI). Collins, too, for all the simplicity and delicacy of such figures as Pity and Mercy, tends to be theatrically melo-dramatic when he describes more violent emotions. Man's woe is "frantic." Fear walks with "hurried step" and looks with "haggard Eye." She creates in her beholder exaggerated and convulsive movements: "Like Thee I start, like Thee disorder'd fly." Genius and Taste in the "Ode to Simplicity" provoke the poet to "some divine Excess." Winter in the "Ode to Evening" yells "thro' the troublous Air" and affrights the "shrinking Train" of Evening and rudely rends her robes. Wan Despair in the "Passions" sings a song that is "sad by Fits, by Starts [is] wild."

For a poet capable of combining melodrama with delicacy, Guido, not Raphael, is the proper parallel. The combination in Guido may be seen in his "Murder of the Innocents" in Bologna, where delicate babes and a sky-borne cherub are contrasted with cruel soldiers and screaming horror-struck mothers (Plate XI). In "Apollo and Mar-syas"—a theme Guido liked and often repeated—a delicately but firmly outlined Apollo, classical in profile, benign in countenance and manner, and completely indifferent to the screaming suffering he is producing, begins his task of flaying alive the hapless Marsyas, whose face and body are theatrically but not unnaturally distorted into an agony of physical pain (Plate XXV B). Moreover, Guido was an allegorist. In his "Fortuna," for example, the figure of the goddess, almost nude, flying through the cloudy sky, her hair and mantle flowing behind her, surrounded by the iconic symbols traditionally attributed to her and accompanied by an attendant

[29] See above, pp. 198–99.

283

winged *putto*, resembles Collins' personae in mood, manner, and iconographic technique (Plate XXV A).

Pictorial analogues alone do not exhaust Collins' affiliations with the plastic arts. The poet Gray, shortly after he had read the "descriptive and allegoric" odes, wrote that Collins had "a fine Fancy, model'd upon the Antique."[30] Gray is sensitive to a quality that Collins himself seems to have cultivated in his own use of the pencil. Collins especially liked to draw medallions and emblems suggesting Greek sculpture and classical decoration. One medallion he intended to illustrate a prose work he had just written entitled "The Friendly Examiner, or Letters of Polémon and Philétus":

> You found by my last that I propos'd the more literary papers should fall under the name of Polémon and the more lusory or comic under that of Philétus. In order to hint this at the head of the Paper I shall have a medallion engrav'd of two elegant Heads *á l'antique* thus (Don't you think 'em *á l'antique?*) over the lower part of the necks of which there shall be a veil thrown, from under which a little Art shall appear writing on a Roman scroll, & a Satyr either in contrast holding up another, or writing on part of the same, or suppose the veil to be upheld by Friendship, who may at the same time point to the Relievo of the medallion while she discovers the ornaments of the base by supporting the veil.[31]

The passage is revealing. Collins is obviously excited by his ability to achieve a quality of antique elegance. Moreover, the design he has drawn seems to suggest the kind of effect he achieves in his poetical allegories.

This leads us to inquire if there is the sculpturesque as well as the picturesque in his poetry and, if so, how it can be discriminated. Such a quality does seem to exist in the odes, but not in clearly separable images like those in the poetry of Pope and Thomson. It is unmistakable marble *à l'antique* that Pope places in his Temple of Fame. Thomson's grieving Celadon and the surprised Musidora become indubitable statues. But in Collins the statuesque is less obvious; it cannot be easily separated from the picturesque and isolated as a thing apart.

And yet it is pervasively present in the odes. There are subtle

[30] To Thomas Wharton, Dec. 27, 1746, *Correspondence*, ed. Paget Toynbee and Leonard Whibley (Oxford, 1935), I, 261.

[31] Quoted in Edward Gay Ainsworth, Jr., *Poor Collins* (Ithaca, N.Y., 1937), pp. 38, 39.

similarities between Collins' figures and the classical figures engraved on the pages of *Polymetis* (Plate XXVIII). Joseph Spence's handsome folio appeared in 1747, too late to have influenced the odes that had appeared some months earlier. But, as we have seen, neoclassical authors admired ancient marbles, coins, and medallions; borrowed images from the sculptures of antiquity; and associated ideal forms with classical marbles.[32] Of these neoclassical habits of mind both the *Odes* of 1746 and *Polymetis* of 1747 are separate embodiments. In the economy and concentration of Collins' allegories, which are stripped of unessential ornament and are free from the floridity and excessive detail of an allegorist like Rubens, one can perhaps see the statuesque. And is not the grace of Collins' figures partly that of sculptured stone? One important equivalent of the poet's personified abstractions, which so often take the form of a nymph, an anchorite, and even the Virgin without being directly Christian or even religious, may be the "moral Venus" of the eighteenth century—the Venus of the Medici transformed into a figure with modesty, elegance, and virginal reserve (Plate XIX B).

There is still another relationship with the plastic arts that should be suggested even though it, like the sculpturesque, cannot be distinctly separated from the pictorial. Collins may not have gone directly to Cesare Ripa's *Iconologia* (see Plate II) or to related moral and allegorical emblems, but there is in the odes a quality that suggests Ripa and other iconologists even when details differ. Collins' Danger is a giant of hideous shape, Ripa's a stripling who treads on a snake and leans on a reed. Collins' personification howls in a midnight storm, and the sky above Ripa's is streaked with lightning. Collins' Danger *sleeps* on a "loose hanging Rock" that impends from a "ridgy Steep," Ripa's *walks* on the edge of a precipice. But perhaps Collins is closer to Otto Vaenius, whose emblems from Horace often strikingly anticipate the figures in Collins and often use the arrangement of Collins, in which the central or subject virtue is accompanied by a train of attendant virtues. The engraving entitled "Virtus inconcussa" presents Virtue trampling on the de-

[32] See above, pp. 144–46, and Addison's discussion of coins and their relevance to literature in "Dialogues upon the Usefulness of Ancient Medals, Especially in Relation to the Latin and Greek Poets," *Miscellaneous Works* (London, 1726), III, 15 ff.

feated Fortune and surrounded by Pity, Justice, Fortitude, Magnanimity, and Temperance[33] (Plate XXIX).

But even this iconological arrangement can be duplicated elsewhere, and it is idle to look for an exclusive influence. Ripa and Vaenius influenced masque, poem, and painting and were themselves influenced by classical poetry and classical sculpture. The web of Collins' pictorialism is of too fine a weave for unraveling. If we wish to see Collins whole, we must see his poetry as at once picturesque, sculpturesque, and emblematic. He has subtly embodied more than one element of the pictorialist tradition.

We have earlier suggested that Thomson's natural personifications differ from Collins' "shad'wy Tribes of Mind." In the *Seasons* the persona is introduced to order and animate a natural scene and is itself a personified natural detail. Thomson's details, personified or not, come originally from nature and rise, as it were, to the poetic scene in which they appear. Collins' come originally from the mind and the imagination, and descend, as it were, to the poetic allegory in which they finally appear. Even in the "Ode to Evening," in which the strategy of presentation is basically that of Thomson, natural detail has been subjected to greater imaginative modification than in any of Thomson's out-of-door descriptions. The personified figure of this lovely ode is more prominent, is attended by a greater number of subsidiary personifications, and is a more efficacious unifying force than are the figures in Thomson's verse. The attitude of poet and reader is not that of a beholder but of a worshiper; and the physical detail is recollected, it would seem, with eyes closed in tranquillity. For Thomson's "clearer Ken" Collins has substituted the "potent Spell" of Fancy. Like his own personified Evening he draws a gradual dusky veil over the real world so that we may not be too long diverted from our exploration of the "World of Soul" and "The dim-discover'd Tracts of Mind."[34]

[33] *Q. Horatii Flacci emblemata . . .* (Antwerp, 1607), p. 8. For Ripa, see above, pp. 91, 92.

[34] These phrases come from Collins' "The Manners: An Ode." In order to apply them to Collins as a whole I am subverting the meaning of this particular poem, in which Collins says farewell to shadowy personifications and subjective writing and turns to observation and nature, the scenes of human life and action, as the future sources of his poetry. This change of program resembles Pope's rejection of "Fancy's maze." But Collins never wrote anything under this aesthetic principle. Certainly the allegorical and descriptive odes are written under the habits of mind and thought that the "Manners" seems to reject.

CHAPTER XI

Thomas Gray

THE MINOR POEMS

Thomas Gray was one of the most learned men of his day. His learning embraced history, criticism, metaphysics, morals, politics, travel literature, botany, zoology, entomology, music, and the plastic arts. His interest in painting was early revealed and early developed. During his tour of the Continent Gray took extensive notes on what he saw in the galleries of Paris, Bologna, Florence, and Rome. He made full appraisals of hundreds of paintings, commenting on the propriety of the subject, the technical qualifications of the artist, his general characteristics, and the state of the picture's preservation. In the notes on Roman collections alone, Gray catalogued more than 250 paintings and commented on virtually each one. His knowledge and judgment in the fine arts went far beyond that of the average poet-traveler of even the antiquarian eighteenth century. A modern critic thinks his account of the frescoes of Domenichino and Lanfranco—written, incidentally, some thirty years before the earliest of Reynolds' discourses—to be "one of the most discerning passages of eighteenth-century art criticism."[1]

It is commonly supposed that Gray's interests ran chiefly to capturing romantic landscape in his "Claude glass" or to discussing

[1] C. F. Bell, "Thomas Gray and the Fine Arts," *Essays and Studies by Members of the English Association*, XXX (Oxford, 1945), 60. Matthew Arnold begins his essay on Gray by paying tribute to his "acquirements" and quoting W. J. Temple, who called Gray "perhaps the most learned man in Europe." See also John Mitford (ed.), *Poems of Thomas Gray with Critical Notes* (London, 1814), pp. xlii, lxi–lxx; Edmund Gosse (ed.), *Works of Gray* (rev. ed.; London, 1902), I, 303–21; Clark S. Northrup, "Addison and Gray as Travelers," in *Studies in Language and Literature in Celebration of the Seventieth Birthday of James Morgan Hart* (New York, 1910), p. 435; Duncan C. Tovey, *Gray and His Friends* (Cambridge, 1890), pp. 205 ff.; Duncan C. Tovey (ed.), *Letters of Thomas Gray* ("Bohn's Standard Library" [London, 1900–1912]), III, 64 ff.

with his "gothic" friend Walpole medieval and early Tudor *objets d'art*. But this is far from being true. Gray's pantheon was that of the other poets we have studied in these pages: the Roman masters of the sixteenth century and the Bolognese masters of the seventeenth. His observations and notes on paintings recorded in Italy during his Grand Tour reveal the fervent admiration of Guido Reni we have already noticed.[2] But they also indicate that Gray admired antique statuary; that Raphael, Titian, Andrea del Sarto, Correggio, Parmigianino, Annibale Carracci, Nicolas Poussin, and Carlo Maratti were his favorites; that, though he usually praised what he saw of Claude and Gaspard, he did not see very much of them and they did not loom large in his mind; and that, like Bellori, whose *Vite* he seems to have had open before him, he found Caravaggio powerful but vulgar, the "very perfection of low nature."[3]

Gray accepted the doctrine of *ut pictura poesis* in criticism and knew the tradition of iconic poetry. He had read the *Greek Anthology*, Philostratus, Vasari, Bellori, Dufresnoy, Du Bos, and Jonathan Richardson.[4] In his stanzas to Richard Bentley, his painter-friend who was preparing illustrations for six of his poems, the poet gives high praise to the power of illustration and views the combination of the two arts as a happy one in which poetry is invigorated and improved.

> In silent gaze the tuneful choir among,
> Half pleas'd, half blushing, let the Muse admire,
> While Bentley leads his sister-art along,
> And bids the pencil answer to the lyre.
>
> See, in their course, each transitory thought
> Fix'd by his touch a lasting essence take;
> Each dream, in Fancy's airy colouring wrought
> To local symmetry and life awake!
>
> The tardy Rhymes that us'd to linger on,
> To Censure cold, and negligent of Fame,
> In swifter measures animated run,
> And catch a lustre from his genuine flame.

[2] Above, p. 167.

[3] "Criticism on Architecture and Painting during a Tour in Italy," *Works of Gray*, ed. John Mitford (London, 1836), IV, 225–305.

[4] Roger Martin, *Essai sur Thomas Gray* (London and Paris, 1934), pp. 126–27.

> Ah! could they catch his strength, his easy grace,
> His quick creation, his unerring line;
> The energy of Pope they might efface,
> And Dryden's harmony submit to mine.[5]

The reference to Dryden and Pope is happy, for Gray, like them, is using the occasion of addressing a painter-friend to interpret the relations of the sister arts and, by implication at least, to identify himself with the tradition of their association. The poems of his predecessors are longer and better. But neither of the other poets has so handsomely complimented the sister art. Gray's view of painting is revealed to be the traditional one: it possesses the power of *enargeia* in even greater measure than poetry—the power of rendering the animation and luster of life itself.

The sensibilities of which we have been speaking were expressed most fully in Gray's youth. They unquestionably underwent some modification during the course of a long life exposed to aesthetic currents radically unlike those that had fructified neoclassical ground. It would be, however, a serious mistake to divide his poetic career into an early classicism and a later romanticism. His highly "romantic" Latin ode on the sublimities of the Grande Chartreuse was, along with his enthusiastic letters on wild and awesome Alpine scenery, written by a very young man on the Grand Tour who was about to admire Guido and Annibale and who had not as yet written his "classical" odes on spring, adversity, and the goldfish bowl. Similarly, the witty, Swiftian neoclassic couplets of the "Candidate" were written in 1764 after the two "sublime" odes and actually during the period that produced those heralds of romanticism, the poems on themes from Norse mythology. Conventional schematization also breaks down in considering the pictorial elements of Gray's poetry. We shall not therefore try to force the matters we are now to consider into a rigid, a priori system.

In the "Ode on the Spring" Gray writes in the manner of Collins but without Collins' peculiar skill. The lack of total structure deprives the personifications of a significant place and function. The requirement of the Wartons that personifications be pictorially

---

[5] "Stanzas to Mr. Bentley." I quote here and elsewhere from the text of Austin Lane Poole (ed.), *Poems of Gray and Collins* (4th ed.; Oxford, 1948). Reference will be made hereafter only to titles of the poems.

rendered is not met with any great distinction. Care possesses a "toiling hand," and Contemplation, a "sober eye." Venus is "fair" and appears, in the loveliest lines of the poem, with a train of "rosy-bosom'd Hours." The natural details remain general and unvisu-alized; the adjectives, derivative and conventional. The sky is "clear blue," the shade is "brown," fortune wears "varying colours," and the year is "purple."

Although much the same would have to be said of the Eton ode and the "Hymn to Adversity," it is obvious that Gray's hand is somewhat more practiced in these poems. The personifications seem more individualized and animated than in the "Ode on the Spring": "Shame sculks behind"; "moody Madness" laughs wildly; Adversity has an "iron scourge" and an "adamantine chain"; Melancholy, a "leaden eye, that loves the ground." The greater profusion of natural detail in these poems, somewhat more skilfully arranged, suggests Thomson: "distant spires" and "antique towers" crown "the watry glade"; and expanses of grove, lawn, and mead with shade and flowers are observed from an eminence.

It is unnecessary to examine all Gray's minor poems in detail since we isolated their two most prominent imagistic effects in consider-ing Thomson and Collins. Gray, like Thomson, presents a natural scene in which pictorial and visual details are subordinated to a quasi-mythological persona whose function is to organize the details and interpret them as manifestations of some kind of animistic order and meaning. In the fragment on vicissitude, written in 1754 and 1755, the first stanza—one of the most beautiful in Gray—personifies the morning and makes it the direct cause of April green-ness.

> Now the golden Morn aloft
>   Waves her dew-bespangled wing;
> With vermeil cheek and whisper soft
> She woo's the tardy spring:
> Till April starts, and calls around
> The sleeping fragrance from the ground;
> And lightly o'er the living scene
> Scatters his freshest, tenderest green.

Gray's other imagistic effect, like Collins' (or the Wartons'), is created by personified abstraction: a pictorially conceived moral quality is presented as in an allegorical painting, attended by a train of minor but related personae. This effect is best exemplified in the "Hymn to Adversity," but it also appears elsewhere. In the "Ode on ... Vicissitude," for example, the following allegorical ideogram, although it lacks the subordination to which Collins usually submitted his grouped allegorical figures, illustrates this tendency to present moral and psychological meaning in visual allegory:

> Still, where rosy Pleasure leads,
>   See a kindred Grief pursue;
> Behind the steps that Misery treads,
>   Approaching Comfort view;
> The hues of Bliss more brightly glow,
> Chastised by sabler tints of woe;
> And blended form, with artful strife,
> The strength and harmony of Life.

This quality is prominent in Collins, but in a less pictorial way it is present also in others, notably Pope. The following lines from the "Essay on Man" must have been in Gray's mind when he wrote the stanza just quoted:

> Love, Hope, and Joy, fair pleasure's smiling train,
> Hate, Fear, and Grief, the family of Pain;
> These mix'd with art, and to due bounds confin'd,
> Make and maintain the balance of the mind:
> The lights and shades, whose well accorded strife
> Gives all the strength and colour of our life
>   [Epistle II, ll. 117–22].

These lines permit us to draw a necessary contrast between the pictorialism of the didactic Pope and the pictorialism of the lyrical Gray—a contrast that, however sharp, yet exists within the boundaries of the neoclassical picturesque. Although Pope uses a metaphor from painting and views life as a picture composed of a tension between light and shade, the verse remains philosophical. The pictorial elements, though present, are the metaphorical overtones of intellectual argument. Pope's lines refer to painting; Gray's lines constitute a painting. Pope, in his abbreviated way, personifies the virtues and then talks about them. Gray asks you to look at them: "See!" His Pleasure, who is described as "rosy," leads; Grief pursues; Misery treads; Comfort approaches.

In Gray's shorter poems the pictorial effects are often exquisitely phrased. But they are usually derivative, their particulars unfreshened by direct observation of either nature or picture. The highly pictorial lines in the "Ode on the Spring" devoted to the "insect youth,"

> Some shew their gayly-gilded trim
> Quick-glancing to the sun,

come from Milton's description in *Paradise Lost* of fish with shining scales who "sporting with quick glance / Show to the Sun their wav'd coats dropt with Gold" (vii 405–6). The pictorially conceived personification of "moody Madness laughing wild" Gray owes to Dryden's "Madness laughing in his ireful mood."[6]

"ELEGY WRITTEN IN A COUNTRY CHURCHYARD"

The "Elegy" consists of a series of alternating descriptions and reflections, a form dear to the neoclassic poet and intimately related to the pictorialist tradition. Gray, like Thomson and Pope before him, places himself in a scene of his own creating, which he then observes and meditates upon. The opening description (ll. 1–28) is followed by a reflection (ll. 29–76). This long passage of moral and sociological comment is in turn followed by a brief description (ll. 77–84) of those "frail memorials," the rude gravestones; and that is followed by a correspondingly brief reflection (ll. 85–92) on the pains of death and the need of comfort. The poem closes with a similar alternation: a description (ll. 93–116) recounts the life and death of a poet and is followed by the concluding reflection (ll. 117–28), which is presented as his epitaph.[7]

The first four stanzas of the first section of the poem are devoted to the outdoor scene in twilight. Its subsequent three stanzas describe the former activities—both during the day and in the evening—of the dead peasants. This second part of the first section, although it consists of several visual details, is not primarily or directly pictorial. In fact, it illustrates that power which Lessing believed the poet alone possessed—the power of "painting with negative traits and, by mixing the negative and positive together, of uniting two appear-

---

[6] See Gray's note to line 79 of the Eton College ode (*ibid.*, p. 34).

[7] For earlier comment on this type of poetic form and its relations to the pictorialist tradition see above, p. 117.

ances in one.''[8] This ability Gray here exploits to the full. The peasants are now dead; the present scene—the scene actually before the poet's and the reader's eye—is a twilit landscape. But by a series of negatives—"*no* more," "*no* children run"—Gray has reconstructed their outdoor daytime life and their indoor evening leisure.

These verses are, by Lessing's standards, unpictorial in still other ways. For example, the details that describe the awakening of the peasants at early dawn are temporally rather than spatially conceived and are presented in order of increasing intensity: "the breezy call" of the morning, "the swallow twitt'ring," "the cock's shrill clarion" accompany and explain the growing wakefulness. Similarly, in the opening description the light is not steady but changing: "*Now fades* the glimmering landscape on the sight." In the course of the succeeding lines the twilight has become complete darkness. Nor is the imagery exclusively visual: the curfew tolls, the plowman plods (here the sense is strongly kinesthetic), there are drowsy tinklings, and the personified morn is "incense-breathing." Gray has had the good artistic sense to remain poet and to animate his scene as only poets can.

Nevertheless, the opening stanzas do constitute a scene, and to concede everything to Lessing would be to lose much of their force. The landscape in fading light is designed with a winding herd and a returning plowman; with ivy-mantled tower, elm, yew tree, and heaving turf. These details—many of which Gray saw and loved in the secluded village of Stoke Poges and in the surrounding Thames Valley with its elms, beechwoods, parish church, and winding lanes—he has composed into a poetical picture of great evocative power. Occasionally he employs words that to the eighteenth-century reader were the signs of the pictorial: the poet points, as it were, to "*yonder* ivy-mantled tower" and uses the demonstrative pronoun in introducing the trees: "*those* rugged elms, *that* yew-tree's shade." The suggestion of pictured landscape is inescapable.

Beautiful though the opening four stanzas are, no eighteenth-century reader would have been content had the poem continued and ended as it had begun—in pure description. Poets and critics as diverse as Swift, Thomas Warton, Beattie, and others had insisted,

[8] *Laokoön* (London, 1914), last paragraph of chap. viii.

in the words of Thomas Twining, that "a poem cannot be founded upon what Pope somewhere calls, an *entire landscape*, without human figures, an image of nature, solitary and undisturbed."[9] This was also true of painting, for, as the Abbé Du Bos once said, "the best painters were so well convinced of this truth, that they have very seldom given us landscapes wholly desert, and without human figures. They have peopled their pictures; they have introduced into them persons employed in some action capable of moving us, and by consequence of engaging our attention. This is the constant practice of Poussin, Rubens, and other great masters."[10] *Ut pictura poesis:* Gray likewise turns from pure scene to human figures and human concerns.

In the long reflective passage that follows the opening description Gray uses a number of personifications. Many of these are only slightly animated: Ambition mocks, Grandeur smiles disdainfully. Nevertheless, plastic suggestions are insistently present and have considerable importance. In drawing the reader's attention to the trophies and statues raised over the tombs of the powerful inside the church under the "fretted vault," Gray fleetingly but unmistakably introduces a note which the attentive reader of these pages will recognize at once as iconic. The phrases "storied urn" and "animated bust" invoke the traditional message of the art epigram—that sculptured stone can, by the miracle of artistic genius, create a sense of vital reality. But here the iconic is ironic—more ironic for being unmistakably iconic: the art object is only life*like*; it is not life itself. What in other contexts would have evoked unmixed praise—the power of art to create *l'illusion de la vie*—here evokes a disturbed reflection. That power, however admirable and availing in art, cannot in life "Back to its mansion call the fleeting breath." Gray's brief invocation of the iconic tradition is one of the most subtle and effective of its many and varied uses.[11]

[9] Quoted by Mitford, *op. cit.* (n. 1), pp. cxlviii–cliii.

[10] Quoted by Joseph Warton in "Reflections on Didactic Poetry," appended to his edition of the *Works of Vergil* (London, 1753), I, 401–2.

[11] Cleanth Brooks's reading of this section of the "Elegy" is remarkably sensitive. He also argues that the function of the personifications is ironic. "This becomes plain when we see that the personifications are actually the allegoric figures, beloved by the eighteenth century, which clutter a great abbey church. . . . They wear the glazed 'disdainful smile' of eighteenth-century mortuary sculpture. They take up the conventional attitudes of such sculpture: . . ." (*The Well Wrought Urn* [Lon-

The next descriptive section, in which the "frail memorial . . . / With uncouth rhimes and shapeless sculpture deck'd" is introduced, differs from the general description that opens the poem in that it concentrates on a simple, typical object. The brief reflection annexed to this description introduces a personification of "dumb Forgetfulness," not visually particularized but placed in a pictorial arrangement—a kind of Eurydice shrinking back to the shades.

In the final pair of descriptive and reflective sections the effect is dramatic. In describing the life and death of the village poet and stonecutter, Gray has obeyed the mandate of Du Bos and brought interest and meaning to his scene by introducing human figures. For, in addition to the sophisticated poet (the "I" of the poem) and the now dead peasant poet (the rustic stonecutter, who must be the "thee" of line 93), Gray has introduced the hoary-headed swain (the voice of the community not entirely sympathetic to the role of the peasant poet) and the literate inquirer (the "kindred spirit" who will some day come and read the sophisticated poet's tribute in the epitaph to the rustic poet's life and death). The "Elegy" is not merely a general reflection on the inevitability of death and the irony of its ways; it is also a new kind of "Lycidas," a creative variant of the pastoral elegy, in which an educated and donnish poet pays tribute to a "mute inglorious Milton," who in his own way had served but at the same time transcended the community that had imperfectly understood and appreciated him.[12]

In the last section of the poem,[13] the most important scenic details are the engraved "stone beneath yon aged thorn" and the three living figures who in differing yet similar ways are morally

---

don, 1949], p. 100). Incidentally, Mr. Brooks' view that these personifications bring us *inside* the church receives support from Constable's illustration of the line, "Can Honor's voice provoke the silent dust?" Two soldiers stand in the church, gazing on the tomb of a crusader, whose reclining figure has been sculptured on the tomb. The scene is lit by light from a mullioned window. Bagg's engraving of Constable is reproduced in the *Connoisseur*, CXXXIV (October, 1954), 81.

[12] I have followed the unorthodox interpretation of Frank H. Ellis ("Gray's *Elegy*: the Biographical Problem in Literary Criticism," *Publications of the Modern Language Association*, LXVI [December, 1951], 971–1008). For another view see John H. Sutherland, "The Stonecutter in Gray's 'Elegy,' " *Modern Philology*, LV (August, 1957), 11–13.

[13] In its revised and final form. See R. W. Ketton-Cremer, *Thomas Gray* (Cambridge, 1955), pp. 97–98, 271–73.

and emotionally related to the humble poet's grave. This contemplation of an engraved tomb is strongly reminiscent of Nicolas Poussin's "The Shepherds of Arcady" now in the Louvre, a painting that enables us with great exactitude to understand the nature of Gray's pictorialism and to appreciate the subtle and easily elusive elegiac tone of the poem (Plate XXVI B).

In Poussin's famous canvas four similar but carefully differentiated figures stand in front of a tomb. Three of them are shepherds bearing staffs, and one is a shepherdess. The oldest of the group, a bearded man, kneels before the tomb and traces with his finger the words *Et in Arcadia ego*, inscribed on the stone. Another of the shepherds, the youngest and most sensitive-seeming of the men, points with an index finger to the inscription but looks at the shepherdess. All the figures express not shocked or outraged surprise but meditative sadness. This is particularly true of the shepherd on the left, whose relaxed, drooping posture suggests resignation.

The parallel between the famous poem and the equally famous painting, which has, to my knowledge, never been drawn by a literary critic, was more than hinted at by Gray's friend and illustrator Richard Bentley. In his illustration of the concluding scene of the poem Bentley seems to have been influenced not only by Gray's text but also by Poussin's painting[14] (Plate XXVII). The tombstone, the old swain, and the inquiring stranger come directly out of Gray. But in his treatment of the swain Bentley has followed Poussin, not Gray, for Gray has the swain beckon to the stranger and point to the stone "beneath yon aged thorn," while Bentley has the swain, like Poussin's kneeling shepherd, trace the letters on the stone. Moreover, the stranger leans on his walking stick in a manner reminiscent of the shepherd who stands farthest to the left on Poussin's canvas and, like the kneeling shepherd in Poussin, casts a shadow across the front of the stone. Bentley had apparently read the "Elegy" and thought of "The Shepherds of Arcady."[15]

[14] *Designs of Mr. R. Bentley for Six Poems by Mr. T. Gray* (London, 1753).

[15] Poussin's figure who traces letters on a tombstone appears also in Blake's illustration of the stanza beginning "Their name, their years, spelt by th'unletter'd muse." The Muse, a female figure bearing a lyre in her left hand, traces with the finger of her right the following "holy text": "Dust thou art" (*William Blake's Designs for Gray's Poems* [Oxford, 1922], Plate VIII). The leading literary source of Arcadian tombs is the inscribed monument to Daphnis in Vergil's fifth ecologue.

The evidence does not permit us to say dogmatically that Gray in writing the "Elegy" thought of Poussin's famous painting, but it does make the suggestion plausible. There can be little doubt that Gray knew the painting. Engraved by Picart, Niquet, Mathieu, and Reindel,[16] viewed by many travelers on the Grand Tour, and discussed by some of the most influential literary and art critics of the period, it had become for European culture of the seventeenth and eighteenth centuries what Gray's poem was to become for that of the late eighteenth and nineteenth centuries, the classical expression of the elegiac mood. It was known and "quoted" by everyone. Like many other themes of seventeenth-century art, it had entered the consciousness of the English people. It could even be parodied without being insulted. When Reynolds painted the double portrait of Mrs. Bouverie and Mrs. Crewe, he unmistakably recalled Poussin by placing both ladies before a tomb bearing the inscription *Et in Arcadia ego.*[17] Richard Wilson also painted an *Et in Arcadia ego,* entitled "Shepherds in the Campagna," in which two shepherds look at a mutilated stele that they have come upon at sundown in the Roman Campagna. Wright of Derby, perhaps recurring to the prototype of all such pictures, the one that had given to the world the famous phrase (Giovanni Francesco Guercino's painting now in the Corsini Gallery, Rome), presented a sentimentalized version of the *memento mori.*[18] And so it was throughout the entire eighteenth century. Poussin's Arcadian theme was diffused by quotation, allusion, and adaptation in both the plastic arts and literature.

Anyone so knowledgeable in the fine arts as Gray was undoubtedly acquainted with the *Et in Arcadia ego* theme in some of its pictorial expressions. Three of those expressions, two by Poussin and one by Guercino, help us discriminate the "tone" of the "Elegy."

[16] Andreas Andresen, *Handbuch für Kupferstichsammler* (Leipzig, 1870–73), II, 293, item 12; John Smith, *A Catalogue Raisonné of the Works of the Most Eminent Dutch, Flemish, and French Painters* (London, 1829–37), Part VIII, p. 139, items 277, 278.

[17] This picture, belonging to the Marquess of Crewe, London, is reproduced in Ellis K. Waterhouse, *Reynolds* (London, 1950), Plate CXXVII.

[18] For a reproduction of Wilson's painting (belonging to the Earl of Stratford) see W. G. Constable, *Richard Wilson* (Cambridge, Mass., 1953), Plate XVII B; for Wright of Derby (now in the Derby Art Gallery) see Ellis K. Waterhouse, *Painting in Britain, 1530 to 1790* (London, 1953), Plate CLXXVI; for Guercino's see Erwin Panofsky, *Meaning in the Visual Arts* (Garden City, N.Y., 1955), Plate XC.

In Guercino's painting two shepherds emerge from the shadows to confront a large human skull that lies on a piece of disintegrating masonry and is accompanied by a fly and a mouse, themselves symbols of death and decay. The mood, extremely dramatic and emotionally powerful, is that of the post-Tridentine baroque. The painting might have influenced Donne or Dryden, but not Thomas Gray. Its mood is too violent; its spirit too dramatically religious.

To a lesser extent the same is true of Poussin's earlier "Et in Arcadia ego" (now in the Chatsworth, Devonshire, collection),[19] itself obviously under the influence of Guercino's moving allegory. Two shepherds and a shepherdess, whose dishabille suggests that the present confrontation has interrupted amorous dalliance, rush in from the left to confront a large sarcophagus on which rests a human skull. One of the two men, the older one, traces the legend *Et in Arcadia ego* with his finger. As if to identify the landscape as that of Arcadia, the river god Alpheus sits in the lower right corner, his head slightly bent in meditative sadness.

Five or six years after painting this baroque piece of agitated surprise at an unexpected encounter with a *memento mori*, Poussin returned to the theme and painted his more famous Louvre canvas. Here the number of shepherds has been increased by one, and the four are now presented in a horizontal frame dictated by the simple rectangular tomb that has replaced the more ornate sarcophagus of the earlier version. The skull has disappeared, as has the allegorical river-god: they would have been inappropriate to a scene in which agitation has been replaced by calm meditativeness and in which the suggestion of interrupted voluptuousness and of a late breathless revelry has been replaced by philosophic melancholy. In the early scene the figures are barefooted; in the latter they are decorously shod. In the earlier the shepherdess displayed one of her breasts; in the later she is fully covered. Mr. Panofsky says of the Louvre version: "Instead of being checked in their progress by an unexpected and terrifying phenomenon, they are absorbed in calm discussion and pensive contemplation. One of the shepherds kneels on the ground as though rereading the inscription for himself. The second seems to discuss it with a lovely girl who thinks about it in a quiet, thoughtful attitude. The third seems trajected into a sympathetic, brooding melancholy."[20]

[19] *Ibid.*, Plate XCI.   [20] *Ibid.*, p. 313.

Precisely this is the general mood of Gray's poem: far from presenting the dramatic discomposure before a *memento mori* conveyed in the baroque pieces, it shares with Poussin's later canvas a mood of meditative, philosophic melancholy.

Gray had, as a very young man, looked upon Poussin as a master of pathos. In an interesting list of proposed themes for painting, he assigns to Poussin a "history" that presents the dying Alcestis surrounded by her weeping children, who hang upon her robe.[21] The youngest boy, who weeps only because the others weep, she embraces with her right arm while her left is extended toward the others. Her lord faints and must be supported by attendants. The figures are mythological, but the story is universally human: a family confronts the impending death of its mother. To Poussin, Gray assigns the power of portraying direct and simple human emotions—the power, that is, of "the pathetic," to use the eighteenth-century critical term employed for just such effects as these. That quality Dr. Johnson found in Gray's "Elegy"—the power of evoking universally felt pathos—a quality that Dr. Johnson and the eighteenth century felt to be characteristic of Vergil: *Sunt lacrymae rerum, et mentem mortalia tangunt.*[22] It would not be fanciful to link the names of Vergil, Poussin, and Thomas Gray.

The interpretations of Poussin's painting that were widely diffused in Gray's lifetime and were certainly known to him stressed the moral ironies that accompanied the coming of death. To Félibien this painting "représente le souvenir de la mort au milieu des prosperitez de la vie"[23]—an interpretation carried in the title of many of the engravings of the painting most popular in the eighteenth century. The comment by Abbé du Bos, of the famous French aestheticians one of the most widely read in England, is worth quoting. After describing the painting, Du Bos says:

And one may perceive, in the midst of the affliction and pity that begin to spread themselves over their features, something of the remains of an expiring joy. We imagine we hear the reflections of these young persons

[21] Tovey (ed.), *Letters* (n. 1), III, 66.

[22] For a discussion of the term "pathetic" in Johnson and elsewhere in eighteenth-century criticism see Jean H. Hagstrum, *Samuel Johnson's Literary Criticism* (Minneapolis, Minn., 1952), pp. 137–44.

[23] *Entretiens sur les vies et sur les ouvrages des plus excellens peintres anciens et modernes* (London, 1705), IV, 70–71.

on the power of death, who spares neither age nor beauty; and against whom the happiest climates can afford no protection. We figure to ourselves what touching things they would say to one another, when they recovered from their first surprize, and we apply these things to ourselves and to those for whom we are concerned. It is in poetry as in painting;[24] and the imitations which poetry makes of nature, touch and affect us, only in proportion to the impression which the thing imitated would make on our hearts, if we saw it in reality.[25]

Such a comment as this could be the very matrix out of which Gray's poem sprang.

Gray's "Elegy" shares with Poussin's painting a moral theme as well as an engraved tombstone with meditative people engaged in conversation clustered about it. But there are likewise important differences between them. By the time Poussin painted his canvas the phrase (*Et in Arcadia ego*) had ceased to mean "I Death am also present in Arcady" and had come to mean "I the deceased person like you lived in Arcady." In Poussin the force of the epitaph seems to be that the shepherds contemplate their own mortality because one like them, one who had also enjoyed the delights of a pastoral Eden, is now dead.[26] Gray's motif is subtler. The speaker of his poem comes from another environment—a higher intellectual and social level—than that of the dead peasant-poet. These two, unlike Poussin's shepherds, have in one sense not shared a past environment. But in a deeper sense they have, and the voice from the peasant's churchyard tomb seems to say: "I too have been a poet as I have been a man, and I too have been marked by Melancholy for her own. *Et ego in Arcadia vixi*." By virtue of this deep spiritual affinity both poets have been enabled to transcend their environments. We as readers, in perceiving this relationship as well as in perceiving the socially undiscriminating triumph of death, have become aware of the ultimate humility of the proud and the equally ultimate pride of the humble.

[24] The very phraseology here reveals the influence of Horace's phrase (*ut pictura poesis*), of which Du Bos's language is an almost literal, though perhaps unconscious, translation.

[25] Quoted by Joseph Warton, *op. cit.* (n. 10), I, 402–3. The values that Du Bos sees in Poussin are precisely those that Johnson found in the "Elegy," which, he said, finds "a mirror in every mind," and to the sentiments of which "every bosom returns an echo" ("Life of Gray," *Works* [Oxford, 1825], VIII, 487).

[26] See Panofsky, *op. cit.* (n. 18).

Poussin's painting provides an important critical commentary on Gray's poem for other than thematic reasons. It reminds us that Gray's poem belongs to the pictorialist tradition. That is borne in upon a reader who comes to it from Milton's more flexible and less static "Lycidas." It also becomes evident to anyone who notices, as we have noticed earlier, that the poem has pictorial reminiscences not only in the descriptive but also in the reflective sections. The very relation between description and reflection is a quality that it derives from the iconic tradition. For what is this poem if not a succession of visually rendered scenes, each leading to a relevant verbalized reflection? That is, do not the passages of moral and philosophical reflection remind one, in all respects except their length, of words engraved under a sculptured or painted scene? The poem is not basically dramatic or narrative; its progress is not that of logical, step-by-step argument or even of emotional effusion guided by the law of free association. A series of pictorially static moments to which reflections have been added, the poem suggests the art of painting and is therefore an example of the neo-classical picturesque. The ideal of *ut pictura poesis* best accounts for the most prominent characteristic of the elegy: its symmetrical alternation of scene and thought, its essential stasis of movement, and the relatively impersonal objectivity of its final form.[27]

It might even help account for its style—for what Professor Sherburn has called its "incisive lapidary diction."[28] The chiseled and classical chastity of Gray's style, like the universality of his theme and scene, may be viewed as the verbal counterparts of the sculpturesque and chromatic simplicities of Nicolas Poussin.

THE "PROGRESS OF POESY"

The first of Gray's great odes reminds Lord David Cecil of "nothing so much as some big decorative painting of the period in which, posed gracefully on an amber-coloured cloud, allegorical figures representing the arts and the passions offer ceremonious

[27] The analogy with Poussin's painting supports Ellis' (*op. cit.* [n. 12]) thesis of the growing depersonalization and increasing objectivity of the successive versions of the poem. The objectivity is accompanied by growing picturesqueness. To the final conclusion and to that alone is the analogy with Poussin valid.

[28] *An Elegy Wrote in a Country Church Yard* (1751) *and the Eton College Manuscript*, with an introduction by George Sherburn (Augustan Reprint Society Publication No. 31 [Los Angeles, 1951]), p. i.

homage to the goddesses of Poetry or Beauty." The section that describes Venus receiving the homage of the Graces recalls "some radiant florid ceiling painted by Tiepolo."[29]

Criticism that saw the pictorial in the great odes began in the eighteenth century shortly after their publication. Count Algarotti, for example, who finds that in general English poets are reflective and didactic and that the warmer-blooded and intenser poets of the South are usually more picturesque and graphic, sees the "sublime" odes of Gray as significant exceptions to the main English tendency. "In this second type of poetry (the *pittoresco*) I should place the poetry of Mr. Gray, who, although born in the North, challenges poets of the warmest blood, who grew up in the regions of the sun."[30]

It is not recorded that Gray himself applied this criterion to his own odes as a whole; but of the "Progress" he said that the two stanzas that follow the first are "very picturesque,"[31] and in a note to the description of the Bard he drew attention to a painting that he claimed was its ultimate inspiration.

Poems themselves, not statements about them, enable us to understand their true nature. The great odes will be found to belong in general to the kind of poetry recommended by the Wartons and the Wartonians as alternatives to the didactic satires and epistles of Pope. They consist so exclusively and rigorously of picture and music as to eliminate virtually all rhetorical statement.

The notion of poetically celebrating a triumphal progress goes back to classical Rome. But during and after the Renaissance the progress was elaborated into many forms that conveyed an impressively large and varied freight of meaning. Progresses appeared in all the arts and even in philosophical argument and historical treatise. The word was sometimes used of scholarly history, as in Ben Jonson's "De progressu picturae" in *Timber*, and the idea, if not the word, was relevant to purely representational allegory. Frescoes on wall and ceiling of *palazzo*, *biblioteca*, and *capella* represented in progressive panels the biographies of historical characters

---

[29] *Poets and Story-Tellers* (London, 1949), p. 65.

[30] Letter to William How, Dec. 26, 1762, in William Mason (ed.), *Poems of Gray* (York, England, 1775), pp. 82–84.

[31] To Richard West, May 8, 1742, *Correspondence*, ed. Paget Toynbee and Leonard Whibley (Oxford, 1935), I, 202.

like Augustine, St. Francis, Aeneas Silvius Piccolomini, and Marie de Médicis; the progresses of mythological characters like Hercules through their successive labors and exploits; the progress of the seasons of the year through their natural course; and even the progress of an idea through its various historical manifestations and intellectual ramifications. By the early eighteenth century the form was so well known and so widely, conventionally, and preposterously used that Swift ridiculed it in a series of mock progresses in verse.[32]

The poet who wished to use the form seriously had an accumulation of impressive precedents in all the arts to guide—or confuse—him. His most general problem was to determine to which of the antithetical poles—philosophic and narrative statement or graphic allegorical representation—he wished to orient his effort. If he chose the first and attempted to tell a story logically or chronologically, he might do what Dryden had done in his brief "progress" of painting in the epistle to Kneller or what Pope had done in his "progress" of criticism in the "Essay on Criticism." But if he was a Gray, writing in mid-century and attempting to free poetry from what he considered the shackles of philosophical and moral statement, he might lean to pictorial representation and, sinking comment in panorama, allow his tableaux to speak more or less for themselves.

To such goals as these Thomson had helped blaze the trail. In his progress of the personified liberty across the vistas of history there are many panoramic pictures. How often Thomson cries out "see! see!" and points to a historical pageant or future prospect! But unfortunately he endowed his goddess with excessive powers of speech, and the thousands of lines of her discourse all but smother the graphic, visual detail. Into that trap Gray is careful not to fall. He has purified his picture of the dross of explanatory comment and rhetorical speech. This aesthetic purification, along with extended and often unnecessary allusiveness, baffled contemporary

[32] Swift wrote three "progresses"—of love, poetry, and beauty. See sepecially his "Progress of Poetry" in Harold Williams (ed.), *Poems of Swift* (Oxford, 1937), I, 230–31. See the check list of "progress pieces" from 1612 to 1821 by Reginald Harvey Griffith, "The Progress Pieces of the Eighteenth Century," *Texas Review*, V (April, 1920), 218–33. Gray's poem came at the crest of the wave. See also Mattie Swayne, "The Progress Piece in the Seventeenth Century," *Studies in English*, XVI (*University of Texas Bulletin*, July 8, 1936), 84–92, and Aubrey L. Williams, *Pope's Dunciad* (Baton Rouge, La., 1955), pp. 42–48.

readers accustomed to poetry of philosophical and ethical statement. Dr. Johnson objected that the opening lines of the poem, which confused "the images of 'spreading sound' and 'running water,' " made no clear, understandable statement about either music or verse, which the landscape scenes were apparently intended to illustrate.[33] But Gray was not interested in stating meaning directly or in giving clear, logical referents for his images. He wanted, first in a Claudian and then in a Salvatorian picture, to protray two antithetical conditions of music, conditions not unrelated to that famous neoclassical pair, the beautiful and the sublime.

All the pictorial effects embodied in the poem need not detain us, but we must consider the first epode, which has been justly celebrated for its exquisite music. As picture it is no less admirable, and Gray's title for it ("Power of harmony to produce all the graces of motion in the body") indicates that he thought of it in terms of the neoclassical picturesque. Had Gray not been silent about Botticelli and had it not been some decades too early in cultural history for an appreciation of the Florentine master, one would be tempted to see in Gray's richly sensuous mythological allegory a reflection of the "Primavera" or the "Birth of Venus." But Poussin's, Giulio Romano's, and Titian's mythologies, which Gray did know and love, will do as well.[34]

The colors are, except for the Pindaric purple of the last line, the unmixed, simple hues of Renaissance canvases: naked feet twinkle on the greensward, the *amori* are crowned with roses, the Pleasures have eyes of blue. The forms are pictorially presented. Dancers describe circles on the grass. Venus walks with the classical *incessus*—the gliding gait —of an Olympian, her arms lifted above her head in the kind of ballet posture that Poussin's deities often assumed. The stanza is worth quoting in full as an example of one kind of eighteenth-century pictorialism at its best—the kind in which the effects of music are plastically realized in the texture and form of the verse itself.

> Thee the voice, the dance, obey,
> Temper'd to thy warbled lay.
> O'er Idalia's velvet-green

[33] *Op. cit.* (n. 25), p. 484.

[34] See, for example, Poussin's "Dance before Pan" in the National Gallery, London, and "Dance to the Music of Time" in the Wallace Collection, London.

The rosy-crowned Loves are seen
On Cytherea's day
With antic Sports, and blue-eyed Pleasures,
Frisking light in frolic measures;
Now pursuing, now retreating,
Now in circling troops they meet:
To brisk notes in cadence beating
Glance their many-twinkling feet.
Slow melting strains their Queen's approach declare:
Where'er she turns the Graces homage pay.
With arms sublime, that float upon the air,
In gliding state she wins her easy way;
O'er her warm cheek, and rising bosom, move
The bloom of young Desire, and purple light of Love.

The second and third ternaries of the "Progress" continue to convey meaning by means of symbolic picture. We proceed from one allegorical panel to another. The poem concludes in the same manner. In the antistrophe of the third ternary Milton is presented as riding through the sky like some huge Rubensian angel or like Raphael's representation of the God of Ezekiel's vision looking at the abyss below (Plate XXX); and Dryden, like Guido's or Poussin's Apollo, appears in the classical car of triumph, drawn by two "Coursers of ethereal race" (Plates XXIV, XXVI A). Fancy itself is presented, not in lower-case statement but in capitalized personification: a bright-eyed goddess, she hovers over an urn that is itself iconically embossed with pictures and from it scatters "Thoughts, that breathe, and words, that burn." At the very end the poet himself rises in flight, like Pindar the Theban eagle, through the "azure deep of air."

Comment on the "Progress" would be incomplete were nothing said of its most obviously pictorial passage, the portrayal of Shakespeare. One learns that Shakespeare was the poet of nature, that he was a descriptive artist of great power, that he was the master of the tragic emotions of pity and fear, that through his comedy he created joy. But here as elsewhere in Gray's great odes these meanings are conveyed in pictorial allegory. It is as though Gray had, before writing these lines, imagined a picture and then had described it in his verse and in describing had interpreted it. To a fully paintable scene—it *was* put on canvas by Romney in his

"Infant Shakespeare Nursed by Tragedy and Comedy," and it is rather closely paralleled by Reynolds' "Infancy of Hercules"[35]— Gray has added only the speech of Nature, the "mighty Mother." Even in that single speech the words are anchored to pictorial detail, for Nature speaks only of the pencil and the keys which she is represented as holding in her hands. Her speech is therefore a kind of pictorial motto.

> Far from the sun and summer-gale,
> In thy green lap was Nature's Darling laid,
> What time, where lucid Avon stray'd,
> To Him the mighty Mother did unveil
> Her aweful face: The dauntless Child
> Stretch'd forth his little arms, and smiled.
> This pencil take (she said) whose colours clear
> Richly paint the vernal year:
> Thine too these golden keys, immortal Boy!
> This can unlock the gates of Joy;
> Of Horrour that, and thrilling Fears,
> Or ope the sacred source of sympathetic Tears.

Although to Gray's contemporaries this passage may have seemed a brilliant tour de force of painterly poetry—Algarotti called it *pittura vivissima*—to the modern reader it can only seem as pompous and affected as the ceilings of Verrio and Thornhill.

"THE BARD"

The "Progress of Poesy" is pictorial only in its individual passages, and there is no single and unifying graphic situation. Episodic in form, it is a gallery rather than a single fresco. But in the "Bard" Gray has achieved unity of pictorial form: he presents in a single scene the entire action of the poem. There is variety, but it comes from slight changes in the scene on one and the same stage. Although Dr. Johnson did not perceive this—perhaps he was too prejudiced about the "sublime" odes to have wanted to perceive it—Gray has in the "Bard" solved the problem of pictorial form which Johnson had elsewhere implied was insoluble.[36]

To accomplish this, Gray followed the example of history painting.

[35] See Chauncey B. Tinker, *Painter and Poet* (Cambridge, Mass., 1938), pp. 67–68.

[36] See above, pp. 256–57.

As a genre this had, during the eighteenth century, attained the greatest prestige of any of the several kinds of painting. Pope had written to Jervas on November 29, 1716: "I long to see you a History Painter. You have already done enough for the Private, do something for the Publick; and be not confined, like the rest, to draw only such silly stories as our own faces tell of us."[37] In 1710 (*Tatler*, No. 209) Steele had drawn at considerable length the specifications for a history piece on the life of Alexander the Great. Joseph Warton had been impressed with the work of the Count de Caylus, who had drawn from Homer's epics "a marvelous variety of subjects proper for history painting."[38] In Sir Joshua Reynolds' discourses the genre retains its traditional prestige as the chief means of expressing the grand style and general nature. Even Dr. Johnson, although he said (*Idler*, No. 45) that he would have grieved to see his friend Sir Joshua desert portraiture for heroes, goddesses, "empty splendours," and "airy fictions," conceded that pictorial "genius is chiefly exerted in historical pictures." In view of the dominance of history painting, it is not remarkable that when poetry modeled itself upon the sister art during this period it frequently turned to paintings of this kind.

Literary influence and cultural context are complicated matters; single sources of a work can almost never be isolated. Before, therefore, we consider the pictorial relationship of the "Bard," we must consider some of its literary antecedents. Relevant to our purposes are the literary antecedents that bear pictorial and graphic suggestion—the works of Ariosto, Milton, and Dryden. Ariosto's contribution is interesting because, Janus-faced, he looks back to the tradition of iconic verse, both medieval and ancient, and ahead to Gray's prophetic telling of history in the future tense. In *Orlando Furioso* history pieces appear on fountain, wall, and hanging. More specifically, Ariosto describes the pictorial representations of future history on the fountain of Merlin, on the walls of the demonically created great hall in the *rocca di Tristano*, and in the ancient *padiglione*, embroidered by Cassandra and magically transported to France as the nuptial chamber of Bradmante.[39] In *Paradise Lost*

[37] *Correspondence*, ed. George Sherburn (Oxford, 1956), I, 377.

[38] *An Essay on the Genius and Writings of Pope* (London, 1806), I, 364–65.

[39] xxvi. 30–47; xxix. 32 ff.; xxxii. 1–58; xlvi. 76–98.

Michael's first method of instruction—a method he later abandons for purely verbal "relation" when he perceives Adam's "mortal sight to faile" (xii. 6–12)—is to present to our first parent's wondering gaze the future history of mankind in a series of tableaux (xi. 423 ff.). Precisely these uses of the iconic tradition and pictorialist form are reflected in the "Bard," in which the souls of the slain bards chant doom upon the successor of Edward and in chanting weave tapestries in which future history is graphically represented.[40]

"Alexander's Feast," discussed at some length in an earlier chapter, is peculiarly relevant to the pictorialism of Gray's poem because Dryden achieves the kind of scenic unity that, as we have seen, characterizes Gray's ode. In both poems changes in scene occur, but they occur within the situation described at the beginning. In the earlier poem Timotheus is placed on high; Alexander and his guests below; and the scenes that pass before the reader's eye are the visible embodiments of the emotions created in the breasts of the heroes by the exalted musician.

There were of course many types of pictorial "history." Some were purely allegorical, in which iconological abstractions from Ripa were grouped together in significant pose, gesture, and relationship. Others were mythological tales that remained intact from Ovid or other ancient sources but had acquired iconic meaning through centuries of use. Still others were illustrations of heroic or epic action from Homer, Vergil, or Tasso. But there were also "histories" that portrayed actual history, that is, paintings that described monumentally the events of the national past and present. For the earlier Rubensian mythological and allegorical "histories" by such men as Verrio, Cooke, Berchet, Ricci, Laguerre, and Thornhill, which had covered the public and private buildings of England during the late seventeenth and early eighteenth centuries, English taste was now beginning to substitute other themes—themes from the English past and present.[41] This development may be related

[40] Gray's poem is, of course, related to the ode of Horace (i. 15) beginning "Pastor cum traheret," in which Nereus stops the boat carrying Helen by calming the wind and then prophesies the future doom of Troy and the house of Priam. But there is nothing in the least pictorial about these prophesies.

[41] Charles Mitchell, "Benjamin West's 'Death of General Wolfe' and the Popular History Piece," *Journal of the Warburg and Courtauld Institutes,* VII (January–June, 1944), 20–33; Edgar Wind, "The Revolution of History Painting," *Journal of the Warburg Institute,* II (1938–39), 116–27.

to the anti-Rubensian critical attacks of Shaftesbury and Spence[42] and to the increasingly forceful attacks on jejune mythology and pretentious allegory that were to culminate in the criticism of Samuel Johnson, who, ironically, directed the attack against Gray himself.

This change in English taste was almost exactly contemporaneous with the creation of Gray's odes. In 1751 and 1752, just a few years before Gray began writing the "Bard," Knighton and Dodsley published the first series of prints derived from English national history. Such pictures were to grow in popularity. By 1770, when Benjamin West began to paint what must surely be the most notable representative of them, the famous "Death of General Wolfe," the English public had been taught to cherish the commemoration in monumental style not only of the past but of the present as well.

Before and during the period in which he wrote the "Bard" Gray was steeping himself in both English chronicle and early English painting and design. Walpole had recently acquired many English Gothic and Tudor paintings and sketches, and in poring over the chronicles Gray devoted much time to identifying the historical figures whose representations he had contemplated at Strawberry Hill. Gray's latest biographer comments that during this period of study "pictures formed themselves in his mind."[43]

It is from this broad and complex background that Gray's poem emerges. We now examine in some detail its pictorial qualities.

One of the most obvious is its outdoor setting. The "Elegy," too, was set in outside nature, but how different is the present scene! Romantic Wales and the Mount Snowdon of Richard Wilson's famous canvas[44] have been substituted for the generalized, classical,

[42] Above, p. 166.

[43] Ketton-Cremer, *op. cit.* (n. 13), p. 132.

[44] I suggest that the setting portrayed in this painting, with a lake in the foreground, darker masses in the middleground to the sides, and a lighter gray for the mountain itself in the center background, would provide an excellent backdrop for Gray's pageantry. Sir George Beaumont said that Wilson's genius had qualities closely akin to Gray's "Bard" (see Myra Reynolds, *Treatment of Nature in English Poetry between Pope and Wordsworth* [Chicago, 1896], p. 235). Although Wilson may have been indirectly inspired by Gray, his painting is not to be regarded primarily as an illustration of the poem. It does seem, however, to be a better visual analogue than Bentley's illustration (Plate XXXII) because it is more spacious and grand. Bentley cramps his characters into too narrow a space and loses some of the breadth

and Poussin-like scene of the earlier poem. Edward's troops, in full medieval panoply, march "down the steep of Snowdon's shaggy side." The venerable and vengeful minstrel stands in full view of the troops on an overhanging rock opposite that overlooks the foaming mountain river Conway. This romantic mountain scene, suffused with the red light of the setting sun, is in part the product of Gray's own sensibility—the love of wild mountain scenery which the Alps had evoked in his youth (the scenes of the Grande Chartreuse and Mount Cenis he had declared "pregnant with religion and poetry") and which the highlands of Scotland had kept alive in his middle age ("none but these monstrous creatures of God know how to join so much beauty with so much horror").[45] Gray's sensibility, somewhat ahead of that of many in his age but by no means out of touch with it, is intimately related to Burke's "sublime" of danger and terror.

The "Bard" is pictorial not only because of its setting but also because of the static position of its characters, who, as in a picture, are within one another's view (see Plate XXXII). Even the spirits of the dead bards are imagined as visible to their last surviving colleague and to their royal murderer—"a griesly band" who sit on one of the cliffs of the mountain. The tapestries that they weave by the very words of their chants of doom are intended to be seen, as those in *Paradise Lost* were seen—these, however, against the backdrop of Welsh mountain and cliff.

> Give ample room, and verge enough
> The characters of hell to trace.

The song of the slain bards is thus iconic: we *see* Edward III on his funeral couch; Richard II's magnificent and wasteful reign is graphically presented as a "gilded vessel" in "gallant trim"; the rose of snow and the red rose of York and Lancaster are actually woven "above, below"; statesmen "appear in bearded majesty," and of

---

of feeling the poem must have. The troops of Edward are barely visible and lack all the impressiveness with which Gray must have regarded them. Bentley's head of the Bard has some merit, and he does place the characters within view of each other. His imagination was not stirred to attempt a representation of the spirits of the slain.

[45] See C. E. de Haas, *Nature and the Country in English Poetry of the First Half of the Eighteenth Century* (Amsterdam, 1928), pp. 230–38.

Elizabeth we *see* "Her lyon-port, her awe-commanding face." We are thus asked to visualize, in the light of the setting sun and against the slope of a Welsh mountain, the future dynastic history of the English that the vengeful minstrels have projected in scenes imagined to be visible to the physical eye.

The Bard is the central character of the scene. In annotating the lines describing his appearance ("Loose his beard, and hoary hair / Stream'd, like a meteor, to the troubled air") Gray says: "The image was taken from a well known picture of Raphaël, representing the Supreme Being in the vision of Ezekiel"[46] (Plate XXX). But in a letter written in 1756 Gray complicates the pictorial origins of the Bard's appearance:

The thought, wch you applaud, in these lines, *Loose his beard* &c: is borrowed from painting. Raphael in his vision of Ezekiel . . . has given the air of head wch I tried to express, to God the Father; or (if you have been at Parma) you may remember Moses breaking the Tables by the Parmeggiano, wch comes still nearer to my meaning[47] [see Plate XXXI].

Gray's comments are extremely interesting, because he not only gives the sources of the image but also throws light on the very nature of the pictorial origins of literary imagery. By mentioning two paintings—one by Raphael and the other by Parmigianino—he shows the futility of trying to determine a single source. As a matter of fact, he looks upon the pictures less as sources and more as illuminating analogues: the second painting "comes still nearer my meaning." He is interested, therefore, not chiefly in showing exactly where the Welsh bard's flowing beard and hair came from but in aiding the visualizing and understanding of the character he has here conceived.

Both paintings represent subjects of the loftiest conceivable nature. Raphael's painting, of which the iconology is complicated and need not detain us now, represents the Supreme Being supported in mid-air under a blaze of glory by the four winged creatures of Ezekiel's vision—four creatures traditionally associated with the four Evangelists (Plate XXX). The face of God seems to have been

[46] Poole, *op. cit.* (n. 5), p. 56.

[47] To Bedingfield, Aug. 27, 1756, *op. cit.* (n. 31), II, 476–77. If Gray refers to pictorial sources in the same manner he does to literary sources, there must be many that remain unspecified.

influenced by classical representations of the head of Jove.[48] Into this painting have been woven strands of the Hebrew, the Christian, and the Greco-Roman tradition. Sir Joshua Reynolds considered it among the most sublime examples of the art, worthy of comparison with Michelangelo's Sistine ceiling.[49]

The other painting to which Gray refers the reader's attention is Parmigianino's "Moses," a fresco in the Chiesa della Steccata of Parma (Plate XXXI).[50] It represents the lawgiver descending from Sinai and, the tablets of the law raised above his head, beginning the angry action that will dash them to pieces. The figure is a fine one: lean and muscular in build, heroic in posture, obviously stirred with righteous indignation.

Gray makes these pictorial annotations in order to enforce the feeling that his poem is one of the greatest exaltation—a vindication of the art of poetry and the dignity of man against royal tyranny. The mood is intended to be one of dazzling elevation. In paintings and poem alike there is sounded a note of divine judgment. The Zeus-like creature presented high above the earthly landscape in Raphael's painting descends to judge—he does not come in mercy. Moses on Sinai, perceiving the idolatry of the people, breaks the tablet of the law in moral anger. Similarly, the Bard, exalted morally as well as physically above the invading armies of Edward, pronounces judgment upon him and his descendants unto the third and fourth generation.

It will be recalled that Sir Joshua Reynolds had conceived of the highest beauty as residing in the "one common idea and central form, which is the abstract of the various individual forms belonging to that class."[51] There is a common form for childhood, another

---

[48] Vasari says that this picture contains "Christ, as Jove, in heaven, surrounded by the four Evangelists as described by Ezekiel, one like a man, one as a lion, one as an eagle and one as an ox, with a landscape beneath." *Lives* ("Everyman's Library" [London, 1950]), II, 236.

[49] Discourse XV.

[50] Gray apparently insisted several times upon the relationship of his Bard to Parmigianino's "Moses." In addition to the letter cited above, there is William Mason's comment that Gray "used to say" that this figure came nearer to his meaning than even Raphael's (*Works*, ed. Mason [London, 1825], I, 49). Gray also recommended that William Palgrave visit the Steccata to observe the "Moses" (March, 1765, Tovey [ed.], *Letters* [n. 1], III, 64).

[51] Discourse III. Reynolds sees Parmigianino's picture as an example of the highest style, the product of a mind "impregnated with the sublimity of Michael An-

for old age; one for maidenly beauty, another for youthful manly strength. For each of these generalized types of beauty one could find instructive exemplification in the Greco-Roman marbles—in statues of Venus, Jupiter, Hercules, Apollo. Both Raphael's God and Parmigianino's Moses belong to that generalized type of venerable manhood that goes back to certain ancient representations of Zeus and Jupiter and that achieved manifold expression during the Renaissance and seventeenth century: in Masaccio's, Ghirlandajo's, Leonardo's, and others' heads of St. Peter; in Guercino's Elijah, in Guido's Moses, and in the St. Jerome of virtually every painter of the Italian baroque.

In his Bard, then, Gray has created a figure that belongs to the species of moral, majestic figures we see portrayed in the canvases to which the poet has referred us. He has thus attempted to achieve that "grandeur of generality," that sublimity of *la belle nature*, to which great neoclassic art has often aspired.

This poem is often considered preromantic because of its Welsh scene and its bardic theme. Yet the pictorial analogues that Gray himself has drawn to it show that classical generality has been attempted and the pictorial tradition, upon which poets from Milton on had consistently drawn, has played an important part. There are few more striking examples than Gray's "Bard" of poetic idealization, which, as we have seen again and again in these pages, was so often during the course of centuries dependent upon pictorial and sculpturesque value.

The pictorial analogues have other meanings as well. They support the conviction that this poem must be visualized to be appreciated. One reason, we may venture to guess, that it has lost its popularity in our time is that we have lost the art of *seeing* it—its magnificent setting, its dramatic arrangement of the principal actors all within each other's view, what Gray has called the "air" of its hero's head and physical presence, the pageant of future history that is unfolded before us.

gelo." He concludes his discussion of this painting and the "grandeur" of its conception by referring to Gray: "As a confirmation of its great excellence, and of the impression which it leaves on the minds of elegant spectators, I may observe that our great lyric poet, when he conceived his sublime idea of the indignant Welsh bard, acknowledged, that though many years had intervened, he had warmed his imagination with the remembrance of this noble figure of Parmegiano" (Discourse XV).

In the concluding lines the eye of the reader is moved from the pictorial stasis of the arrangement that has hitherto prevailed to sudden, plunging motion.

> He spoke, and headlong from the mountain's height
> Deep in the roaring tide he plung'd to endless night.

These words describe an action imposed, as it were, on a canvas. They animate a hitherto static figure and constitute a climax, not of narrative action, but of pageant and tableau. Our attention has been fixed on relatively motionless, though not of course *e*motionless, figures and objects—on the venerable poet standing on a rock, on the mountainside itself, on the red sky of the sunset. But now, in a stroke, the bard and the sun have disappeared. The impoverished world is left to darkness—to "endless night" and the sound of roaring waters. The last effect of the poem, which Gray intended to be his greatest and of which he said, "I felt myself the Bard,"[52] is thus to dissolve its own visual fabric and to leave not a rack behind. If this action possesses force, it is because of the plastic solidity of the forms that are now destroyed.

[52] Ketton-Cremer, *op. cit.* (n. 13), p. 134.

Conclusion

Conclusion

In the painting reproduced as Plate IV, "Nature Adorned by the Graces," Rubens has attempted to say in visual language that "True wit is nature to advantage dressed." Nature, who recalls the many-breasted Ephesian Diana (Plate V A), has been stylized into a classical statue on a classical pedestal. The three Graces, also in classical attitude, drape her head with a mantle and adorn her neck with chains, while two winged cupids descend with wreaths of flowers and gently break into a natural scene already framed by art. For below, above, and all around Nature there runs a border of elaborately entwined fruit, leaf, and flower, itself adorned with nude figures from the classical pantheon. Rubens has displayed a nature that is methodized but that remains nature still.

It might seem at first that Rubens has done no more than anticipate the artificial ornamentation of neoclassical taste and provide a visual epigraph for superficial decoration. But mere ornament does not usually arouse the enthusiasm and claim the devotion that English neoclassical civilization accorded the idea here embodied. It would be a serious misreading of an important era of English civilization to see in it no more than a taste for style, a desire merely to decorate life and nature. Far more than that was involved; the values of society, the dignity of man, and civilization itself were all related to the methodization of nature. The art of the period bore a profound, though unexpressed, relationship to the "pleasing illusions" of Burke's political thought—illusions that "made power gentle and obedience liberal" and that constituted the "decent drapery of life" necessary to cover "our naked shivering nature."

Literary pictorialism was one of the most attractive means of achieving style in poetry, of transcending without deserting nature. If the Graces were meant to adorn Nature not only for aesthetic and social but also for moral and political purposes, we can better

317

appreciate the tenacity with which the mind of neoclassical man adhered to pictorialist aesthetics. Bearing the prestige of a continuous tradition that extended from Homer to modern centuries, nourished by love of ancient sculpture and modern Italian art, energized by the new philosophical empiricism of Locke and Newton, literary pictorialism was more than a decorative device. It was one of the supporting pillars in what Thomson, referring to the cultural tradition, once called the "palace of the law."

But apart from its relevance to basic cultural value, a knowledge of literary pictorialism helps us read and understand neoclassical poems. Even the youngest and least experienced teacher of poetry knows how necessary it is to impress students with the importance of seeing while reading. Nothing can so effectually destroy poetic pleasure as the unvisual and imprecise response too often accorded even the sharpest and most effective visualizations of poetry.

The creation of precise visual responses to poetry is of course the business of all of us. But for reading eighteenth-century neoclassical verse properly, more than seeing is required. We must see pictorially. Our vision must be prepared by knowledge of pictorialist criticism, of the conventions of iconic verse, and of the masterpieces of the pictorial pantheon. All these elements constitute the visual context of the neoclassical poet, and it is no exaggeration to say that this context is fully as important as his philosophical and purely literary relationships.

We need not today accept the eighteenth-century evaluation of pictorial verse, but we must attempt to understand it if we wish to enter more deeply into an important period of our cultural past. Perhaps, therefore, one final illustration will be permitted of the joy with which the man of the eighteenth century greeted "poetical pictures." When Parson Abraham Adams was prodded by Mr. Wilson to discuss "what kind of beauty was the chief in poetry," the lovable curate worked himself up to a pitch of enthusiasm that reached its climax in praising the "Opsis" (that is, the scenery and painting) of Homer, the greatest of all poets:

But did ever painter imagine a scene like that in the Thirteenth and Fourteenth Iliads? where the reader sees at one view the prospect of Troy, with the army drawn up before it: the Grecian Army, camp, and fleet; Jupiter sitting on Mount Ida, with his head wrapt in a cloud, and a thunderbolt in his hand, looking towards Thrace; Neptune driving through the sea, which divides on each side to permit his passage, and then seating himself on Mount Samos: the heavens opened, and the deities all seated on their thrones.

Parson Adams had pictorialized the *Iliad* and responded with fervor to his own tableau: "This is sublime! This is poetry!" His honest delight English neoclassical poets were fully prepared to share.

Index

early poems, 289–92
"Elegy," 292–301
Eton College ode, 290
"Hymn to Adversity," 290
"Ode on the Spring," 289–90, 292
"Ode on . . . Vicissitude," 290–91
  and plastic arts, 287–89
  and Pope, compared, 291
  and Poussin, 299–301
"Progress of Poesy, The," 301–6
  and Thomson, 290
Greek Anthology, 22, 24, 47, 48, 75, 226, 288
Greek romances, 31–33, 48, 78, 117, 222
Green, Matthew, 271
Griffith, Reginald Harvey, 303 n.
Grifolus, Jacobus, 60 n.
Grosart, Alexander B., 114 n.
Guarini, Giovanni Battista, 107
Guercino (Giovanni Francesco Barbieri), 241, 252, 257, 260 n., 297–98, 313
Gürninger (i.e., Grüninger), J. R., 60 n.
Guidi, Domenico, 238
Guido; *see* Reni
Guillaume de Lorris, 42

Haas, C. E. de, 264 n., 310 n.
Hadas, Moses, 33 n.
Hagstrum, Jean H., 64 n., 140 n., 143 n., 299 n.
Ham, Roswell G., 177 n.
Hamilton, Charles, 133
Hamm, Victor M., 161 n.
Handel, George Frederick, 193, 193 n.
Hanford, James Holly, 109 n.
Hard, Frederick, 76 n., 77 n.
Hardie, R. P., 8 n.
Harington, Sir John, 114 n.
Harmon, A. M., 15 n.
Harris, James, 135, 163 n.
  frontispiece of *Three Treatises*, 135, Pl. V B
Harrison, Jane E., 21 n.
Harte, Walter, 163 n., 165 n.
Haselmayer, Louis A., 43 n.
Haskins, Charles Homer, 40 n.
Hatzfeld, Helmut, xv, xvi
Hauser, Arnold, 17 n., 67 n.
Haydocke, Richard, 71 n.
Hazlitt, William, 110, 143, 157, 158, 170 n.
Helbig, Wolfgang, 145 n.

Hephaestus, 19, 20, 20 n., 21, 25
Herbert, George, 98–100
  "Posie, The," 98–99
Herculaneum, 17, 26, 28
Hercules, 26, 303, 313
  Farnese Hercules, the, 145, 224, 224 n., 248, Pl. XVIII A
  "Hercules at the Crossroads" (also "The Choice of Hercules"), 190–95, Pl. VI, Pl. VII A
  "Here" (with "there," "yon," and "yonder," sign of pictorial verse), 215, 215 n., 223, 236–37, 293
Herford, C. H., 90 n., 91 n., 193 n., 274 n.
Herodas, 24
Herrick, Robert, 110
Hertford, Francis Seymour, Countess of, 245
Hervey, James, 264 n.
Hesiod, 21 n., 25, 27, 35, 190
Heydenreich, Ludwig H., 68 n.
Highet, Gilbert, 5 n.
Hilliard, Nicholas, 75
History painting, 116, 146, 180, 186, 306–9
Hobbes, Thomas, 136, 150, 198
Hoby, Sir Edward, 58
Hoffleit, Herbert B., 23 n.
Hogarth, William, 132, 193, 199 n.
Holbein, Hans, 75, 110, 173
Holstenius, Lucas, 109
Homer, xix, 6 n., 15, 17, 18, 19–22, 24, 25, 27, 28, 28 n., 34, 35, 49, 53, 57, 58, 59, 61, 63, 79, 99, 148 n., 155, 184, 226, 229, 308, 318, 319
  and Pope, compared, 230–33
Hooker, Edward N., 179 n., 225 n.
Horace, xviii, 3, 9–10, 12, 13, 16, 26, 40, 40 n., 41, 55, 57 n., 58, 59, 59 n., 60, 61, 68, 95–96, 99 n., 131, 174, 175, 176 n., 180, 226, 285, 308 n.; see also *Ut pictura poesis*
Hotson, Leslie, 69 n., 86 n.
Hottinger, M. D., 158 n.
Hourticq, Louis, 176 n.
How, William, 302 n.
Howard, William Guild, 111 n., 152 n., 153 n., 176 n., 186
Howe, P. P., 143 n., 158 n.
Hughes, John, 163 n., 216 n., 274, 274 n.
Hughes, Merritt Y., 125 n.

327

PLATE I. Engraved title page of Pierre le Moyne, *Les peintures morales* (Paris, 1645) (see pp. 33, 105, 117, 181, 238).

Vecchia si dipinge, perciòche gl'è ordinario de'giouani stare allegri, & i vecchi malenconici, però ben disse Virg. nel 6.

Pallentes habitant morbi, tristísque senectus.

E mal vestita senza ornamento, per la conformità de gl'alberi senza foglie, & senza frutti, non alzando mai tanto l'animo il malenconico, che pensi à procurarsi le commodità per stare in continua cura di sfuggire, ò proueder à mali, che s'imagine esser vicini.

Il sasso medesimamente oue si posa, dimostra che il malenconico, è duro, sterile di parole, & di opere, per se, & per gli altri, come il sasso, che non produce herba, ne ascia, che la produca la terra, che gli stà sotto : ma se bene pare otiosa al tempo del suo verno, nell'attioni Politiche, al tempo nondimeno della Prima uera, che si scuopre nelle necessità de gl'huomini sapienti, i malenconiosi sono trouati, & esperimentati sapientissimi, & giudiciosissimi.

M A N S V E T V D I N E.

DONNA coronata d'oliuo, con vn Elefante à canto, sopra del quale posi la man destra.

La mansuetudine secondo Aristotele nell' Ethica lib. 4. è vna mediocrità determinata con vna ragione circa la passione dell'ira in fuggirla principalmente, & in seguirla ancora in quelle cose, con quelle persone, come, & quando, & doue conuiene per amor del buono, & bello, e pacifico viuere.

L'Elefante nelle lettere de gl'Antichi Egittij, perche hà per natura di non combattere con le fiere meno possenti di esso, nè con le più forti se non è grandemente prouocato, dà gr.ã de inditio di mansuetudine, & ancora perche caminando in mezzo d'vn armento di Pecore, che le vengono incontro si tira da banda, acciò che imprudentemente non le venissero offese, & porta tanta osseruanza à così debili animali, che per la presenza loro, quando è adirato tocca

PLATE II. "Melancholy," from Cesare Ripa, *Nova iconologia*, Part II (Padua, 1618) (see pp. 91, 99, 148, 219, 285).

PLATE III. Correggio, "The Madonna of St. Jerome" (see pp. 169, 220)

PLATE IV. Rubens, "Nature Adorned by the Graces" (see pp. 14, 150, 202 n., 317)

PLATE V B. "Nature and the Arts," Frontispiece of James Harris, *Three Treatises* (2d ed.; London, 1765) (see p. 135).

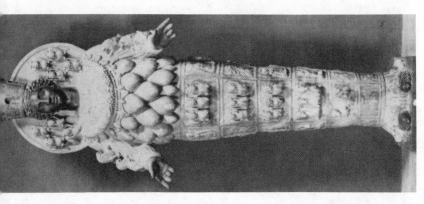

PLATE V A. Diana of Ephesus (see pp. 135, 317).

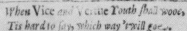

ILLVSTR. XXII.   Book. I.

MY hopefull *Friends* at thrice five yeares and three,
Without a *Guide* (into the World alone)
To seeke my *Fortune*, did adventure mee;
And, many hazards, I alighted on.
First, *England's* greatest *Rendevouz* I sought,
Where VICE and VERTVE at the highest sit;
And, thither, both a *Minde* and *Bodie* brought,
For neither of their Services unfit.
Both, woo'd my *Youth*: And, both perswaded so,
That (like the *Young man* in our *Emblem* here)
I stood, and cry'd, *Ah! which way shall I goe?*
To me so pleasing both their Offers were.
VICE, *Pleasures* best Contentments promist mee,
And what the wanton *Flesh* desires to have:
Quoth VERTVE, *I will Wisdome give to thee,*
And those brave things, which noblest Mindes doe crave.
Serve me said VICE, *and thou shalt soone acquire*
All those Atchievements which my Service brings:
Serve me said VERTVE, *and Ile raise thee higher,*
Then VICES *can, and teach thee better things.*
Whil'st thus they strove to gaine me, I espyde
Grim *Death* attending VICE; and, that her Face
Was but a painted *Vizard*, which did hide
The foul'st Deformity that ever was.
LORD, *grant me grace for evermore to view*
Her Vglinesse: And, that I viewing it,
Her Falshoods and allurements may eschew;
And on faire VERTVE *my Affection set;*
  Her Beauties contemplate, her Love embrace,
  And by her safe Direction, runne my Race.

PLATE VI. "Hercules," from George Wither, *A Collection of Emblemes* (London, 1635), Book I, Illustration 22 (see pp. 95, 192, 193 n.).

National Museum, Naples; Photo Alinari

PLATE VII A. Annibale Carracci, "Hercules at the Crossroads" (see p. 192)

Uffizi Gallery, Florence; Photo Alinari

PLATE VII B. Rubens, "Hercules between Vice and Virtue" (see p. 192)

Corsini Gallery, Rome; Photo Anderson

PLATE VIII A. Guido Reni, "Mary Magdalen" (see pp. 189,

Pitti Gallery, Florence; Photo Alinari

PLATE VIII B. Guido Reni, "Cleopatra" (see pp. 189, 196, 237, 275, 276)

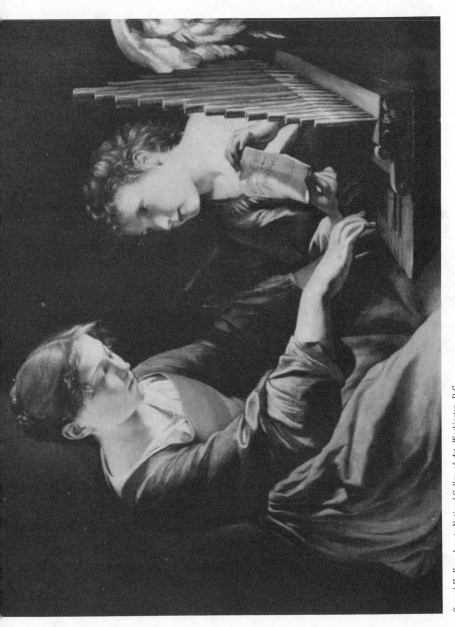

PLATE IX. Orazio Gentileschi, "St. Cecilia and an Angel" (see pp. 205, 237)

PLATE X. Caravaggio, "Head of the Medusa" (see p. 199)

PLATE XI. Guido Reni, "The Massacre of the Innocents" (see pp. 199, 283)

PLATE XII. Raphael, "Ecstasy of St. Cecilia" (see pp. 204, 222, 237)

PLATE XIII. Orazio Gentileschi, "Saints Valerian, Tiburtius, and Cecilia" (see pp. 204, 237)

PLATE XIV. Rubens, Sketch for the ceiling of the Banqueting Hall, Whitehall, London (see p. 203).

PLATE XV. Frontispiece of Account of Castlemaine's Embassy (London, 1688) (see p. 208).

PLATE XVI. Rubens, "The Toilette of Venus" (see p. 221)

PLATE XVII. Joshua Reynolds, "Lady Sarah Bunbury Sacrificing to the Graces" (see p. 222).

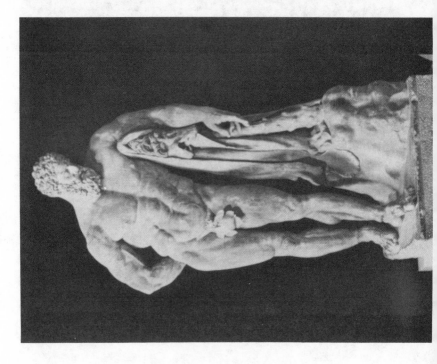

PLATE XIX A. Apollo Belvedere (see pp. 145, 248)

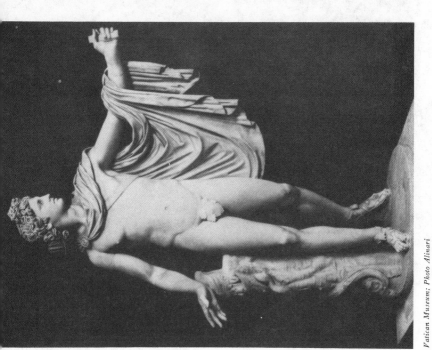

PLATE XIX B. Venus de' Medici (see pp. 248, 285)

PLATE XX. Dürer, "Melancholy I" (see p. 219)

PLATE XXI. Titian, "Mary Magdalen" (see pp. 222, 237)

PLATE XXII. Domenichino, "The Communion of St. Jerome" (see p. 242)

PLATE XXIII. William Kent, Frontispiece of *The Seasons* by Mr. Thomson (London, 1730) (see p. 263)

PLATE XXIV. Guido Reni, "Aurora" (see pp. 125 n, 260, 278, 305)

Bayerischen Staatsgemäldesammlungen, Munich

PLATE XXV B. Guido Reni, "Apollo and Marsyas" (see p. 283)

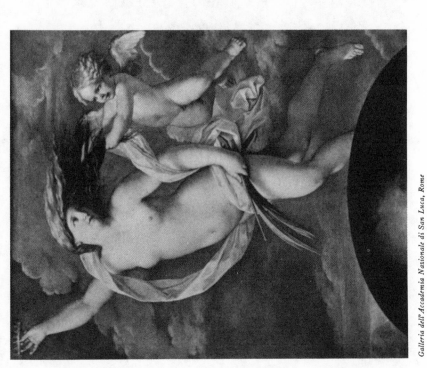

Galleria dell' Accademia Nazionale di San Luca, Rome

PLATE XXV A. Guido Reni, "Fortune" (see pp. 283–84)

PLATE XXVI A. Nicolas Poussin, "The Kingdom of Flora" (see pp. 263, 305)

PLATE XXVI B. Nicolas Poussin, "The Shepherds of Arcady" (see p. 296)

PLATE XXVII. Frontispiece for Gray's "Elegy in a Country Churchyard," in *Designs of Mr. R. Bentley for Six Poems by Mr. T. Gray* (London, 1753) (see p. 296).

PLATE XXVIII. L. P. Boitard, Engraving of ancient air nymphs, zephyrs, aurae, and sylphs, in Joseph Spence, *Polymetis* (London, 1747) (see p. 285).

PLATE XXIX. Otto Vaenius, Virtus Inconcussa, in *Emblems of Horace* (Antwerp, 1607) (see pp. 285–86).

PLATE XXX. Raphael, "The Vision of Ezekiel" (see pp. 305, 311)

Chiesa della Steccata, Parma; Photo G. F. N.

PLATE XXXI. Parmigianino, "Moses" (see pp. 311, 312)

PLATE XXXII. Richard Bentley, Design for Gray's "Bard" (see pp. 309 n., 310).